OFFICE AUTOMATION: A SOCIAL AND ORGANIZATIONAL PERSPECTIVE

John Wiley
INFORMATION SYSTEMS SERIES

Editors

Richard Boland
University of Illinois at Urbana-Champaign

Rudy Hirschheim
Oxford University

Hirschheim: *Office Automation: A Social and Organizational Perspective*

OFFICE AUTOMATION: A SOCIAL AND ORGANIZATIONAL PERSPECTIVE

R. A. Hirschheim

Templeton College
Oxford University

 John Wiley
INFORMATION SYSTEMS SERIES

JOHN WILEY & SONS
Chichester · New York · Brisbane · Toronto · Singapore

Copyright © 1985 by John Wiley & Sons Ltd.

Library of Congress Cataloging in Publication Data:
Hirschheim, R. A. (Rudy A.)
  Office automation: A social and organizational
  perspective.
  (John Wiley information systems series)
  Includes bibliographies and index.
  1. Office practice—Automation. 2. Business—Data
  processing. I. Title. II. Series.
  HF5547.5.H58 1985   650'.028'5   85–22756

  ISBN 0 471 90909 2

British Library Cataloguing in Publication Data:
Hirschheim, R. A.
  Office automation: A social and organizational
  perspective.
  (John Wiley information systems series)
  1. Office practice—Automation   2. Office
  management
  I. Title
  651   HF5548.2

  ISBN 0 471 90909 2

Printed and bound in Great Britain

To Geoffrey and Katie

Series Foreword

In order for all types of organization to succeed, they need to be able to process data and use information effectively. This has become especially true in today's rapidly changing environment. In conducting their day-to-day operations, organizations use information for functions such as planning, controlling, organizing, and decision making. Information, therefore, is unquestionably a critical resource in the operation of all organizations. Any means, mechanical or otherwise, which can help organizations process and manage information presents an opportunity they could ill afford to ignore.

The arrival of the computer and its use in data processing has been one of the most important organizational innovations in the past thirty years. The advent of computer-based data processing and information systems has led to organizations being able to cope with the vast quantities of information which they need to process and manage to survive. The field which has emerged to study this development is *information systems* (IS). It is a combination of two primary fields: computer science and management, with a host of supporting disciplines, e.g. psychology, sociology, statistics, political science, economics, philosophy, and mathematics. IS is concerned not only with the development of new information technologies but also with questions such as: how they can best be applied, how they should be managed, and what their wider implications are.

Partly because of the dynamic world in which we live (and the concomitant need to process more information), and partly because of the dramatic recent developments in information technology, e.g. personal computers, fourth-generation languages, relational databases, knowledge-based systems, and office automation, the relevance and importance of the field of information systems has become apparent. End users, who previously had little potential of becoming seriously involved and knowledgeable in information technology and systems, are now much more aware of and interested in the new technology. Individuals working in today's and tomorrow's organizations will be expected to have some understanding of and the ability to use the rapidly developing information technologies and systems. The dramatic increase in the availability and use of information technology, however, raises fundamental questions on the guiding of technological innovation, measuring organizational and managerial productivity, augmenting human intelligence, ensuring data integrity, and establishing strategic advantage. The expanded use of information systems also raises major challenges to the traditional forms of administration and authority, the right to privacy, the nature and form of work, and the limits of calculative rationality in modern organizations and society.

The Wiley Series on Information Systems has emerged to address these questions and challenges. It hopes to stimulate thought and discussion on the key role information systems play in the functioning of organizations and society, and how their role is likely to change in the future. This historical or evolutionary theme of the Series is important because considerable insight can be gained by attempting to understand the past. The Series will attempt to integrate both description—what has been done—with prescription—how best to develop and implement information systems.

The descriptive and historical aspect is considered vital because information systems of the past have not necessarily met with the success that was envisaged. Numerous writers, most notably Henry Lucas, postulate that a high proportion of systems are failures in one sense or another. Given their high cost of development and their importance to the day-to-day runing of organizations, this situation must surely be unacceptable. Research into IS failure has concluded that the primary cause of failure is the lack of consideration given to the social and behavioural dimension of IS. Far too much emphasis has been placed on their technical side. There are good historical reasons why this has been the case, as discussed in Chapter 5 of this first book of the Series. The result has been something of a shift in emphasis from a strictly technical conception of IS to one where it is recognized that information systems have behavioural consequences. But even this misses the mark. Writers such as Goldkuhl, Lyytinen, Land, Mumford, Mowshowitz, Kling, Klein, Boland, and Hirschheim suggest that information systems are more appropriately conceived as social systems which rely, to a greater and greater extent, on new technology for their operation. It is this social orientation which is lacking in much of what is written about IS. The first book in the Series, *Office Automation: A Social and Organizational Perspective*, goes some way in attempting to correct this imbalance. Future books will go even further.

The Series seeks to provide a forum for the serious discussion of IS. Although the primary perspective is a more social and behavioural one, alternative perspectives will also be included. This is based on the belief that no one perspective can be totally complete; added insight is possible through the adoption of multiple views. Relevant areas to be addressed in the Series include (but are not limited to): the theoretical development of information systems, their practical application, the foundations and evolution of information systems, and IS innovation. Subjects such as systems design, systems analysis methodologies, information systems planning and management, office automation, project management, decision support systems, end-user computing, and information systems and society are key concerns of the Series.

July 1985   Rudy Hirschheim
                                                                     Richard Boland

Preface

The application of new technology to the office—variously referred to as office automation, the office of the future, the electronic office, office information systems, etc.—has captured the imagination of many people of late. New products are being announced virtually every day, books on how to obtain the many benefits of office systems are proliferating, and the general hype behind this new technology is probably greater than any previous computing-related technological development. Much of the interest in office automation stems from technological achievements—in particular, the application of the ubiquitous microprocessor, which is directly responsible for the emergence of products such as word processors, personal computers, intelligent copiers, and management workstations. The most important technological achievement, however, is probably the convergence of these products with telecommunications, allowing the linking together of previously stand-alone devices and the sharing of resources. The new office technologies and systems have been heralded as the solution to the many problems associated with today's offices, particularly the so-called 'productivity problem'.

If all this sounds like something you have heard before, you are right! As far back as the 1950s people were writing about how the computer would revolutionize the office. The hardware and software might have been less advanced, but the general concept was the same. The result, however, was not exactly as thought. Computers did change the way offices and organizations worked, but not to the extent that was widely predicted. There are, of course, many possible reasons why this was the case: the technology was not sophisticated enough, the applications were not sufficiently well understood, etc., and, concomitantly, why it will be different with office automation.

However, there is another possible reason why computing may have had little 'real' effect; viz. that the social domain into which it was placed was not sufficiently understood. Research undertaken over the past ten years has concluded that it is the social rather than the technical aspects of a technology which are responsible for its effects. This may seem intuitively obvious and to many it may be, but the simple truth is, no matter how obvious the importance of the social domain, it is largely ignored. The literature and discussions on office systems are almost entirely technical in nature. Although lip service is paid to the 'behavioural' dimension (e.g. user-friendly interfaces, user involvement, and the like), little serious attention is given to the social domain.

This then is the motivation for this book. It is an attempt at counterbalancing the wealth of available material on the technical side of office automation. It acts as a dialectic, to provide a serious treatment of the social and organizational aspects of office systems. The work draws on historical argument in an attempt to persuade the reader that much can be learned from the lessons of the past. In a sense the old adage 'he who does not learn from history is destined to repeat it', provides the *raison d'être* for this work. Just as computer-based information systems have met with limited success, so too will be the case with office information systems unless a more social view is taken. This book attempts to suggest why a social and organizational perspective is needed, and what the result is if such a perspective is adopted.

If adopted, a number of dramatic changes become evident. Firstly, the conception of the office changes—from one which sees the office as largely deterministic, rational, and overt to one which is largely non-deterministic, political, and covert. Secondly, the models and methodologies appropriate for office automation move from the highly formal and abstract to the less formal and participative. Thirdly, implementation is transformed from the mechanical process of installing some particular office system/technology to a process of social and organizational change where participation is the key ingredient. Fourthly, the implications of office automation become recognized as not simply the logical and rational outcome of technological use, but the product of social forces which often have little to do with any particular piece of technology. Lastly, the ability to predict the effects of any technological intervention is not one which can be undertaken with simple, empirical cause–effect models, but needs interpretive approaches such as those involving hermeneutic analysis. These are the fundamental conclusions reached by this work. How they have been reached is the subject matter of this book.

September 1985   Rudy Hirschheim
                                                                                    Oxford

Acknowledgements

There are many people who have directly helped with the production of this book. I should like to acknowledge their support and thank them for their assistance. Before mentioning who they are, I would like to note the importance of the indirect help which has been so vital to the conceptual base of this work. Fundamentally, this book is the synthesis of many ideas which have been lying around (often dormant) in the information systems field for quite some time. These ideas, coupled with sociological and philosophical concepts, have provided the basis of the work undertaken here. It is thus difficult to acknowledge all those whose ideas are sprinkled liberally throughout the book. Six individuals in particular, however, are responsible for the motivation behind many of the arguments which lie at the foundation of this work. Rob Kling's cogent writings on the social analysis of computing have, in many ways, been the model for my analysis of office automation. I have drawn on a number of his arguments to motivate my social theoretic perspective. Dick Boland's insightful use of an interpretivist or phenomenological perspective has largely driven the subjectivist philosophical viewpoint adopted here. Although many others have advocated such a perspective, Boland's work has been a constant source of inspiration. Enid Mumford's writings on sociotechnical systems and participative design have provided the *raison d'être* for the heavy emphasis placed on implementation. Her adamantine support for participation along with her success with ETHICS have been instrumental to my treatment of office system methodologies and implementation. Heinz Klein's insistence on the social nature of information systems and the dysfunctional consequences of not recognizing this fact has been a theme adopted throughout. Moreover, his advocation of the need to consider philosophical issues during inquiry has been at the core of the social theoretic perspective adopted here. Dick Welke's suggestion that research in information systems needs to be both eclectic and insightful has provided the 'spirit' of inquiry in that this work has drawn upon historical, sociological, philosophical, and information systems arguments. Finally, Frank Land's guidance and support through the difficult times has allowed the work to reach its completion.

A number of individuals have been more directly responsible for the production of this book and deserve my utmost thanks: firstly, Heinz Klein, who has allowed me to use one of our papers as the base for Chapter 7;

secondly, Dick Boland and Frank Land for their insightful and helpful comments on earlier drafts of the manuscript; thirdly, Ian Shelley for his foresight on recognizing the need for a Series in Information Systems of which this book is the first; fourthly, Sue Coles for typing the original version of the manuscript, Dick Baskerville for his assistance in its editing, and my wife Sally for her help in proofreading the final version; fifthly, the staff at John Wiley & Sons for their technical assistance and support; and last but not least, my family, who have seen too little of me over the past two years during the preparation of this book.

Contents

Chapter 1

JUSTIFICATION AND RATIONALE FOR A SOCIAL THEORETIC PERSPECTIVE OF OFFICE AUTOMATION

INTRODUCTION

Throughout history, man has sought to apply his intelligence to improve work and the working environment. The result has been a vast range of tools (e.g. hoes, hammer, axes) and techniques (e.g. masonry, carving, sculpturing) which have helped raise the material standing and well-being. In recent history, the tools and techniques have become quite sophisticated (e.g. internal combustion engines, computers, programming). Along with the development of these new tools and techniques have been a growth in the use of the term 'technology' to describe these developments. Technology may be thought to be the particular tools and techniques used by a culture. More generally, it is a set of ways by which a social group provides itself with the material objects of its civilization. Its widespread use within the context of describing recent progress has meant it has become closely associated with material products, particularly those which are machine or computer related. So close has been the association that today most people tend to equate technology with microprocessor-based products. Technology connotes sophisticated items, too complex for the common man (indeed virtually all of society) to understand. Technologists — those who work with and understand the technology — are something of an elite. Not only do they possess knowledge of the technology but a jargon-filled language which is incomprehensible to all others. This is a source of power which can be marshalled to obtain desired outcomes. (Other technologists — in the broadest sense of the term — e.g. doctors, lawyers, educators, possess the same power except theirs is associated with different forms of technology.)

Technology has also become associated with advancement: new medical achievements, improved transport, better weapon systems, and the like. It is generally portrayed to the masses in a favourable light as the vehicle with which to improve society. As people do believe it has had positive effects on their way of life and material well-being in the past, there is no reason to suspect it will be different in the future.

Technology does, however, appear to have a numbing and seductive effect. Numbing in the sense that people come to expect that it is (or can be) the cure for the world's ailments (largely independent of what they might be) and seductive in the sense that people seem to become enamoured with technology almost to the exclusion of everything else. There is a concentration on the physical and material aspects of the technology instead of the human and social dimensions. There is also a belief in 'technological determinism' or 'the technological imperative', the view that technology will inevitably continue to develop more or less irrespective of what man does. Once started, it can not be stopped. Martin (1981) makes the point: 'It is technology that has created the dilemmas, and yet the only way out of the dilemmas is more technology' (p.3).

Part of the seductive appeal about technology lies in the belief that new developments are somehow markedly different from what preceded them and thus will have dramatic effects. A seemingly innate property of the technological development is the adjoining belief that it is in some manner revolutionary; things previously impossible now become possible. Of course not all advancements are portrayed in a revolutionary light, but even if they are not, there is still considerable enthusiasm exhibited about them. The seductive appeal of technology is such that optimisms and unreal expectations often accompany its development. It is to this latter point that this work is addressed.

One of the latest achievements in the ever-advancing field of computing is that of office systems, the application of computing and telecommunications to the office domain. Much has been made of the potential benefits of these new systems and products but, as yet, few of the postulated benefits have been widely experienced. In fact a number of organizations have experienced dysfunctional effects. The simple truth is that while much has been written about the positive consequences accrued through the use of new office systems, little empirical evidence exists with which to back it up. User experiences in the United Kingdom, reported in Hirschheim (1985), suggest that organizations have not obtained the beneficial effects hoped for. Contrary to expectations, widespread productivity improvements, changes in personal working habits, and the like were not in evidence. Moreover, while most organizations experimenting with office system technology claimed in public that the systems were successful, many in private reported that the claims were rather more apocryphal than real.

To those who have been involved in the computer-based information systems area such a situation must bring a sense of *déjà vu*. Similar claims were made for management information systems and with similar results. Obtaining the predicted benefits of computer-based information systems has always proved elusive. It is always harder than conventional wisdom seems to suggest; the same is true with office systems. The history of computing is replete with examples of extravagant claims about new technology which could not be realized. Management information systems, database systems, decision support systems, expert systems, and fifth-generation computer systems have all had turns at capturing the imagination of prospective users and making claims about widespread effects. Office automation is simply one of the latest technological developments which is being pushed hard by vendors, consultants, and the like. In the drive to promote office systems, considerable effort has been expended to highlight the technological aspects of the systems, i.e. the hardware and software. Productivity gains are construed as the logical outcome of the application of a particular technology to a particular office activity. There is a familiar kind of rationality underlying these arguments. It is precisely the same one used in the 1960s to promote management information systems; and it is the same for all the other aforementioned computer-based systems as well.

There is clearly a sense of history repeating itself (yet again!) with scarcely any notice being taken of the lessons learned from the past. In the thirty or so years of experience with computing, a number of realities have emerged. These are largely based around the realization that information systems are not technical systems but social systems and must be developed within a social and organizational context. Technical interpretations have proved largely unsuccessful (see Mowshowitz, 1976, who noted that in excess of 40 per cent of information systems were failures). The basic contention of this work is simply that if a technological orientation is taken of office automation, failure is likely to follow. Yet it is precisely this orientation which is so pervasive. Office automation is discussed in terms of a major technological achievement — one which will revolutionize the office. Even the term itself conjures up an image of office work being automated through the application of computer-based devices. New technology is portrayed as the instrument to make the office more productive and efficient. However, this is hardly a new idea. One of the first commercial computer ventures in the United Kingdom during the 1950s was LEO (Lyons Electronic Office) — the application of computers to the office. Hoos (1960), in the same period, wrote about office automation in the sense of the computer taking over the office. Rhee (1968) used the same term — office automation — to describe the impact of computers in offices.

By taking a more historical view about office systems a number of important points emerge. Firstly, the office systems (office automation) is not a new or revolutionary development. Some of the technical components are, of course, new but the general concept is not. If dramatic changes in productivity, efficiency etc., were not experienced in the past why should they be expected now? Office automation is not the automation of office functions, by and large, but the development of information systems in the office. Thus the term office information systems (OIS) is more appropriate than terms such as office automation, the office of the future, and so forth. However, because of the widespread adoption of the term office automation (OA), it is used throughout this work.

Secondly, because it is fundamentally to do with information systems rather than automation it is possible to understand OA by considering the past lessons of developing computer-based information systems. A large body of literature exists, largely under the rubric of implementation research, which has explored the reasons for information systems failure. The general conclusions are that failure is much more widespread than people would like to admit, and the primary cause of failure has to do with the general state of ambivalence towards the social and human side of information systems. The systems are conceived of in technical terms, designed in technical terms, and implemented in technical terms, with little attention paid to social aspects. If the human side is considered, the understanding of this dimension is so primitive and naive that the effect is almost worse than if no consideration had been made at all.

Thirdly, the technical bias apparent in the literature and discusssions on OA is a product of historical tradition. When new technologies are developed, their technological sophistication becomes the focal point of interest. This is partly due to the enamouring effect technology has (see above), partly to the type of person who wishes to be involved with its design, development, and use (those who have a fascination with new tools and instruments often to the exclusion of social aspects; cf. Bjorn-Andersen and Hedberg, 1977), and partly to the reasons for considering its use (to make organizations more productive through technological means). These in combination with the 'technological imperative' make the technical orientation of OA, and other new technologies, irresistible. However, as noted above, this technical bias associated with new technologies such as OA has led to an almost complete neglect of their social dimension. As Sackman (1971) notes: 'Technical matters turn computer professionals on, human matters turn them off.' It is not surprising, therefore, to find virtually the whole of OA literature concentrating on technical issues, with very few serious treatments of the social domain.

Fourthly, because of the technical bias, some fundamental social and societal issues have been given very scant attention. Work, for example, is written about as though it was little more than the performance of certain tasks. An office worker travels to meetings, performs calculations, writes letters and reports, answers and makes telephone calls, and so forth. Work is seen as the rational process by which business functions are carried out. People engage in work because they need to earn a living. It is usually not perceived as anything elegant; rather work conjures up images of boring activities, i.e. drudgery. This image, however, is extremely narrow and misses the social richness of work. People engage in work not just for economic reasons but for the social interaction and stimulation which accompanies it. A question posed long ago regarding the relationship between man and work needs to be considered. Simply put, it asks: 'Does man work to live, or live to work?' The technological view seems to hold to the former, but from a more social view the latter interpretation is more likely.

This book is an attempt to provide a counterbalance to the current situation, to place OA in a social context. This is done by adopting a social theoretic perspective.

NEED FOR AND EXPLICATION OF A SOCIAL THEORETIC PERSPECTIVE

For too long now, office automation has been considered a technical innovation which could be applied with relative impunity from the social domain. Token social and human considerations such as user-friendly interfaces, ergonomically sound design, and the like have been thought to be sufficient considerations of the social and human realm. But are they? The contention proposed here is that simplistic considerations such as these mask the complexity of and do no justice to the reality of social and organizational life. Work is conceived of as observable activities: meetings, telephone conversations, travel, typing, etc., which are performed to realize some particular office or business function. Office workers are rational beings who engage in those tasks which are necessary for the performance of their organizational duties. Some 'enlightened' OA researchers have attempted to broaden the office focus to include goals which can be determined by the tasks which are performed. (See, for example, 'the office semantics view' in Chapter 3.) However, even here there are serious flaws and philosophical confusion. The simple fact is that the field of office automation has given scant attention to the human and social domain of offices and organizations. The reason for this state of affairs is not surprising; those working in OA are, by and large, technically inclined and motivated. The requirement, therefore, is for a serious treatment of the human and social aspects of office information systems. This is the motivation for adopting a social theoretic perspective.

The social theoretic notion is to connote a more conjectural analysis of the social side of office systems. It is put forward as a dialectic to the classic technical interpretation. The treatment will hopefully serve as a basis for argument through which a better appreciation of OA can be attained. No claims are made that this analysis will be 'theory producing' in the conventional sense. Instead, what is hoped for is a more 'emergent' knowledge (in the Glaser and Strauss, 1967, and Mintzberg, 1979, conception) — one which produces a better sense of understanding. The analysis will be considered effective if it provides new insight into OA, if the essential structures of OA are re-thought or added to. The validity of the analysis rests on the self-validation of those insights which are communicated clearly and completely to the reader. If what is communicated adds meanings to OA in the mind of the individual reader, then knowledge has been gained, and the process of inquiry is successful.

The social theoretic perspective concentrates on the social and behavioural components of the office. The work which people do in offices is perceived in a social context; it is governed by social convention and gives meaning through shared conceptions of reality, yet is the product of conflicting goals, beliefs, values, and the like. Offices are often conceived as stable, almost immutable structures in the standard OA literature, but this is strikingly naive from a social theoretic perspective. Offices may indeed *appear* to be stable and structured on the surface, but behind this veneer lies an exceedingly complex existence. Viewing the office in terms of a 'negotiated order' seems a much better description of the reality of office life.

The social theoretic perspective focuses on the group and its interactions rather than the individual as the key to understanding the office. This is the classic structuralist–individualist dichotomy. Briefly put, the individualist would contend that offices (and organizations in general) do not exhibit behaviour, it is the individual people that do. By focusing on larger collectivities (i.e. offices) the researcher neglects the individual processes that occur which produce the observed actions. Individualists, such as Collins (1981), argue that the activities of the larger collectivity are simply aggregates and are insufficient as empirical explanations of social processes. Structuralists, on the other hand, postulate that collectivities are more than simply the aggregation of the individuals or activities which constitute them. They possess emergent properties which cannot be explained through an individualist interpretation (Mayhew, 1980). By focusing on the individual one loses the emergent properties of group existence. (See Pfeffer, 1982, for a detailed treatment of this debate.) Because of the need to conceive of the office in terms of social and group interactions, and the sharing of meanings, a structuralist orientation is adopted within the social theoretic perspective. The result is an analysis which is much more sociological than psychological in nature. In fact, psychological 'theories' have been ostensibly excluded from consideration in this analysis as they were felt to be inadequate and inappropriate for dealing with the richness of social interaction.

STRUCTURE OF THE BOOK

This first chapter has set out the primary deficiency inherent in current treatments of office automation, viz. the failure to consider the importance of the social dimension. The knowledge gained over the past fifteen to twenty years through implementation research has been conspicuously ignored. Because of this, it is unlikely that the proposed benefits of OA will be realized. In fact, the long-term impacts might be dysfunctional. In order to go beyond simple technical analyses of office systems and to explore the wider area of office automation, a social theoretic perspective has been proposed. It provides not only the motivation for a social analysis of OA but also a general conception of what needs to be considered. The rest of the chapters in the book address those key areas which are essential for a detailed understanding and appreciation of office automation.

Chapter 2 provides a background to OA. It is not essential to the social theoretic argument but does offer a general and, to some extent, historical overview of the field. It outlines why there appears to be so much enthusiasm for office automation, some views on its historical development, and the problems associated with its definition. The primary reasons for the growth of interest in OA are also discussed, as are its predicted benefits. This chapter does not take a critical view of the postulated benefits nor their underlying assumptions. In fact, one of the main purposes of the chapter is to highlight the rather simplistic view taken of, for example, office productivity, particularly as it is the cornerstone of much of the interest in office systems. It is an archetypical view of OA which sets the stage for its social theoretic critique.

Chaper 3 begins the social theoretic analysis by exploring the nebulous concept of the office. It is hard to imagine how OA could be successfully applied, without a detailed understanding of the environment into which it is placed, i.e. the office. Yet, this is precisely what has been happening. Conceptions of the office have focused around the manifest activities performed by people. Understanding the office has been equated with the measurement of activities or 'functions'. This seems incredibly naive. The purpose of this chapter is to suggest alternative conceptions of the office. It begins by providing a brief history of the office and a survey of various writers' thoughts on the nature of the office. Because of the large number of office conceptions available in the literature, the chapter attempts to impose a structure which allows the key features of the conceptions to become apparent. This is done by describing the various office conceptions in terms of 'views' of which there are seven: activities, semantics, functions, work roles, decision taking, transactional, and language action. These views, however, are simply variations of more global or fundamental positions which are termed 'theoretical perspectives'. Two broad perspectives are identified: analytical and interpretivist. They represent fundamentally and markedly different notions of the office. The former conceives of offices as largely deterministic, rational, and overt; the latter as mostly non-deterministic, political, and covert. The analytical perspective is the dominant position adopted by the information systems community but a case is made for a shift in direction, away from the analytical to the interpretivist.

Chapter 4 addresses the area of OA models and methodologies. The theoretical perspectives and the associated views identified in the last chapter have direct equivalents in the available models and methodologies. This is hardly surprising. In the development of an OA model/methodology, the developer must have some underlying conception of the office. Again, not surprisingly, the dominant office conception upon which the OA models and methodologies have been based is the analytical perspective. The chapter explores the notion of 'methodology' as well as the similarity and difference between and OIS and conventional information systems methodology. The notion of 'model' is similarly explored, as is the connection between model and methodology. A number of OA models and methodologies are surveyed and an analysis is undertaken. The analysis involves the potential relationship of model to methodology, and their relationship to office views. Additionally, an evaluation of the various models/methodologies is undertaken. A variety of social and technical criteria is used in the evaluation with the result being that those methodologies which take into account the social domain have been more favourably assessed.

Chapter 5 covers the area of OA implementation. It is considered to be one of the key issues for successful information systems, yet is presented in a most naive and simplistic way in most of the literature. Because of the importance attached to implementation, it is not surprising that the most highly rated methodologies were those which explicitly considered and could satisfactorily deal with this issue. The chapter begins by exploring what implementation is and why it is critical for the success of OA. User resistance to change is portrayed as a natural and expected reaction to any new technological intervention and should be recognized as such. Conventional 'behavioural' approaches to overcome this resistance are shown to neglect the richness of social interaction. Planned change models, for example, miss the plurality of offices and assume a rationality on the part of organizational actors which is unlikely to exist. Counterimplementation and counter-counterimplementation strategies suffer a similar fate. While they recognize the political nature of implementation, they offer no sensible way to effectively deal with it. Moreover, they perpetuate the notion that implementation is simply a game in which there are winners and losers. Behavioural approaches such as these are felt to be too simplistic as they generally neglect the political and social processes inherent in organizational change. The implementation advocated in Chapter 5 is based on sociotechnical system ideals and effected through participation. Through participative development, the social and political aspects of change can be most effectively dealt with.

Chapter 6 discusses the broad area of OA implications. Although there have been dramatic claims about the widespread changes which will occur through office system use, there is apparently little empirical evidence to support these contentions. From a historical perspective, there is great reason to doubt their validity as similar claims were made for previous technological developments which ended in notable disappointment. This chapter takes a detailed look at the individual, organizational, and societal impact of OA. In so doing, it uncovers a variety of underlying (and usually hidden) assumptions associated with the various studies reporting OA implications. These assumptions are tied to philosophical positions which are never discussed. In reviewing the litera-ture, it is noted that there are three broad positions on impact: optimism, pessimism, and pluralism, which appear to have more to do with beliefs and values than empirical fact. They act as frameworks for reporting what is likely to happen, gathering support from confirming reports while ignoring discon-firming evidence. These positions are really independent of any particular technology. The relationship between *a priori* beliefs and reported impact is shown to be a powerful way of understanding the literature on OA implications.

One of the primary conclusions drawn in this chapter is that OA, on its own, does not necessarily have any particular effect; rather it is the underlying ideals and values that guide its management and implementation which are the major influence. Thus the connection between OA implementation and implications becomes evident.

Chapter 7 addresses the area of consequence prediction. Because OA impacts have been postulated to be related to values and beliefs which guide its management and implementation, it becomes feasible to contemplate consequence prediction. If the beliefs and values are understood in advance then it is possible to explore potential implications. This chapter draws on the work in the previous chapters to outline both a perspective and approach to analyse potential impacts. The perspective advocated is termed a 'consequentialist perspective' to connote the need for considering the possible effects of OA use before it is introduced. Simply put, it argues that the desirability of a technological intervention is to be determined by assessing the consequences the intervention brings about, irrespective of whether these were intended or unintended. The problems of agreeing on a set of values by which to assess desirability and how to predict consequences is explored. An approach for consequence prediction, grounded in hermeneutic process, is developed. It is based on role play. The result of an OA case study using the role-playing approach is reported and its potential for prediction is discussed. The conclusion put forward in the chapter is that hermeneutic analysis is a potentially fruitful way to deal with OA consequence prediction.

Chapter 8 summarizes the results of the social theoretic perspective applied to OA. The chapter reviews the discussions which took place on understanding the office, OA models and methodologies, implementation approaches, implications analysis, and consequence prediction, highlighting the major conclusions and points reached in each. Areas which might be considered contentious are explored, and support for the approach taken is offered. Potential criticisms of the work are anticipated and responded to. A fundamental disagreement on the degree of structure in the office is seen to be the source of the different views of office automation. The implications of this disagreement are taken up, resulting in the plea for a less deterministic view of the office to be adopted. Finally, avenues for further and future research are outlined.

Appendix A explores the relationship between the office views noted in Chapter 3 and various views of organizations. A number of organizational theory frameworks are discussed and an attempt is made to compare these with the proposed office perspectives and views. The result of the comparison suggests an underlying structure which is consistent across both.

Appendix B provides a checklist of key questions to be asked before implementing office automation. It involves the consideration of technical, organizational, communications, job, work group, training, safety, ergonomic, employment, and recommendation matters.

Figure 1.1 depicts how the key elements of office automation are related and how they are treated in this book. The most basic element is that of the 'office'. How the office is conceived lies at the heart of office automation. Its spatiotemporal and socioeconomic dimensions dictate what, when, where, how, and why the actions of an office take place. Office work, depending on the view held about these office dimensions, can be interpreted along the continua: structured/unstructured, overt/covert, rational/political, and pragmatic/symbolic. The belief that office work lies mostly on the structured, overt, rational, and pragmatic ends of the continua is at the root of the *analytical office perspective* discussed in Chapter 3, and is the conventional conception of the office. The alternative belief, that office work is largely unstructured, covert, political, and symbolic, reflects the *interpretivist office perspective*, and is the office conception advocated here. The way the office is conceived directly affects the notion of an office system. If a more analytical office perspective is embraced then the view of an office system is generally more technical in nature, i.e. it is a technical (computer-based) system which has (or may have) behavioural effects. If a more interpretivist perspective is adopted, it is likely to be conceived as a social system which to a greater or lesser extent relies on technical components for its efficient and smooth operation. The office system notion in turn dictates the appropriate models and methodologies to be used for its development: formal, deterministic ones for a technical conception of an office system; less formal, participative models and methodologies for a social system conception. They

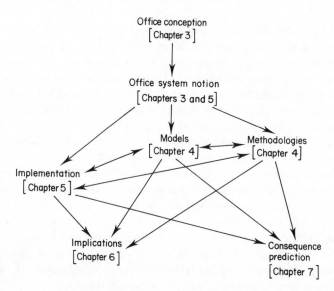

FIGURE 1.1   *How the key elements of office automation are related*

are also strongly related to the notion of implementation. Formal models and methodologies tend to promote a static and mechanical view of implementation; it is simply the 'putting in place' of the developed system. More informal models and participative methodologies reflect a process-oriented, social conception of implementation. The notion of implementation can be the result of or the reason for the choice of a particular model/methodology. These in turn are directly responsible for the implications of office automation — whether beneficial or dysfunctional effects result. They are also related to the way consequences are conceptualized and predicted: mechanistic–causal analysis for an analytical office perspective, hermeneutic analysis for an interpretivist perspective.

REFERENCES

Bjorn-Andersen, N., and Hedberg, B. (1981) 'Designing information systems in an organizational perspective', in *Prescriptive Models of Organizations* (Eds. P. Nystrom and W. Starbuck), TIMS Studies in the Management Sciences, Vol. 5.

Collins, R. (1981) 'On the microfoundations of macrosociology', *American Journal of Sociology*, **86**.

Glaser, B., and Strauss, A. (1967) *The Discovery of Grounded Theory: Strategies for Qualitative Research*, Aldine Publishing Company, Chicago.

Hirschheim, R. (1985) 'User experiences with office automation: lessons and conclusions', Working paper 85–02–1.0, London School of Economics, February.

Hoos, I. (1960) 'When the computer takes over the office', *Harvard Business Review*, July–August.

Mayhew, B. (1980) 'Structuralism versus individualism: Part I, Shadowboxing in the Dark', *Social Forces*, **59**.

Martin, J. (1981) *Telematic Society: A Challenge for Tomorrow*, Prentice Hall, Englewood Cliffs.

Mintzberg, H. (1979) 'An emerging strategy of "direct" research', *Administrative Science Quarterly*, **24**, No.4, December.

Mowshowitz, A. (1976) *The Conquest of Will: Information Processing in Human Affairs*, Addison-Wesley, Reading.

Pfeffer, J. (1982) *Organizations and Organization Theory*, Pitman, Boston.

Rhee, H. (1968) *Office Automation in Social Perspective: The Progress and Social Implications of Electronic Data Processing*, Basil Blackwell, Oxford.

Sackman, H. (1971) *Mass Information Utilities and Social Surveillance*, Auerbach Publishers, New York.

Chapter 2

A BACKGROUND TO OFFICE AUTOMATION

INTRODUCTION

The development of the microprocessor and the concomitant ability to apply it to a variety of products have dramatically increased the rate of change in the development of office technology and systems. This has given rise to products such as word processors, personal computers, intelligent copiers, management workstations, and PABXs. The greatest change, however, will likely lie in the convergence of these technologies with telecommunications, allowing the linking together of previously stand-alone products and the sharing of resources. This convergence is depicted in Figure 2.1. It attempts to present the emergence of a so-called 'integrated information resource' function which is the result of a confluence of three previously separate functions: data processing, telecommunications, and office services. Figure 2.1 also suggests how the four major means of information communication, voice, image, text, and data, are evolving and converging into one integrated resource.

These developments have led — and are increasingly leading — to the emergence of a variety of products which do not require the sanctity of an air-conditioned computer room nor the deployment of highly skilled computer operators and analysts. Rather, the products can be operated in ordinary offices by ordinary office staff.

The predicted concourse of the various technologies listed in Figure 2.1 with the office at the hub has caused many people to rethink the functions and activities of offices as well as their potential support by new office technology and systems. The term most generally used to describe this rethink is, and has been, office automation (OA). However, it is by no means universally accepted. Other terms have been offered as an alternative to office automation: office information systems (Ellis and Nutt, 1980), the office of the future (Uhlig, Farber, and Bair, 1979), the electronic office (Price, 1979), the paperless office (Strassman, 1985), integrated office systems (Naffah, 1980), and office support (Panko and Sprague, 1982), but none is as widely used.

Although the term office automation is in widespread use today, most are not particularly happy with it. OA conveys a rather narrow picture of an office, where tasks have been taken over by computers and computer-supported devices; the emphasis is on *automation* rather than *support*. It is this automation aspect which bothers many people about the term, and almost inherently leads

FIGURE 2.1 The integrated information resource

to a concentration on the technology rather than the social and work aspects of the office. For this reason the terms office support or office information systems would be better as they project a connotation which is much broader than office automation; however, neither is as widely used nor as known as office automation. (This is perhaps less true in the academic community. Quite a number of papers and journals refer to the area under rubric of office information systems rather than office automation; see, for example, ACM's publication *Transactions on Office Information Systems*.)

OFFICE AUTOMATION DEFINITION

As there is no universally accepted term to describe the application of new office technology and systems in the office, neither is there a universally accepted definition of office automation. Definitions offered in the literature range from the very broad and general to the specific. Some attempt to draw on the history of technological innovation in the office; others prefer to concentrate more on the nature of office work and the possibilities of new working arrangements. Still others do not even bother to define it, as they feel the term is too ambiguous or is so much related to individual perceptions that any attempt at a universal definition would be pointless. Nevertheless, a definition of the term is needed if office automation is to be adequately understood.

Hammer and Sirbu (1980) provide one of the most general definitions of office automation. They define it simply as:

> ...the utilization of technology to improve the realization of office functions.

Unfortunately this definition is so general that it is hard to exclude anything from being 'office automation'. According to their definition, office automation has been going on since the dawn of the office. Although this 'process oriented' or evolutionary view is a useful one, it does not sufficiently differentiate between what is and what is not office automation.

Ellis and Nutt (1980) in an attempt at a more specific definition of office automation state:

> An automated office information system attempts to perform the functions of the ordinary office by means of a computer system.

This definition tries to attach a significance to the new technology, although it seems to be limited to 'a computer system'. This, most would argue, is too limiting as it would tend to exclude products such as local area networks, intelligent copiers, video conferencing, and the like. Additionally, the aspect of 'to perform the functions of the ordinary office' seems misplaced as well. Most would take issue with the notion of 'the performing of office functions' as a key ingredient of office automation. Rather, the *support* of office functions is a more appropriate criterion than that of *automation*.

A variation of the Ellis and Nutt definition is offered by Uhlig, Farber, and Bair (1979). They discuss office automation more in terms of the types of tools needed by office workers. They consider an automated office as:

> ... an office in which interactive computer tools are put in the hands of individual knowledge workers, at their desks, in the areas in which they are physically working.

The authors provide a definition which differentiates between office workers — in this case 'knowledge workers' and 'non-knowledge workers'. (The term 'knowledge worker' tends to be rather loosely used to mean those office workers who spend a considerable part of their day performing unstructured and varied tasks which often require a high degree of tacit knowledge. In general, knowledge workers are thought to include managers, professionals, and the like.) The mention of 'interactive computer tools' is conspicuous as it is more specific than 'a computer system'. It still does not seem general enough to embrace local area networks, video conferencing, etc.; nor does this definition allow for a 'process-oriented' view to be taken of office automation. The definition also leaves out how the automated office affects those who are not 'knowledge workers'.

Many of the shortcomings of the previous definitions are corrected in the one offered by Olson and Lucas (1982). They state:

> Office automation refers to the use of integrated computer and communications systems to support administrative procedures in an office environment.

This definition emphasizes the notion of 'support' rather than automation and makes reference to the 'integration of computer and communications systems' — a point lacking in many definitions. However, the definition makes no mention of OA's historical background — particularly the growth of a multidisciplinary approach to office automation.

A definition which does take the historical background into account is one proffered by Zisman (1978). He notes that although office automation is a relatively new phenomenon, it is really an old term which has been given a new meaning:

> In the late sixties, the term referred to the application of computers to well-structured, high-volume office tasks.... In its present reincarnation, office automation refers to the application of computer technology, communications technology, systems science and behavioural science to the vast majority of less structured office functions which have not been amenable to traditional data processing technology. In both cases, however, the objective of office automation is to improve the productivity of our white-collar labour force.

The only major point which seems to be left out by Zisman is the notion of the *convergence* of the technologies being the primary instigation of the 'reincarnation'. One of the other potential sticky points of Zisman's definition is his notion that office automation tackles the 'less structured office functions'. As will be shown later, this is not something which everyone would agree with. There are a considerable number of people who ascribe to the notion that managerial or knowledge work is too unstructured to be amenable to technology (cf. Stewart, 1971; Mintzberg, 1973). Thus, to think that office automation can deal with the tasks of the knowledge worker is fallacious.

In sum, no one definition appears to capture the entirety of office automation. However, the amalgamation of Olson and Lucas and Zisman's definitions provides a reasonable alternative. It is presented below and will be used throughout this work:

Office automation, in its current form, refers to the application of integrated computer, communication, and office product technologies and social science knowledge to support the myriad activities and functions in an office or office environment.

OFFICE AUTOMATION HISTORY

The history of office automation, according to Meyer (1982), is a long and rich one. Meyer notes a number of innovations and product evolutions occurring in various fields relating to information systems, data processing, and office practices which have all contributed to its emergence. The following, adapted from Meyer, is one view of OA's history:

1870s. The first successful typewriter commercially produced. It provided the basis for mass written communication and the essence of the office. 'Its impact during the following 100 years on the Western world, particularly the United States, ranged from the restructuring of business practices to the emancipation of women, and, as suggested by some, even to the change of a prosaic writing style. Its history is a colourful one, filled with triumphs, as well as with disappointments' (Yamada, 1980).

1920s. The invention of the telephone as the foundation to the telecommunications infrastructure.

1930s. The adoption of 'scientific management', particularly for task specification and optimization. It provided a vehicle for a rational look at business practices and was the foundation of systems analysis.

1950s. The application of operations research to the decision-making process.

1950s. The emergence of the photocopier as the basis for rapid document reproduction. It greatly enhanced the ability to proliferate and disperse information throughout an organization.

1950s. The introduction of electronic data processing for the efficient processing of business transactions.

1960s. The development of telecommunications management which provided the foundation of telecommunications networking.

1960s. The emergence of management information systems (MIS) '... deals with all informational and decision-making activity associated with operating an organization ... to encourage better organizational efficiency and effectiveness through facilitating information provision and decision support to management' (Dickson, 1981).

1970s. Digital networks emerge to facilitate the communication among computers, particularly across great geographic distances.

1970s. Distributed processing emerges to provide the basis for local processing and storage.

1970s. The application of word processing for text editing and document preparation. Word processing is presented as a central feature of the so-called 'automated office'.

1970s. The practical application of behavioural science as a tool for the management of organizational change.

1980s. The development of the personal computer, a device which brings the computer to the individual and offers the possibility of complete distributed computing.

1980s. Decision support systems (DSS) emerge to support the decision-making process of management. 'Decision support implies the use of computers to:

1. Assist managers in their semi-structured decision tasks.
2. Support, rather than replace, managerial judgement.
3. Improve the effectiveness of decision-making rather than its efficiency' (Keen and Scott Morton, 1978).

1980s. The emergence of management workstations as new information manipulation tools for managers and professionals.

An alternative perspective on the historical development of office automation is offered by Panko and Sprague (1982). It is a more comprehensive view, and is based on two alternative options for dealing with the growth of information technology in organizations.

Panko and Sprague see the history of office automation starting in the office of the past. They note that in the early 1960s only the telephone was ubiquitous but computers were beginning to stake a claim to data-processing applications, thereby replacing the older electronic accounting machines. During the 1960s, whitecollar work flowered and so electric typewriters and photocopiers became commonplace. However, at the same time, the industrial segment plummeted. Panko and Sprague describe four major specializations that emerged from a fragmented approach to information management geared to manage the increased spending towards office technology:

1. *Data processing, management reporting.* Computing invariably meant data/records processing and was put under the umbrella of the Chief Financial Officer, with control primarily in the hands of the users. The introduction of new technology necessitated the employment of so many DP specialists, such as programmers and operators, that a powerful and rather independent DP centre evolved with its own DP manager. Applications began to extend beyond normal payroll functions, increasing the DP centre's hold on the organization.

2. *Specialized office products.* These products include mailing equipment, duplicators, and microfilm, and were generally purchased by the individual offices using them.

3. *Telecommunications.* Telephone and telex services were supplied by ven-

dors who relieved the user organization of most administrative burdens. This precluded the presence of large internal staff and also removed telecommunications from the spotlight that its outlay might have justified.
4. *General office products.* The spending on these items, e.g. typewriters, facsimile terminals, and answering machines, was provided for by annual budgets, but considerable initiative was left to individual departments.

Thus, the four major specializations of the 1960s placed control fairly near to the users, and since their technologies were so diverse, there was no need for a unified information management structure.

The impetus for a unified management structure gained momentum towards the end of the 1960s for the following reasons. Firstly, the outlay on information technology was steadily increasing, so much so that it necessitated closer scrutiny and tighter controls — a process not aided by scattered management accountability principles. Secondly, the technological barriers among the various tools were rapidly disintegrating. In fact, it may now be difficult to find any office product or equipment that is not microprocessor based and cannot be programmed to handle tasks that cut across authority boundaries in the firm. Additionally, the recent advances in networking have enabled office products to be linked in decentralized office communication systems and also have facilitated the recent trend in DP towards distributed data processing.

Panko and Sprague suggest two solutions open to organizations:

1. *The DP solution: information resource management (IRM).* The central theme of this solution is the treatment of data/information as a primary resource. Thus data/information must be managed across the organization in an integrated manner. However, IRM is historically conditioned, for it grew out of DP's file management and data management tradition, thus explaining its bias towards information repositories. Although IRM may claim to be a total philosophy of corporate management, in practice it is the DP manager's idea of total corporate information management.
2. *The office automation solution: small products and integrated office systems.* In early 1970s, new office products greatly expanded the role of small information tools in areas yet untouched by information technology. Such products included word processors, solid-state facsimile devices, and intelligent copiers. The era of office automation had begun, and its concept had now broadened to encompass a myriad of new tools.

Whatever the view on OA history, one point which all seem to agree with is its expanding focus. While this expansion in focus is healthy, and it is generally true that office automation is moving beyond traditional general office products, there is widespread disagreement over what it encompasses. According to

Hammer and Sirbu (1980), there are presently four conceptual models through which office automation may be viewed, and which may be helpful in the implementation of computer and communication technology in the office:

1. *Extension of DP tools.* The first model views office automation simply as an extension of DP functions, updated to take account of new hardware and software possibilities. This is an incomplete view in that traditional DP focuses on highly structured and data-intensive applications, while offices, in general, are often text intensive, highly interactive, and constantly changing.
2. *Paperless office.* The second model focuses on the concept of a paperless office, whereby the basic clerical tasks of information handling have been mechanized with the aid of computer-based tools such as word processors, electronic filing cabinets, and electronic mail. This view concentrates on office activities (see Chapter 3) and on the savings to be made by the application of modern technology to these tasks.
3. *Knowledge worker support.* The third model aims at augmenting the knowledge worker with powerful and intelligent tools which allows him/her to perform tasks of information manipulation. These tools include aids for composition, spelling correction, and document sharing. Recently, the scope has broadened to include facilities for group work such as computer conferencing.
4. *Decision support.* The last approach is that of decision support, whereby decision makers are provided with tools that assist them in accessing and analysing information. These tools theoretically support an unstructured or semi-structured decision process through the provision of calculations, displays, and other aids.

ANTECEDENT DEVELOPMENTS LEADING TO THE INTEREST IN OFFICE AUTOMATION

Without question there exists considerable interest in new office technology. Offices have been thought to be inefficient and costly. With the current concern for cost-consciousness, new information technology is perceived to be the vehicle for 'bringing the office into the twentieth century'. Yet the reasons for the interest in office automation are wider than just the development of some new technology. It has much more to do with attitudes, societal development, and so on.

1. The Coming Information Age

It is generally accepted that for the past two to three decades society has been undergoing an information explosion and entering an age where more and more people are working in the information sector (Machlup, 1962; Bell, 1973; and Porat, 1977). Figure 2.2, taken from Strassmann (1980), depicts this diagrammatically.

Panko (1981), based on US Department of Labour statistics, states that in 1980, 51.4 per cent of the US labour force were employed in white collar occupations whose work is largely information based. In a more recent analysis (Panko, 1984), white collar work is divided into two categories: 'information workers' and 'non-information workers'. He estimates that over 40 per cent of the 1982 US labour force were information workers.

A similar contention is made by Schement and Lievrouw (1984) who anticipate that well over 50 per cent of the labour force is engaged in information work. This is based on their finding that 40 per cent of all formal occupations are in fact 'information occupations' (p. 332).

As part of the information age, the world has experienced an unprecedented 'explosion' in the amount of textual or narrative information — easily confirmed when one looks at the number of pages printed in the various professional society journals during the past two decades, or by looking at the number of pages being printed by the publishers of the world, or by any organization for that matter.

The amount of information being stored on computers has concomitantly increased to meet the need to store and process the information. However, the gap between digital information, accessible from computers, and the total information being generated in the world is becoming wider. This gap is largely made up of narrative kinds of information and it is in the area of textual

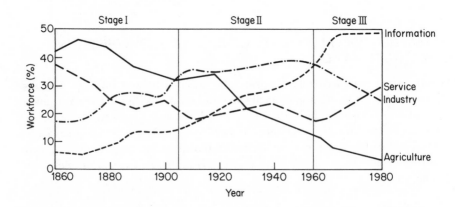

FIGURE 2.2 Changing composition of US workforce (%) from 1860 to 1980. Stage I is primarily agricultural; Stage II is an industrial economy; and Stage III is the information economy (Strassmann, 1981)

information that new technologies can be expected to make the greatest contribution to society in the future. Since much of the work that is conducted in offices involves narrative information, new office systems can be seen as a potentially valuable aid in its processing. This is a theme adopted by Bell (1980) who notes:

Obviously, the information explosion can only be handled through the expansion of computerized and subsequently automated information systems.

2. Advances in Technology

The concept of automating office tasks is not a new one — the first typewriter was developed in England more than two hundred years ago (*circa* 1714). Since that time, the office has been evolving; the process has been slow but continuous, incorporating relevant new technologies as they became available, in the systematic search to improve efficiency and extend the capabilities of office staff.

Recent technical advances like the microprocessor and telecommunications have had a more dramatic impact on the office than anything since the typewriter; they are now creating possibilities for information creation, storage, retrieval, distribution, and communication which were not even dreamed of a few years ago. The developments have virtually all had their basis in semiconductors and it is perhaps useful to briefly look at this industry.

The business of producing semiconductors now constitutes a major growth industry. According to Branscomb (1982), the compound growth rate of semiconductor industry shipments, in the United States, is 25 per cent per annum. The same trend has been reported in Japan where the sales of semiconductors by the two major companies — Hitachi and NEC — are growing at over 20 per cent a year.

The developments in semiconductor chips and of large-scale integration (LSI) has had a major impact on much of today's new technology and will influence future developments. The recent significant progress made in very large scale integration (VLSI) circuits indicates an advance in the achievement of higher chip density and lower cost, and an increase in the level of intelligence of the resulting systems.

The rapid development of semiconductors from transistor or integrated circuits (IC), followed by LSI and VLSI, has made it possible to realize a merger of computers and communications, a move towards digitalization, and the eventual reduction in cost of the systems equipment, both in the case of computers and communications. Figure 2.3, taken from Kobayashi (1981), is a generally accepted view of the trends in cost and integration of semiconductors.

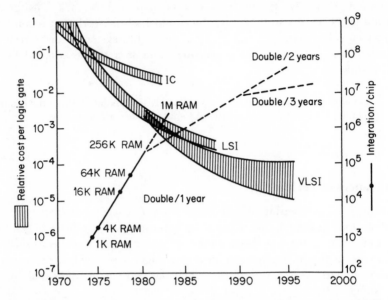

FIGURE 2.3 Trends in cost and integration (Kobayashi, 1981)

Kobayashi refers to this integration as 'C & C', the result of a unification of computers and communications. The recent trends of communication networks indicate the future combination of transmission systems and switching systems with digital technologies capable of creating integrated digital networks. This combination will result in a general-purpose network, referred to as an ISDN (integrated service digital network). Figure 2.4, also from Kobayashi, depicts this trend where the horizontal axis indicates the movement in communication technology (representing the degree of digitalization) while the vertical axis shows the degree of systematization.

Branscomb (1982) agrees. He sees the improvement in density and performance of semiconductors continuing for at least the next five to ten years. These trends are depicted in Figure 2.5.

Recent developments in semiconductors have also had other effects. For example, Figure 2.6 shows how semiconductors are dramatically reducing cycle times while concurrently reducing the cost of memory (Figure 2.7). These improvements have been accomplished through variations of memory LSI configurations and through high-density assembly techniques.

Interestingly, the falling prices of computer components, e.g. memory, logic, and circuitry, contrasts sharply with the cost trends associated with the people who use the technology. According to Burns (1977), the yearly cost reductions in computer memory, computer logic, and communications technology are 40,

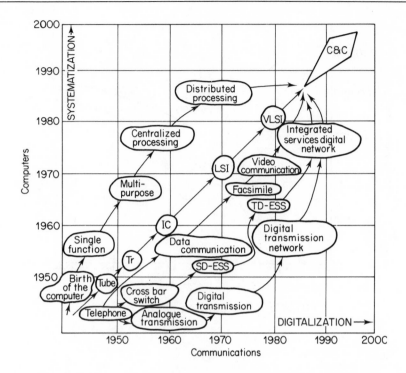

FIGURE 2.4 The integration of computers and communication
SD–ESS: space division electronic switching system
TD–ESS: time division electronic switching system
Tr: transistor

25, and 11 per cents respectively, whereas the cost of the labour force is increasing at 6 per cent per annum. Figure 2.8 presents these trends diagrammatically.

The importance of falling computing equipment costs in the growth of office automation was a theme discussed in Price (1979) as well. He noted that there has been a 20 per cent increase per annum in the price/performance of computer processors. For small computer systems, the increase is even more dramatic, viz. 35 per cent per year. Price contends that manufacturers will continue to be able to offer more and more powerful computers with increased performance at lower and lower prices.

One of the implications of the new technology is that it is now economical to incorporate microprocessors into many 'dumb' devices (such as terminals), which can then perform tasks previously covered by people or mainframe computers.

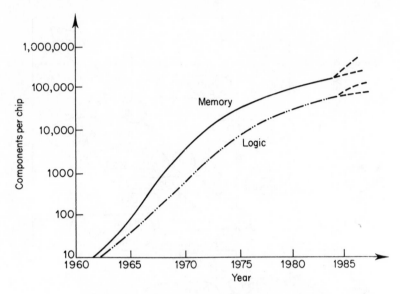

FIGURE 2.5 Integrated circuit density

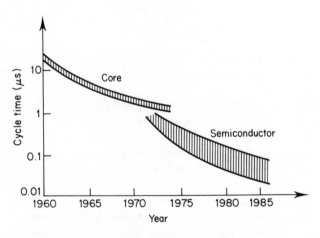

FIGURE 2.6 Cycle time of memory devices

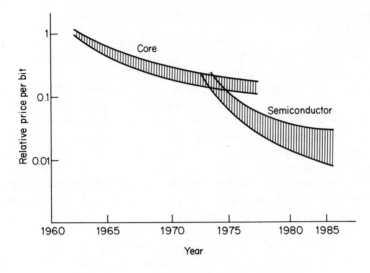

FIGURE 2.7 Price of memory devices

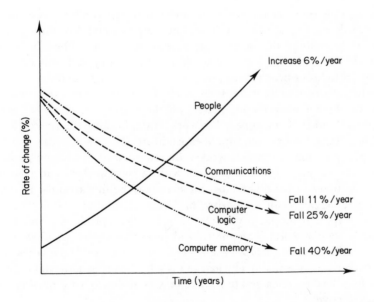

FIGURE 2.8 Rate of change of technologies

3. The Search for Ways to Improve Office Productivity

Perhaps the primary impetus behind office automation is the desire to improve office worker productivity. A considerable amount has been written about this subject and one of the key phrases of today is the 'productivity problem'. Office automation has been proclaimed to be *the* solution to the productivity problem but, as will be discussed shortly, this problem may be more imagined than real.

In a study published in *Business Week* (30 July 1975), it was asserted that over the past decade industrial productivity has risen by almost 90 per cent while office productivity has managed less than a 4 per cent increase. Operating costs in the office, over the same period, have nearly doubled. The result has been an increase in the overall proportion of total corporate running costs attributed to the office from 20–30 per cent to the present 40–50 per cent. Traditionally, corporations have made little capital investment in their office workers; estimates suggest the figure to be between $2,000 and $4,000 per office worker. Panko (1981) calculates the average capital expenditure per office worker to be $3,000. By comparison, the average capital expenditure for the industrial (factory) worker is estimated to be about $25,000.

The conclusion which many draw is that the reason for such a low office productivity increase is the small capital expenditure per office worker. Thus, an increased capital expenditure in the office could lead to higher office productivity.

Although the conclusion is widely believed, there are two caveats which need to be considered. One, the assumption that higher capital expenditure leads to higher productivity in the factory may or may not be true. There have clearly been cases where the implementation of new machinery and technology have actually led to lower productivity, worker unrest, sabotage, and the like. In the cases where there was an increase in productivity, how much of it is actually due to the higher expectations placed on the workers by management? Or perhaps the workers felt compelled to work harder because they feared for their jobs. The correlation between capital expenditure and productivity — although not spurious — may be much weaker than suspected. Two, comparing the productivity increases in office workers with factory workers and concluding that productivity in the office must increase may be unwarranted in that the relative starting points for comparison may be totally different. It is conceivable that ten years ago the factory worker was highly unproductive but through technology, better working methods, and procedures, etc., productivity rose markedly. This may not be the case with the office worker. If ten years ago the office worker was reasonably efficient in his job, then it is understandable why productivity has not risen greatly. There may be little scope for making the job more productive.

Moreover, there is reason to doubt the validity of these figures altogether. Grant (1984) contends that the capital expenditure figure is totally wrong.

Based on his assessment, the actual figure is between $15,000 and $20,000 per office worker. He also considers the 4 per cent office worker productivity increase over the past decade to be nothing more than a myth. He estimates the 'real' increase to be comparable with other occupations. Support for Grant's contention comes from Panko (1981) who in studying US federal government statistics calculated governmental office productivity to have increased by approximately 1.3 per cent per annum during the 1970s. This, Panko felt, was reasonable considering the overall economy's annual productivity growth was only 1.7 per cent. In a further analysis of the data, Panko (1984) reports that the 'real' compounded growth rate of the US federal government offices was closer to 2.8 per cent per annum — almost twice the overall economy's average. Between the period 1967 and 1981, office productivity had increased by 48 per cent.

These assessments cast some doubt on the relationship between capital expenditure and productivity. Whatever the relationship is, it is far from clear if a change in one will bring about a comparable change in the other. Nevertheless, the belief that further capital expenditure will cause office worker productivity to increase is widely held.

4. The Concern about the Growing Number of Office Workers

Another important reason for the interest in office automation is associated with the explosive growth in the numbers of office workers, which is a world-wide phenomenon. It suggests the need for office technology because of the sheer number of people involved in office and administrative jobs.

The number of people who make their living in the office or office-related jobs is rising every year. Zisman (1978) reported that 22 per cent of the US labour force was involved in office work. Other figures are more dramatic. Based on a 1981 UK study, 7,791,400 British workers — 34.2 per cent of the labour force — are engaged in office, professional and technical occupations (UK Department of Employment, 1981). In the United States, the figures is even higher: 37,151,000 workers comprising 50 per cent of the labour force, with a total wage bill of almost $600 billion per annum (US Bureau of Labor Statistics, 1981).

The trend also holds in the Federal Republic of Germany. According to a Siemens study, reported in Morgenbrod and Schaertzel (1980), the proportion of office workers in relation to the total number of employees has risen from 35 per cent in 1960 to 43 per cent in 1970 to approximately 53 per cent in 1980. Not only is this trend continuing but office workers secure a disproportionate amount of payroll costs. Figure 2.9 shows the disproportionate escalation of payroll costs in relation to the rise in the number of office employees.

One of the important aspects associated with the rising number of office workers is that of salaries — particularly those of managers and other

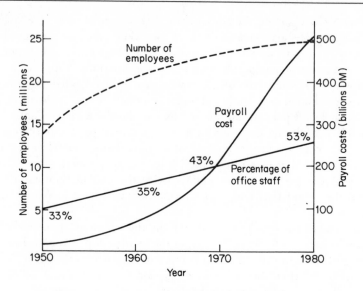

FIGURE 2.9 Office staff versus payroll costs in Germany

professionals. White collar salaries constitute a significant amount of the running costs of a business. Poppel's (1979) study of US businesses reported that $600 billion out of $800 billion spent on the support of office-based white collar workers was attributable to 'knowledge' workers, i.e. managers and other professionals (see Figure 2.10).

Poppel also suggested that by 1990, the direct cost of white collar workers could rise to $1.5 trillion. He proposed that a $300 billion yearly savings could be obtained, however, if new office technology were exploited (see Figure 2.11). Much of the $300 billion savings would come from reduced salary bills. This becomes apparent when one considers the true salary costs of a typical employee. It is a point that Haider (1979) claims too few people realize when they commit themselves to employing an individual. Based on his figures (see Figure 2.12) the total corporate commitment to an individual employed in an organization is approximately $2.5 million.

There are two additional concerns associated with the growing number of office workers. One, as the number grows, a greater and greater proportion of total corporate costs will be based on office costs; the present figure is reported to be between 40 and 50 per cent. These costs are expected to continue rising at between 10 and 15 per cent per annum, and involve increases in: salaries, cost of office supplies, cost of transportation, fuel, rental charges, postal charges, and the like.

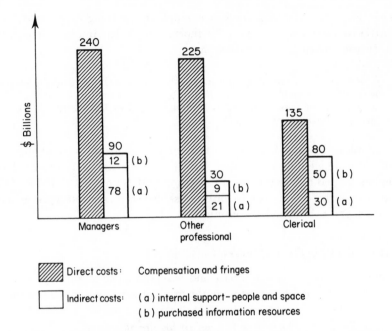

FIGURE 2.10 Breakdown of $800 billion spending in 1979 of US businesses to support their office-based white collar workers

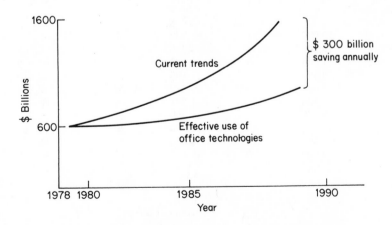

FIGURE 2.11 Saving potential of office technologies

Two, even with the high rates of unemployment being experienced by the industrialized nations, there is still a shortage of skilled and experienced office staff. It was reported in *Datamation* that:

> ... a shortage of secretaries is putting heavy burdens on highly skilled professionals who otherwise could be delegating up to 30% of their work. Without that support, we have a situation where industry finds itself with $30,000 to $40,000 a year clerks (*Datamation*, April 1980).

As examples, a recent UK Department of Employment study reported that there were 35,994 vacancies for clerical and related staff in the United Kingdom. Alfred Marks Bureau, a UK secretarial agency, estimated that in the London area, there were six jobs for every skilled secretary and typist available. Reports suggest this trend is continuing.

5. The Spiralling Office Market

The spiralling office market is part and parcel of office automation and is, in some sense, self-fulfilling. That is, as the need for new office systems grows, the

TABLE 2.1 Cost of an employee

Assumptions:
- 20 years old
- $10,000 p.a. salary at start
- works 30 years
- receives 8% p.a. increase
- retires on half salary
- lives to age 75

Year	Salary $	Year	Salary $	Year	Salary $
1	10,000	11	21,589	21	46,609
2	10,800	12	23,316	22	50,338
3	11,664	13	25,182	23	54,365
4	12,597	14	27,196	24	58,715
5	13,605	15	29,372	25	63,412
6	14,693	16	31,721	26	68,484
7	15,869	17	34,259	27	73,964
8	17,138	18	37,000	28	79,881
9	18,509	19	39,960	29	86,271
10	19,990	20	43,157	30	93,172

Total salary	$1,132,828
Benefits @ 30%	339,848
	$1,472,676
Retirement income for 25 years	1,004,430
Total salary: income plus related overhead expenses	$2,477,106

information technology industry will expand to meet the demand. As the industry grows, it will, through advertising, publicity, etc., cause the demand for office technology to grow, and so on.

Market forecasts for the office technology area vary substantially, but no matter which forecast is read, the predicted expenditure is substantial. *Business Week* (30 July 1975), for example, predicted the market for office system technology would reach $85 billion in the United States by the middle to late 1980s. A Canadian Department of Communications study (Coates, 1981) predicted the Canadian market alone would be worth $10–15 billion by the end of the 1980s. The study also expected the US market to exceed $220 billion by 1988. Current predictions suggest the figure to be in excess of $300 billion by 1990.

6. The Need to be Competitive

Improving the quality of an organization's output, speed of response to customers' requirements, speed of entry to markets, and accuracy of information to enable markets to be exploited may also be motivating forces which drive an organization towards office automation.

Organizations are aware of the need to create an advantage over their competitors, and are constantly searching the environment for opportunities and threats. Some organizations are prepared to be innovative in their outlook and willing to pay the cost of being in a position to take those opportunities as they arise. However, most organizations tend to adopt a 'wait and see' attitude and take advantage of new opportunities only when other companies have demonstrated the benefits.

There is a growing awareness that information is an integral part of the production of goods and the provision of services — take away a company's database and it will not be able to operate effectively. Information, the argument goes, should be treated as another of an organization's resources such as the more familiar ones of land, labour, and capital. Some experts believe that the value of information will be the most powerful long-term force in motivating the development and growth of office automation.

7. Familiarity with Computing Equipment

The increased familiarity with computers and computer-related products and the knowledge acquired from the use of electronic equipment, such as calculators, video games, and personal computers in the home, will facilitate user experience and lead to expectations of seeing such equipment in use within a work environment.

Branscomb (1982) predicts a reduction in the ratio of employees per terminal from forty-eight people per terminal within the US workforce in 1980 to an

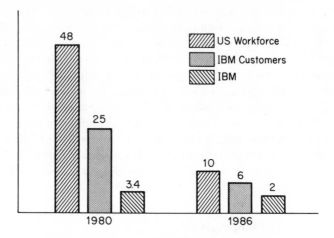

FIGURE 2.12 Employees per terminal

estimated ten people per terminal in 1986 (see Figure 2.12). He contends this can only be accounted for if one considers the increased familiarity of the general public with computers and computer-related products as well as trends internal to business and industry.

OFFICE AUTOMATION BENEFITS

The potential benefits resulting from office automation have been predicted to be many and varied. They range from increases in productivity, to reduced costs, to improvements in the quality of working life of office personnel. The arguments are aimed mostly at management and thus have a distinctive economic flavour to them. A number of more prominent benefits are briefly outlined here and taken up again, in a more serious fashion, in Chapter 6.

One of the key areas where benefits are predicted is in the area of office worker productivity — and not just the productivity of the clerical worker. Abraham (1981) asserts that the major gains may well occur with managers and other office professionals. He sees productivity enhancements occurring in five areas:

1. Better utilization of human resources — by reducing the number of employees or by having the same number perform more work
2. Increased performance — through the increase of output per person
3. Increased quality of decisions, work, products, and services — through improvements in the handling and dealing of information

4. Increased efficiency — through the performance of tasks in less time
5. Increased effectiveness — through, for example, improved organizational communication

Abraham provides a comprehensive (and some might say unrealistic) list of benefits for the professional or knowledge worker which divides the benefits into two categories — tangible and intangible:

1. *Tangible benefits.* Tangible benefits generally save either time or labour (or both) and are usually observable and quantifiable. Abraham notes benefits in eight areas: (a) fewer transfers of control over work; (b) decreased need for travel; (c) decreased need for meetings; (d) decreased number of phone calls; (e) eliminated shadow functions (i.e. unpredictable, time-consuming activities that do not contribute to productivity, such as incorrectly dialling a telephone number); (f) increased output; (g) fewer media transformations; and (h) elimination of labour via automation, or elimination of a procedure or steps in a procedure.
2. *Intangible benefits.* Intangible benefits can also save time or labour, but they are less susceptible to quantification and are more subtle. Abraham notes twelve areas of improvement: (a) better control over events and, hence, over time; (b) reduced dependency on other parts of the organization; (c) decreased need for procedures and forms to track work as it travels through the organization; (d) attitude and morale improvement, leading to increased job satisfaction; (e) decreased dependence upon management style for effective management; (f) increased goodwill and customer satisfaction; (g) quicker decisions; (h) better decisions; (i) more effective and timely communications; (j) higher quality work; (k) increased span of control; and (l) better and more timely information.

Uhlig, Farber, and Bair (1979) present an alternative way of looking at the potential office automation impact on management productivity (see Figure 2.13). It is based on how the various technologies of office automation replace or augment present office tasks, leading to a savings of 2 hours 45 minutes in an eight hour working day.

A similar view of OA benefits is offered by Lodahl (1980) who calls them 'value-added' benefits. These are extra facilities provided to the office worker which extend his or her capabilities. Price (1979) notes four value-added benefits resulting from office automation:

1. *Increased information accessibility*, from an information management system (IMS) which can provide information that is more up to date and accurate and can also provide the means to search, define requirements, and retrieve relevant information quickly and cheaply.

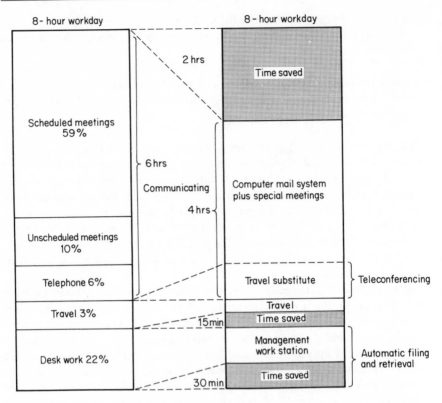

FIGURE 2.13 Potential office automation impact on management productivity

2. *Increased people accessibility*, from, for example, an electronic message system which can provide the possibility of non-simultaneous contacts (e.g. store and forward communication). It will permit people to communicate efficiently even though both of the parties are not at the same place or are not simultaneously available — a great advantage given the fact that up to 70 per cent of business calls fail because of the inavailability of the person at the other end.
3. *Increased control over personal activities* is realized through the possibility of working from different locations by, for example, using portable terminals. The use of electronic message systems will enable individuals to be able to control when they wish to look at messages rather than having to endure constant telephone interruptions while trying to concentrate.
4. *Increased individual contribution.* Individuals can spend more time on their primary tasks, rather than auxiliary (but essential) support tasks.

CAUSE FOR CONCERN

Whether office automation *will* yield benefits such as those predicted above will depend on a variety of social and behavioural aspects related to work and general organizational life. If it is predicted that OA will lead to better decision making and greater productivity then it must be assumed that some understanding of what people do in offices is held. If it is predicted that OA will lead to, for example, less travel then it is assumed a knowledge of personal preferences is possessed. People will only travel less if that is their preference. It is simply fallacious to posit that because video, audio, or computer conferencing lessens the need for travel, therefore there will be less travel. Even if the contention that the technology lessens the need for travel is correct, it is still up to the individual workers to decide whether they want to travel less.

Sweeping predictions such as those presented above are not only dubious but are dangerous as well. They heighten expectations, further fuel purely economic considerations of OA, and perpetuate the technical bias of office automation. The following chapters offer a social conception of OA, in an attempt to provide a richer understanding of the office, how office systems can be applied, and what their implications are likely to be.

REFERENCES

Abraham, S. (1981) 'The impact of automated systems on the productivity of managers and professionals', *Proceedings of the 1981 Office Automation Conference*, Houston, March.

Bell, D. (1973) *The Coming of Post-Industrial Society*, Basic Books, New York.

Bell, D. (1980) 'The social framework of the information society', in *The Computer Age: A Twenty-Year View* (Eds. M. Dertouzos and J. Moses), MIT Press, Cambridge, Mass.

Branscomb, L. (1982) 'Bringing computing to people: the broadening challenge', *Computer*, **15**, No.7, July.

Burns, J. (1977) 'The evolution of office information systems', *Datamation*, April.

Coates, S. (1981) 'The office of the future', Department of Communications, Government of Canada, Ottawa.

Dickson, G. (1981) 'Management information systems: evolution and status', *Advances in Computers*, Vol. 20, Academic Press, New York.

Ellis, C., and Nutt, P. (1980) 'Computer science and office information systems', *ACM Computing Surveys*, **12**, No.1, March.

Grant, K. (1984) 'The "folklore" of office automation', *Office Systems Research Journal*.

Haider, R. (1979) 'Planning for office automation', *Proceedings of the Infotech State of the Art Conference*, Vienna.

Hammer, M., and Sirbu, M. (1980) 'What is office automation?', *Proceedings of the 1980 Office Automation Conference*, Atlanta.

Keen, P., and Scott Morton, M. (1978) *Decision Support Systems: An Organizational Perspective*, Addison-Wesley, Reading.

Kobayashi, K. (1981) 'Computer, communications and man: the integration of computer and communications with man as an axis', *Computer Networks*.

Lodahl, T. (1980) 'Cost–benefit concepts and applications for office automation', *Proceedings of the 1980 Office Automation Conference*, Atlanta.

Machlup, F. (1962) *The Production and Distribution of Knowledge in the United States*, Princeton University Press, Princeton.

Meyer, N. (1982) 'Office automation: a progress report', *Office: Technology and People*, **1**, March.

Mintzberg, H. (1973) *The Nature of Managerial Work*, Harper and Row, New York.

Morgenbrod, H., and Schaertzel, H. (1980) 'The degree of office automation and its impact on office procedures and employment', *Computer Networks*.

Naffah, N. (Ed.) (1980) *Integrated Office Systems — Burotics*, North-Holland, Amsterdam.

Olson, M., and Lucas, H. (1982) 'The impact of office automation on the organization: some implications for research and practice', *Communications of the ACM*, **25**, No.11, November.

Panko, R. (1981) 'Facing basic issues in office automation', *Computer Networks*, **5**.

Panko, R. (1984) 'Office work', *Office: Technology and People*, **2**.

Panko, R., and Sprague, R. (1982) 'Towards a new framework for office support', *Proceedings of the SIGOA Conference*, Philadelphia, June.

Poppel, H. (1979) 'The automated office moves in', *Datamation*, November.

Porat, M. (1977) *The Information Economy*, Publication 77–12, US Department of Commerce, Washington, May.

Price, S. (1979) *Introducing the Electronic Office*, NCC Publications, Manchester.

Schement, J., and Lievrouw, L. (1984) 'A behavioural measure of information work', *Telecommunications Policy*, December.

Stewart, R. (1984) *How Computers Affect Management*, Macmillan, London.

Strassmann, P. (1980) 'The Office of the future: information management for the new age', *Technology Review*, December/January.

Strassmann, P. (1985) 'The paperless office', *Information Technology Training*, February.

Uhlig, R., Farber, D., and Bair, J. (1979) *The Office of the Future*, North-Holland, Amsterdam.

Yamada, H. (1980) 'A historical study of typewriters and typing methods', *Journal of Information Processing*, **2**, No.4.

Zisman, M. (1978) 'Office automation: evolution or revolution', *Sloan Management Review*, Spring.

Chapter 3

UNDERSTANDING THE OFFICE

INTRODUCTION

Although there exists considerable literature on the technical aspects of office automation, the social environment into which it is placed has been far less explored by researchers. In particular, the tasks which are performed in offices have received biased attention. There exist a number of office activity task taxonomies but they do little more than provide a simple structure through which to conceive of an office. From a social perspective this appears to be overly simplistic and misses the richness of social action in an office. To focus on the overt and manifest aspects of the office may very well lead to its misrepresentation. This chapter takes a critical look at the way offices are conceived in the office automation literature and suggests alternatives which may provide a better understanding of the real functions of an office.

HISTORICAL DEVELOPMENT OF THE OFFICE

According to present-day commentators such as Daniel Bell and Alvin Toffler, the age within which we live is continuously undergoing change. The change is rapid and refers not only to technology but to all aspects of our way of life. The office of today is different from what it was in the past and will be different again in the future. In order to better understand the concept of 'the office', it is perhaps useful to look at its evolution. It should be noted that this evolutionary view is only meant to be a very brief treatment of an historical account of the office and is based on the classic analysis of Rhee (1968). The historical perspective is meant to convey the fact that offices are not immutable objects; rather they evolve according to technological progress and social conditions.

1. Pre-Industrial Age

The history of the office reaches far back into the annals of human history, probably to the start of man's economic activities. As man found the need to record economic activity, certain forms of specialization (e.g. record keeping) surfaced. Man found it advantageous to group many of the specializations at a particular location and thus the notion of an office having some geographical connotation emerged. Concomitant with the physical locating of individuals at one site came the need to manage and organize their activities. Hence, the emergence of the office — a place where people engaged in certain economic activities in some organized manner.

Until the age of the industrial revolution, office workers — in contrast to factory workers — were characterized as a prestigious labour class closely linked with management and/or the owners of businesses. They were involved in activities that required a variety of skills, not the least of which were skills associated with functions of management. Clerical work was completely paper based and individualized, even after the development of the telephone and typewriter. As the complexity of society grew, office activities and skills increased. Job content changed and the social distinction between white collar and blue collar workers became more pronounced.

2. Industrial Age

The development and perfection of the steam engine in the eighteenth century brought about a substantial increase in capital resource expenditure in industrial organizations along with a dramatic rise in the labour force of both the factory and the office. The all-purpose clerk of the pre-industrial age began to disappear and was replaced by a more specialized clerk who concentrated on only one or a few office tasks. This came about due to concerns about productivity. Writers such as Taylor, Gilbreth, and Gantt stressed the need to apply scientific techniques to standardize and rationalize work. Decision making — a major time-consuming operation — was removed (whenever possible) so that a person had more time to spend on the task(s) that remained. The work which remained was some standardized fragment of some larger piece. It was also more routine and repetitive. The application of Taylors' 'scientific management' principles led to improved productivity of both the factory and office worker. The office itself became a myriad of islands of specialization, where each function was as standardized and rational as possible.

3. Information Age

As the need for more sophisticated information was recognized as essential if organizations were to survive in the post-industrialized age, offices were forced to process even greater quantities of information. Information had to be utilized more effectively. Information technology was seen as the key. Technology such as computers, electronic typewriters, and PABXs allowed office workers to better handle the problems of obtaining, classifying, storing, retrieving, and processing information. Information networks sprang up to help organizations exchange information. The notion of information overload was recently recognized and has led many offices to pay more attention to information analysis, information presentation methods, and the quality of information. The office of the information age places a great reliance on information technology; as such, a variety of technical skills have to be possessed by the office workers of the information age.

In a sense, the office worker has come full circle: from a generalist in the pre-industrial age, to a specialist in the industrial age, and now back to a generalist. Getz (1978) writes: ' ... where technology once divided us into many fields of speciality, we now find that technology is eliminating the need for some specialists and the generalist is again on the rise....'

NATURE OF THE OFFICE

On the surface, the tasks which are performed and thus what occurs in the office seem apparent. Everyone has a conception of what an office is and the views are, most likely, similar. However, differences start to creep in when one attempts to structure the activities in some meaningful fashion. Carter and Huzan (1981), for example, discuss the nature of the office in terms of work processes where 'paper' is the accepted basis of these work processes. They note that an office contains three basic elements (people, paper, and files) which are involved in five general activities:

1. People to people communication (e.g. telephone)
2. People to paper communication (e.g. typing)
3. Paper to paper transfer (e.g. copying)
4. Paper to file transfer (e.g. storing)
5. Files to people transfer (e.g. information retrieval)

Carter and Huzan also mention:

> The essential resource being processed is information and the transference process involves communication.

Kent (1979) views the nature of the office differently. He sees the office as producing 'products' which involve various office tasks and functions. 'Products' are defined as the output produced by the office workers in performing their duties in the organization. For instance, the products from the administrative department are mostly paper: documents, reports, etc. 'Tasks' are defined to be the activities professional people do (Table 3.1) and 'functions' to be those that clerical people perform (Table 3.2).

Price (1979) offers an alternative classification for structuring the nature of the office. He breaks up office operations into four categories:

TABLE 3.1 A collection of tasks applicable to all 'products'

1. Plan	7. Coordinate
2. Consult	8. Obtain approvals
3. Collect data	9. Disseminate
4. Analyse, sort, and evaluate data	10. Maintain records
5. Review and revise drafts	

TABLE 3.2 A series of functions performed by clerical staff to support professional staff

1. Typing	8. Communication
2. Dictation	● voice
3. Transcription	● record
4. Files maintenance	● data
5. Duplication	● post
6. Inter-office distribution	9. Data processing
7. Printing	

1. Document preparation. This covers activities associated with the preparation of documents and includes dictation, typing, shorthand, duplicating, copying, and the use of typesetting services.
2. Message distribution, which covers the activities associated with the distribution of information and includes using telephones, telex, mail services, and travel for meetings.
3. Personal information management, which covers the activities related to organizing personal information and includes the use of filing cabinets, index cards, in/out trays, diaries, planning boards, and the like.
4. Information access, which involves activities related to the access of information and includes the use of directories, timetables, catalogues, libraries, bibliographic services, and corporate databases.

The Office Management Association (1958) provides a more simple view of the nature of the office and sees offices as providing services to organizations. In particular, they see offices as providing two types of services:

1. General services dealing with copying, correspondence, telephone, and other general activities essential and common to all organizations.
2. Information services are all services dealing with information such as producing reports.

It should be noted that even though the Office Management Association view concentrates on services rather than activities; all services — in one way or another — still involve information. Information is seen as the basic commodity of the office. This is a point which has not escaped the attention of Mokhoff (1979) who suggests that office functions can be classified into two fundamental information activities: information processing and information handling. Information handling activities are made up of oral data, text, and graphics exchanges while information-processing activities consist of text production, data collection, documentation and storage, and graphics production.

In terms of the views summarized above, offices can be thought of as centres of organizational information handling and processing. Many therefore conclude that the nature of an office can be considered within the context of what an office does, namely: (1) receives information; (2) records and stores information; (3) structures information; (4) processes information; and (5) provides access to the information.

It is because offices are fundamentally conceived as information handlers and processors that there has been so much interest in office automation. Office automation is seen as a vehicle for dramatically enhancing information handling/processing capabilities. However, this conception may be problematic. Even though many consider that the nature of the office revolves around information, this still does not explain what *actually* happens in the office. There is a pressing need to have a better appreciation of what does happen in offices.

OFFICE TAXONOMIES

Researchers have sought a richer understanding of the office through the development of two types of taxonomies: one associated with the kinds of offices which exist; the other, with the various observable office activities. The former attempts to categorize the office into specific and different types, the latter tries to uniquely classify office activities or tasks. Examples of the former are Panko and Sprague's (1982) Type I and II offices, Panko's (1984b) enhancement, and Gunton's (1983) typology. This type of taxonomy has currently not provided a great deal of insight into the inner workings of offices. The office categorizations, although interesting, have been too simplistic to be of much value. This chapter will therefore concentrate on those taxonomies which focus on the functions performed by individuals in an office.

Numerous taxonomies, each with its own terminology to define and classify the activities of an office, have been proposed (Stewart, 1967; Klemmer and Snyder, 1972; Mintzberg, 1973; Engel et al., 1979; Uhlig, Farber, and Bair, 1979; Christie, 1981; Conrath et al., 1981a; Cook, 1981; Poppel, 1982; and Kurke and Aldrich, 1983) Although each classifies activities in its own particular way, from a more global perspective such classifications are fundamentally the same. This is a point suggested by Higgins and Safayeni (1984) and substantiated by Dodswell (1983) who had little difficulty in synthesizing six different studies each with its own specific taxonomy. The simple fact is that these types of taxonomies are relatively straightforward: easy to conceptualize and easy to understand how observable office activities could be classified under such a scheme. However, the simplicity of these taxonomies raises considerable concern. Higgins and Safayeni (1984), for example, note three problems associated with such taxonomies: (1) office activities may not be classifiable in any meaningful way; (2) the idea of mutually exclusive categories does not necessarily reflect reality; and (3) office activities may not be mappable onto different technologies. Suchman (1983) worries that these taxonomies reflect a view where office activities are seen to be the product of some enduring structure that stands behind office work, rather than the product of social action. From a social theoretic perspective, the activities (or procedures, functions, tasks, as they are loosely referred to in the literature) performed in an office are largely social in nature. An office, therefore, is a social environment involving social action. Manifest behaviour, the basis of all the taxonomies cited above, provides only one perspective from which to conceive of office activities. There are others. The next sections of this chapter critically analyse the foundations of the various ways an office can be conceived, highlighting the implicit assumptions underlying each.

OFFICE PERSPECTIVES

In attempting to develop an understanding of the operations of an office, it is necessary to first explore the notion of 'office'. This, however, proves most difficult. Dodswell (1983), for example, laments: 'it is extraordinarily difficult to provide a concise and clear definition (of office)' (p.8). Pava (1983) writes:

> The term 'office' is a misnomer. It implies a false homogeneity. Office work denotes a wide assortment of functions that include everything from processing ticket stubs to strategic planning. People working in offices do a great many different things. They hold different jobs, run different sorts of operations, and draw upon a variety of skills and equipment (p.46).

Hammer and Zisman (1979) share a similar concern:

> ... we find these definitions (of an office) fundamentally inadequate. First, they suggest a vision of an office as a free-floating room containing a 'manager' and a 'secretary' whose job descriptions can be expressed in terms of generating documents, conversing on the telephone, and attending meetings. Second, they refer to 'the office' as though all offices were the same, instances of a canonical archetype (quoted in Panko 1984a, p. 206).

Viewing the office as a place where white collar work is conducted or as a set of functions and activities whose output is written and oral communication, is likely to lead to an unacceptably narrow focus. The former view focuses on geographical constraints whereas the latter concerns itself only with what people appear to do in offices. Neither view sufficiently takes into account the fact that offices are not isolated entities, but rather independent bodies which interact and exist within some larger context — the organization. Offices serve a variety of purposes, many of which are highly informal and not easily understood. Moreover, they are in a dramatic state of flux. The advent of remote work, for example, has removed the geographical boundaries associated with offices. The functions carried out by the office can now be dispersed across the social and geographic landscape. Thus, the term 'office' may very well be an unsatisfactory label for where, how, when, and what work is performed in the emerging information society. This, of course, is particularly true given the increasing role information technology plays in the evolution of the office. Nevertheless, as Delgado (1979) notes, the concept of 'office' is deeply ingrained in our culture. He writes:

> The concept of the office can be seen as one of the most consistent threads in any culture, for systems of government and manufacture may change beyond recognition, but in any organization of human beings which extends beyond the smallest group, the word 'office', and the ideas it represents, emerge as stable components of language (quoted in Dodswell, 1983, p.9).

Although the concept 'office' poses considerable difficulty in terms of definition, there are a number of dimensions or levels through which an office could be conceived. For example, offices are thought to have a geographical dimension (its physical placement); a temporal dimension (hours of or at work); an activity dimension (tasks which are performed); a structural dimension (worker reporting relationships); a spatial dimension (the area where a person works relative to his coworkers); an economic dimension (the economic criteria which drives the organization and by which the worker is assessed); and a social dimension (the social and psychological reasons which motivate people to work in offices). This list is not exhaustive; it is simply meant to suggest the complexity of what is involved in attempting to acquire an understanding of the office. Exploring offices in terms of these dimensions, however, tends to mask the fundamental conception of an office; i.e. underlying the dimensions is a more basic notion, viz. a theoretical perspective.

The assertion proposed here is that there are two different theoretical perspectives of the office: *analytical* and *interpretivist*. These perspectives represent two markedly different notions of what goes on in an office. The former sees the office as an environment where people perform a variety of functions to support the successful running of the organization. The functions are conceived of in terms of largely formal and structured actions or activities. The latter conceives of the office in terms of mostly unstructured and informal human action. In some ways these perspectives are not dissimilar from Kling's (1980) two perspectives on the social impact of computing, i.e. 'systems rationalism' and 'segmented institutionalism'. He defines systems rationalism as assuming a consensus on major social and organizational goals. It possesses a relatively synoptic account of social behaviour and places extreme weight on both organizational and economic efficiency. Segmented institutionalism, on the other hand, sees intergroup conflict as the norm and is thus disinclined to believe in any consensus about organizational goals. Social behaviour is dynamic, hard to understand and define, yet the key ingredient of organizational life. The sovereignty of individuals and social groups over critical aspects of their lives is considered the dominant issue instead of economic efficiency.

The analytical and interpretivist office perspectives differ on a number of dimensions. For example, the former sees office functions (activities) as largely deterministic, rational, and overt whereas the latter conceives of them as mostly non-deterministic, political, and covert. The analytical perspective metaphorically conceives of the organization as 'structure'; the interpretivist conceives of the organization as 'agent' or 'culture'. This metaphorical difference (based on Argyris and Schon's, 1978, 'theories of organizational learning') reflects two alternative views of organizations. The 'structure' view sees organizations as 'an ordered array of role-boxes connected by lines which represent flows of information, work, and authority' (Argyris and Schon, 1978, p. 324). The 'agent' or 'culture' view notes that organizations are both instruments for achieving social purposes and small, restricted societies where 'people create for themselves shared meanings, symbols, rituals, and cognitive schemes which allow them to create and maintain meaningful interactions among themselves and in relation to the world beyond their small society' (p.327).

The analytical perspective sees office action in terms of manifest behaviour; the interpretivist, in terms of the shared social meaning of the actors. The former is observable and empirical, the latter is symbolic and largely non-empirical. It follows, therefore, that the appropriate measurement instruments and research paradigms must also differ. The analytical perspective adopts formal models using empirical methods as the appropriate measurement instrument, while the interpretivist uses phenomenological study. The former embraces a quantitative research paradigm; the latter, a more qualitative one. This is similar to the Burrell and Morgan (1979) dichotomy of 'objectivism' versus 'subjectivism' (see Chapter 6). Lastly, the two perspectives differ in their focus: for the analytical, the focus is on analysis; for the interpretivist, it is 'verstehen' or understanding. The former seeks to analyse office operations and functions by breaking them down into their constituent parts. Knowledge is acquired through the scientific endeavour of reductionism. The latter is less concerned with analysis and more concerned with understanding; knowledge is available only in the context of understanding the social actions and meanings of the participating actors in a social setting. The focus is on understanding (verstehen) these social actions and meanings. Table 3.3 summarizes the differences between the two theoretical perspectives.

TABLE 3.3 *Comparison of the analytical and interpretivist perspectives*

	Analytical	Interpretivist
Office functions	Largely deterministic, rational, overt	Largely non-deterministic, political, covert
Metaphor	Organization as 'structure'	Organization as 'agent' or 'culture'
Office action as:	Manifest behaviour	Social meaning
Appropriate measurement instrument	Formal models	Phenomenological study
Research paradigm	Quantitative	Qualitative
Focus	Analysis	Verstehen

Although these perspectives are very broad, it is felt that they do reflect the general archetypal notion of an office which exists in the published literature. The perspectives are operationalized through *office views*, which are more specific approaches or conceptions of an office (and/or office actions).

OFFICE VIEWS

An office view refers to the particular way an individual conceives of an office. It is likely to be related to a person's world view or Weltanschauung (Checkland, 1981), which itself is the product of a person's education, environment, cultural background, experiences, and the like. An office view reflects those aspects of an office which are thought to be most important in the eyes of the perceiver. Views are likely to be overlapping and not as clearly defined as what follows. Nevertheless, the archetypes presented below do seem to reflect the general constructs presented in the literature. They also fall neatly into the two theoretical perspectives presented above.

The *analytical* perspective is reflected in three different, although popular, views of the office: *office activities, office semantics,* and *office functions.* The first conceives of an office as a place where a variety of activities are performed to support the successful operation of the organization. The second centres on office behaviour as a reflection of organizational goals. The third places primacy on the functions which go on in an office. Functions are analysed through office procedures. A procedure, in this context, is the unit of analysis which allows one to study the fundamental operations of an office. All three views focus on *manifest behaviour* as the key element or primitive of the office. That is, the most effective way of understanding the office is to see it in terms of observable behaviour. Because the office is perceived as largely deterministic and structured, a methodology which is more formal in nature is considered appropriate. Thus, methodologies based on recognized systems analysis approaches, e.g. entity–attribute–relationship formalisms, data flow diagrams, and other data analysis techniques, are embraced. Examples of these office methodologies are OAM (Sirbu *et al.*, 1982), OADM (Sutherland, 1983), MOBILE (Dumas *et al.*, 1982), OBE (Zloof, 1982), OPAS (Lum, Choy, and Shu, 1982), SOS (Bracchi and Pernici, 1984), and OFS (Cheung and Kornatowski, 1980). They represent a fairly formal office model/system; cf. SCOOP (Zisman, 1977), ICN (Ellis, 1979), and OMEGA (Barber, 1982). (The issue of methodologies and models is taken up in Chapter 4.)

The *interpretivist* perspective is observable in four alternative office views: *work roles, decision taking, transactional,* and *language action.* The first views offices in terms of a series of work functions which are performed by organiztional actors. Its basic focus is on the *roles* of the actors. The second sees offices in terms of decisions which have to be taken by various decision makers, each having his own particular cognitive style. The focus here is on cognition. The third conceives of offices as arenas where information transactions occur. Office workers are viewed as information exchangers who behave opportunistically while bargaining amongst themselves for information. The focus is thus on *information exchange.* The fourth looks at offices in terms of social action mediated through language. Organizational actors engage in dialogue or language action in the course of their work. As it is imperative to comprehend the meaning of such action for the office to be truly understood, the focus is on *language.* Since the office is conceived of as largely non-deterministic, formal office methodolo-

TABLE 3.4 Comparison of the office views

	Views	Focus	Methodologies	Model
Analytical perspective	Office activities		OAM	SCOOP ICN
		Manifest be- haviour	MOBILE	OPAS OFS
	Office semantics		OFFIS	OBE OMEGA SOS
	Office functions			
Interpretivist perspective	Work roles	Roles	ETHICS	
	Decision taking	Cognition	Sociotechnical	
	Transactional	Information exchange	Soft systems	No formal models
	Language action	Language	SAMPO	

gies are more problematic. Classic systems analysis methods are inappropriate in this circumstance. Instead, methods based on, for example, sociotechnical systems principles and participation appear more appropriate. Methodologies such as Mumford and Weir's (1979) ETHICS, Pava's (1983) sociotechnical approach, Checkland's (1981) soft systems, and Goldkuhl and Lyytinen's (1982) work on SAMPO offer possibilities which need to be explored in the office context. It is apparent that the office model embraced in these types of methods is nothing like the formal model of the analytical approaches. Any model would be a loose one, providing little more than a structure or framework through which to consider offices. In fact, the interpretivist perspective notes that it is not possible to develop a formal model of the office since its underlying assumption — that offices are non-deterministic — negates the possibility of a formal, structured model. Table 3.4 attempts to depict the different views diagrammatically.

ANALYTICAL PERSPECTIVE

1. The Office Activities View

By far and away the most prevalent view of the office is the activity view. It conceives of the office, not so much as a place, but as an environment where certain activities are performed to support the successful operation of the organization. The important concept in this view is *what* activities are undertaken and by whom. The time taken to perform an activity and the procedures followed in carrying it out are both crucial aspects. Frederick W. Taylor's (1911) conception of work rationalization provides the motivation and basis of this view. The major criticism of this view is that it does not attempt to understand *why* these activities are performed, i.e. for what underlying reasons. Nevertheless, the popularity of this view can not be denied and its use in the context of office automation, where one looks for specific tasks which the technology can support, is unmistakable.

A number of studies have been carried out to find out what activities office workers perform and what proportion of their time is spent on each activity. It should be stated at the outset that although there have been numerous studies on office activities, detailed comparisons between them are problematic. This is due to a number of facts. Firstly, many studies use job categorizations which are incompatible with others; or worse, there is no description of what the job categories entail. Secondly, studies treat non-working or personal time in different ways; some exclude it from their calculations, others do not. Thirdly, the method of data collection varies considerably between studies. Some use self-recording techniques, others employ observational methods. Fourthly, the studies have occurred at various points in time and for varying durations; thus, it would not be surprising that some difference could be attributable to time differences. Nevertheless, this has not stopped people from trying to compare the various studies; see, for example, Dodswell (1983).

What follows is a brief review of some of the more well-known studies on office activities.

Office Activity Studies

Perhaps the most widely quoted office activity study is that of Engel *et al.* (1979). Their study attempted to elicit the various activities performed by office workers and the amount of time spent on each. The authors divided office workers into three primary groups: secretarial and typing, clerical, and principal (which included both managerial and professional workers). Their results are shown in Tables 3.5 to 3.7.

Poppel (1982), reporting on a large Booz, Allen, and Hamilton study, notes that knowledge workers (principals) spend a considerable portion of their time (18–30 per cent) on fairly unproductive activities. These include: travelling, waiting for meetings to start, searching for information, typing, making reservations, filing, and photocopying. Meetings — both scheduled and unscheduled — take up between 60 per cent (for senior managers) to 40 per cent (for junior managers) of their time. Poppel claims that approximately 20 per cent of

TABLE 3.5 Time spent by principals on various activities

Activities	Top management only, %	All principals, %
Writing	9.8	15.6
Mail handling	6.1	4.4
Proofreading	1.8	2.3
Searching	3.0	5.6
Reading	8.7	7.3
Filing	1.1	2.0
Retrieving filed information	1.8	3.6
Dictating to secretary	4.9	1.9
Dictating to a machine	1.0	0.6
Telephone	13.8	12.3
Calculating	2.3	6.6
Conferring with secretary	2.9	1.8
Scheduled meetings	13.1	7.0
Unscheduled meetings	8.5	5.4
Planning or scheduling	4.7	4.3
Travelling	13.1	6.4
Copying	0.1	0.9
Using equipment	0.1	4.4
Other	3.2	7.6

TABLE 3.6 Time spent by secretaries on various activities

Activities	Percentages, %
Writing	3.5
Mail handling	8.1
Bulk envelope stuff	1.4
Collating/sorting	2.6
Proofreading	3.9
Reading	1.7
Typing	37.0
Telephone	10.5
Copying or duplication	6.2
Conferring with principals	4.3
Taking shorthand	5.5
Filing	4.6
Pulling files	2.8
Keeping calendars	2.6
Pick-up or delivery	2.2
Using equipment	1.3
Other	1.8

TABLE 3.7 Time spent by clerical staff on various activities

Activities	Percentages, %
Writing	7.3
Telephone	9.2
Meetings	1.9
Typing	7.8
Copying and printing	3.9
Filing and retrieving	5.9
Information searches	10.2
Routine transactions	23.9
Calculation and data processing	16.6
Other	13.3

all meetings are conducted over the telephone. Intellectual work comprises only 29 per cent of the knowledge workers' time. Figure 3.1 summarizes these findings.

Mintzberg (1973) in a comprehensive study on managerial work found managers spending a considerable portion of their time in both scheduled and unscheduled meetings (69 per cent). A similar result was noted by Kurke and Aldrich (1983). Figure 3.2 summarizes Mintzberg's and Kurke and Aldrich's findings.

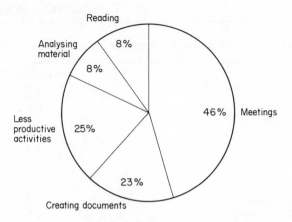

FIGURE 3.1 How knowledge workers spend their time

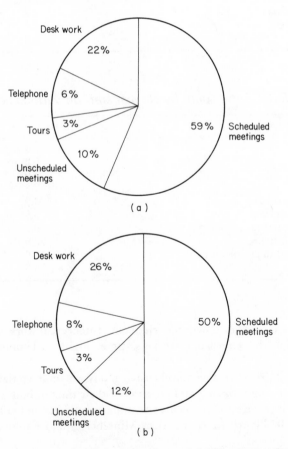

FIGURE 3.2 Managerial work distributions: (a) Mintzberg; (b) Kurke and Aldrich

Dodswell (1983) attempted a synthesis of a number of the management work activity studies and came up with the conclusions summarized in Table 3.8. Dodswell used four job categories: manager, professional, secretary, and clerk. He defined 'professionals' as those who performed staff functions and 'managers' as those who had the responsibility for coordinating and directing the activities of all the others. 'Secretaries' and 'clerks' were not defined as they were felt to be self-explanatory.

Figure 3.3 depicts the conclusions of Stewart's (1967) detailed study of 160 managers in terms of activities and proportions of time.

Klemmer and Snyder (1972) in an analysis of over 3,000 professional, technical, administrative, and clerical personnel noted the activities and times shown in Figure 3.4.

More recently, Christie (1981) and his colleagues performed a large survey of the office activities engaged in by 178 officials of the Commission of the European Communities. Christie divided office activities into two categories:

TABLE 3.8 Proportion of time spent on various activities

Activities	Manager, %	Professional, %	Secretary, %	Clerk, %
Interpersonal communication (telephone, travel, meetings)	60	33	15	12
Document creation	18	23	60	40
Document handling	20	40	20	40
Other	2	4	5	8

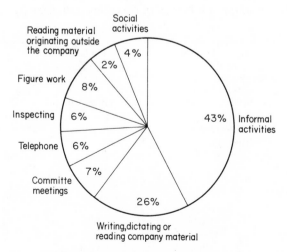

FIGURE 3.3 Stewart's results

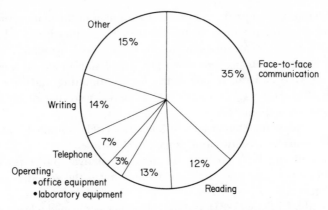

FIGURE 3.4 Klemmer and Snyder's conclusions

activities associated with communication (e.g. telephone, writing, meetings) and non-communication activities (e.g. planning, travelling). Further, he suggested two distinct types of communication: Type A communication referred to those office activities which were of a direct conversational manner involving two-way communication and usually entailing an immediate response (e.g. telephone conversation, meetings); Type B communication referred to those activities which were not of a conversational nature but involved the use of some storage function (e.g. writing, reading, copying).

The Christie study used three different job categories: level 1, upper management; level 2, other management; level 3, non-management. The results are presented in Table 3.9.

TABLE 3.9 Percentage of time spent on office activities by various levels of officials

	Type A communication	Type B communication	Other
Characteristics	Direct manner Spoken information	Involve storage written information	Non-communication
Activities	Telephone Conferring Meetings	Reading Writing Dictating Researching Filing Copying Proofreading	Calculating Planning Scheduling Travel Equipment use
Time spent by			
Level 1	40%	42%	18%
Level 2	33%	35%	32%
Level 3	30%	31%	39%

Conrath *et al.* (1981a), in a slight variation of the office activity theme, performed a Canadian study of office work. In their study, the authors collected data from 164 office workers in four companies. The study was different from other office activity studies in that the categories of work were based on 'office tasks' rather than activities. As such, the categories are somewhat different from other office activity studies. Table 3.10 presents the various categories used in the study and its results.

As can be seen, the office activity view of the office is very popular. There are two primary reasons why this is so. One, it is easier to quantify and measure the functions of office when they are defined in terms of independent activities. The activities are observable and, hence, relatively straightforward to measure. Moreover, there is less chance of ambiguity or misinterpretation. If a person is talking on a telephone this fact is easy to note with little chance that someone else would perceive it differently. Contrast this with a work role view where office functions are seen as various organizational roles (to be discussed later). Here, considerable ambiguity and confusion could arise as any specific task might be seen by different individuals to represent different roles.

Two, not only is the office activities view the simplest view of the office, but also the most logical when the concern is one of technology use. It is far easier to see where office technology could be used when the office is conceived in terms

TABLE 3.10 Percentage of time spent on various tasks

Task code	Keyword task descriptors	Percentage
A	Advising, counselling, assisting, recommending, problem solving, instruction, acting as liaison (two-way flow)	6.9
B	Bookkeeping, accounting, calculating, inventorying, invoicing (number crunching at clerical level)	14.9
D	Deciding, authorizing, approving (action oriented)	11.1
E	Evaluating, auditing, controlling, coordinating (non-people oriented comparison against standard)	13.5
F	Completing forms, filing, recording, logging (algorithm oriented)	2.0
G	General administration, paperwork (managerial level)	7.0
H	Human relating, supervision, appraising performance, staffing, motivating people (people oriented)	12.8
I	Informing, reporting (one-way flow)	4.2
M	Interactive formal meetings	2.7
O	Orders, requests, invoices, bills	1.5
P	Planning, budgeting, analysing (future oriented)	12.4
Q	Arranging scheduling of meetings, appointments (secretarial level)	5.5
S	Selling, convincing, persuading, advertising (change oriented)	3.8
T	Typing, transcribing, copying, writing (moving from one medium to another)	2.6

of activities instead of more subjective elements such as roles and/or functions. Thus, from an office automation seller's viewpoint, office activities makes the most sense. To highlight this, one need only look at the Siemens' study (Morgenbrod and Schaertzel, 1980) where office activities were looked at in terms of their potential for formalization and automation. Tasks (activities) which could be formalized, i.e. described in terms of instructions or algorithms, were considered capable of being automated. The authors noted, however, that not all tasks which were formalizable could be automated. Only a portion of office activities which were capable of formalization had the potential for automation. Figure 3.5 presents the Siemen's study results across a number of functions in a variety of organization types. Figure 3.6 summarizes the results across various industries.

It can be seen from Figures 3.5 and 3.6 that there is considerable variation between the percentage of activities which are capable of being formalized and those which are automatable among the different organizations and functions. On average, however, Morgenbrod and Schaertzel note that 43 per cent of office activities are formalizable with approximately 25 per cent capable of being automated.

In sum, the office activity view of the office is very popular among office automation proponents for the reasons discussed above. Further, this view has a long tradition. The history of office activity measurement is a rich one, pre-dating even Frederick Taylor, and can be traced back to Weber's early writings on bureaucracy. With the emergence of Taylor's 'scientific management', however, activity measurement became widespread. It is little wonder that, even today, Taylor's concept of work rationalization is still the primary basis for how offices are perceived.

Moreover, the popularity of the office activity view is manifested through the various office automation systems currently developed or in the process of development. For example, Xerox's 8010 information system is based on the notion of 'records processing' (Purvy, Farrel, and Kose, 1983). This is where office work is conceived of as a series of activities which manipulate structured information (records). The system supports these activities by supplying a vehicle which allows records to be easily processed. OFS (office form system) (Cheung and Kornatowski, 1980) has a similar conception of the office except that its basis is on a 'form' rather than a 'record'. A form is any paper or electronic representation of an office procedure. Forms have a stylized format and have areas called 'fields' which hold the form's contents. Although Purvy, Farrel, and Kose (1983) claim forms are 'aimed at a more structured environment than Star (Xerox 8010)', they both view offices in terms of activities. Similar viewpoints can be found in Office-By-Example (Zloof, 1981), OmegaForm (Attardi, 1981), and Gehani's (1983) high-level form language.

However, as will be discussed later, this view suffers from the extreme simplicity by which it conceives of offices. While it is a relatively simple way of

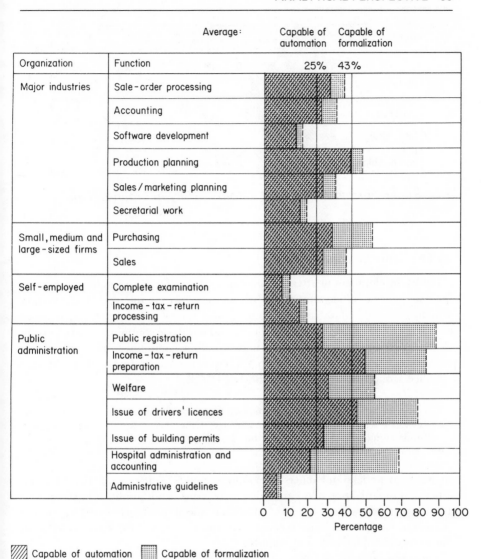

FIGURE 3.5 Percentage of working time capable of formalization and automation for various organizations

addressing office work, it provides no vehicle for understanding why people perform the manifest activities they do nor what they believe the effects will be. Additionally, this view provides no mechanism for comprehending the social aspects of work — the social interaction which is part and parcel of office work.

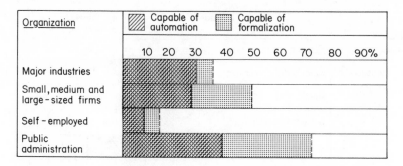

FIGURE 3.6 Formalizability and automatability in organizations

2. The Office Semantics View

A recent development in attempting to understand the office and its operation is
the emergence of office semantics. It is an outgrowth of the work done on data
semantics by the database community and borrows heavily from artificial
intelligence (AI) thought. Just as the AI and database communities are looking
closely at semantics as the basis for understanding communication, a number of
office researchers are attempting to apply what is known in an office setting.

Office semantics, as defined by Barber (1983):

> ... is the study of information-intensive organizational work (and) ... reflects the
> concern with the intent behind the act. Office semantics is concerned with
> understanding the reasons behind the physical tasks that are performed in
> organizational work.

In order to understand office behaviour it makes a distinction between two
aspects of organizations: 'organizational structure' and 'application structure'.
The former refers to informal and formal social relations occurring in the
organization while the latter is concerned with the explicit rules associated with
the particular office task under study.

According to Barber (1983), office semantics views office work as containing
four fundamental characteristics:

(a) Open-ended knowledge world. This suggests that the list of actions
    available to an office worker cannot be articulated. It is, in a word,
    unknowable. The manifestation is office behaviour which is surprising and
    unpredictable. Barber states: 'This is as much a property of the perceiver of
    the world as it is the world itself since it is our assumption that the perceiver
    is of limited cognitive capabilities.'

(b) Evolutionary environment. Organizations are in a continuous state of change. Thus, any attempt at understanding office behaviour must take into account the dynamic, evolving system.

(c) Perceiving cognitive processes. Office tasks cannot be understood by simply watching someone carrying out an action. As noted in Klein and Hirschheim (1983): 'The description of the physical aspects of behaviour does *not* describe human action, only people doing things ... it fails to analyse what lies behind (the action, i.e. intent).'

(d) Describing cognitive processes. In order to understand cognitive processes they must be describable. Yet this is extremely difficult for two reasons. Firstly, it is not usually possible to describe all the mental processes a person uses in making a decision. Secondly, even if it were possible, the description would be of little use as many of the mental processes are idiosyncratic to that individual and irrelevant to the general case of decision making. The goal of describing cognitive processes, according to Barber (1983), is 'to describe the individual's task-relevant knowledge and thought processes in a way that — taken in aggregate — explains organizational behaviour'.

Office semantics' primary focus is to develop an understanding of not only how an individual performs a certain task but also the reasons why it is performed. It sees office work as being much more complex than just simple activities. Office semantics relies on procedures and goals; i.e. problem solving (office work) is characterized as a search for a procedure (sequence of actions) which will achieve some desired goal. It contends that it is necessary for goals to be known. This may come about in one of two ways: (1) goals could be specified by the user or (2) they could be inferred from the sequence of actions (procedures) performed (cf. Suchman, 1979). Goals provide the mechanism for understanding office behaviour. As Attardi (1981) notes:

> Office workers are able to handle ... their daily work because they know the goals of the office work. ... Explicit representation of the goals exposes hidden assumptions about the office work and makes the actions performed by an office worker more understandable.

Unfortunately, goal anticipation is far from straightforward. Goals, other than the most trivial, are difficult to describe in any meaningful way. Often they can only be discussed in very broad terms. There is also the misconception that all organizational members share the same goals; this is far from true, as Perrow (1961), Clegg and Dunkerley (1980), and many other organizational theory writers note. Moreover, the view that intent can be inferred from action — where intent reflects some goal — is misguided. This is a point strongly argued in Klein and Hirschheim (1983). They state:

The purpose (intent) of an action is indeed the goal to which it is directed, but this cannot be identified with the results it brings about because this would involve two assumptions which are not necessarily true: one, the individual believed — correctly — that his movements would have that result; two, the individual consciously desired that the result should come about. The difficulties involved here are self evident.

The office semantics view, even with the inherent difficulties associated with goals, offers an interesting alternative to the activity view. Moreover, this view forms the basis of a number of experimental systems. (See, for example, the write-up on OMEGA in Chapter 4.) The office semantics view can be found in the writings of Attardi (1981), Hewitt, Attardi, and Simi (1981), Barber and Hewitt (1982), Jakob (1982), and Barber (1982, 1983).

3. The Office Functions View

In this view, offices are conceived of in terms of procedures and functions. To understand what goes on in an office, it is necessary to analyse the procedures and functions which make up office work. Procedures can be combined into higher level functions which can be defined as 'aggregates of all the detailed activities that collectively manage and maintain some resource that relates to the business goals of the larger organization' (Sirbu *et al.*, 1982). These high-level functions do not usually lend themselves to analysis and thus it is the procedures which become the centre of focus. A procedure can be thought of as a description of the historical sequence of events that an office object or operation progresses through to reach its intended goal. The realization of its goal in combination with the completing of other procedures leads to the successful operation of some higher level function and (ultimately) the business.

From a more social/organizational perspective, the office functions view embodies an impersonal focus on functions as the basic element of the office. Functions are interrelated and aggregated into higher level functions and larger subsystems in such a way that they instrumentally achieve some office or organizational goal. Functions are structured by prescribing the tasks, roles, behavioural expectations, duties, and responsibilities associated with each office function. It is the prescribed roles, rather than individuals, that are structured. Individuals occupy these roles and must therefore be selected and trained to meet the set requirements. Individuals are thereby immersed as component parts of a structured, interlocking system that shapes their activities. Functions are the products of organizational goals which are considered to be predetermined. Performance constraints and technical principles govern the design of jobs, groups, offices, departments, and the overall organization. Functions are performed and governed by rational laws which guide the behaviour of the office worker in undertaking a function. This underlying belief in the rationality and deterministic nature of office work is the reason why the office functions view embodies an analytical perspective.

There are a number of writers who adopt an office functions view in their conception of the office. Sirbu *et al.* (1982) and Sutherland (1983), for example, have developed methodologies for office automation which are based on functions. They employ three primitives: (a) objects, abstract or tangible entities of the office; (b) procedures, the structure of what has to be done to realize an office goal; and (c) functions, a collective of office tasks which is responsible for the managing of some organizational resource. Their approaches employ functional analysis, a vehicle for documenting the primary functions which need to be supported in the office domain. Aklilu (1981) also maintains an office functions view, although he concentrates on different operations. For Aklilu, office functions are most appropriately conceived of in terms of information products, which can be structured into three categories: data creators, data convertors, and information users. See also Hammer and Zisman (1979) for an example of a methodology which adopts an office functions view. (For more information on these methodologies and the office function-based approach see Chapter 4.)

Hammer and Sirbu (1980) offer a general conception of the office which incorporates some interesting observations about the nature of office work. Firstly, Hammer and Sirbu note that offices and their activities tend to be distributed in terms of both time and space. They involve the continuous coordination of parallel activities in various places. Secondly, office activities, although often routine in nature, are more often in a perpetual state of change. Office workers must constantly revise their actions to cope with the dynamic environment of today's organizations. Thirdly, office tasks and activities are largely interactive. Rarely are problems solved except by the action of several persons in an interactive exchange of ideas and commitment. In fact, much of what occurs in the office is group work involving the simultaneous participation of a number of people, rather than sequence of events performed by autonomous actors. They suggest that a more appropriate way to understand the office is by focusing on functions rather than activities. Functions are the root causes of activities; as such, it makes more sense to analyse them — particularly considering the distributed, dynamic, and group nature of office activities.

INTERPRETIVIST PERSPECTIVE

1. The Work Role View

A number of individuals have expressed concern over the narrowness of the more deterministic views. They contend these views might be useful in documenting what is being done in offices but not why. Mintzberg (1973), for example, asserts that even with all the work done on what managers do, there is still considerable confusion over what managers *actually* do. He writes:

> ... as a child, I wondered what my father did at the office. He was the president of a small manufacturing firm, but his job was not at all clear .... Some people operated machines, others typed letters. All he ever seemed to do was sit in his office, sign an occasional letter, and talk. What did managers do?

This question has bothered many people. The activity view, for instance, provides only a narrow conception of what he does, e.g. spends 59 per cent of his time in scheduled meetings, 6 per cent on the telephone, 10 per cent on unscheduled meetings, and so on. (It should perhaps be mentioned that the activity view could be considered a major improvement over previous conceptions of what managers did. For most of this century managers were thought to perform four basic activities as described by Fayol in 1916, namely, planning, controlling, organizing, and coordinating.) It was this narrow view which led a number of individuals to attempt a more detailed treatment of what people actually do in offices.

Foremost among these attempts was the study performed by Mintzberg (1973). In this comprehensive work, Mintzberg sought to describe the precise nature of managerial work. He concluded that the broad view of managerial work where a manager supposedly plans, controls, and organizes was too simplistic to be of much value, and the activity view provided no understanding of why a manager engaged in certain activities. Mintzberg proposed an alternative view in which a manager's job can be described in terms of various work roles.

Roles, according to Weinstein and Weinstein (1972), are the 'sets of rights and duties relating to the performance of a function in accomplishing a task' (p. 11). They apply to particular situations and are understood by those in the situation. Moreover, they define the expected behaviour of any person in a social setting. The rights and duties are social constructs performed in a social arena and govern a person's behaviour. However, it is here that there exists some disagreement about the notion of 'role'. Simon (1964), for example, conceives of role in a very deterministic way. He writes:

> Roles in organizations ... tend to be highly elaborated, relatively stable, and defined to a considerable extent in explicit and even written terms. Not only is the role defined for the individual who occupies it but it is known in considerable detail to others in the organization who have occasion to deal with him (p. 4).

This narrow conception of role is shared by Clegg and Dunkerley (1980) who suggest that organizational life is more realistically discussed in terms of 'hegemony and control rather than roles and goals' (p. 309). Boulding (1956) defines role as 'that part of the person which is concerned with the organization or situation in question'.

Roles are important from an organizational perspective because there is a need to divide complex tasks into simpler activities which can be performed by individuals. According to Argyris and Schon (1978), this division of complex tasks is a natural feature of organizations. Organizational roles refer to:

> ... the cluster of component tasks which the (organization) has decided to delegate to individual members. The organization task system, its pattern of interconnected roles, is at once a design for work and the division of labour.

This conception of roles, however, does not take into account their dynamic nature. They change over time and are shaped by the personality, values, and beliefs of the role holder as well as his perception of the role and the expectations of others interacting with him. It is not surprising, therefore, that others offer an alternative interpretation of role. Banbury and Nahapiet (1979) and Weinstein and Weinstein (1972), for instance, conceive of role in a more interpretive and socially determined fashion. Silverman (1970) states: 'Roles ... exist as an expression of the meanings which men attach to their world.'

Generally speaking, work roles can be thought of more in terms of a continuum. Jaques (1967) suggests that a role can vary from 'prescribed' to 'discretionary'. The behaviour attached to a role may be either specifically articulated and defined — leading to little or no discretion — or vaguely defined, allowing the individual role holder considerable discretion and flexibility. The notion of the work role portrayed here is of a more discretionary and symbolic nature. Mintzberg (1973) also adopts this more interpretivist orientation.

Instead of perceiving office work in terms of simple activities, Mintzberg felt that understanding the work roles of managers would provide a richer picture of the office and its operation. He suggested the existence of three 'interpersonal' roles that give rise to three 'informational' roles which in combination yield four 'decisional' roles.

Interpersonal Roles

These are roles which arise directly from a manager's formal authority and involve interpersonal relationships and interaction.

(a) Figurehead role. Because of his organizational position, a manager must perform a number of duties which are of a ceremonial nature, e.g. greeting important people, attending special functions such as employees' weddings, etc.

(b) Leader role. A manager is responsible for the work of the people in the organizational unit. As such he is responsible for the motivation of subordinates as well as the training and staffing of the unit.

(c) Liaison role. A manager needs to make and maintain contacts outside the vertical chain of command. This self-developed network of outside contacts provides the manager with his own external information system.

Information Roles

These are roles which are a direct outgrowth of the fact that managers are the 'nerve centres' of their organizational units; they fundamentally receive, process, and transmit information.

(d) Monitor role. A manager perpetually scans the environment for a wide variety of information to develop an understanding of the organization and its environment. Much of the information collected by the manager is current, informal, and 'soft' in nature. Thus, he emerges as a 'nerve centre' of internal and external information of the organization.

(e) Dissemination role. A manager needs to share and distribute much of the information received from the information channels to other members of the organization. Some of the information transmitted is factual in nature, some is more subjective and involves interpretation and inference.

(f) Spokesman role. A manager transmits some of the information to individuals outside the organizational unit. Usually this kind of information involves an organization's plans, actions, policies, results, etc.

Decisional Roles

These are roles associated with the need to make decisions which are based on a manager's formal and informal authority and the fact that he is the nerve centre of the organization.

(g) Entrepreneuer role. A manager continually searches the organization and its environment for opportunities to improve the organizational unit. He often initiates, designs, and supervises 'improvement projects' to bring about changes.

(h) Disturbance handler role. A manager spends a considerable portion of the time responding to high-pressure changes. He is responsible for corrective action when the organization encounters unexpected disturbances.

(i) Resource allocation role. A manager is responsible for deciding who in the organizational unit receives what resources. Additionally, he authorizes the important decisions of the unit prior to their implementation.

(j) Negotiation role. A manager spends considerable time in representing the organization in negotiations. Usually the negotiations are routine but quite often they are non-routine and the source of much stress.

Mintzberg notes that the roles are not easily separable; rather they form a gestalt — an integrated whole. Moreover, managers do not necessarily give equal attention to each role. Mintzberg's conception that managerial activity is best described in terms of roles they perform rather than simple, objective actions is a good example of a work role view of the nature of the office.

Suchman and Wynn (1984) share Mintzberg's distaste for simplistic conceptions of office work, feeling instead that roles are a better mechanism for understanding action. Roles, fundamentally, permit the realization that the actual procedures of the office are not the ones formally defined. Rather, they are largely socially determined and behavioural in orientation. They write:

> The problems involved in accomplishing office tasks ... are ignored in procedural formulations of how the work gets done (p. 139).

Their recommendation is to broaden the conception of the procedural understanding of the office to include the informality and discretionary nature of office work and the work roles which support it.

Although roles describe the rights and duties associated with office work, it is not altogether clear how they come about. Banbury and Nahapiet (1979) offer one of the few frameworks which can be used to understand roles within the context of individuals' beliefs, values, and assumptions. They see these as interacting and causing the individual to exhibit certain behaviour. According to Banbury and Nahapiet, there are six primary aspects of beliefs relevant for the understanding of roles: three which refer to their source and three which relate to their content.

Source

(a) Those beliefs which derive from the actor's cultural background.
(b) Those beliefs which derive from the actor's professional background which pull him towards a certain line of thinking.
(c) Those beliefs which derive from the actor's status or position in the organization and which tend to be similar to his peers. These beliefs are likely to influence an actor's interpretation of organizational goals.

Content

(d) Beliefs about the constraints which the actor sees operating in the organization (e.g. technology used, reporting relationships, and resource availability).
(e) Beliefs about the function and value of office automation in the organizational context.

(f) Beliefs about the function and value of particular office systems the actor is to use (or has used).

It is the beliefs, values, and assumptions which impact on roles and make office work more symbolic and ritualistic. It is clear that such a view is consistent with the interpretivist perspective.

2. The Decision-Taking View

An alternative to the work role view can be found among the many researchers who focus on the decisions which are made and the decision-taking process in an office environment. Here, the central issue is decision taking — what decisions are made, by whom, for what reasons, the decision maker's cognitive style, and such like. Cognition, an important element in decision making, refers to 'the activities by which an individual resolves differences between an internalized view of the environment and what is actually perceived in the same environment' (Zmud, 1979, p. 967). There are two complimentary components of this view: 'cognitive style' and 'decision-making models'. The former reflects the particular cognitive preferences of the individual decision maker by examining the cognitive processes involved in problem solving and the use of information. More specifically, Huber (1983) defines cognitive style as:

> ... the process behaviour that individuals exhibit in the formulation or acquisition, analysis, and interpretation of information or data of presumed value for decision making. The cognitive style paradigm emphasizes the problem-solving process rather than the cognitive structure and capacity. It categorizes individual habits and strategies at a fairly broad level and essentially views problem-solving behaviour as a personality variable (p. 567).

Various models exist by which to categorize the different cognitive styles, many of which are based on Jung's (1923) psychological types.

Mason and Mitroff (1973) describe Jung's psychological types framework as being characterized by four major modes or psychological functions. Two of the modes relate to how an individual takes information in, i.e. the psychological functions used to perceive or sense the objects of the world, and two pertain to how an individual makes decisions on the information received, i.e. the psychological functions used to evaluate or judge the objects of perception. The two modes associated with perception are 'sensation' and 'intuition'. *Sensation* refers to the kind of individual who typically takes in information from the senses, i.e. is fundamentally empirical in nature. There is a preference for concrete, specific facts and a desire to attend to the details of any situation. *Intuition*, on the other hand, relates to the kind of individual who typically takes information in by means of the imagination and is interested in seeing the 'whole situation'. Somewhat non-empirical in nature, this individual tends to prefer the hypothetical possibilities of any situation to the 'actual facts'. The two modes associated with evaluation are 'thinking' and 'feeling'. *Thinking* refers to the process of reaching a decision through the use of analytical modes of reasoning. *Feeling* refers to the process of reaching a decision through the use of personalistic value judgements, often highly unique to that particular individual. Jung maintains that the psychological functions for perception are independent of the ones for evaluation, thus leading to four perception–evaluation combinations: (a) sensation–thinking (ST); (b) sensation–feeling (SF); (c) intuition–thinking (NT); and (d) intuition–feeling (NF). These four personality types are meant to reflect the general cognitive styles of individual decision makers. Mason and Mitroff note, however, that these four types are not as 'pure' as depicted. They state:

> The human personality is too diverse, rich and complicated to be explained in terms of only four modes. Nevertheless, even as *caricatures*, these types prove to be useful heuristic devices characterizing personalities and managerial styles (p. 478).

A similar classification can be found in McKenney and Keen (1974), who categorize cognitive styles along two continuums which can be mapped onto one another: an information-gathering one and an information-evaluation one. The former relates to how an individual's mind organizes sensations. At one extreme, focus might be made on the relationship between sensations and their potential generalization — this is referred to as 'perceptive'; at the other extreme, focus might be made on sensation details in an attempt to derive specific knowledge — this is referred to as 'receptive'. The latter continuum (information evaluation) relates to how an individual analyses sense impressions. At one extreme, an individual might follow an ordered procedure to yield an analytic solution (referred to as a 'systematic' or 'analytical' approach); at the other extreme, he might use intuition, act spontaneously, etc. (referred to as an 'intuitive' or 'heuristic' approach). McKenney and Keen suggest that individual decision-making behaviour will reflect some point in this two-dimensional space.

Other examples of cognitive style typologies abound. Churchman (1971), for example, lists six categories of cognitive type: (a) the 'mathematical type' who interprets all decisions as mathematical ones, (b) the 'realist' who interprets reality with hard, quantitative facts, (c) the 'idealist' who interprets reality in terms of imagination, (d) the 'pragmatist' who interprets reality in terms of feasibility and possible solutions, (e) the 'consensual type' who sees reality in terms of what can be generally agreed upon, and (f) the 'conflictual type' for whom reality is what results from dialectic debate. These types formed the basis of Churchman's inquiring systems (i.e. evidence generator and guarantor methods).

Hunsaker and Hunsaker (1981) propose an alternative typology similar in orientation to McKenney and Keen's. Their two dimensions are: decision-making focus (either fixed on a single issue or multiple issues) and information use (either minimum or maximum usage of available information). The result of the two-dimensional mapping is four cognitive styles: decisive, flexible, hierarchical, and integrative (see Figure 3.7). The 'decisive' decision maker is one who uses a minimal amount of information, arrives at the one correct decision, and respects the organizational rule system. 'Flexible' decision makers also use a minimal amount of information but are more adaptable. Their decision-making process does not necessarily lead to the 'best' solution but to a satisfactory one. 'Hierarchical'-style decision makers use great quantities of data which are carefully analysed to arrive at the 'best' solution. They value perfection, precision, and thoroughness. 'Integrative' style decision makers also use a large amount of information but they generate a variety of simultaneous interpretations and many possible solutions. They are the most adaptive of the various styles.

(See Keen and Bronsema (1981) for a review of recent cognitive style research.)

'Decision making models' focus on the models adopted by decision makers and their decision-making behaviour. This is related to cognitive style but is more comprehensive. It addresses conceptual ways people make decisions.

Simon (1960) provided one of the classic (and simplistic) models of the decision-making process. He contended there were three phases in the process: 'intelligence', relating to the environment search for problems and opportunities; 'design', developing and analysing various courses of action to solve the

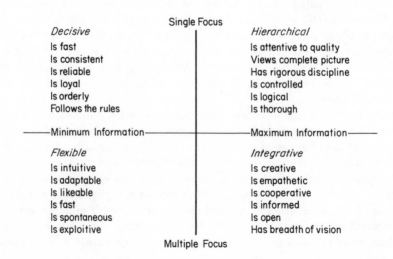

FIGURE 3.7 Hunsaker and Hunsaker's typology of cognitive styles

problem; and 'choice', selecting and implementing the most appropriate course of action. Others such as Pounds (1969), Kilmann and Mitroff (1979), and Checkland (1981) note that problem formulation is not the straightforward process depicted by Simon. Both problem finding and formulation are fraught with difficulties, and need to be given much greater attention in the decision-making process.

Davis and Olson (1984) suggest the importance of developing a correct model of the decision maker — one which takes into account the way an individual examines a problem and arrives at a solution. They outline three such models:

(a) Classical economic model. Here the decision maker exhibits normative behaviour in reaching a purely economic solution. It assumes that the alternatives and outcomes are known in advance by the decision maker, who seeks to maximize profit or utility, behaves in a 'rational' fashion, and is sensitive to the differences in utility between the outcomes. Decision making under this model is prescriptive and seeks to identify the optimal solution in any situation.

(b) Administrative model. Here the decision maker is seen to exist in only a partially known world and, due to cognitive limits, does not behave in a totally rational way. Simon (1960) refers to this as 'bounded rationality'. It assumes that all alternatives are not known in advance; the decision maker undertakes a limited search to uncover a few satisfactory alternatives and a decision is taken which leads not to an optimal solution but a 'satisficing' one. Decision making under this model is descriptive and is more of a heuristic conception of the decision-making process.

(c) Human expectations model. Here the decision maker is seen more as an individual with specific psychological traits. He possesses a particular cognitive style and exhibits behaviour consistent with it. Decision making is largely based on expectations which can be understood through the theory of cognitive dissonance, commitment theory, and the theory of anticipatory regret. Like the administrative model, decision making under this model is descriptive but is more behavioural in orientation.

Keen and Scott Morton (1978), in an analysis of the various decision-making 'schools of thought', present a framework which is similar to Davis and Olson, but extends the behavioural orientation to include more interpretive elements. They note five major schools of thought:

(a) The rational manager model. This mirrors Davis and Olson's 'classic economic model' where decision making is conceived of as purely economic and objective choices. The decision maker is thought to act rationally using accepted analytical techniques.

(b) The 'satisficing', process-oriented model. This model is similar to Davis and Olson's 'administrative model' where the decision maker, because of bounded rationality, seeks satisfactory rather than optimal solutions. Decision making is seen in terms of improving the current situation, and the focus is more on the processural nature of decisions.

(c) The organizational procedures model. Decision making under this model is seen as the result of standard operating procedures invoked by various organizational units or departments. To understand decision making, one must focus on identifying what procedures are followed, the various channels of communication and relationships, and the like.

(d) The political process model. Decision making here is seen as a bargaining process between organizational members and units. It is the power and influence which determine the decisions to be made and their eventual outcome. To understand decision making, it is important to see how the various interests and constraints are meshed together and guide the behaviour of organizational actors.

(e) The individual differences model. Decision making under this view reflects the problem-solving and information-processing behaviour of the office worker. The individual decision process is related to the decision maker's personality, cultural and professional background, social pressures, and the like. This model has much in common with the cognitive style aspects of decision making.

Other frameworks on decision making can be found in Lindblom (1959), Cyert and March (1963), Schroder, Driver, and Steufert (1967), Wilensky (1967), Allison (1971), Newell and Simon (1972), Mintzberg, Raisinghani, and Theoret (1976), Sprague (1980), and Nutt (1984).

3. The Transactional View

This view conceives of offices as arenas for information exchanges which operate on the basis of contracts (Williamson, 1975). Organizations are perceived as stable networks of transactions which are regulated, through the processes of coordination and control, by a set of contracts. These govern the transactions which occur between organizational units.

The transactional view is largely based on the work of Williamson's (1975, 1979) 'new institutional economics' which has its roots in Commons' (1934) 'institutional economics'. Williamson, like Commons, regards the transaction as 'the ultimate unit of economic investigation' (Commons, 1934, p. 6). It is transactional considerations, rather than technology, which typically determine which mode of organization will materialise. Williamson contends there are typically two modes of organization: the market and the hierarchy. The former deals with coordination and control through its ability to precisely measure and reward individual contributions; the latter, through a mixture of formal reward mechanisms coupled with a socialized acceptance of common objectives

(Ouchi, 1979). Institutions, in this context, produce order, but out of conflict. Order is conceived of as 'working rules of collective action' (Commons, 1934, p. 6). The transaction view notes that order is not a simple matter because individuals behave opportunistically and have bounded rationality (see above). Order becomes even more complex due to what Williamson (1975) refers to as 'information impactedness' — where one party in a transaction is much better informed than the other, and the latter cannot achieve information parity or cannot achieve parity except at great cost.

Transactions occur through the process of bargaining, and Williamson (1979) notes three types of bargaining or contract models: (a) contingent claims contracts, where the terms of the contract are related to how the future unfolds, e.g. a particular service is provided contingent upon certain conditions; (b) sequential spot contracts, where a particular service is provided on the basis of continually bidding for the job in the spot market, i.e. what appears as a long-term relationship is in fact a continuously bid arrangement involving the spot market; and (c) authority relation contracts, when there is a contract such that A agrees to accept the authority of B in return for some compensation.

Since the costs of writing and executing complex transactions vary with the characteristics of the human decision makers and the properties of the mode of organization, the choice between market and hierarchy is non-trivial. It is dependent upon which provides a better mechanism for the undertaking of a particular set of transactions. The choice, according to Williamson (1975), has to be based on two sets of factors: environmental and human. The former are concerned with uncertainty/complexity and small numbers; the latter with opportunism and bounded rationality. He notes that the combination of bounded rationality and uncertainty may make the writing of contingent claims contracts infeasible in many circumstances such that the hierarchy mode of organization may be preferred as it tends to reduce complexity.

The transactional view notes that the human factors of bounded rationality and opportunism play an important role in transaction formulation. Bounded rationality can manifest itself in that participants to a transaction may not be able to successfully communicate about the contract through the use of words and symbols which are contractually meaningful. Opportunism is reflected in man's self-seeking interest. Williamson (1975) refers to it as 'self-seeking with guile'; it makes an individual's transactional behaviour 'subtle and devious', and can involve information distortion or 'the making of self-disbelieved promises'. Ciborra (1983) defines such behaviour as:

> ... an attribute of the human agent related to his/her proclivity to manipulate ... information, misrepresent goals and intentions in a context where self-enforcing promises cannot be secured (p. 138).

A recent extension to and application of Williamson's ideas has been proposed by Ouchi (1979, 1980). Ouchi used the transactional notion specifically to explain organizational control and evaluation mechanisms. He extended Williamson's modes of organization to include a third type: the clan. It relies on a set of shared beliefs between members and requires a high level of commitment on the part of each individual in the group to behave by socially prescribed behaviours. Information, necessary for office action and control, is often contained in rituals, stories, and ceremonies which convey the organization's values and beliefs.

Of fundamental importance to the transactional view is the belief that organizational (and office) goals are complex, social constructs and not the simple procedural-oriented functions adopted in, for example, the office semantics view. Clegg and Dunkerley (1980) state: 'the real goals are the results of negotiation and conflict between individuals and groups at different organizational levels: the outcome of process rather than formal function' (p. 304).

Offices are thus seen as 'negotiated orders' and the product of continuous contractual arrangements. Examples of the 'negotiated order' and/or transaction view can be found in Strauss *et al.* (1963), Day and Day (1977), and Ciborra (1981).

4. The Language Action View

This view sees offices in terms of social action where language is the mediating force. The language action (LA) or rule reconstruction view is so called because office action is conceived of in terms of communication (Goldkuhl and Lyytinen, 1982). This view revolves around the need to reconstruct the social interaction or activity which goes on in an office, and the determination of the goals which frame the activities. In particular, it is interested in the communication rules that govern the interaction. The physical attributes of a given human activity and the rules of human interaction are framed as linguistic phenomena. Language, therefore, is one important category of human action and is a social artifact whose primary function is to support social interaction. The regularities of language and its use are governed by its constitutive rules. Meaning is the result of rule-following behaviour on the part of social actors, conceptualized in terms of speech acts that mediate the speaker's intentions. A speech act is defined as 'a minimal meaningful unit of information exchange in language' (Lyytinen, 1985, p. 70).

There are four assumptions which underlie the language action view (Lyytinen, 1985):

(a) Natural language sentences correspond to the performance of social acts; these are the speech acts.
(b) The speech act is the basic unit of linguistic communication.
(c) The meaning of sentences for the actors in a social setting (such as the office) is revealed by describing the kinds of acts that have been performed through their utterance.

(d) Speech acts obey socially determined rules. Since the rules govern the performance of speech acts, they permit the systematic study of meaning, and more generally, linguistic behaviour.

The language action view maintains the belief that office systems development is basically concerned with modelling the *rules* of human communication, but it has a distinctive underlying philosophical framework. The LA view explicitly relates itself to the critical social theory of Jurgen Habermas (1984; McCarthy, 1982). Basically, the LA view proposes that office (or information) systems development must serve the three knowledge interests of critical social theory: (a) technical control, (b) improvement of communication among participants in social action, and (c) emancipation from unnecessary social or natural constraints of human freedom. From this perspective the central goal of system development is to overcome the barriers to consensual social action by improving human communication and supporting the rationality of social action. Social action is called 'rational' if it is justified by reasons which can stand the test of critical, informed debate. If the forces which channel individual behaviour are themselves not based on valid reasons, for instance, if they are based on vested interests or mere conventions, they cannot stand the test of a universal, informed debate. Therefore, consensual human discourse is crucial for creating the knowledge which alone can distinguish between rational and merely accepted social action. The fact that social action is based on agreement does not mean 'true' consensus is achieved, since such agreement may be fallacious or illegitimate. The consensus about the legitimacy of social action must be 'grounded' on valid knowledge. Office systems should be designed such that they help to 'ground' social action on valid reasons through improving communication. Office information systems are thus defined as 'formal linguistic systems for communication between people which support their actions' (Goldkuhl and Lyytinen, 1982, p. 14).

Since there exists a number of barriers to effective communication, the LA view notes that rational social action needs to be 'supported' through special efforts of systems development. Rational social action requires undistorted communication. To achieve this, the 'intersubjective intelligibility' (or understanding) of messages needs to be high. Rational social action may be supported through three strategies: (a) improving the social conditions for communication, (b) improving the language (or message formalisms) used by the social actors, and (c) improving the means through which the information needs of the individuals can be modelled and dealt with.

For undistorted communication to occur, four types of *validity claims* (Giddens, 1982) must be said to exist. That is, for consensual interaction to be carried out, communication must be 'intelligible', 'truthful', 'adequate', and 'accurate'. A situation where it is possible to freely test these validity claims is called an *ideal speech situation*. Communication carried out under an approximation of the conditions of ideal speech is called *rational discourse*. The LA view sees the following barriers to rational discourse: (a) subjective bias which includes lack of understanding; (b) inability to obtain proper information due to physical constraints (e.g. distance, time pressures, mechanical calculation errors, and the like); and (c) distortion of information by social conditions, in particular by the effects of conflict of interest and power.

A first step to creating the conditions of rational discourse is to improve the intersubjective intelligibility of messages. This can be done by modelling the intended meanings of messages for social action, and the most promising avenue for effecting such a strategy is through the use of speech act theory.

The basic tenet of speech act theory is that the meaning of messages cannot be adequately understood without analysing the human intent behind communication. The same words or data can mean different things depending on the intent with which they are communicated and the consequences which are expected in different social contexts. This contrasts sharply with alternative views which hold that the meaning of messages can be derived from the syntactic elements of speech, e.g. words and phrases.

From speech act theory, the following four levels of analysis can be applied to office communications:

(a) *Syntax description.* It is concerned with the rules which differentiate well-formed messages from ill-formed ones. This is similar to the concept of a well-formed formula in logic and mathematics. (Code checking, data transmission protocols, are concerned with this level.)

(b) *Description of propositional content.* This level is concerned with the rules of prediction and reference. It is similar to various data modelling approaches based on entities, attributes, and relationships.

(c) *Description of performative meanings or illocutionary forces.* This is accomplished by applying an exhaustive classification of possible 'illocutionary effects' of communication; e.g. factual assertions, directives or instructions, declaratives, commitments, and expressives (Searle, 1971). (The LA view sharply criticizes the existing office modelling approaches in that they tend to deal with all data as if they were simply factual descriptions when in reality other types of illocutionary effects are present.)

(d) *Description of the perlocutionary effects of the message.* This aspect of language analysis focuses on specifying the consequences (behavioural and physical) which are to be expected through the act of communicating. Frequently, but not always, this is aimed at influencing the receiver, e.g. by a memo expressing concern over some contemplated action. Ordinary language conveys intended 'perlocutionary effects, by using such verbs as warning, advising, threatening, reassuring, inviting a response, etc. The intended effects, however, may be different from those which actually occur. For example, if someone shouts 'fire' the intended effect may be to warn and prevent harm; the actual effect, however, may be to create chaos and cause the precise opposite of what was intended.

It should be noted that as speech act theory is evolving, so too is the LA view. The precise nature of its concepts and the methods and tools for implementing its form of communication analysis are discussed in more detail in Goldkuhl and Lyytinen (1982), Lyytinen (1985), Lyytinen and Lehtinen (1984), and Lehtinen and Lyytinen (1983, 1984).

DISCUSSION

Whereas the analytical views on the nature of offices take a more 'task-oriented' approach, i.e. office workers perform certain tasks or take on certain roles, the interpretivist views are more 'social-oriented', i.e. looking at office work within the context of behavioural and social interaction. They call into question a number of the underlying assumptions held by others. For example, none of the analytical views consider whether the goals (whatever they are) of the organization are shared by the various organizational units and the individual employees. There is an implicit assumption that there is a set of goals which are shared by all organizational members. Yet the conventional wisdom of present-day organizational theory suggests otherwise. Goals are not shared; in fact, many are in conflict with one another. The goals of one individual are often diametrically opposed to another. The same is true of organizational units. (See, for example, the oft-cited case where the accounting department seeks to keep inventory low to reduce carrying costs but the sales department tries to keep inventory levels high to enhance sales prospects.)

Closely related to the above point is the notion of conflict. Most office views ascribe to a 'cooperative' or 'conflict-free' view of organizations. That is, organizations are relatively stable, embracing an objective and rational coop-eration among members. An alternative conception, well discussed in Burrell and Morgan (1979), suggests that organizations are not stable forces. On the contrary, they are in a constant state of conflict — conflict over power, prestige, information, resources, etc. (see Table 7.1 of Chapter 7).

The conflict view sees organizations as bargaining systems where individuals and groups bargain with one another. Organizations are, in a sense, 'negotiated orders' and the product of continuous contractual arrangements (see the transaction view).

Another point, also related to the others, is whether organizations (in general) and office work (in particular) can be considered rational. The analytical views implicitly treat office work and workers as rational. This may, however, be too simplistic. As has been mentioned above, there is considerable evidence that even if man is rational the craving for power, resources, influence, and social recognition — along with the fact that personal goals may not be consistent with organizational ones — may make actions appear irrational. Thus, it is important to understand an individual's intentions regarding why a particular action is performed in the way it is.

Additionally, the interpretive views start from a totally different perspective on work and why people engage in it. They question the 'economic, rational man' notion of work which contends that man, fundamentally, works to earn a living. While man may indeed work to earn money, it is not the only reason why man works. In fact, it may not even be the main reason. Man engages in work to keep the mind active, to achieve self-satisfaction in the fruits of labour, to experience the social company and interaction of working with others, and so on. To put it in the context of the proverbial question of whether 'man works to live or lives to work', the interpretive perspective sees man needing work to live — and not just from an economic standpoint. Work is how man satisfies many — if not most — of the primary human needs. These are, for example, the need for: freedom (autonomy, independence, etc.), affection (solidarity, cohesion, love, etc.) recognition (success, achievement, respect, etc.) and meaning (orientation, identity, consistency, etc.) (Etzioni, 1967). Take away work and a person becomes unfulfilled. This is, perhaps, the primary reason why so many social scientists are so outspoken about unemployment. As Jenkins and Sherman (1979) note:

> The work ethic is so deeply ingrained in British and other industrialized societies that work has acquired a value in itself, even though it is widely regarded as unpleasant.

It is this notion of the importance and overall character of work rather than the particular tasks which make up work which differentiates the interpretive from analytical views.

The two theoretical perspectives and their associated views have important implications for the development of office automation methodologies. An analytical perspective provides a more ready basis for the development of formal methodologies due to its focus on overt, rational office tasks. Indeed, the recent proliferation of office methodologies and models make this a *fait accompli*. There has been a similar growth in information systems methodologies as well. However, there are some nagging doubts about the efficacy of such approaches. For one, they tend to neglect the social aspect of office work. Offices are really sociotechnical systems; methodologies based on the analytical perspective concentrate on the technical, to the detriment of the social. The implementation research literature is rife with examples of what happens when there is such an imbalance (see Chapter 5). The interpretivist perspective, on the other hand, holds the promise of a more balanced treatment, as much more importance is attached to social issues. Approaches based on this perspective are likely to lead to more successful office automation implementation (Hirschheim, 1984). Chapter 4 explores the types of office automation models and methodologies available and attempts an evaluation of them. Appendix A analyses the relationship of the analytical/interpretivist perspectives (and their associated views) with the existing organizational theory perspectives.

REFERENCES

Aklilu, T. (1981) 'Office automation — office productivity — the missing link', *Proceedings of the Office Automation Conference*, AFIPS, Houston, March.
Allison, G. (1971) *Essence of Decision*, Little Brown, Boston.
Argyris, C., and Schon, D. (1978) *Organizational Learning: A Theory of Action Perspective*, Addison-Wesley, Reading.
Attardi, G. (1981) 'Office information systems design and implementation', Paper presented at the SOGESTA School on Office Information Systems, Sogesta, August–September.
Banbury, J., and Nahapiet, J. (1979) 'Towards a framework for the study of the antecedents and consequences of information systems in organizations', *Accounting, Organizations and Society*, **4**, No. 3.
Barber, G. (1982) 'Embedding knowledge in a workstation', in *Office Information Systems* (Ed. N. Naffah), North-Holland, Amsterdam.
Barber, G. (1983) 'Supporting organizational problem solving with a work station', *ACM Transactions on Office Information System*, **1**, No.1, January.
Barber, G., and Hewitt, C. (1982) 'Foundations of office semantics, in *Office Information Systems* (Ed. N. Naffah), North-Holland, Amsterdam.
Boulding, K. (1956) 'General systems theory — the skeleton of science', *Management Science*, **2**.
Bracchi, G., and Pernici, B. (1984) 'The design of office systems, *ACM Transactions on Office Information Systems*, **2**, No. 4, April.
Burrell, G., and Morgan, G. (1979) *Sociological Paradigms and Organizational Analysis*, Heinemann, London.
Carter, L., and Huzan, E. (1981) *Microelectronics and Microcomputers*, Teach Yourself Books, London.
Checkland, P. (1981) *Systems Thinking, Systems Practice*, J. Wiley and Sons, Chichester.
Cheung, C., and Kornatowski, J. (1980) *The OFS User's Manual*, Computer Systems Research Group, University of Toronto, March.
Christie, B. (1981) *Face to File Communication: A Psychological Approach to Information Systems*, J. Wiley and Sons, Chichester.
Churchman, C. (1971) *The Design of Inquiring Systems*, Basic Books, New York.
Ciborra, C. (1981) 'Information systems and transactions architecture', *Policy Analysis and Information Systems*, **5**, December.
Ciborra, C. (1983a) 'Management information systems: a contractual view', in *Beyond Productivity: Information Systems Development for Organizational Effectiveness* (Ed. T. Bemelmans), North-Holland, Amsterdam.
Clegg, S., and Dunkerley, D. (1980) *Organization, Class and Control*, Routledge and Kegan Paul, Henley.
Commons, J. (1934) *Institutional Economics*, University of Wisconsin Press, Madison.

Conrath, D., Higgins, C., Irving, R., and Thachenkary, C. (1981a) 'Determining the need for office automation: methods and results', CECIT working paper, University of Waterloo.

Conrath, D., Higgins, C., Thachenkary, C., and Wright, W. (1981b) 'The electronic office and organizational behaviour — measuring office activities', *Computer Networks*, **5**, No. 6.

Cook, C. (1981) 'Organizational and office analysis', *Proceedings of the Office Automation Conference*, AFIPS, Houston, March.

Cyert, R., and March, J. (1963) *A Behavioural Theory of the Firm*, Prentice Hall, Englewood Cliffs.

Davis, G., and Olson, M. (1984) *Management Information Systems: Conceptual Foundations, Structure, and Development*, 2nd ed. McGraw-Hill, New York.

Day, R., and Day, J. (1977) 'A review of the current state of negotiated order theory: an appreciation and critique', *Sociological Quarterly*, **18**.

Delgado, A. (1979) *The Enormous File*, Murray, London.

Dodswell, A. (1983) *Office Automation*, J. Wiley and Sons, Chichester.

Dumas, P., du Roure, G., Zanetti, C., Conrath, D., and Mairet, J. (1982) 'MOBILE-Burotique: prospects for the future', in *Office Information Systems* (Ed. N. Naffah), North-Holland, Amsterdam.

Ellis, C. (1979) 'Information control nets: a mathematical model of office automation flow', *Proceedings of the 1979 Conference on Simulation, Measurement and Modelling of Computer Systems*.

Engel, G., Groppuso, J., Lowenstein, R., and Traub, W. (1979) 'An office communications system', *IBM Systems Journal*, **18**, No. 3.

Etzioni, A. (1967) *The Active Society*, Free Press, New York.

Gehani, N. (1983) 'High level form definition in office information systems', *The Computer Journal*, **26**, No.1, February.

Getz, C. (1978) 'DP's role is changing', *Datamation*, February.

Giddens, A. (1982) *Profiles and Critique in Social Theory*, Macmillan Press, London.

Goldkuhl, G., and Lyytinen, K. (1982) 'A language action view on information systems', *Proceedings of the Third International Conference on Information Systems*, Ann Arbor, December.

Gunton, T. (1983) 'Moving fast up the learning curve', *Computing (Europe)*, Special Report on Office Automation, June.

Habermas, J. (1984) *The Theory of Communicative Action: Volume 1 — Reason and the Rationalization of Society*. Translated by T. McCarthy, Beacon Press, Boston.

Hammer, M., and Sirbu, M. (1980) 'What is office automation?', *Proceedings of the 1980 Office Automation Conference*, Atlanta, March.

Hammer, M., and Zisman, M. (1979) 'Design and implementation of office information systems', *Proceedings of NYU Symposium on Automated Office Systems*, New York, May.

Hewitt, C., Attardi, G., and Simi, M. (1981) 'Knowledge embedding in the description systems OMEGA', MIT draft paper.

Higgins, C., and Safayeni, F. (1984) 'A critical appraisal of task taxonomies as a tool for studying office activities', *ACM Transactions on Office Information Systems*, **2**, No. 4, October.

Hirschheim, R. (1984) 'A participative approach to implementing office automation', *Proceedings of the Joint International Symposium on Information Systems*, Sydney, April.

Huber, G. (1983) 'Cognitive style as a basis for MIS and DSS design: much to do about nothing?', *Management Science*, **29**, No. 5, May.

Hunsaker, P., and Hunsaker, J., (1981) 'Decision styles — in theory, in practice', *Organizational Dynamics*, Autumn.

Jakob, F. (1982) 'First implementation step toward embedding office semantics in the Buroviseur', in *Office Information Systems* (Ed. N. Naffah), North-Holland, Amsterdam.

Jacques, E. (1967) *Equitable Payment*, Penguin, Harmondsworth.

Jenkins, C., and Sherman, B. (1979) *The Collapse of Work*, Eyre Methuen, London.

Jung, C. (1923) *Psychological Types*, Routledge and Kegan Paul, Henley.

Keen, P., and Bronsema, G. (1981) 'Cognitive style research: a perspective for integration', *Proceedings of the Second Internation Conference on Information Systems*, Boston, December.

Keen, P., and Scott Morton, M. (1978) *Decision Support Systems: An Organizational Perspective*, Addison-Wesley, Reading.

Kent, R. (1979) 'Office automation and product methodology', *Proceedings of the LACN Symposium*, May.

Kilmann, R., and Mitroff, I. (1979) 'Problem defining and the consulting intervention process', *California Management Review*, **21**, No.3, Spring.

Klein, H., and Hirschheim, R. (1983) 'Issues and approaches to appraising technological change in the office: a consequentialist perspective', *Office: Technology and People*, **2**, No.1.

Klemmer, E., and Synder, F. (1972) 'Measurement of time spent communicating', *Journal of Communication*, **22**.

Kling, R. (1980) 'Social analysis of computing: theoretical perspectives in recent empirical literature', *Computing Surveys*, **12**, No. 1, March.

Kurke, L., and Aldrich, H. (1983) 'Mintzberg was right!: a replication and extension of the nature of managerial work', *Management Science*, **29**, No.8, August.

Lehtinen, E., and Lyytinen, K. (1983) 'SAMPO project: a speech act based IA methodology with computer aided tools', Department of Computer Science, University of Jyvaskyla, Report WP-3.

Lehtinen, E., and Lyytinen, K. (1984) 'A model theoretical interpretation of information systems using illocutionary logic', Department of Computer Science, University of Jyvaskyla, working paper.

Lindblom, C. (1959) 'The science of muddling through', *Public Administration Review*, **19**, No. 2, Spring.

Lum, V., Choy, D., and Shu, N. (1982) 'OPAS: an office procedure automation system', *IBM Systems Journal*, **21**, No. 3.

Lyytinen, K. (1985) 'Implications of theories of language to information systems', *MIS Quarterly*, March.

Lyytinen, K., and Lehtinen, E. (1984) 'On information modelling through illocutionary logic', *Proceedings of the Third Scandinavian Research Seminar on Information Modelling and Data Base Management*, Tampere.

McCarthy, T. (1982) *The Critical Theory of Jurgen Habermas*, MIT Press, Cambridge.

McKenney, J., and Keen, P. (1974) 'How managers' minds work', *Harvard Business Review*, May–June.

Mason, R., and Mitroff, I. (1973) 'A program for research on management information systems', *Management Science*, **19**, No. 5.

Mintzberg, H. (1973) *The Nature of Managerial Work*, Harper and Row, New York.

Mintzberg, H., Raisinghani, D., and Theoret, A. (1976) 'The structure of "unstructured" decision processes', *Administrative Science Quarterly*, **21**.

Mokhoff, N. (1979) 'Office automation: a challenge', *IEEE Spectrum*, **16**.

Morgenbrod, H., and Schaertzel, H. (1980) 'The degree of office automation and its impact on office procedures and employment', *Computer Networks*.

Mumford, E., and Weir, M. (1979) *Computer Systems in Work Design: The ETHICS Method*, Associated Business Press, London.

Nutt, P. (1984) 'Types of organizational decision processes', *Administrative Science Quarterly*, **29**, September.

Office Management Association (1958) 'Office administration', Report of the Office Management Association.

Ouchi, W. (1979) 'A conceptual framework for the design of organizational control mechanisms', *Management Science*, **25**, No. 9, September.

Ouchi, W. (1980) 'Markets, bureaucracies and clans', *Administrative Science Quarterly*, **25**, March.

Panko, R. (1984a) 'Office work', *Office: Technology and People*, **2**.

Panko, R. (1984b) '38 Offices: analyzing needs in individual offices', *ACM Transactions on Office Information Systems*, **2**, No. 3, July.

Panko, R., and Sprague, R. (1982) 'Towards a new framework for office support', *Proceedings of the SIGOA Conference*, Philadelphia, June.

Pava, C. (1983) *Managing New Office Technology: An Organizational Strategy*, The Free Press, New York.

Perrow, C. (1981) 'Markets, hierarchies and hegemony', in *Perspectives on Organizational Design and Behaviour* (Eds. A. Van de Ven and W. Joyce), J. Wiley and Sons, New York.

Perrow, C. (1961) 'The analysis of goals in complex organizations', *American Sociological Review*, **26**.

Poppel, H. (1982) 'Who needs the office of the future?', *Harvard Business Review*, November–December.

Price, S. (1979) *Introducing the Electronic Office*, NCC Publication, Manchester.

Purvy, R., Farrel, J., and Kose, P. (1983) 'The design of star's records processing: data processing for the noncomputer professional', *ACM Transactions on Office Information Systems*, **1**, No.1, January.

Rhee, H. (1968) *Office Automation in Social Perspective: The Progress and Social Implications of Electronic Data Processing*, Basil Blackwell, Oxford.

Schroder, H., Driver, M., and Steufert, S. (1967) *Human Information Processing*, Holt Rinehart, New York.

Searle, J. (1971) 'What is a speech act', in *The Philosophy of Language* (Ed. J. Searle), Oxford University Press, Oxford.

Silverman, D. (1970) *The Theory of Organizations*, Heinemann Educational Books, London.

Simon, H. (1960) *The New Science of Management Decision*, Harper and Row, New York.

Simon, H. (1964) 'On the concept of organizational goal', *Administrative Science Quarterly*, **9**.

Sirbu, M., Schoichet, S., Kunin, J., and Hammer, M. (1982) 'OAM: an office analysis methodology', MIT Office Automation Group Memo OAM-016.

Sprague, R. (1980) 'A framework for research on decision support systems', in *Decision Support Systems: Issues and Challenges* (Eds. G. Fick and R. Sprague), Pergamon Press, Oxford.

Stewart, R. (1967) *Managers and Their Jobs*, Macmillan, London.

Strauss, A., Schatzman, L., Bucher, R., Ehrlich, D., and Satshin, M. (1963) 'The hospital and its negotiated order' in *The Hospital in Modern Society* (Ed. E. Friedson), The Free Press, New York.

Suchman, L. (1979) 'Office procedures as practical action: a case study', Xerox Palo Alto Research Centre, Technical Report.

Suchman, L. (1983) 'Office procedure as practical action: models of work and system design', *ACM Transactions on Office Information Systems*, **1**, No. 4, October.

Suchman, L., and Wynn, E. (1984) 'Procedures and problems in the office', *Office: Technology and People*, **2**.

Sutherland, J. (1983) 'An office analysis and diagnosis methodology', Unpublished M.Sc. thesis, MIT, February.

Taylor, F. (1911) *Principles of Scientific Management*, Harper, New York.

Uhlig, R., Farber, D., and Bair, J. (1979) *The Office of the Future*, North-Holland, Amsterdam.

Weinstein, D., and Weinstein, M. (1972) *Roles of Man: An Introduction to the Social Sciences*, The Dryden Press, Chicago.

Wilensky, H. (1967) *Organizational Intelligence*, Basic Books, New York.

Williamson, O. (1975) *Markets and Hierarchies: Analysis and Antitrust Implications*, Free Press, New York.

Williamson, O. (1979) 'Transaction–cost economics: the governance of contractual relations', *Journal of Law and Economics*, **22**, No. 2, October.

Zisman, M. (1977) 'Representation, specification and automation of office procedures', Ph.D. thesis, Wharton School, University of Pennsylvania.

Zloof, M. (1981) 'QBE/OBE: a language for office and business automation', *Computer*, **14**, No.5, May.

Zloof, M. (1982) 'Office-By-Example: a business language that unifies data, word processing and electronic mail', *IBM Systems Journal*, **21**, No. 3.

Zmud, R. (1979) 'Individual differences and MIS success: a review of the empirical literature', *Management Science*, **25**, October.

Chapter 4
OFFICE AUTOMATION METHODOLOGIES AND MODELS

INTRODUCTION

Although there exists great interest in office automation, there is considerable confusion about the appropriate methods for office system development. Office systems have been developed in an *ad hoc* manner, often with little consideration of any formal or structured approach to systems analysis, design, and implementation. Some office automation proponents suggest it is possible to use standard systems methodologies; others contend the need for specific office automation methodologies. This chapter explores the area of office models and methodologies: outlining what they are, how they differ, a review of current approaches, and their evaluation.

METHODOLOGIES

1. The Process of Systems Analysis and Development

Systems analysis is the process of collecting, organizing, and analysing facts about a particular system and the environment in which it operates. The complete range of activities involved in such a process and the information needed and generated by these activities refers to the general area of *systems development*. There is great variation as to which detailed activities are actually performed, the sequence in which they are performed, the documentary output which is produced from each, and the extent to which they are prescribed and formalized. There are historical reasons for such variation and a long history of attempts to achieve greater understanding, formalization, and control of systems development. This has led to the emergence of *systems analysis and development methodologies* which are (supposedly) coherent and integrated sets of methods, techniques, and tools to assist the developer.

A methodology usually tries to depict: (a) the activities to be performed, (b) the relationships and sequence of these activities, and (c) the various evaluation and decision milestones which must be reached for systems development. Fundamentally, the aim of an OA methodology is to make the development process easier and more reliable.

2. Phases in Office Systems Development

According to Bracchi and Pernici (1984), the development phases for office systems are similar to those found in conventional systems. In the requirements analysis phase, the office 'reality' is studied and requirements investigated. These requirements are then formally specified using a conceptual model of the office. This is the office requirements specification phase. An office systems design is then generated which meets the identified requirements. Next, the system is put together and implemented. An ongoing process of evaluation is used to monitor the development, generating modifications as and when required. Figure 4.1 depicts the OA development process.

Most effort to date has been focused on the problem of formally specifying office elements in a model, rather than the development of a complete methodology. Therefore, most existing so-called office automation methodologies are really only partial methodologies, emphasizing only a subset of the OA systems development process. Table 4.1, from Bracchi and Pernici (1984), describes some of the more popular conceptual office models/methodologies.

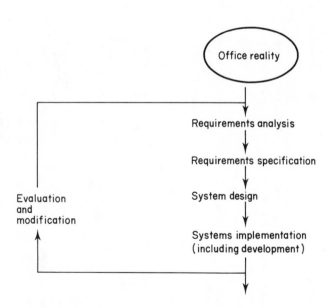

FIGURE 4.1 Phases in OA systems development

TABLE 4.1   OA conceptual methodologies and models (Bracchi and Pernici, 1984). Copyright 1984 Association for Computing Machinery, Inc., reprinted by permission

	Model	Authors' references	Year	Type of model	Required analysis	Basic elements	Comments
Data-based models	OFFICETALK-ZERO	Xerox	1976	Descriptive	tech. prot.	Forms	Minicomputer-based workstation
	OMEGA	MIT	1980	Highly formal descriptive	tech. prot.	Forms	Knowledge-based system
	OFFIS (methodology)	Univ. of Arizona	1980	Highly formal analytical	tech. prot.	Objects, attributes, relations	System for support of office system design, consistency and completeness, technical methodology
	OBE Office-By-Example	IBM	1981	Highly formal descriptive (analytical)	tech. prot.	Forms, two-dimensional objects	Many functions: 1 language extension of Query-By-Example and System for Business Automation
Process-based models	SCOOP System for Computerization Of Office Processing	Univ. of Pennsylvania	1977	Formal descriptive (analytical)	tech. prot.	Procedures, transitions/states	Concurrent asynchronous processes, Petri nets + production systems
	ICN Information Control Nets	Xerox	1979	Highly formal analytical	tech. prot.	Procedures, activities, repositories	Streamlining, information structure, control structure
	OAM Office Analysis Methodology	MIT	1980	Analytical	decis. tech. soc.	Procedures, functions + resource	Operational and technical semi-structured activities, complete methodology based on OSL model, required analysis
	OSL Office Specification Language	MIT	1980	Descriptive	decis. tech. soc.	Application domain procedures	Evolution of BDL Analyst oriented
	Ticom-II	Univ. of Minnesota	1981	Formal analytical	tech.	Task-transactions, repositories,	Graph theory, auditing methodology, minimize cost for inter-

	Name	Institution	Year			Concepts	Description
Process-based models	Office MAPS (methodology)	ELEA (Firenze)	1981	Descriptive	tech.	Functions, process flow	Organizational structure, complete methodology (organizational)
	MOBILE-Burotique (methodology)	KAYAK Project	1982	Formal analytical	tech.	Tasks; functions and hierarchical levels, cost/benefit an.	Meta-methodology (set of design tools), requirements analysis (socio-technical)
Agent-based models	Structural model	Univ. of Ancona	1981	Highly formal descriptive	tech. decis.	Agents	Office in form of functions and personal databases of agents
Mixed models	OFS Office Form System	Univ. of Toronto	1980	Highly formal analytical	tech. prot.	Forms, messages, procedures	Form=relation=message
	IML Information Management Language	GMD (Bonn)	1981	Highly formal descriptive	tech.	Predicate/transition nets + inscriptions	Control structure and data structure, same nature
	OPAS Office Procedure Automation System	IBM	1982	Highly formal descriptive	tech. prot.	Forms, abstract procedure specification, authorization form	Specification through forms
	Semantic models	Univ. of Toronto	1982	Highly formal descriptive	tech.	Office objects, procedures	Semantic model, extension of Taxis
	OFFICETALK-D	Xerox	1982	Formal analytical	tech. decis. prot.	Forms, procedures	OFFICETALK-ZERO + ICN
	SOS Semantic Office System	Politecnico di Milano	1982	Formal descriptive	tech. decis. prot.	Agents, documents, dossiers, activities, rules	Procedures and form-based model, rule-based control

3. Methodology Definition

Because the terms 'methodology' and 'model' are widely used yet loosely defined in the office automation literature, there is a need to provide a more rigorous definition of them. This section will concentrate on the notion of methodology, while the next will focus on model.

Checkland (1972) defines methodology as 'an explicit, ordered, non-random way of carrying out an activity ... independent of the content of that activity'. This is elaborated upon in his book *Systems Thinking, Systems Practice* (1981) where he distinguishes between 'method' and 'methodology'. He states a methodology is 'a set of principles of method which in any particular situation has to be reduced to a method uniquely suited to that particular situation'. Checkland (1981) notes that a 'methodology' can be conceived of as intermediate in status between 'philosophy' and 'technique' (or method). 'Philosophy', in this context, is defined as 'a broad non-specific guideline of action'. For example, the statement 'all science is based on a nomothetic inquiry process' is seen as a 'philosophy'. A technique, on the other hand, is a 'precise specific programme of action which will produce a standard result: if you learn the appropriate technique ... you can ... serve a tennis ball so that it swerves in mid-air'. Checkland states: 'A methodology will lack the precision of a technique but will be a firmer guide to action than a philosophy. Where a technique tells you "how" and a philosophy tells you "what", a methodology will contain elements of both "what" and "how".'

Welke (1981), in a detailed treatment of the information systems development process, defines a methodology as 'a comprehensive procedural framework directed towards accomplishing a particular change in the object system'. Welke describes the 'object system' as that which one is interested in perceiving (and developing). A person perceives an object system through a filtering apparatus, called a 'perception schema' or simply 'schema'. The schema acts to identify certain aspects of the object system of interest while rejecting others. Welke calls the result of viewing an object system through a particular perception schema an 'image'. Schemas are, of course, time dependent, and an individual may apply numerous schemas to an object system yielding many images. A collection of these images of the same object system is referred to as 'the perceived object system'. It exists in the mind of the perceiver. When he attempts to externalize the images, he does so through a 'representational model' or simply 'model'. It is a symbolic representation of (perceived) reality. Images are manifest through what Welke calls 'representational forms', e.g. diagrams, text, tables, lists, and the like. They are organized, for the purpose of external communication, through an adopted framework or 'frame'. To put it differently, a 'model' is the result of applying a representational form to a perceived object system using a particular frame (see Figure 4.2).

Returning to methodologies again, Welke notes they are comprised of predetermined sets of tasks which are grouped into stages according to some

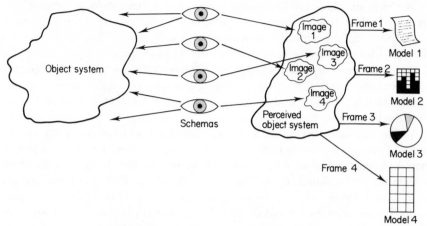

FIGURE 4.2 The notion of a model

prespecified set of methods (using various tools and techniques). 'Tasks' are defined as single pieces of work which usually have predetermined deliverables associated with them. 'Stages' are sets of prespecified tasks undertaken to obtain some needed intermediate result. 'Techniques' are ways of accomplishing certain goals through the performance of simple steps. Techniques are human skills and tools. 'Tools' are specific objects or operations employed in the use of a particular technique, which can exist independently from the techniques which use them. A 'method' is defined as a description of a specified technique in some symbolic language (see Figure 4.3).

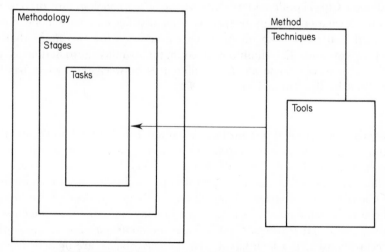

FIGURE 4.3 Representation of methodology

Welke posits there are two distinct aspects of a methodology: 'process' and 'framing'. The former refers to the tasks, tools, and techniques used to accomplish the procedural component of a methodology. The latter refers to how the object system is perceived and the types of changes which take place. These two aspects of a methodology, when taken collectively, 'form a teleological system for change directed at achieving a certain set of objectives according to an underlying ethic, and in relation to both the object system and to the developers engaged in the process'.

Welke also notes that a methodology should support two necessary components of information systems development: change process, and schema perception and representation. The former relates to how the changes to the object system are to be managed; the latter, how the object system is perceived and represented. While considerable attention has been paid to schema perception and representation in current methodologies, very little has been given to the change process.

Both Checkland's and Welke's definitions of 'methodology' share a view that sees it as more comprehensive than the term 'method' which implies techniques and/or tools. This conception of methodology appears to be widely used and accepted by the information systems community, even though it is not necessarily consistent with the standard dictionary definition where method is seen as a way of doing something and methodology as the study or science of methods. Maddison *et al.* (1983), for example, note that information systems methodologies came about as a collection of methods which proved to be valuable. They state: 'Where ... such methods were successful their originators and practitioners may have enhanced their supporting practices, techniques and tools, thus forming a methodology.' Because of its comprehensive nature and clarity, Welke's classification of method/methodology will be adopted here.

Although Checkland's and Welke's views of methodology are driven more from an information systems perspective than an office automation one, it could be argued that there is so much similarity between the two areas that it is proper to consider the definitions meaningful to office automation as well. There are, however, some potential differences between the two as has been pointed out by Bracchi and Pernici (1984):

(a) Focus. Conventional systems focus on automating manual processes and/or providing management information. OA systems focus on providing individualized tools for the wide range of office workers to increase their efficiency and effectiveness (e.g. multifunction intelligent workstations).
(b) Office data. The conceptual models on which methodologies must be based need to be semantically rich and take into account all office elements with their particular features. Conventional methodologies reflect the world of record constructs which has driven the way objects are modelled. Every-

thing is perceived as a record, thereby inheriting the poor semantics of this ubiquitous structure.

(c) Office activities. The work performed in offices may be classified as either: (1) procedural (the same sequences of tasks take place and they are algorithmic by nature), (2) semi-procedural (the tasks consist of subsets of procedural activities but the choice of the subsets is not algorithmic by nature), or (3) non-procedural (neither the tasks nor their sequences are algorithmic by nature). Conventional methodologies can only satisfactorily deal with procedural activities, yet all three are necessary for OA systems.

(d) Scope. The scope of office automation is much greater than conventional systems. Office systems have the capability of transforming the way people and organizations operate. Conventional methodologies tend to focus their attention on the hardware and software components of a system, whereas office methodologies need to effectively deal with both technical and social aspects.

(e) Cost justification. Traditional methodologies can rely on more straightforward approaches to system cost justification. Office systems are far more difficult since their greatest potential lies in adding value to work, instead of cost displacement. This problem is exacerbated by the fact that OA applications are extremely diverse, embracing decision support systems, expert systems, electronic messaging, computer conferencing, and the like.

Ballou and Kim (1984) also note differences. They see office automation methodologies having to contend with more complex environments than their data-processing counterparts. Differences can be found in: (a) interaction with technology — OA systems need to possess a much higher level of user friendliness, as the OA system operator and end user are normally the same person; (b) nature of projects (as noted by Bracchi and Pernici, 1984) — OA systems need to deal with office activities which are more unstructured and varied than the classic transactions supported in DP systems; (c) basic unit of information processed — in OA systems the basic unit is the office document, a variable and often unstructured item, in contrast to the highly structured data record; (d) role of communication — whereas DP systems do not normally disrupt interpersonal communication, OA systems can directly affect both formal and informal interpersonal communication; and (e) implementation strategies — because OA systems are relatively immature, there is little experience with how to successfully implement them which is in direct contrast with the proven strategies used in implementing DP systems (but see the next chapter for a detailed treatment of the implementation issue). Table 4.2, adapted from Ballou and Kim (1984), summarizes the differences in OA and DP environments, thereby suggesting the need for alternative methodologies. (It should be noted that their view of DP has a distinct 'batch' orientation and

TABLE 4.2 Difference in DP/OA environments

Factor	DP environment	OA environment
Interaction with technology	Low level of user interaction	High level of user interaction
Nature of projects	Structured and without variation	More unstructured and varied
Basic units of information processed	Data record	Office document
Role of communication	Unaffected	Directly and indirectly affected
Implementation strategies	Strategies well established	Strategies not established

thus seems a bit contrived. The general tenor of the argument, however, is probably correct.)

According to Bracchi and Pernici (1984), an office automation methodology should: (a) allow a complete description of an office to be obtained — the office model used in the methodology should be able to describe as many aspects of the office as possible, with little or no ambiguity; (b) permit the location of those office functions which would directly and indirectly affect the goals of the office — in particular, it should facilitate the discovering of those functions which are important for social and organizational reasons; (c) act as a guide in providing alternative technical solutions suitable for the office under study; and (d) offer some guidelines in evaluating possible solutions and in choosing design tools and techniques. Moreover, it should provide direct interfaces to the subsequent implementation phases.

In addition to these more specific goals, there are more general or global goals which a methodology should seek to achieve. They are: (a) wide applicability — a methodology should be applicable in a large number of diverse environments; (b) easy to use — it should be relatively straightforward to use, not requiring vast amounts of documentation nor needing the help of a specialist (e.g. the methodology's originator) to apply; (c) comprehensive — it should be able to provide a detailed treatment of the subject of study in terms of both breadth and depth; (d) easy to teach — it should also be relatively simple to teach; a methodology which cannot be readily comprehended by a potential user is of little value; (e) economical — in the sense that it should not necessitate the expenditure of disproportionately large amounts of resources; (f) fundamentally sound — it should be based on tools and techniques which have a firm logical foundation; and (g) clarity, precision, and conciseness — a methodology should have clearly defined steps, which are both precise and concise, with clearly defined deliverables as their end products.

OFFICE MODELS

1. Model Definition

Welke's definition of 'model' provides a firm base by which to discuss the general properties a model should have. It was, however, developed from an information systems perspective and is not necessarily consistent with definitions offered by writers in the office systems area. Researchers in this field have sought to define 'model' within the specific context of the office. Given the difficulty in defining 'office' it is not surprising, therefore, that the notion of 'model' has no universally agreed meaning. Newman (1980), for example, contends that office models are hypotheses about the way offices function. He sees office models being based mostly on the information-processing function of offices: information flow, information storage and retrieval, and the use of information in decision making. For Newman, the aim of office modelling 'should be to construct a single model, or a consistent set of models, that provides an accurate and complete description of office activity'. Ellis and Limb (1980) offer a broad definition of 'model'; they state: 'A model is a limited abstraction of reality. The limitation is expressed by selecting a subset of the relevant attributes and structures.' Gibbs (1982) is similarly broad. He suggests that an office model is an information model that is designed specifically for the office domain.

Because of the importance of having some specified meaning of the term 'model', it will be thought of as a conceptual structure which provides the apparatus for describing some particular situation. More specifically, it is the product of applying some representational form using a particular frame. It is an interpretive description which, hopefully, will provide valuable insight into the situation the model is attempting to reflect. Modelling, by extension, is the process of constructing a model. In the data-processing community, much effort has been expended in the theoretical and practical development of data models and data-modelling techniques. The effort has now been extended into the office automation area. Some suggest there is no difference between office modelling and data modelling, i.e. the tools for data modelling can be used in the office as well. Others agree in principle but note that the tools have to be modified somewhat to reflect the difference in focus. Others feel that the current data models and data-modelling approaches are inappropriate for use in the office, and hence the need for alternatives.

Most office models currently in existence share a fundamental notion, namely that offices can be conceived of as transaction-oriented systems. Although many transactions are performed concurrently, the activities associated with each type of transaction can be processed sequentially. Specific knowledge about how an individual type of transaction is processed can be used to infer a richer understanding of the parallel operation of an office.

2. Types of Office Models

To help produce a better understanding of office models, various authors have developed taxonomies through which the classification and comparison of office models is made possible. Newman (1980), for example, notes five types of office models: (a) information flow models, which seek to represent office work in terms of units of information that flow between offices; (b) procedural models, which attempt to represent office work in terms of procedures that are executed by office workers; (c) decision-making models, which seek to describe the office in terms of the decision-making activities of managers and other office personnel; (d) database models, which posit that office work can be described in terms of information records that are created, modified, and manipulated by means of transactions; and (e) behavioural models, which describe office work in terms of social activities involving groups and individual action, woven into the information-processing tasks of the office.

Tapscott (1982) distinguishes between five types of office models, which are somewhat similar to, yet distinct from, Newman's:

(a) 'Organizational communication models' are models which view the office as a communication system. For these models, communication is the key to understanding organizations. Deutsch (1952) notes that communication and control are the two critical processes in organizations. He writes:

> Communication is what makes organizations, ... control is what regulates their behaviour. If we can map the pathways by which information is communicated ... we will have gone far toward understanding that organization (quoted in Tapscott, 1982).

Goldhaber (1976) agrees; he feels communication is central to the workings of an organization since it connects the paths of the organization together and to the outside world. Organizational communication models try to model this activity in terms of communication networks.

(b) 'Functional models' focus on the underlying functions the office exists to fulfil. Hammer and Zisman (1979) define a function as an end to be realized through the performance of activities (tasks) (see the 'office functions view' in Chapter 3). Functional models tend to focus on the form rather than the content of office work.

(c) 'Information resource management models' seek to accentuate the need for effective management of the organization's information resource. These models are an outgrowth of information systems thinking and quite often contain or are driven by technological development. Tapscott (1982) suggests that the information resource management models, because of the primacy given to information, attempt to determine (quantify) the value of information, although not necessarily successfully.

(d) 'Decision support systems models' seek to place office systems within the context of supporting the judgements of office managers and others who make decisions. In particular, they attempt to model the semi-to unstructured decision tasks which require some balance between judgement and analysis. The decision support system notion, according to Keen and Scott Morton (1978), involves the assisting of office managers in their decision making, supporting rather than replacing judgement, and improving the effectiveness rather than the efficiency of decision making.

(e) 'Quality of working life models' focus on the meaning and nature of office work. They also are concerned with the structure of work organizations, the process of organizational change, and the result of the change process. Notions such as sociotechnical systems, job satisfaction, job design, industrial democracy, and organizational design tend to be part of the quality of working life models.

Bracchi and Pernici (1984) propose a completely different taxonomy for classifying office models (see Table 4.1). It is based on the fundamental elements that the models take into consideration. They note four types: data-based models, process-based models, agent-based models, and mixed models. 'Data-based models' are those which group data into 'forms', which emulate paper forms common in traditional offices. The basic elements of these models are data types and operations (e.g. storage, manipulation, and retrieval). Office activities are equated with operations. 'Process-based models' analyse and describe office work by focusing on the various office activities concurrently performed by the users and the system. 'Agent-based models' attempt to describe the office in terms of the functions performed by the active entities of an office environment — the 'agents'. Key considerations of these models are: the different roles agents take on in carrying out specific tasks, the domains in which they have the authority to act, and the sets of relationships which link the various agents together. 'Mixed models' are usually some combination of the other three. Bracchi and Pernici note that a variety of elements are requied for office system design; their taxonomy defines the relationships between the various chosen elements.

REVIEW OF CURRENT OFFICE MODELS

The following is a brief review of some of the current office models and modelling approaches which have been developed. They are presented in a descriptive and neutral fashion, and are assessed later in the chapter.

1. Tapscott's Model

According to Tapscott (1982), an office model needs to conceptualize what takes place in the office and organization. It needs to be hierarchical to reflect the overall goal structure of the organization. His model depicts an office as a system which receives inputs, processes them, and turns them into outputs. The model embodies a hierarchy of levels:

(a) Mission (or goals). These are the articulated global objectives which the organization attempts to achieve.
(b) Key results areas. These are the critical areas which have to be successful for the organization to achieve its global objectives. Examples of such areas may be organizational growth, worker satisfaction, organizational stability, and high productivity.
(c) Functions. These are particular independent operations (functions) which have predetermined and specific inputs and outputs. Examples of such functions are accounting, marketing, personnel, and administrative services.
(d) Processes, procedures, and jobs. These are the three particular kinds of operations which are undertaken in the execution of the functions. 'Processes' refer to the relationships between the series of work activities performed in executing a function. 'Procedures' are the actual groups of work activities performed to achieve a specific purpose. Examples are procedures for invoicing, writing programs, collective bargaining, and the like. 'Jobs' reflect the way the work activities are actually aggregated into divisible units, i.e. assigned to people with particular titles — jobs. It can be noted that while office activities are not exclusively assignable to a particular job, a given job can be described in terms of the activities it is to perform. Similarly, functions can be discussed in terms of the specific jobs which enable their execution.
(e) Work activities. These are the physical and mental tasks actually undertaken to carry out a given function. For example, a communications process would involve the performance of a number of related activities such as typing, dictation, travelling, writing, and scheduling.

Figure 4.4 depicts Tapscott's model diagrammatically. As can be seen, Tapscott's model is a fairly high-level one and does not provide much detail on the sequence of activities, how they are performed, and so on. It is for this reason that others have developed more procedural models.

2. Information Control Nets Based Model

Ellis' (1979) information control nets (ICN)-based model is a mathematical flow model which is used for the analysis and description of information flow within an office. By means of a network representation, a detailed description of office activities can be achieved. Specific data about the office is gathered using an iterative approach, involving interviews, observation, and analysis. Ellis

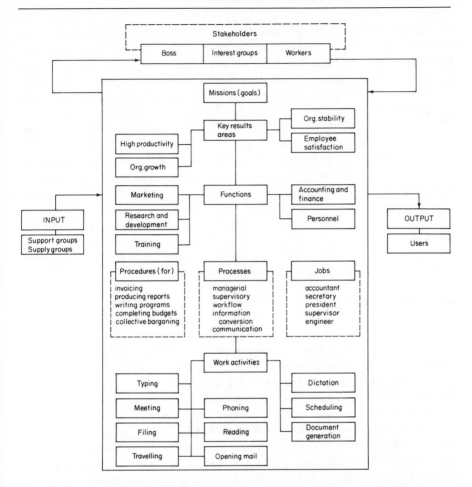

FIGURE 4.4 Tapscott's office model (Reproduced by permission of Plenum Press from Tapscott, 1982)

suggests that his ICN-based model is able to detect flaws or inconsistencies in the underlying office description and even perform office restructuring.

All ICNs have three basic requirements; they must be: (a) mathematically tractable, (b) simple (for easy manipulation and understanding by office workers), and (c) extensible (to enable it to include theoretical analysis and simulation). Ellis contends that it is the mathematical orientation and rigour of the ICN which sets it apart from other office models.

The ICN-based model defines an office as a set of interrelated 'procedures' which can be further divided into a set of 'activities' that access and update information stored in what are called 'repositories'. The execution sequence for the activities are determined through 'precedence constraints'. These are simple rules stipulating the immediate successor activity for each parent activity. Upon completion of an activity, one of its successor activities is allowed to proceed. The execution of a successor activity need not be immediate after the completion of its parent activity. It is possible that the subsequent activity may be busy, e.g. the telephone may be in use, in which case it has to go into a wait state until the resource becomes free.

In the ICN model, the four primitives (i.e. procedures, activities, repositories, and precedence constraints) are usually represented graphically or as a set of mappings defined over groups of activities and repositories. ICN diagrams normally use the following conventions: rectangles represent permanent repositories; triangles, temporary repositories; labelled circles, activities; small unfilled circles, conditional branches; small solid circles, start (or end) of parallel activity sequence; light arrows, repository accesses and updates; and dark arrows, precedence constraints (see Figure 4.5a and b).

According to Ellis, proper utilization of the ICN can help restructure the office. This restructuring can be achieved through three types of transformations: automation, office reorganization, and office streamlining. The use of automation simply substitutes activities with similar (or identical) activities which can be completed by mechanical means (or assistance). Office reorganization involves parallelism and the rearrangement or shifting of activities through decision nodes. Within the realm of parallelism it is possible to identify 'Abelian activities'; that is, activities in which the order of processing can be switched around without changing the end result. 'Streamlining', the primary method for restructuring offices (Cook, 1980; Ellis, 1979; Ellis, Gibbons, and Morris, 1980), is a set of transformations providing different views of the basic office activities. It identifies the origin and destination of the information involved in a procedure. Although it has several goals, streamlining's foremost aim is to produce a clear and concise picture of the underlying office information flow, discarding any redundant activities in the process. Other goals include reducing communication costs and alterations in the efficiency of local information flows, e.g. a reduction in the number of files and forms. Streamlining is made up of three sets of transformations. The first set is called the 'office normal form' which clarifies information flow by isolating individual subsets of activities. The second set is the 'minimal form' which presents the 'fundamental' information flow. The last set is the 'information flow necessary conditions diagram' which establishes the relationships between inputs and output by means of a probabilistic function. Transformations such as data rollback, where data previously used is no longer required, and data rollforward, where activities are moved forward, can be used to help reduce office communication overheads.

Ellis contends that the ICN model is useful in analysing the possible effects of introducing parallelism into the office, in answering questions regarding group

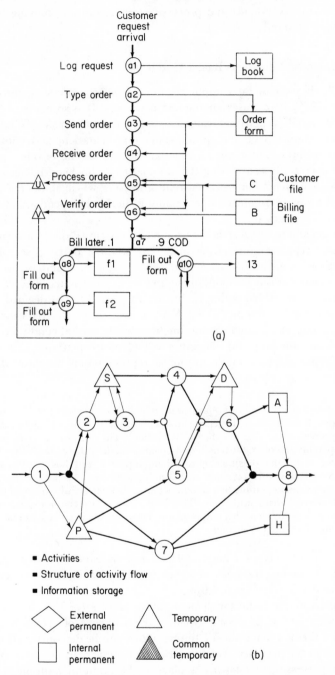

FIGURE 4.5 Examples of ICN diagrams: (a) order processing (Ellis and Nutt, 1980); (b) information control net diagram (Cook, 1980)

and individual workloads and processing times, and for studying the office's throughput characteristics.

3. Augmented Petri Nets Based Model

SCOOP, the system for computerization of office processing, developed by Zisman (1977, 1978), uses augmented petri nets. It is so named because the system is based on petri nets augmented by production rules. SCOOP places particular emphasis on the specification, representation, and automation of office procedures. The main focus is on the automating of office procedures without necessarily considering the automating technology. It views the office as a system of asynchronous concurrent processess, which allows the office to be regarded as an environment where many primarily independent, event-driven tasks occur concurrently.

Fundamental to SCOOP is the production system (PS) — the formalism for knowledge representation. It is made up of three parts: a set of rules or 'productions' constituting a condition → action; a database or 'context' allowing state data to be maintained; and a rule interpreter. The PS functions by testing the condition within each rule; if the condition is deemed to be true the consequent action is performed. Many conditions may be required to trigger a single action and a single action might result in several conditions.

The second fundamental element of SCOOP is the petri net, a formalism for process representation whose graphical representation has been defined by Miller (1973) as follows:

> A petri net is a graphical representation with directed edges between two different types of nodes. A node represented as a circle is called a 'place', and a node represented as a bar is called a 'transition'. The places in a petri net have the capability of holding tokens. For a given transition, those places that have edges directed into the transition are called 'input places', and those places having edges directed out of this transition are called 'output places' for the transition. If all the input places for a transition contain a token, then the transition is said to be active. An active transition may fire. The firing removes a token from each input place and puts a token on each output place. Thus, a token in a place can be used in the firing of only one transition.

Because it has two types of nodes, 'places' and 'transitions', with an arc passing between the nodes, the petri net may be termed a bipartite directed graph (Peterson, 1977) (see Figure 4.6).

The petri net is useful for demonstrating process coordination, and choice and conflict within processes. Because the sequence of events has no time constraint the non-deterministic timing notion can be demonstrated within the formalism of the petri net. Another advantage of the petri net is the connection between processes by allowing a place to be input to multiple transitions; simply put, more than one transition can be activated concurrently. Likewise,

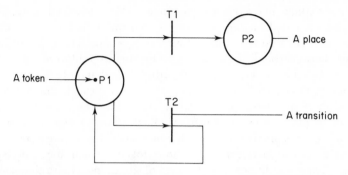

FIGURE 4.6 A graphical representation of a petri net showing conflict

production rule actions are able to activate, simultaneously, several augmented petri nets. The ability of the petri net to generate multiple processes is a valuable feature considering the dynamic nature of office systems.

Strict requirements for inter-process communication and coordination mean the production system alone cannot model asynchronous concurrent processes. In order to model these processes the production system models the individual processor events while the petri net models the relationships between the asynchronous concurrent processes. In this manner the model can accommodate most problems (Zisman, 1977).

SCOOP is particularly useful for problems with flow characteristics because it has the advantage of viewing the process representation and the knowledge representation independently. It allows the analyst to determine from the current state of the system (the synthesis of all enabled transitions), the likely 'chunks' of knowledge relevant to the decision for further action.

Each transition in the petri net represents a process and each process is constructed as a set of rules. Therefore each transition is a 'home' for the rules which describe that process. When a particular transition is enabled, its firing is dependent on the rules 'residing' in it. Because more than one transition can be enabled simultaneously, it is possible to have numerous sets of activated rules, each in its respective transition. The rules in all enabled transitions taken together constitute the active rule set. Membership of this set is merely temporary because the PS's rule interpreter continuously cycles through the active rule set to see that all conditions are satisfied. As soon as a rule condition is met, the corresponding rule actions are executed, thus instigating the firing of the transition from which the rule originated. As the process progresses some transitions become enabled while others become disabled, resulting in modification of the active set. The firing of a rule provides for direct rule interaction because it passes information (via the petri net) to the rule interpreter regarding other rules to be applied subsequent to a transition being fixed.

The information management language (IML)-inscribed nets (Richter, 1981) is also founded on the petri net formalism. It is based on predicate/transitions nets (PrT-Nets) — themselves variants of petri nets. There are many similarities between the PrT-Net and the petri net as used in SCOOP. Richter defines a PrT-Net as an ordered graph with labelled arcs. It has the ability to specify how complexes of data — 'tokens' — pass through the network. Like petri nets, there are two types of nodes: places and transitions. Tokens pass from place to place through transitions. Each place represents a 'predicate' which is a set of tokens with specific characteristics. Each transition designates an operation to be performed on those tokens which meet pre-specified conditions. These conditions take the form of situation–action rules, sometimes referred to as 'transition formulae' or 'firing expressions'. When a token is assigned to a labelled arc entering a transition it is said to be 'consumed'. If it is assigned to a labelled arc leaving a transition, it is said to be 'generated'. More precisely, the IML-inscribed net is a PrT-Net utilizing 'objects' with transitional net symbols inscribed on them; these objects are used as 'high-level tokens'. Within the PrT-Net, there are two types of abstract objects: 'constructs' and 'forms'. A 'construct' is an abstraction used to model the information contents of physical objects which may be subjected to operations defined within these contents. These operations may take the form of abstract data management operations or content manipulation functions (e.g. for text editing). Construct operators and language elements together make up the construct processing segment of IML; they form the basis for all further development of more complex inscription expressions. By contrast, a 'form' attempts to model the representation of a physical object by exhibiting all of the relevant structural properties of its inputs on some applicable physical system. This type of form refers only to those found in text-processing systems and includes both database input and output. They use a two-dimensional field structure so as to form a rectangular arrays of 'cells'.

Because they are deemed to be a more explicit and realistic system model, IML-inscribed nets are considered by Richter (1981) as an improvement over 'token nets' like SCOOP. They are designed to aid in the production of information system models, particularly where structured information objects must be taken into consideration. Research on the model continues with emphasis on the construction of a specification technique to be used in the production and interpretation of complex plans for information systems used in engineering.

4. Form Flow Model (FFM)

The FFM views the office as 'a network of stations through which forms flow' (Ladd and Tsichritzis, 1980). Information is collected on 'forms' as structured data, and processed at one of several stations. A 'station' is the term for an abstract entity which relates a person, or their role with a physical location and device through which to operate. A form is initiated at a station within the network, processed as it moves through various stations, and ultimately terminated at a station within the network. The coordination of the route which forms take between stations is accomplished by the network. Currently, networks cannot coordinate among forms; thus forms moving between stations are assumed to be completely independent from each other.

In defining the notion of 'form', Tsichritzis (1982) distinguishes between four aspects of forms: 'form types', 'form instances', 'forms', and 'form templates'. A 'form type' refers to a data type defined for a particular form. A 'form instance' represents an occurrence of a form type. 'Form' refers to the values of the attributes of a form instance. 'Form template' is a mapping from a form instance to an actual business message (or business form). Forms contain three parts: 'type', 'key', and 'contents'. Form type denotes the kind of fields a form contains; form key alludes to its unique identifier; and form contents refers to the values residing in the fields.

Stations possess in-trays and out-trays into which forms are placed. Forms from the in-tray are taken and an operation-selection function is applied to determine the immediate destination of the form. All stations are assumed to be consistent in the processing of forms (i.e. if a form should return to the same station with identical values it will be treated the same). Termination of a form occurs if a station keeps it or deletes it. Any duplication of that form is treated as a new form.

All forms within a network originate from an initial tray and terminate in a final tray. Communication between two stations can take place when the network takes a form from a non-final out-tray of one station and transfers it to the in-tray of another station. Such movement is achieved through what Tsichritzis calls the 'routing flow arcs' associated with the non-final out-tray. Since 'forms are neither created nor destroyed, only transformed' (Ladd and Tsichritzis, 1980), the network can be called a true flow network.

In order to keep the model simple some restrictions have been imposed upon it:

(a) *The network must be deterministic.* A deterministic transformation of the form's contents will occur due to the sequence of operations performed on it from the initial introduction into the network to its final state.

(b) *The network must be isolated from all external factors.* No external data is referenced unless it has been deliberately included in the contents of a form already within the system. No external actions can be triggered unless they are recorded in the contents of the output form. The operation and routing-selection function and operations are assumed to be separate from each other as well as from the current state of the network.

(c) *The network must be memoryless.* No form contents can be recorded for future reference; stations only record contents of forms as they pass through. Once a form is out of the network the station deletes any information recorded. The FFM may be broken down hierarhically into subnetworks which can be analysed individually before being mapped onto stations. The mapped stations can then be reassembled as a more simplistic network for analysis. Various aspects of the model can be interpreted through the application of mathematical analysis. The graph theoretic approach (GTA) is applied to locate the flow paths. The depth first search (DFS) algorithm is then used to enumerate the flow paths and calculate the average processing time as well as the frequencies of the flow paths. The 'commodity flow analysis' (CFA) reveals any troublesome bottlenecks in the network and 'queuing network analysis' (QNA) locates the longest queue in the network.

When the GTA is applied, the FFM is considered a directed graph of in-trays, out-trays, and flow arcs. A flow path is a sequence of incident flow arcs moving from the initial tray to the final tray, thus defining a sequence of stations and a sequence of operations. The primary goal of this analysis is to calculate the optional flow path as closely as possible to the 'followable flow paths' (i.e. the paths which forms actually take during processing). Sometimes when using the concept of followable flow paths the problem of looping arises. This occurs when a sequence is infinite and followable — the form becomes trapped in the network forever, indicating an error in the network. It may be more convenient to group flow paths into equivalence classes to study the characteristics in terms of a small group of classes.

The FFM may be analysed as a 'commodity flow network' (CFN) using CFA to determine the capacity constraints. The CFN is able to determine maximum loading factors for forms, stations, and communication channels. Because the number of forms being input into the system can be estimated, the needed capacities of the stations or communication channels can be determined, thus averting potential bottlenecks.

The FFM may be called a 'multiclass queuing system' (Ladd and Tsichritzis, 1980). A form is viewed as a job, and a station as a server with a single queue for its set of in-trays. Each operation within a station corresponds to a unique job class. The problem is then formulated in terms of how to optimally service the jobs in the queue. The solution is obtained using QNA. Several assumptions must be made prior to arriving at the solution. They are: one-step behaviour, server homogeneity, and routing homogeneity. Ladd and Tsichritzis define these as follows:

(a) One-step behaviour. The only observable change in the system is the result of a single job entering the system, flowing between servers, or leaving the system.

(b) Server homogeneity. The service time distribution of a server is dependent only on the state of its queue.
(c) Routing homogeneity. The routing frequencies may depend only on the total number of jobs in the system currently.

There are several variations on the use of forms, such as office-by-example (OBE) (Zloof, 1981, 1982) and the high-level form definition language (Gehani, 1983). OBE is a language developed specifically for the description and manipulation of various types of office objects. The office is regarded as a collection of objects which can be manipulated by office workers. OBE is an evolution of the consideration of forms as simple two-dimensional objects (data structures). The objects are set out in the form of tables and retain the image of paper forms. The high-level form definition language is formulated on the concept of abstract types in programming languages. As of yet, no other form-based model has provided such a language or the definition of forms. Gehani's definition of form is slightly different from Tsichritzis (1982). Gehani defines a 'type' as a set of values plus a set of operations which may be performed on the values. An abstract data type is described as a user-defined type, and a form type is defined as a set of values corresponding to all methods of filling a form correctly along with the operations which can be performed on these values. He also defines a form to be an instance of a form type. Other examples of office form-based models/systems are OPAS (Lum, Choy, and Shu, 1982), FADS (Rowe and Shoens, 1982), and FORMANAGER (Yao *et al.*, 1984).

5. OMEGA

OMEGA is an outgrowth from the field of artificial intelligence (Barber, 1982, 1983). Technically it is a knowledge-embedding language used to embed specific office job descriptions into an office worker's workstation support of problem solving. OMEGA's viewpoint mechanism (a general contradiction-handling facility which stores statements of rules) is used to reason about change and contradiction. When a contradiction does arise the viewpoint mechanism is utilized to reason why it occurred.

The use of OMEGA provides a record of the activities involved in the performance of specific office tasks. This description includes mental as well as physical activities relevant to a task and the reasons for the activities. Because OMEGA characterizes work by an explicit representation of goals and actions, it can expose hidden assumptions and implicit goals about office work. This form of representation proves a useful aid in handling unexpected contingencies, as well as making the actions performed by an office worker more comprehensible. Office workers are better equipped to handle unexpected contingencies because they know the specific goals of the office work and the actions necessary to achieve these goals. They may elect to use the OMEGA to suggest an alternative plan of action or to examine the goals the alternative action must take on if the action is unable to be performed. The user's actions can also suggest what the current goals are and thus narrow the choices for solving the problem as well as reducing the solutions space (see the 'office semantics' view in Chapter 3).

OMEGA uses a problem-solving support paradigm represented in Figure 4.7. The problem-solving support paradigm is an extension of the classical view of problem solving in artificial intelligence. The paradigm is applied by the user (office worker) as follows. OMEGA either attempts to establish or refute a particular goal, based on its knowledge of the goal. If a goal cannot be established, OMEGA notifies the office worker that contradictory information is present. The office worker can then either modify the goal or insert more relevant information in order to establish the goal once again. The cycle is repeated until the goal becomes established. The analysis above is achieved by OMEGA's viewpoint mechanism — the heart of the problem-solving support paradigm.

The 'description lattice' (Barber, 1983) of OMEGA is used to embed knowledge (in the form of descriptions) which are the basic elements of OMEGA's system of reasoning. The descriptions are of objects in the system and relationships between objects. This method of information storage allows for great flexibility in data stored as well as permitting individual office tasks to be singled out for reasoning. Because the descriptions are a general facility they provide a great deal of functionality. For example, descriptions are provided of the structures of office activities and problem-solving processes, a specification of the application and organizational structures, as well as viewpoints for reasoning.

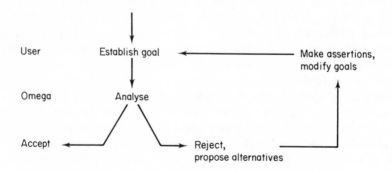

FIGURE 4.7 Problem-solving support paradigm

Viewpoints may be thought of as a type of storage for descriptions and statements. More precisely, they are objects within the system (i.e. goals and assertions) that may be reasoned about and described, like any other descriptions found in the system. An integral characteristic of viewpoints is that the only change that can be made is the *addition* of information. Viewpoints can allow rules to be implemented in such a way that further deductions or inferences can be made as information is added to them. Whenever information in a viewpoint is changed the resulting actions are controlled by 'sprites'. Sprites are procedures which fire when a predetermined condition in the knowledge base has been detected. Generally, a sprite fires when an assertion is made or when a goal is stated.

The viewpoint mechanism of OMEGA has a history-keeping capability which allows it to maintain a globally consistent database. If an inconsistency arises a valid conclusion can still be reached by pinpointing the inconsistency to within a particular viewpoint. Reasoning can continue to take place outside of the inconsistent viewpoint. The ability to limit the effect of contradiction to within viewpoints is achieved by explicitly keeping track of assertions and justifications. Information deemed to be true is called an assertion. A justification is that information which supports and explains why an assertion is deemed to be true. If a contradiction occurs the causal factors can be analysed by the reasoning mechanism, instead of using techniques such as backtracking or other types of search mechanisms. When a statement is presented, OMEGA responds to the truth or falseness of it, supplies its reasons for the decision, or even that it does not know. Figure 4.8 illustrates how viewpoints handle the process of contradiction.

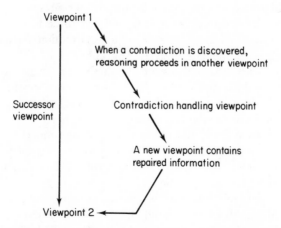

FIGURE 4.8 Handling contradictions with viewpoints

The figure illustrates a contradiction found while reasoning in viewpoint 1; it ceases all activity and initiates the contradiction-handling viewpoint. It is here that the justification for the assertions within the contradiction are analysed. New assertions, along with some of the assertions from viewpoint 1 (depending on where the contradiction initiated), are then input into viewpoint 2. This new viewpoint (viewpoint 2) is known as the successor of viewpoint 1 and continues the reasoning process where viewpoint 1 ceased.

REVIEW OF SELECTED CURRENT METHODOLOGIES

The following is a brief review of various methodologies which have been proposed for office automation. They are presented in a descriptive way and are assessed later in the chapter.

1. ISAC

ISAC (Lundeberg, Goldkuhl, and Nilsson, 1981) is an approach to information systems and OIS specification, developed in Sweden, which is based on the traditional process of taking an object system and reducing it into manageable and meaningful chunks. The object system is decomposed into smaller and smaller subsystems until information-processing activities are defined as separate entities within the subsystem. Since reductionism is considered a natural aspect of man's thought process, this decomposition process is thought meaningful. The major advantage of this kind of process is its structured and coherent nature. Most information systems development methodologies embrace this process but few provide as comprehensive an approach as ISAC.

The ISAC methodology is particularly strong on the specification side. It uses a graphical description technique for the visual representation of activities. In carrying out the design process ISAC adopts three levels of abstraction, starting from activity analysis (A graphs) to information systems analysis (I graphs) through to component analysis (C graphs).

ISAC begins with an analysis of the activities in the object system. Subsystems are similarly analysed so that information-processing activities can be noted. The analysis is performed through the use of A graphs. Associated with the A graphs are tables summarizing the need for change, special considerations, system goals and objectives, and the properties of the system. The A graphs are supplemented by tables of properties, processes, and tasks. The information system is then analysed in terms of data structures, program structures, equipment, and operation.

In the ISAC approach, information systems are specified along three levels: (a) change analysis, (b) activity studies, and (c) information analysis. The function of *change analysis* is to discover the changes which should be made to improve the operation of the organization. It starts with an analysis of problems and needs which includes a description of the current situation and objectives.

It continues with an analysis of change alternatives and ends with a recommendation of whether or not to change. If the end product of change analysis is the need for change, it recommends a particular option. In *activity studies*, the particular situation (system) is described in terms of the activities of the organization. The activity studies delimit the system in question and partition it into subsystems which are more readily analysed. These subsystems are studied in detail to provide a richer understanding of them and their connections with other organizational systems. The purpose of *information analysis* is to describe what the proposed system will contain and how it will perform. It provides a vehicle for communication between the affected interest groups. Information analysis presents what is needed to arrive at the desired output (precedence analysis), the structure of the desired information system (component analysis), and, finally, the necessary processes in the designed system (process analysis).

ISAC is a fairly comprehensive (and complex) methodology, capable of providing detailed user information requirements. One of its primary strengths lies in the heavy user input associated with developing the various A, I, and C graphs. The end result should closely reflect user needs. The methodology also appears to be relevant for the development of a logical office systems design. Although it was not developed specifically with office systems in mind, its high degree of flexibility to adapting to multiple social and technical contingencies is promising for OIS. Figure 4.9 provides an overview of the ISAC approach.

2. Checkland's Soft System Methodology

Checkland (1981) has developed a general methodology which could be used for information systems analysis and, by extension, office automation. Checkland states that it was designed for use in broad problem-solving situations, but its relevance to systems analysis is clear. His approach has its roots in the 'systems movement', which is an alternative to the more orthodox 'reductionist' approach, and contends it is more fruitful to study 'wholes' rather than 'parts' since a reductionist approach fails to appreciate the existence of synergy, where the whole is different from the sum of·its parts. Checkland contends that traditional information systems development is based on reductionist principles, on what he calls 'hard systems thinking'. It tends to take an overly simplistic view of the world — one where there is no apparent disagreement over organizational objectives and problems. As an alternative, he offers 'soft systems thinking', a general approach to problem solving which denies the existence of a recognized and agreed set of organizational objectives, needs, and performance measures. Checkland suggests that the universe of problems can be divided into those where hard systems thinking is appropriate and those where soft systems thinking is necessary. Information systems (and office systems) belong in this latter category.

Checkland sees information systems within the realm of social systems which he states are composed of rational assemblies of linked activities and sets of

1. *Change analysis*
   1.1 Analysis of problems, current situation, and needs
       — problems experienced, problems to be examined
       — affected interest groups are consulted
       — crude activity model developed
       — compare what is wanted with what is available
   1.2 Study of alternatives
       — generate and describe change alternatives
       — evaluate change alternatives by social and technical objectives
   1.3 Choice of change approach
       — reasons for choice
       — development measures, e.g. OA development, organizational
                 development
       — parallel measures to assist change

2. *Activity studies*
   2.1 Partition into information subsystems
       — detail activity model
       — identify the subsystems that need different types of aid or different
                 degree of automation
       — classify the identified subsystems according to their formalizability
                 and type of processing:
           — those that are impossible to formalize
           — those that are not suitable to formalize
           — those that are formalizable and, hence, automatible
       — delimit the subsystem
           — to match various user perspectives
           — to meet time requirements, e.g. response time
   2.2 Study of information subsystems
       — analysis of contribution towards fulfilment of goals
       — generate alternative levels of ambition, e.g. quality of information,
                 accuracy
       — test levels of ambition to see that they are realistic and realizable
       — cost/benefit analysis
       — choice of ambition level
   2.3 Coordination of the system
       — analyse the relationships between different systems
       — prioritize the different system alternatives

3. *Information Analysis*
   3.1 Precedence and component studies
       — suitable extent of information analysis for each subsystem (depends
                 largely on the degree of formalizability)
       — precedence and component analysis to analyse information needs
   3.2 Process analysis
       — identification of processes
       — detailed description of processes
   3.3 Property analysis
       — the value of the system properties are determined
       — qualitative and quantitative values are distinguished

FIGURE 4.9 Overview of the ISAC approach

relationships. Checkland refers to these as 'human activity systems'. He recognizes that in order to regulate the behaviour of organizational role holders and create shared expectations among individuals in an office, formal systems are designed. Further, the heterogeneity of human behaviour and values influence the character of the total organizational system and its supporting information systems. However, Checkland notes a problem. He states:

> A purely behavioural approach based upon the idea of man as a gregarious animal will neglect the power and influence of rational design, (while) an approach which assumes human beings to be rational automata and ignore the cultural dimension will also pass the problem by.

Thus, there is need for an approach which is formal yet captures the behavioural richness of organizational life. Checkland contends his soft systems methodology is such an approach.

Overview of the Methodology

The methodology is meant for addressing fuzzy, ill-defined problems — precisely those of social systems. Hard systems thinking, which is goal directed in the sense that goals (objectives) are stated at the outset, is inappropriate as such articulated goals do not exist in social systems. Soft systems thinking starts from the point of view that human activity systems possess goals which are not quantifiable. In human activity systems, problems are manifestations of mismatches between the perceived reality and that which is perceived might become actuality.

Checkland's methodology is different from the traditional approaches in that it does not prescribe specific tools and techniques, only general problem formulating approaches. It is a framework which does not force or lead the systems analyst to a particular 'solution', rather to an understanding. The steps within the methodology are categorized as 'real world' activities and 'systems thinking' activities. The steps in the former are executed by the people in the real world or problem situation; the steps in the latter attempt to provide a conceptual model of the real world which is in turn modified by discussion with the concerned people. It is therefore a highly participatory approach.

The methodology is shown diagrammatically in Figure 4.10. (It should be noted that although the stages are described in sequence, Checkland claims a project can be started at any stage; further, backtracking and iteration are not only possible but essential.)

Stages 1 and 2: The Problem Situation

The function of these stages is to outline the situation so that a range of possible and relevant views can be revealed. As many different perceptions of the problem situation, from people with a wide range of roles, are collected, the

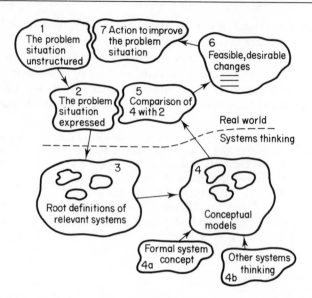

FIGURE 4.10 Overview of Checkland's methodology (Checkland, 1981)

views will, hopefully, reveal patterns of communication (both formal and informal), power, hierarchy, and the like. These early stages should not attempt to 'define' the problem, only to build up an understanding of the 'situation in which there is perceived to be a problem' without imposing any particular structure on it or assuming any structure exists.

Within these stges, it is recommended that each problem situation be described in terms of 'structures' and 'processes'. The former refers to those relatively immutable structures identified in terms of physical layout, reporting structure, formal and informal communications, etc. The latter reflects those elements which are continually changing. They are often identified in terms of basic activities such as planning to perform some task, understanding it, monitoring how well it is done, analysing its external effects, and so on. The relationships between structures and processes are studied to ensure they operate in harmony. (Checkland calls this 'climate' and claims it is a 'core characteristic' of many problem situations.)

Stage 3: Root Definitions of Relevant Systems

By the conclusion of stage 2, different perceptions of the problem situation should have been sufficiently clear to enable 'notional systems' to be named.

These are systems which are relevant to the problem. Stage 3 is concerned with choosing the appropriate notional systems from the stated systems in stage 2. The choice is done through the help of what is known as a 'root definition', which Checkland defines as a concise description of a human activity system that captures a particular view of it. To put it differently, it is a definition of the basic nature or purpose of the system thought by a particular actor to be relevant to the problem at hand. The construction of the root definition is at the core of the methodology. Checkland notes that the task of root definition construction is a non-trivial one, and contains a large element of intuition and experience. He does, however, offer a six-element checklist which all root definitions should explicitly contain, known conveniently by the acronym CATWOE:

(a) Ownership (O): the agents who have a prime concern for the system, systems owners, system control, or sponsorship
(b) Transformation (T): the process by which defined inputs are transformed into defined outputs
(c) Actors (A): the agents who carry out, or cause to be carried out, the transformation activities of the system
(d) Customer (C): clients, beneficiaries, or victims of the system's activities
(e) Environmental constraints (E): environmental impositions — features of the environment or wider system which have to be taken as given
(f) Weltanschauung (W): an outlook, framework, image, etc., which makes the particular root definition a meaningful one

Checkland suggests that the omission of any element from the development of a root definition could cause the definition to be 'wrong' unless there is good reason for omitting it.

Stage 4: Making and Testing Conceptual Models

Conceptual models, according to Checkland, are models which will accomplish what is defined in the root definition. If the root definition is viewed as an account of what the system is, then the conceptual model is an account of the activities which the system must perform in order to be the system named in the definition. Conceptual models are not descriptions of any part of the real world, only the structured set of activities sufficient to account for the system as defined by the root definition. It does not follow, however, that only one conceptual model can be developed from any particular root definition. A conceptual model is considered complete if it conforms to the conditions necessary and sufficient for a system to be 'formal'. The 'formal system' model is a compilation of management components which arguably have to be present if a set of activities is to comprise a system capable of purposeful action. These compo-

nents include: having a purpose or mission, resources, a measure of performance, a decision-making process whose elements are also systems which interact
with one another, a boundary separating it from its environment, and some
guarantee of continuity.

The sequence of events which occur in the generation of a conceptual model
is depicted in Figure 4.11.

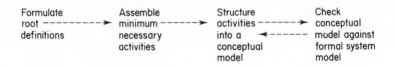

FIGURE 4.11 Generation of the conceptual model

Stage 5: Comparing Conceptual Models with Reality

At this stage, conceptual models are compared with the problem situation
analysed in stage 2. There are four approaches for making such a comparison:
(a) use the conceptual model as a basis of ordered questioning, in particular, to
open up a debate about change; (b) trace through the sequence of events that
have produced the present problem situation and compare what had happened
with what would have happened if the conceptual models had been implemented; (c) ask what features of the conceptual models are particularly
different from the present reality, and why; and (d) develop an alternative
conceptual model of the problem situation with the same 'form' as the first, then
'overlay' one onto the other and reveal mismatches which are the source of
discussion of change.

The purpose of the comparison stage is to generate debate about the possible
changes which might be made within the perceived problem situation.

Stages 6 and 7: Implementing 'Feasible and Desirable' Change

Checkland states that the changes likely to be recommended through his
methodology will probably be more modest in nature than what would be
recommended by a 'hard' methodology. (The latter is likely to advocate the
creation and implementation of a new system.) Changes should be desirable as
a result of the insight gained from building and selecting root definitions, and
creating conceptual models. They should be culturally feasible, taking into

account the characteristics of the situation, the people in it, and their shared experiences and beliefs. There are three types of changes possible: changes in structure, in procedures, and in attitudes. The first refers to changes made to those parts of reality which will not readily change in the short term, e.g. organizational groupings, functional responsibilities, and reporting structures. The second are changes to dynamic elements, e.g. the process of reporting and informing. The third refers to the changes in attitudes as a result of the other two changes. These are changes to the intangible characteristics which reside in the individual and collective consciousness of human beings. It includes changes in the expectations which people have of the behaviour appropriate to various roles.

Changes generated from this stage are debated by those people in the problem situation who care about the perceived problem. Once changes have been agreed, they can be implemented. This process may be straightforward or problematic — in which case the methodology itself may be used to help in the implementation process.

3. Mumford's ETHICS

ETHICS, an acronym for effective technical and human implementation of computer systems, is a methodology developed largely by Enid Mumford and has been evolving over the past fifteen years. It is quite different from the traditional approaches to information system development in that it is based on the ideals of sociotechnical systems (STS). Mumford (1981) defines STS as:

> ... an approach to work design which recognizes the interaction of technology and the people, and produces work systems which are both technically efficient and have social characteristics which lead to high job satisfaction.

Technology, when viewed from this perspective, is much more flexible and less 'given' than is the case with traditional approaches.

A key aspect of the methodology is its participative nature; users play a very large and important role in systems development. While user involvement is important in any methodology, it is absolutely vital in ETHICS. It must be stated, however, that the participative nature of ETHICS should not be overemphasized, as it sometimes is in the literature. The methodology attempts to operationalize the sociotechnical philosophy; participation is only one ingredient among many.

ETHICS is also an evolving methodology. There have appeared a number of different versions over the years: some more comprehensive, others more conceptual in nature. The version discussed here is probably the most comprehensive of the ones published.

The Detailed Steps of the Methodology

The ETHICS methodology contains six stages divided into twenty-five steps:

Stage	Title	Steps
1	Essential systems analysis	1–11
2	Sociotechnical systems design	12–20
3	Set alternative solutions	21–22
4	Set compatible solutions	23
5	Rank sociotechnical solutions	24
6	Prepare detailed work design from chosen solution	25

Stage 1: Essential Systems Analysis

STEP 1. Identify problem or opportunity
In this step, the question 'why are we changing?' is posed. The purpose is to identify the particular opportunities available by a new system or a problem which needs attention.

STEP 2. Identify system boundaries
Users are asked to identify those departments and units of the organization and its environment which are likely to be directly affected by the proposed change. Mumford suggests four areas for consideration: (a) business activities affected, e.g. sales, finance, and personnel; (b) existing technology affected, e.g. computer systems and office systems; (c) parts of the corporation affected, e.g. departments and sections; and (d) parts of the corporation's environment affected, e.g. suppliers and customers.

STEP 3. Description of existing system
This is undertaken to help ensure that the design team understands how the existing system works. It is concerned with defining what happens now. There are two approaches to providing such a description:

(a) Simple input–output analysis, where the principle inputs and outputs are identified and analysed; and
(b) Activity analysis, where the system needs and activities are identified under five headings:
  (1) Operational activities. These are the most important day-to-day tasks, i.e. the necessary activities.
  (2) Problem avoidance/correction activities. These are the key problems (or variances) that must be prevented or rapidly corrected if they occur.

(3) Coordination activities. These activities must be coordinated in the system or with other systems.

(4) Development activities. These activities, products, services, etc., need to be developed and improved.

(5) Control activities. These show the system is presently controlled, e.g. how the targets are set, progress monitored, key objectives met, and so on.

STEPS 4 and 5. Identify key objectives and tasks
The purpose of these stages is to identify the key objectives and tasks which the new system must support. It starts by eliciting the key objectives of the department, section, or functional area which is the focus of study, describing why these objectives exist and how close they are to being met. Next, the tasks which must be carried out if the objectives to be achieved are identified. Mumford suggests that these should be specified in broad terms, without going into too much detail.

STEP 6. Identify unit operations
Related sets of tasks that can be integrated into what Mumford calls 'unit operations' are noted. These are subsystems associated with each objective identified in step 4.

STEP 7. Identify key information needs
The key information required if each key task is to be successfully completed is set out. This could be carried out through input–output analysis where the principal requests for information coming from outside and the information collected by departments within the system boundaries are noted, as well as where the information processed in the system is passed on to.

STEP 8. Diagnose efficiency needs
Efficiency needs are identified by looking for examples of variances in the system which is being redesigned. According to Mumford, a variance is a tendency for a system to deviate from some desired norm or standard. Variances caused by a shortage of information are particularly noted. The areas where discrepancies are likely to be identified are: variances due to inadequate resources; variances due to errors which originate outside the system boundary; and variances due to the complex nature of external demands.

STEP 9. Diagnose job satisfaction needs
Job satisfaction is defined by Mumford as the 'fit' between what people would ideally like to have as a work situation and what they perceive they are receiving. Needs arise from a 'bad fit' between the present and the ideal, and must be corrected in the new system. Job satisfaction is seen to be achieved when three types of needs are met in the work situation; personality needs,

competence and efficiency needs, and needs associated with personal values. 'Personality needs' can be divided into two primary needs: knowledge needs — the wish to be able to use one's knowledge in the job — and psychological needs — the desire for status, responsibility, recognition, job security, social relationships, promotion, and achievement. 'Competence and efficiency needs' reflect individuals' desire for: (a) support and control — support and control services which allow them to exercise their talent; and (b) task structure — job and task structures which individuals find motivating, interesting, and challenging. 'Personal values needs' refers to the individual's desire for fair and ethical treatment by the firm's management.

To carry out this diagnosis Mumford recommends a job satisfaction questionnaire.

STEP 10.   Forecast future needs
Because the environment changes so rapidly, most work systems have only limited lives. To prolong their lives for as long as possible, it is necessary to be able to adapt to change. Thus, those factors in the environment which are likely to change, and to which the new system must adapt, need to be identified. This is done through a technique called 'future analysis'. It attempts to address: (a) changes in the available technology, (b) changes in legal requirements, (c) changes in economic and other environmental factors, (d) changes in attitude, expectations, tastes, or in opinion climates, and (e) changes within the organization.

STEP 11.   Set and rank efficiency and job satisfaction needs
All groups with an interest in the system should take part in this exercise. The users are given a list of objectives and invited to rank each one on a scale of 1–5. The suggested occupational groups who would be involved in the ranking are data-processing staff, and user managers and staff from the relevant user departments. Each group would rank the objectives according to their own preferences.

Stage 2: Sociotechnical Systems Design

STEP 12.   Identify technical and business constraints
In this stage, the technical and organizational constraints on the design of the system are set out. Examples of these constraints are security, back-up and recovery, and availability of hardware.

STEP 13.   Identify social constraints
Here, the social constraints on the design of the system are outlined. An example of a social constraint is the desire to reduce the overall number of staff but without forced redundancies. This is the human counterpart to the technical constraints identified in step 12.

STEP 14. Identify resources available for the technical system
This step sets out the resources available for the technical system. Examples of these resources are availability of personnel, equipment, and finance.

STEP 15. Identify resources available for the social system
Similar to the previous step, it identifies those resources which can be used for the social system. Availability of personnel, training, consultancy, finance, etc., are all examples of such resources.

STEP 16. Specify the priority of the technical and business objectives
From the list of objectives outlined in step 11, the different occupational groups are expected to reach a consensus on a priority list for the objectives. Only technical objectives which are feasible, given the cited constraints, should be considered.

STEP 17. Specify the priority of the social objectives
Again, similar to step 16, it is the social objectives which are addressed.

STEP 18. Check for compatibility
In this step, the objectives discussed in the previous two steps are checked to ensure they are compatible. If not, the objectives have to be revised in light of the incompatibility. As the result needs to be agreed by the various occupational groups, it is possible that the process may be iterative.

STEP 19. Take technical system decisions
For the technical system, a variety of decisions will need to be taken — decisions about input, the computer, output, and the like. Input questions relate to how the input would be handled, what equipment to use, and so on. Computer decisions relate to what the machine will do, what it will not do, and what will be handled manually. Output decisions are concerned with output, media, format, frequency, and the like.

STEP 20. Take social system decision.
For the social system, the human counterpart to the above decisions are considered. For example, choices about input jobs (e.g. how to organize jobs associated with the input of data to the system) and output jobs (how to organize jobs which are both connected and unconnected to the computer, and how to integrate them) are discussed.

Stage 3: Setting Out Alternative Solutions

STEP 21. Set out alternative technical solutions
In this step, a maximum of four or five different technical solutions are outlined, each of which is compatible to the stated objectives. For each alternative

solution, both the technical and social advantages and disadvantages are set out in a matrix, which facilitates comparison. Each technical solution is evaluated against the following criteria:

(a) Does the solution achieve all the priority technical and business objectives which were specified in step 16? Does it achieve all or some of the non-priority items?
(b) Is the solution limited in any way by the constraints identified in steps 12 and 13?
(c) Are the various resources identified in steps 14 and 15 adequate to realizing the solution?

STEP 22. Set out alternative social solutions
In step 11, a comparison between the social desires and the perceived reality was carried out on five needs: knowledge, psychological, support/control, task, and ethical. Those areas of poor 'fit' would be the central focus of the alternative social solutions. When setting out the alternative social solutions, it is important to consider them independently of the technical solutions at this step. Mumford suggests thinking about social systems in two ways: (a) the organization of the total work flow into the various departments or sectons and (b) the design of the actual work which is undertaken in each of these departments. She feels it is better to concentrate on the former in this step and leave the latter to step 24.

As in the previous step, each social solution should be evaluated against the three criteria: priority, constraints, and resources. Doubtful solutions should be eliminated and a shortlist drawn up (alongside of a shortlist of technical solutions).

Stage 4: Setting Out Compatible Solutions

STEP 23. Set out compatible sociotechnical solutions
In this stage, the shortlists of technical and social solutions are merged to see which pairs of solutions are compatible with one another. Those which are incompatible are discarded. When a technical and social solution is found to be able to operate together, the combination is entered into an evaluation matrix which is used in the next stage.

Stage 5: Ranking Sociotechnical Solutions

STEP 24. Rank the matched solutions
The compatible pairs of technical and social solutions entered in the evaluation matrix in the previous stage are now ranked using the information generated in steps 21 and 22. It is important that the proposed sociotechnical solution still meets the criteria outlined in stages 1 and 2, namely:

(a) Does the chosen solution meet both technical and social needs?
(b) Are sufficient resources available to achieve both the technical and social dimensions of the solution?
(c) Are there any constraints which make the solution infeasible?
(d) Does it meet other technical and social objectives set out in step 11 but did not become priority objectives?

Stage 6: Prepare a Detailed Work Design

STEP 25. Prepare a detailed work design for the sociotechnical solution
In this step, a list and description of all the tasks which people will perform if the particular sociotechnical solution is implemented is developed. These tasks are ranked in terms of simplicity and checked to see if there is any way of combining or arranging them into jobs to provide a balanced spread of required skills and complexity of tasks. The arrangement of tasks needs to be checked to make sure the created jobs are as interesting and satisfying as possible. Issues of concern are:

(a) Are there acceptable feedback loops for each job, informing the workers of their performance?
(b) Can workers easily identify the targets they need to achieve?
(c) Are there clear boundaries between the different jobs so that workers have a sense of identity with their job?
(d) Is the cycle time of the tasks long enough to avoid a feeling of routine and repetitive work, yet short enough to allow workers to feel they are making progress?

If the highest ranking sociotechnical solution scores high on these issues, while still achieving the technical objectives, then it is accepted as the final solution. If not, one of the other shortlisted solutions is tried. Figure 4.12 depicts the process diagrammatically.

4. Tapscott's User-Driven Design Methodology

Tapscott's (1982) user-driver design (TUDD) methodology is a practical approach to office automation. It is based on a three-phased, evolutionary design process involving the use of pilot studies to provide the necessary knowledge for successful office automation. The three phases are the pre-pilot phase, the pilot phase, and the operational system phase. TUDD is depicted in diagrammatic form in Figure 4.13. There are two stages in the methodology: stage 1, data collection and analysis, and stage 2, design. Each phase of TUDD contains both stages, where the results of the first stage are usually fed to the second (although, on occasion, results from stage 2 of a particular phase are passed directly to stage 2 of the subsequent phase).

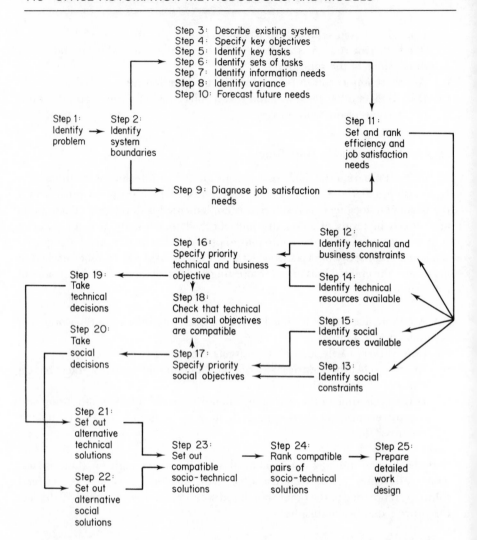

FIGURE 4.12 Schematic of the stages of the ETHICS methodology

Pre-Pilot Phase

In this phase, a variety of data is collected for the purpose of identifying an appropriate site for a pilot system. In general, the pilot should entail low-risk but high profile. There are three components to stage 1 of the pre-pilot phase: the organizational scan, the diagnosis, and the pilot systems analysis:

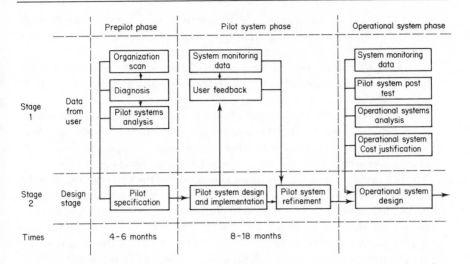

FIGURE 4.13 Tapscott's user-driven design. (Adapted from Tapscott, 1982)

(a) The organizational scan. The organizational scan provides the background information which is used to decide whether office automation is appropriate for the organization. Discussions about the opportunities for office systems, likely effects, time frame, costs, etc., are undertaken. Tapscott notes three types of information gathering associated with the scan. Firstly, discussions with senior management are held for the purpose of obtaining a broad picture of the organization — its objectives, environment, culture, history, plans, and so on. Secondly, structured interviews are conducted with a number of office personnel to discover various areas where office automation may help; for example, in communication, worker job satisfaction, administration, decision making, and information storage and management. Thirdly, secondary sources of information, such as corporate documentation — organizational charts, job descriptions, etc. — and external information, are obtained to provide a richer picture of the organization. The information generated from the organizational scan is used to design the measurement instrument (questionnaire) used in the diagnosis.

(b) The diagnosis. In this component of the pre-pilot phase, an attempt is made to determine the likely areas where office systems may improve the effectiveness of the organization. To obtain this information, a questionnaire is developed and administered to a number of key office personnel. Typical improvement areas, as identified in the organizational scan, are job satisfaction, communications, administrative support, decision making, and information management. The diagnosis tries to quantify the effects of particular improvements, e.g. what proportion of time could be saved by a new office system. In addition, the questionnaire can be used to provide a variety of attitudinal information about the office workers which may prove invaluable when planning the pilot systems design, carrying out pre-test/ post-test evaluation, and the like.

Tapscott states that the output of the organizational scan and diagnosis is to be contained in an 'opportunity report', which typically has four sections: (1) an introduction to office automation, (2) opportunities available, (3) possible pilot alternatives, and (4) recommendations.

(c) The pilot system analysis. The third component of the pre-pilot phase is the pilot systems analysis. An analysis of the possible office system structures is performed along with a discussion of pilot site prospects, costs, and ways to undertake pre- and post-test evaluations. The end product is the production of a pilot system feasibility report. This report contains details on: opportunities for improvements, pilot alternatives, pilot proposal, description of hardware and software requirements, expected costs and benefits, and the overall plan. See Figure 4.14 for an outline of a typical pilot system feasibility report.

The pilot system feasibility report
1. Summary of opportunities for improvement
2. Summary of pilot alternatives
3. Pilot proposal
   - Configuration
   - Functions of the system
   - Size of pilot group
4. Functional description of the pilot
5. Proposed hardware and software description
6. Description of approximate costs and anticipated benefits
   (Costs and anticipated benefits specified in the pilot system feasibility report are estimates only.)
7. What's next?
   (Outline of the specific steps leading to the pilot system specification report.)
   - Executive briefing and demonstration for some key subgroups within the proposed pilot group.
   - Final determination of the pilot group must be made at this time.
   - Prepare a draft report covering the system specification. This should include:
     organization design considerations, technical specifications, cost, acquisition plans, and possible patterns for future growth of the system.

FIGURE 4.14 Outline of the pilot system feasibility report. (Reproduced by permission of Plenum Press from Tapscott, 1982)

In the second stage of the pre-pilot phase, the pilot system feasibility report is taken and developed into the pilot system specification. Its purpose is to provide a detailed functional specification of the pilot system. The specifications are outlined in a report which is given to the technical staff who will be in charge of constructing the pilot system. The system specification report contains details on: system architecture (both technical and social), hardware and software components, organizational design, implementation plan, training, and evaluation. See Figure 4.15 for an outline of a pilot system specification report and Figure 4.16 for a representation of the pre-pilot phase of Tapscott's methodology.

1. System architecture
   (a) Technical
       ● System components
       ● System interfaces
       ● Overview of hardware/software
       ● Context—relationship to existing systems
   (b) Social
       ● Procedures
       ● Job design
       ● Environment
2. Hardware components
   ● Configuration/detailed equipment specification
   ● System site plan—physical environment for system resources
   ● Specification of any hardware construction
3. Software
   ● Appropriate packages
   ● Detailed specification of software to be written (applications, user inter-face, interconnections, etc.)
4. Organization design
   ● Workflow, etc., procedures
   ● System responsibilities
   ● Job design
   ● Physical environment (lighting, workstations, etc.)
5. Implementation plan
   ● Implementation steps
   ● Organization and responsibilities during implementation (user commit-tees, role of consultant, etc.)
   ● Management of change (unfreezing, change, consolidation, refreezing)
6. Training
   ● Training responsibilities (vendor, client, consultant, individual users)
   ● Outline of training program
   ● Evaluation plan for training program
7. Evaluation
   ● System monitoring, accounting plans
   ● Procedure for refining, extending pilot system
   ● Post-test evaluation plan

FIGURE 4.15 Outline of pilot system specification report. (Reproduced by permission of Plenum Press from Tapscott, 1982)

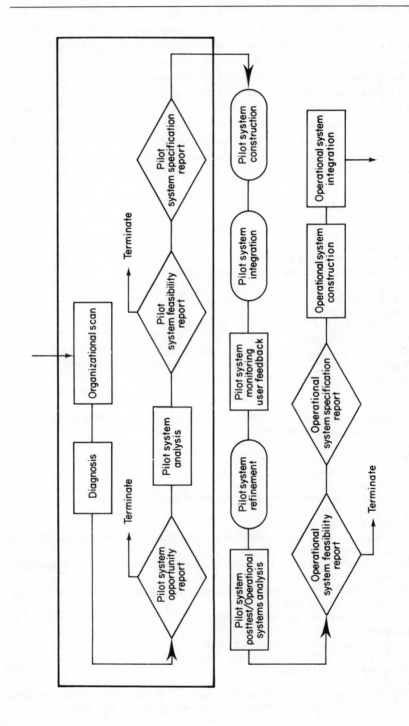

FIGURE 4.16 TUDD: pre-pilot phase (Reproduced by permission of Plenum Press from Tapscott, 1982)

Pilot System Phase

The pilot system phase report is taken in this phase, and converted into a live system. The recommended hardware and software are purchased or developed, the training is undertaken, the office is redesigned as specified, and the system is installed and integrated into the office environment. Once implemented, system monitoring begins. Information on system use, down time, data accessed, facilities used and not used, etc., is collected and retained for analysis. User feedback on the system is required and may be obtained through structured interviews, questionnaires, observation and informal conversations. The information obtained in systems monitoring and through user feedback is used to analyse ways to refine the pilot system. The refinement may take the form of simple system tuning, modification of system components, or addition/deletion of particular applications. See Figure 4.17 for a representation of the pilot system phase.

Operational System Phase

After the pilot system has performed its task, i.e. provided the knowledge and information needed to make informed organizational decisions about office automation, an operational system can be contemplated. Components of this phase include: (a) the analysis of pilot system monitoring and user feedback data, which provides valuable information on overall system utilization, those applications and facilities which were felt to be useful, the learning curves associated with the various aspects of the system, and so on; (b) a pilot system post-test, which involves the readministering of the questionnaire used in the pilot phase of the project to check for changes in people's perceptions about the office system after having experience with it; (c) an operational systems analysis, which provides the requirements of the operational system; and (d) the cost justification for the operational system. It is envisaged that much of the justification will come from the results of the pilot phase. Should the pilot show negative cost/benefit, it would be more difficult to justify an operational system. Figure 4.18 depicts the operational system phase of the methodology.

To operationalize the methodology, Tapscott notes four roles in the office systems development process: the architect, analyst, designer, and programmer. The role of the office systems architect is not dissimilar to that of a building architect. The architect is expected to understand the basic human, social, and functional needs of the people who will use the building. It is his or her job to oversee and guide the entire design and development process. In like fashion, the office systems architect would ensure the needs of the office staff were catered for as well as oversee the definition and implementation process. The office systems analyst acts as the change agent, responsible for eliciting user requirements, analysing and interpreting data obtained in pre- and post-tests,

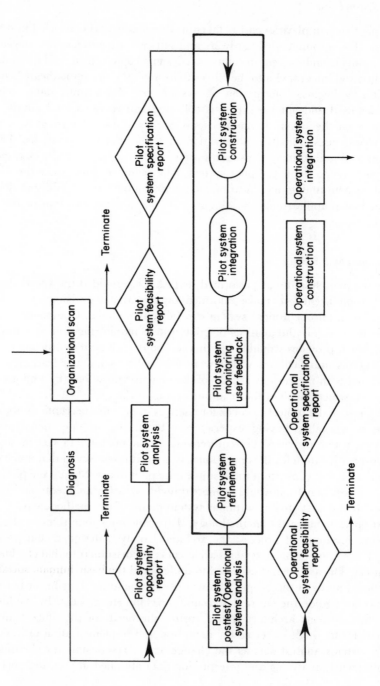

FIGURE 4.17 TUDD: pilot system phase (Reproduced by permission of Plenum Press from Tapscott, 1982)

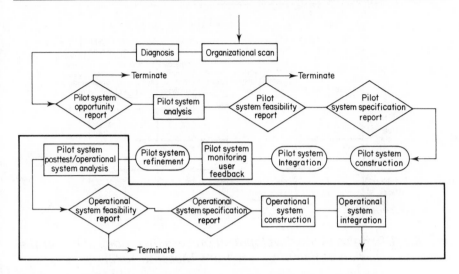

FIGURE 4.18 TUDD: operational system phase (Reproduced by permission of Plenum Press from Tapscott, 1982)

performing an evaluation of the pilot, and helping the designer produce the pilot and operational system feasibility and specification reports. The office systems designer acts as an intermediary between the analyst and programmer. With the analyst, he works on the functional description and specification of the pilot and operational system and, with the programmer, ensures the system is constructed according to its stated specification. The designer also interacts with the vendors, to ensure commitments are met. The office systems programmer performs the usual tasks of coding plus constructing the interface between the office system and the organization's data-processing systems (and corporate database). Figure 4.19 shows the various roles in the office systems development process.

5. Pava's Sociotechnical Design Methodology

Pava (1983) has developed an approach to office system analysis and design which is also based on sociotechnical system theory. In many ways it is similar to Mumford and Weir's (1979) ETHICS but it specifically extends the sociotechnical notion into the office domain. The office, from a sociotechnical perspective, needs to be conceptualized as an open system. Pava notes that although it is relatively straightforward to view factory work as an open system, office work is another matter. Factory work is characterized by routine transactions involving inputs of people, raw materials, and production information as well as transformation processes which yield finished products. Office

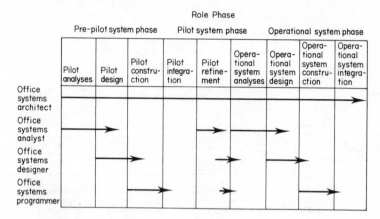

FIGURE 4.19 Roles in the development process (Reproduced by permission of Plenum Press from Tapscott, 1982)

work, on the other hand, is far less routine and defies comparison with factory work. Moreover, the roots of the difference are multifaceted and complex, involving social class distinctions, educational and attitudinal differences, and historical variations. Yet, for the sociotechnical systems viewpoint to be successful, it must be able to handle the non-routine aspects of office work. Pava (1983) states:

> ... predominantly routine office work is well suited for established socio-technical design. Primarily non-routine office work requires a new analytic method grounded in sociotechnical theory but able to accommodate non-sequential free-flowing work. In between these extremes are jobs with relatively equal proportions of routine and non-routine tasks. A method that incorporates elements of both the conventional and the emergent procedures of sociotechnical analysis is likely to be most valuable here (p. 49).

Pava lists three reasons why traditional sociotechnical analysis is not amenable to non-routine office work: (a) multiple, concurrent transformation processes, because non-routine office work requires the person to typically manage a number of transformation processes simultaneously; (b) non-linear transformation flow, which means that non-routine work embodies transformations completely beyond rational, fixed, or final solutions; and (c) operational separatism, which notes the educational, authority, expertise, and career aspiration differences between routine and non-routine office workers. These differences lead to a highly individualistic orientation which is not consistent with the work group notion so fundamental to traditional sociotechnical design.

To overcome these differences, Pava outlines a six-step method for analysing non-routine office work.

Step 1: Mapping the Target System

Although there is no one correct way to analyse non-routine work, a useful approach is to start with the 'tracing of sequences of deliberations'. Deliberations are defined as: 'reflective and communicative behaviours concerning a particular topic. They are patterns of exchange and communication in which people engage with themselves or others to reduce the equivocality of a problematic issue' (p. 58). Deliberations involve: (a) topics, which are the important problems of 'critical success factors' (Rockart, 1979) that face an organization; (b) forums of exchange, where individuals discuss the various 'topics'; and (c) participants — the individuals who take part in such 'forums'. These deliberations are thought to be effective units of analysis since they cut across the organization, and often reveal hidden, non-obvious, or counterintuitive patterns of office work. They are as central to the analysis of non-routine work as linear conversion is to routine work.

Step 2: Structuring for Maximum Self-Design

Since sociotechnical design is only effective when there is a great degree of user self-design, the second stage of Pava's approach involves 'entry, sanction and startup'. 'Entry' refers to the need to gain access to the office and the senior people whose support and approval is necessary. 'Sanction' entails the obtaining of formal approval from the organization's senior management. 'Startup' relates to the establishment of a design group made of key departmental members along with someone who can act in the capacity of a 'facilitator'. This person is often an outside consultant (see Chapter 5). In addition to the design group, Pava recommends the establishment of a steering group, made up of senior organizational managers to oversee the process, who can help in promoting and gaining approval for the final design proposal.

Step 3: Initial Scan

This can be thought of as the first stage in the actual analysis process, and is similar to that in traditional sociotechnical design. Its objective is for the design group to develop a shared and broad image of the office and the organization as a whole. (Checkland, 1981, might refer to this as a 'rich picture'.) In undertaking an initial scan, design group members need to: (a) reach a consensus on the global mission of the organization and the goals of their individual department or unit; (b) develop a statement regarding the organization's philosophy on managing its people; (c) identify the key internal and external factors which influence the organization and their unit; and (d) concern themselves with the important historical, social, and physical features of the organiztion and their unit.

Step 4: Technical Analysis

This iterative process involves the analysis of the technical subsystem. Here the tools and procedures used to convert inputs into outputs are examined. The focus should be on the management of deliberations (including their defects and opportunities for improvement) instead of the traditional variance matrix used for routine work. The design group should: (a) list the current deliberations, setting priorities on the deliberations and selecting the major ones which require the greatest amount of scrutiny; (b) note the various forums of exchanges for each major deliberation; (c) identify the participants and the information they deposit and withdraw for each major deliberation; (d) identify the inaccuracies, gaps, and other errors which arise in the forums in the discussion of deliberations; (e) analyse the manifest constituent elements (activities) of office work (e.g. typing, reading, telephoning, travelling, and the like); and (f) compare and contrast the identified activities and deliberations in a matrix format to allow for a systematic analysis and diagnosis, useful for the next stages.

Step 5: Social Analysis

This stage involves the analysis of the social subsystem which uses the technical subsystem to convert inputs into outputs. Its main task is to identify divergent values, interdependent parties, role networks, and discretionary coalitions. Once identified, the goal is to create mutual understanding and shared meanings rather than eliminate differences. This would allow intelligent trade-offs to be made on an ongoing basis. Pava notes four requirements of social analysis: (a) the development of a role network which maps out the parties who participate in the various deliberations; (b) the specification of values which the parties typically adopt; (c) the identification of divergent values between parties which continuously obstruct deliberations; and (d) the recognition of interdependent parties who forge 'discretionary coalitions' for their long-term interest and survival. Pava contends that it is these discretionary conditions which are the norm in non-routine office work, just as work groups are the social norm for routine work.

Step 6: Work System Design

This stage involves the identification of the best fit between the technical and social subsystems. Finding the best match is not always easy but is critical for the development of successful office systems. The objective, according to Pava, is to create a variety-increasing work system which embraces the notion of 'redundant functions' (i.e. where more than one person possesses any one skill and each person possesses more than one skill). Pava outlines a five-step process for matching the technical with the social subsystem: (a) identify and acknowledge the major deliberations and their associated discretionary coalitions; (b) for each deliberation specify the responsibilities of each discretionary coalition; (c) develop office worker policies which support effective deliberations between discretionary coalitions; (d) list organizational structural changes which might enhance coordination and responsibility aspects to facilitate major deliberations; and (e) propose technical improvements, including new procedures and new hardware.

To these five steps, Pava adds a sixth: approval and enactment. This involves getting the proposed sociotechnical design approved by senior management and then implemented. The design must also be accepted by the rest of the organization.

Pava advocates a similar process when dealing with routine office work. The major differences occur in step 4 with its focus on variance analysis instead of deliberations, and step 5 which analyses psychological job criteria in place of discretionary coalitions. Figure 4.20 outlines both routine and non-routine work aspects of Pava's sociotechnical design methodology.

6. Office Analysis and Diagnosis Methodology (OADM)

OADM is a data-gathering tool which assists the analyst on decisions about the introduction of OA technology into an office (Sutherland, 1983). It is actually a refinement and extension of OAM (Sirbu *et al.*, 1982). As well as describing the current operations in the office, an OADM study collects a great deal of quantitative data (necessary for cost justification) and enumerates the problems and opportunities within the office.

The Office Model

OADM and OAM use the same model, a function/procedure model of the office. The model demonstrates that the office has structure and it attempts to describe the office using high-level constructs. The model is descriptive in nature and has three primitives: objects, procedures, and functions.

The model focuses on the *object* which is an abstract concept related to the overall functioning of the office. The object is usually associated with a series of activities.

A *procedure* describes the operation of the office in terms of what is done and when. It has a local object related to it and expresses the progress of this object through successive stages called *states*. A state represents the point at which no further activity can occur until an *event* takes place. An event is something that

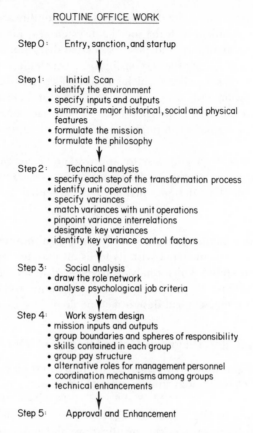

ROUTINE OFFICE WORK

Step 0: Entry, sanction, and startup

Step 1: Initial Scan
• identify the environment
• specify inputs and outputs
• summarize major historical, social and physical features
• formulate the mission
• formulate the philosophy

Step 2: Technical analysis
• specify each step of the transformation process
• identify unit operations
• specify variances
• match variances with unit operations
• pinpoint variance interrelations
• designate key variances
• identify key variance control factors

Step 3: Social analysis
• draw the role network
• analyse psychological job criteria

Step 4: Work system design
• mission inputs and outputs
• group boundaries and spheres of responsibility
• skills contained in each group
• group pay structure
• alternative roles for management personnel
• coordination mechanisms among groups
• technical enhancements

Step 5: Approval and Enhancement

FIGURE 4.20 Pava's sociotechnical design methodology

happens causing some work (called a step) to move the object to the next state.

In OAM AND OADM a *function* has three parts: (a) an 'initialization phase' which creates a particular instance of an object, (b) a 'management phase' concerned with the control of objects during their life-cycle, and (c) a 'termination phase' in which a particular instance of an object is disposed of. A function provides the framework for a specific set of office procedures and indicates when the procedure has been performed. Business operations of several offices can be linked together in a function. The principal difference between a function and a procedure is that a function manages objects by describing the complete life-cycle of the object, whereas a procedure changes the state of the object by describing the steps necessary to bring about the change.

The cause (or reason) for an event not occurring is called an *exception*. It prevents the normal performance of the procedure and requires some response.

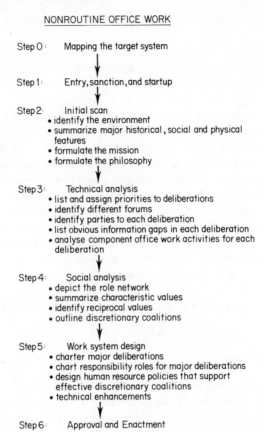

NONROUTINE OFFICE WORK

Step 0 :   Mapping the target system

Step 1 :   Entry, sanction, and startup

Step 2 :   Initial scan
• identify the environment
• summarize major historical, social and physical features
• formulate the mission
• formulate the philosophy

Step 3 :   Technical analysis
• list and assign priorities to deliberations
• identify different forums
• identify parties to each deliberation
• list obvious information gaps in each deliberation
• analyse component office work activities for each deliberation

Step 4 :   Social analysis
• depict the role network
• summarize characteristic values
• identify reciprocal values
• outline discretionary coalitions

Step 5 :   Work system design
• charter major deliberations
• chart responsibility roles for major deliberations
• design human resource policies that support effective discretionary coalitions
• technical enhancements

Step 6 :   Approval and Enactment

FIGURE 4.20 (continued)

This is not the same as a *variation*, which is simply a modification of the procedure.

Anything in the office which office staff or the analyst feels is not satisfactory is termed a *symptom*. A *cause* is the reason why a symptom occurs. An aspect of the office which everyone feels is functioning at an optimum level (given the current state of the office), but might be improved by new possibilities, is called an *opportunity*.

A Summary of the Methodology

Before embarking on an OADM study the following areas must be examined:

(a) *The reasons for undertaking the study.* Any preconceived initial expectations should be known at the outset as the analyst may place emphasis on other areas causing the study to fall short of the expectations of those who have commissioned it.

(b) *The constituencies of the office* — specifically the office personnel, the office manager, and all senior management. Since issues to be discussed vary greatly between offices, a variety of approaches can be used by the analyst in contacts with these people (see Sutherland, 1983.)

(c) *Who should actually do the study.* Such a study can be performed by a single person or a team; they can be from within the office or outsiders. Whoever performs the study would greatly benefit by having the following skills: organizational sensitivity, system perspective, analytic ability, good communication skills, an understanding of office work, a sensitivity to people, as well as persistence blended with tact.

(d) *The suggested unit of study.* Usually this is a function. Since an office may carry out several functions, the function's definition may be dependent upon the scope of the study and overall automation effort. Theoretically, an entire function (regardless of what offices it encompasses) should be studied. Practically, this is usually beyond the scope of the study.

Once the above have been discussed and agreed upon, the OADM study may proceed.

Steps in the OADM Study

STEP 1. Preparation and distribution of background questionnaires
The initial stage of an OADM study involves the development of a questionnaire to elicit a broad understanding of the office and the organization of which it is a part. The questionnaire is distributed to a wide variety of people in an attempt to obtain a sound background to the study.

STEP 2. Reviewing questionnaire results and any background information about the office that is available
The completed questionnaires are analysed with the specific intention of spotting anomalies. Additionally, other background information — corporate records, organizational charts, etc. — is scrutinized to supplement the knowledge obtained through the questionnaires.

STEP 3. Interview with the office manager.
During the interview with the office manager the following issues need to be discussed:

(a) *The establishment of ground rules for the study.* This provides the manager and analyst with a chance to clarify details of the study's operation and expectations. It also gives the manager insight into his role, the time required of him and his staff, and duration of the study.

(b) *The functions and resources of the office.* The analyst must check the accuracy of information regarding this and any hypotheses that may have been made. The following areas need specific attention:

   (i) The basic mission of the office. The mission often states the official purpose for improvement; it is therefore necessary to work with this in mind if the study is to be truly beneficial.

   (ii) The functions of the office. The manager can provide an overview for the analyst to use as a starting point with detailed information being obtained during staff interviews.

   (iii) The major resources of the office. The office manager can once again provide some, though generally not all, information from which to begin the study

   (iv) The staffing levels for each function. These numbers can provide some insight into the present staffing level a function is afforded. No direct conclusions should be made from this, but hypotheses can be developed for further analysis.

(c) *Verifying the organizational context.* Much of this information will have been given in the background questionnaire, but the analyst needs to verify the accuracy. Additional information may be needed from the manager. This may include:

   (i) The system of reporting relationships to senior management.

   (ii) The internal office organization.

   (iii) The staffing and support levels for job categories (this is vital information for identifying areas of improvement and cost–benefit analysis).

   (iv) The key interfaces to other offices.

(d) *Identifying who to interview.* Based on the background interviews, the analyst will have decided what kinds of people he needs to interview; the manager may suggest who should be interviewed within groups. Each analysis process necessitates interviewing two or three people from each job type. Larger offices may have several layers of management and the analyst will need to interview all managers. Additionally, people from outside the office may have to be interviewed. These may be people who interact closely with the office under study or who use products of that office, as well as anyone the office manager reports to. The manager should be asked to suggest who to interview in the cases outside of the office. This reveals any communication which may involve only the manager. Outside interviews should never take place until the first round of interviews with the office staff have been completed. These may reveal any low-level communication and/or contacts between the office staff.

(e) *Identifying success factors.* Critical success factors (Rockart, 1979) are somewhat difficult to identify; nevertheless, OADM applies them to individual offices.

(f) *The manager's job.* Much of the manager's job is spontaneous (unexpected tasks) and therefore difficult to categorize. The function/procedure model is not particularly useful here as it fails to describe managerial work. Nevertheless, the analyst must make an effort to understand and summarize the manager's job within the office function.

STEP 4. Interview the staff

(a) *Interview preparation.* The analyst should be conversant with the problem, symptoms, and causes, as well as other information about the office before the interviewing begins.

(b) *Interview process.* All interviews should be restricted to the interviewer and interviewee, as other people can interfere with the flow or prevent the interviewee from speaking openly. The interviewer should clearly state the goals of the study, emphasizing that it is not a performance evaluation but a study of the whole office. The interview must be, and be understood by the interviewee to be, a process of two-way communication.

The first step of the interview consists of the interviewee and analyst becoming acquainted, as well as the analyst informing the interviewee of the study's goals, progress, etc. The next step consists of two stages. In the first the analyst tries to elicit and comprehend the interviewee's work and perspective on current operations of the office. The second stage involves obtaining information about what the interviewee feels should or can be changed. Throughout the interview the analyst should keep the office model in mind and be certain that all data necessary is being gathered.

(c) *Observation.* This is frequently used as a tool to confirm the accuracy of the interviewee's perceptions. The analyst's observations of how staff utilize time, symptoms of problems, the physical character of the office, as well as social organization, all ensure that no activity of the office in the study is omitted.

STEP 5. Interviews with outsiders

Interviewing outsiders attempts to achieve two purposes: to determine the use and usefulness of the products the office under study produces and to view symptoms and/or opportunities from a different perspective.

STEP 6. Analysis of information

The analysis process is made up of two stages and should begin as soon as possible after the first interview:

(a) *Stage 1.* This involves fitting the data into the function/procedure model of the office. This helps to illustrate what information is missing so can be obtained in the second round of interviews. It also points up exceptions to procedures or procedure steps.

(b) *Stage 2.* At this point the analyst begins to concentrate on less structured material, such as: the causes of office problem symptoms, measures of various types of procedures, and the intentions behind the procedures. The analyst particularly focuses on what problems are encountered. Once the symptoms are known the problem can be identified. The OADM model suggests that since several symptoms can be the result of a single problem, there will be fewer problems than symptoms.

Identifying all problems at this stage of the study is not possible but the second round of interviews should help uncover them. Once again, at this stage the definition of problems is largely dependent on the analyst and office staff, making it a normative process as opposed to a purely descriptive one.

STEP 7. Production of draft descriptions
Draft descriptions should be recorded immediately after the first few interviews to minimize the loss of information. The descriptions are made up of two parts within a standardized format: a procedure description of how the office is currently functioning and a description of the problems in the office:

(a) *The procedure description.* This is broken down into a number of chapters:
   (i) The first chapter describes the mission of the office, the organizational context of the office, any information concerning the overall physical environment that is special or noteworthy, and a brief overview of the major office functions. Much of this information will have come from the interview with the manager, and is necessary in order to understand the function and procedure descriptions that follow.
   (ii) Chapter 2 is optional; if included it should discuss any matters of the office environment that may be crucial to understanding how the office works.
   (iii) Then follows several chapters discussing office functions. Each procedure has its own section describing what is done, why it is done, and statistics concerning the procedure (i.e. how many, how much, and how long).
   (iv) The final chapter will contain information concerning exception handling techniques as they are applied to the entire office. This information is obtained in the final interview with the manager.
   (v) Generally speaking, there will be several appendices in the procedure description. The number included depends on the individual study and its purpose. These appendices would include such details as lists of databases, logs and lists used in the office, copies of standard forms used in the office, a table of titles and people, quantitative questionnaire results, sample questionnaires, and the like.

(b) *Problem description.* Though the descriptions of problems encountered in the office may be similar in structure to the current operations, they should be handled separately. Along with the problem description, answers to specific questions, e.g. what if the function or procedure was eliminated (or improved), should be added where appropriate.

Upon completion of the two types of descriptions, they should be passed back to the interviewees for review before the second round of interviews.

STEP 8. Preparation and administration of quantitative questionnaire
Information obtained in the quantitative questionnaire will be used later to help justify costs of any changes suggested. Along with the questionnaire there is a log to be kept.

The *questionnaire* itself is based on self-reporting and collects data about office activities including: mail handling, file storage, typing, etc. Questionnaires may be prepared in many ways (cf. Sutherland, 1983). The questionnaires are to be completed by the entire staff, including the manager.

The *log* is much more geared towards office statistics; e.g. the collection of data about the number of objects handled for each step of a procedure, within a set time frame. The analyst must decide the type of information to be collected in the logs. The logs should be kept between the interview rounds so any noted situation otherwise unforeseen can be examined during the second interview.

The collected results of the questionnaires and logs should be incorporated into the descriptions of current operations by the analyst.

STEP 9. Iterate the interview process
The format of the second interview is very much like the first, with the addition of the draft description. The analyst should confirm that the draft description is accurate and ask the interviewee for general comments, before discussing any specific comments. The analyst should then ask questions regarding any information that has been left out from the procedures. These are usually about the handling of exceptions in the procedure and causes of the symptoms.

STEP 10. Final interview with the manager
Upon completion of the draft documents, the analyst should send copies to the office manager and make an appointment for another interview. The aim of the interview with the office manager is manifold:

(a) To present the results of the study of current operations.
(b) To ask the manager about the general exception handling in the office.
(c) To go through the problem/opportunities list with the manager for his agreement as well as to find out if any measures have recently been taken to remedy some of the noted problems.

(d) To check that the described intentions behind the procedures are correct.
(e) To discuss the nature of the rough proposal; specifically, which problems they should start to address. The analyst may suggest some technological solutions to these problems.

STEP 11. Presenting options and preparing plans
The options for improvement are presented to the office staff and feedback is obtained. The analyst then prepares a plan for future action and alternatives.

The preparation and descriptions of plans is not, however, the end of the automation process. Next comes the system design, cost justification, system selection, the development of a particular implementation strategy, user training, the actual changeover to the new, and finally the development of procedures for modifying the system (as necessary).

In sum, OADM has three purposes: (1) it establishes a good working relationship with the office manager and staff through the provision of guidance in techniques for the creation of a positive atmosphere; (2) it elicits a complete description of the current operations in the office; and (3) it provides for the collection of information necessary for cost–benefit analysis and design stages of the automation process. Sutherland (1983) notes that OADM would be very useful for the description of small semi-structured offices, but may be less beneficial for overviews of large organizations.

7. Additional Office Automation Methodologies

There have been other 'methodologies' developed specifically with office automation in mind, but they have not been extensively written up in the literature or are not as fully developed as the ones previously covered. Three prime examples of such methodologies are MOBILE-Burotique developed as part of Project KAYAK at the French Research Institute INRIA, OFFIS developed at the University of Arizona, and Information Manufacturing developed at Xerox.

MOBILE-Burotique

MOBILE-Burotique has been defined as a 'flexible, meta-methodology serving several purposes and used by different people who perceive a modular application of Burotique (office automation)' (Dumas, du Roure, and Zanetti, 1982). It was the product of several field studies which attempted to establish a basis for a unified methodology that would help in the specification, introduction, and evaluation of office automation. Fundamental to the development of the methodology was the need to: (a) take into account both human and organizational factors and (b) use several methods and instruments in carrying out organizational analysis. The result was a methodology which could be used by three different groups of people: clients, who need precise and detailed information about their individual offices; manufacturers, who require valid statistical information on a given market; and researchers, who wish to obtain a better understanding of offices in general.

The MOBILE-Burotique methodology is intended to be a comprehensive one, supporting the office analyst in each stage of office systems development. This support is provided in a six-phase framework including not only office analysis, but also office system specification, selection, and implementation. The phases are: (a) intelligence — the identification of the objectives and context of the investigation as well as the office objects to be investigated; (b) observation — a description of all parts of the office under study and profiles of the activities undertaken; (c) conception — the development of a number of alternative office scenarios; (d) choice — the choice of one of the scenarios; (e) implementation — the implementation of either a pilot or final system; and (f) evaluation — the evaluation of the implemented office system (MOBILE Guide, 1982). Moreover, for each phase MOBILE provides an approach for determining: goals, outcomes, procedures to be followed, prerequisites, and instruments for data collection and analysis. The office analyst can select the instruments and procedures which are appropriate for investigating a particular office.

MOBILE-Burotique attempts to be a unified methodology, instead of a single method of study, and is made up of a collection of interchangeable instruments for studying offices, which can be used to produce several coherent methods geared for a particular study, taking into account its needs and constraints. The choice of the appropriate instruments to use in a particular study is guided by several instrument constraints: cost, value of obtaining results, time, and acceptability to the organization. The most suitable instruments are determined via a 'cost–benefit analysis'.

According to Dumas, du Roure, and Zanetti (1982), there are eight categories of office system instruments which might be appropriate for use in MOBILE:

(a) Observation of existing documentation
(b) Preliminary observation of the organization, to provide the researcher with some insight about existing problems and directions to follow
(c) Questionnaires with different degrees of structures
(d) Captors, which may be automatic (part of the technology) or manual (logged by the user)
(e) Activity diaries completed by the users
(f) Third-party observation, which can be used in combination with an activity diary to get different data from an objective viewpoint

(g) Interviews, with different degrees of structure (aimed mainly at getting details difficult to obtain with other instruments)
(h) Role-playing exercises and simulation techniques.

The specific instruments used in MOBILE-Burotique, according to Conrath *et al.* (1982), are: (a) questionnaires for obtaining user perceptions on usage patterns and needs; (b) task records for providing details on the tasks performed, elapsed time, relative importance, and such like: (c) communications diaries for eliciting information on communications activities; and (d) detailed task analysis (Thackenkary and Conrath, 1982) for facilitating the analysis of specific task performance. Marcus, Roubier, and Zanetti (1982) note that detailed task analysis is valuable in that it yields the following information, useful for office system development: (a) an input/output schema showing details of inputs to and outputs from the office; (b) a task procedure schema representing the procedures followed in turning inputs into outputs; and (c) tables showing volumes and frequencies of the various communication-based activities in the office. It must be noted, however, that the task procedure schema does not necessarily generate an understanding of what is being done in the transformation of inputs into outputs, only that some procedures are being followed. Why they are being followed or how they might be improved is not always apparent. Moreover, although in the intelligence phase of the methodology the objectives of the office are identified, the analysis instruments do not attempt to relate these objectives to the discovered procedures.

OFFIS

OFFIS is, fundamentally, an office system design aid rather than a 'methodology', but will briefly be covered here because it has been referred to by some commentators (Bracchi and Pernici, 1984) as an office automation methodology. It is a computer-based system supporting interactive (and iterative) office analysis and design, primarily at the physical design level (Konsynski, Bracker, and Bracker, 1982). The system is based on the 'OFFIS model' which is specified by office system designers using the non-procedural 'OFFIS language'. The OFFIS approach could be thought of as a flexible method for analysing office system features and constraints.

The office system design process using OFFIS proceeds in the following manner. The system designer (typically thought to be an office manager) attempts to determine system requirements and constraints. These are fed into the system through the OFFIS language: a simple syntax, non-procedural language. They lead to an incremental development of the OFFIS model: a conception of the office specified in terms of objects, attributes, and relationships. Specifications fed into the OFFIS system are checked for consistency;

those which are incorrectly specified are returned with an error diagnostic. The OFFIS statements are also stored in the OFFIS database. The database can be analysed, through the OFFIS analyser, to produce analysis reports which provide the designer with a snapshot of the current version of the proposed system design. Through a set of specified rules, the analysis reports can pinpoint any inconsistencies or incompleteness in the design. The design could then be modified by manipulating old and creating new OFFIS statements. The new design can also be analysed, thus giving OFFIS its iterative feature. Design proceeds through iterative stages, moving closer to the optimal each time.

The OFFIS model, as was noted earlier, is based on three well-known and used primitives: objects, attributes, and relations. (Most database models use the same primitives, although instead of the term 'object', 'entity' is used.) An 'object' is a static element describing agents or data (i.e. an entity). 'Attributes' relate to the properties of objects. 'Relations' depict interconnections and associations among objects. They can also depict temporal arrangements, conditions, and organizational reporting relationships.

The OFFIS language provides the designer with a simple and convenient means of specifying office system requirements. OFFIS language statements apply to OFFIS object categories called 'sections'. Each section begins with a section header, consisting of the keyword 'section-type' and one or more user supplied names for the section. All statements following the section header provide a description for the section. A sample OFFIS language specification, taken from Konsynski, Bracker, and Bracker (1982), is provided in Figure 4.21.

Information Manufacturing

An extreme view of an office information system is considering it as an 'information manufacturer'. Aklilu (1981) developed his methodology on this view. Information, as a tangible product of the office, has to be designed and produced with a predetermined specification, quality, and schedule — just like a product produced in a manufacturing organization.

Aklilu's information manufacturing view is based on three stages: data creation, data conversion, and information use. Figure 4.22 depicts the stages diagrammatically.

Stage I. Data creators

Stage I of Aklilu's model is made up of operations and line functions. In manufacturing, raw data elements, such as direct labour hours, units produced, material used, etc., are recorded by various line organizations within the plant. The major paper work in Stage 1, he believes, is documentation and bookkeeping.

SCENARIO

'The office secretary schedules a meeting based on the president's and vice-president's calendars. Notices are placed in each employee's mail box notifying them of the quarterly report meeting. A copy of the notification is filed. The secretary must also write and send meeting notices to the company accountants, who are external to the organization. The quarterly report meeting is a regularly held event which happens four times yearly; it lasts about 2 hours each time it is held.'

        JOB-TITLE OFFICE-SECRETARY
          CREATES QUARTERLY-MEETING-NOTICES
          SCHEDULES QUARTERLY-MEETING
            USING P-CALENDAR, VP-CALENDAR

        MEETING QUARTERLY-MEETING
          HAPPENS 4 TIMES YEARLY;
          ATTENDED BY PRESIDENT, V-PRESIDENT
            ACCOUNTANTS;
          DURATION 2 HOURS;

        DATAFILE QUARTERLY-MEETING-NOTICE
          UPDATED BY OFFICE SECRETARY
            USING QUARTERLY-MEETING-NOTICE;

        LETTER QUARTERLY-MEETING-NOTICE
          HAPPENS 4 TIMES YEARLY
          SENT TO ACCOUNTANTS
          ROUTED TO P-MAILBOX, VP-MAILBOX
            EMPLOYEE-MAILBOX

        EXTERNAL-NAME ACCOUNTANTS

FIGURE 4.21 OFFIS language specification (Konsynski, Bracker and Bracker, 1982)

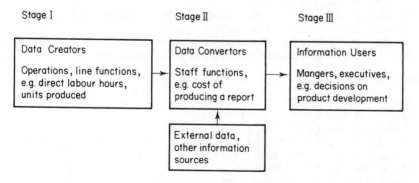

FIGURE 4.22 Aklilu's information manufacturing view

Stage II. Data convertors
The major responsibility of Stage II is the conversion of raw data into information that can be used as an input to Stage III for decision-making purposes. Aklilu feels that knowledge workers are the main actors at this stage.

Stage III. Information users
The activities of the knowledge worker in Stage II is driven by the requirements of Stage III — the decision-making body. All the energy and effort of Stage II should be directed towards the need specification set by management. Aklilu contends that the process of data creation, data conversion, and information usage (decision making) clearly indicates that the target population for the office automation market is the knowledge worker in Stages I and II.

Based on the above view, Aklilu proposes a methodology in skeletal form consisting of three phases; it is depicted in Figure 4.23. The fifteen steps in the methodology are fairly general and it is therefore difficult to see how Aklilu's approach will work in practice. Its skeletal nature and the lack of any examples of its use makes it a more dubious methodology. It has been briefly discussed here because of its novel approach to office automation.

PHASE I: Macrofunctional analysis

1. Understand overall character and objectives of the office and organization
2. Determine primary operations by major functional and reporting areas
3. Perform 'top-down' analysis
   — Develop input/output profile
   — Understand information management process
   — Determine data base for Phase II

PHASE II: Microactivity analysis

1. Obtain management feedback
2. Develop generic list of activities that describe current operations
3. Develop technology indicator log
4. Conduct technology indicator log time tracking
5. Analyse results and determine activities to be transferred

PHASE III: Concept formulation and implementation

1. Obtain management feedback
2. Develop overall automation concept
3. Technology evaluation and selection
4. Develop before and after scenarios for each activity to be automated
5. Prepare final recommendation package
6. Obtain management agreement
7. Recommend implementation plan

FIGURE 4.23 Aklilu's information manufacturing methodology

ANALYSIS OF OFFICE AUTOMATION MODELS AND METHODOLOGIES

It can be seen that there exists a number of alternative office automation models and methodologies. Yet the OA literature has been remiss in not adequately defining what it means by 'model' and 'methodology' nor specifying the linkage between the two. The OFFIS system, for example, uses an office model (based on objects, attributes, and relations) to develop an office system design but never explicitly states the relationship between model and methodology; nor, for that matter, do the authors refer to OFFIS explicitly as a methodology. Tapscott (1982) describes an approach (methodology) for developing office systems as well as an office model, but the connection between the two is never articulated. Others discuss approaches for building office models and modelling formalisms which are to be used to develop automated office systems. But, again, the connection with methodology is tenuous. Others, such as Pava (1983), discuss various methodologies for developing office systems but make no mention of a model.

1. Comparison of Model/Methodology

Although the OA community has not bothered to articulate the relationship between model and methodology, it is felt that if one exists, it should be made explicit. There are four possible relationships between the two:

(a) No relationship between model and methodology. One possibility is that there is no specific association between the two — that the development of a model/methodology is independent from the other. If Welke's (1981) comprehensive framework for systems development is embraced, as was advocated earlier in the chapter, then this view seems unlikely. Since a model is the result of imposing a particular frame of reference on perceived reality it must be intimately related to the approach one takes in the analysis and design of a system. It is difficult to imagine how model development and methodology use could proceed independently of one another.

(b) Methodology use generates a model. A second alternative implies that there is an association between the two in that a model is the result (perhaps by-product) of methodology use. One chooses an appropriate methodology and a model follows. This would seem to be the position adopted in, for example, OFFIS. The use of the OFFIS system leads to the generation of an office model. The difficulty with this view, however, lies in the subservient nature of model to methodology. A model, which is a frame of reference applied to an object system, is no longer freely chosen but rather imposed on the designer (user) by the methodology. The concern is: what happens if the methodology's frame of reference is inconsistent with the particular designer's? Should one be forced into a view which is different from one's own? It could, of course, be argued that the designer may not have any specific view, or that his view is inferior to the one adopted by the methodology. However, any such argument would be problematic and should be avoided if possible. The best way to avoid the argument is for the model not to be seen as an output of a methodology.

(c) Model development dictates the methodology to be used. A third alternative is to see a connection between the two but in the opposite way of point (b) above. In this view, the choice of an office model or modelling approach automatically implies the methodology to use. This appears to be the case in, for example, Ellis' (1979) information control nets model and Zisman's (1977) SCOOP. The methodology used to develop an office system is directly related to the adopted model; there is no real choice of a methodology independent of the model. This view may be more in line with Welke's framework in that the designer's (user's) frame of reference is given primacy. The designer just chooses an office modelling approach which mirrors his conception, and the methodology is automatically chosen. Although this view is more in line with the advocated conception of model and methodology, it is perhaps too extreme. Methodology use should be consistent with model choice but it need not necessarily be automatic. It is possible that a variety of methodologies could be appropriate with a particular model, which leads to the fourth alternative.

(d) Choose a methodology which is consistent with a model. This follows on from the discussion in the previous point where it seems sensible to advocate the choice of a methodology which reflects a designer's frame of reference and, hence, choice of model. Since there may be a number of methodologies consistent with a particular model, it would appear not only unnecessary but also inappropriate to suggest only a particular one be used. It should be left up to the designer to choose a methodology which feels comfortable and is consistent with his modelling approach.

2. The Relationship Between Model/Methodology and Office View

As was mentioned in the previous chapter, there is a direct link between office views and office models/methodologies. The connection is a simple and straightforward one. An office view refers to the particular way an individual conceives of an office and is related to his world view or outlook (Weltanschauung). Since a model is the output of a particular schema (based on an individual's frame of reference) applied to some perceived reality, it must be directly related to his office view. If it is assumed that the individual chooses an office model which reflects his frame of reference, then the link is clear. Further, the choice of a methodology consistent with an office model (as advocated in point (d) above) completes the inextricable link between office view, model, and methodology.

The most common office view, office activities, is reflected in many office models/methodologies: OFFIS, SCOOP, ICN, OPAS, OFS, OBE, and SOS. The office semantics view is adopted in the OMEGA office modelling approach. The office functions view is adopted by OAM, MOBILE, and OADM. Interpretivist office views, such as work roles, decision taking, transactional and language action, are less developed and generally not that well known. It is therefore not very surprising that there are fewer models/methodologies. Pava's sociotechnical design, Checkland's soft system methodology, Mumford's ETHICS are examples of methodologies which reflect interpretivist thinking. They can be seen as reflecting the general interpretivist's view rather than a particular office view, and are thus appropriate for a broader and more social or behavioural office conception.

3. Methodology Appraisal

Given the substantial number of models/methodologies available for office systems development, an appraisal of their features would help potential adopters choose the most appropriate one for their particular application. Unfortunately, model/methodology appraisal is extremely problematic. Recent attempts at information system methodology evaluation (Maddison et al., 1983; Olle, Sol, and Verrijn-Stuart, 1982) have proved particularly contentious. Evaluation turns out to be highly subjective, largely because of the evaluation criteria chosen and the way they are applied. For example, must a methodology be appropriate for all types of systems or just a few, should anyone be able to use it or must it be a trained specialist, is there a choice of steps to be performed or are they set, and so on? (See Olle, 1983, for a list of similar criteria which might be applied to a methodology.) Then there are criteria such as efficiency, effectiveness, quality of the design produced, and the like, all of which are highly subjective. Moreover, there is the problem of whether to evaluate a methodology on its own independent of its output (the designed system), or to judge it by evaluating what it produces. This is clearly a non-trivial matter which poses difficult choices. Attempting to appraise a methodology on its own presents an air of artificiality about it, since its function is the production of a system (or at least its specification). On the other hand, evaluating the resulting system is also problematic for two reasons: (a) there are few real objective measures of system quality, most are subjective; and (b) it is impossible to say that the resulting system is the product of the methodology solely. There are a host of factors (independent of a methodology) which contribute to system development, e.g. the idiosyncratic characteristics of the designer(s). (See

Hirschheim, 1984, for a further treatment of the issue of methodology evaluation.)

Although methodology appraisal is problematic, the process of evaluation itself yields insight into the important characteristics of the methodology. It is for this reason that an office automation methodology appraisal is attempted. The appraisal is of a more conceptual type, involving an analysis of the methodology itself rather than the office system it produces. Since office automation methodologies are relatively new, there is little available experience with them, or with their resulting systems.

4. Methodology Appraisal Framework

The criteria used in the appraisal are based on Wasserman and Freeman's (1983) evaluation framework, modified and extended for office automation. The framework used here involves four classes of evaluation criteria: (a) technical, which are features associated with the more technical aspects of a methodology; (b) usage, involving those features related to a methodology's usability; (c) economic, involving those features related to a methodology's ability to generate economic data for system evaluation: and (d) behavioural, associated with a methodology's ability to adequately deal with the social aspects of systems design.

(a) *Technical criteria*

There are a number of characteristics of a methodology which pertain to its ability to successfully deal with the more physical aspects of systems analysis and design. They can be divided into nine categories:

(1) Function hierarchy — the ability to take a high-level function, decompose it into several lower level functions which can be specified in greater detail.
(2) Data hierarchy — the ability to do the same decomposition with data.
(3) Interfaces — the ability to specify distinct boundaries betwen systems and subsystems, and to specify their interconnections.
(4) Control flow — the ability to specify and represent the sequence in which functions are to take place.
(5) Data flow — the ability to specify and represent the flow of data between functions.
(6) Data abstraction — the ability to abstract into a higher level the data used in the system.
(7) Procedural abstraction — the ability to specify a function independent of the means by which it is performed.

(8) Parallelism — the ability to specify the coexistence of two or more functions carried out at the same time.
(9) Comprehensiveness — the extent to which the vast array of functions, procedures, and office characteristics can be represented.

(b) *Usage criteria*

The usage characteristics of a methodology pertain to its ability to be easily and successfully used to develop office systems. There are twenty categories:

(1) Understandability — the ease with which a specialist can understand how to use the methodology.
(2) Comprehensibility — the ease with which the output of the design process can be comprehended.
(3) Transferability — the ease with which the methodology can be taught to non-specialists.
(4) Reusability — the ease with which the outputs of the methodology can be reused either for other systems or for modifications in the longer term.
(5) Computer support — the existence of computer support for the use of the methodology.
(6) Life-cycle support — the extent to which the methodology covers the various stages of the system's life-cycle.
(7) Project range — the ability to handle a variety of projects.
(8) Cohesiveness — the extent to which the tools and techniques of the methodology are interrelated.
(9) Ease of phase transition— the ease of moving from one stage to another of the methodology.
(10) Extent of usage — the extent to which the methodology has been applied in real world settings.
(11) Observability — the extent to which the key stages or decision points are highlighted and readily observable.
(12) Controllability — the degree to which the methodology's user(s) can control the choice of tools and techniques rather than having to follow some preordained sequence.
(13) Relevance — the general ability of the methodology to handle problems in the office domain.
(14) Consistency — the extent to which the results of the methodology's application are similar when applied to similar situations.
(15) Complexity — the degree of complexity associated not only with the methodology itself but also its documentatiion.
(16) Modifiability — the ease with which the results of prior stages of the methodology can be modified in light of the results of later stages.

(17) Completeness — the capability of the methodology to yield results which are both correct and complete and to be able to completely specify the requirements.
(18) Sensitivity — the degree to which minor perturbations in the problem situation dramatically alter the outputs or the application of the methodology.
(19) Formality — the degree to which the methodology is firmly grounded in mathematics or logic.
(20) Team work — the extent to which the methodology supports team work.

(c) *Economic criteria*

The economic criteria of a methodology pertain to its ability to be used cost-effectively and generate economic data. There are four general categories:

(1) Manageability — the degree to which the methodology lends itself to normal management control and monitoring techniques.
(2) Life-cycle benefits — the extent to which the methodology's outputs at various system life-cycle stages are beneficial on their own.
(3) Cost of use — the extent to which the operating costs of using the methodology are not prohibitive.
(4) Cost–benefit analysis — the degree to which the methodology can be used to generate cost–benefit information to help analyse the work of a proposed office system.

(d) *Behavioural criteria*

The behavioural criteria relate to a methodology's ability to adequately handle the social and behavioural aspects of systems development. These are likely to be extremely important when considering office systems — perhaps more so than with conventional data-processing systems. There are nine categories:

(1) Structured task capability — the ability of the methodology to adequately handle structured office tasks.
(2) Unstructured task capability — the ability of the methodology to adequately deal with unstructured office tasks.
(3) Social action — the capability of the methodology to consider the social action which occurs in offices.
(4) Job design — the extent to which the methodology can influence job design, particularly the social component.
(5) Multiple problem perceptions — the ability of the methodology to handle multiple perceptions and formulations of the problem situation.

(6) Implementation — the extent to which the methodology considers the implementation of its product; i.e. strictly technical considerations, or social as well.
(7) User participation — the degree to which the methodology permits true user participation in the office systems development process.
(8) Primary focus — the particular way the methodology focuses on and represents office work.
(9) Office view — the specific view which the methodology is based on.

Table 4.3 attempts to appraise the various office models/methodologies outlined in this chapter on the basis of the criteria proposed. Although the appraisal has an air of objectivity about it, there is, nevertheless, a high degree of subjectivity associated with it as there is with *any* evaluation (as was discussed earlier). The models/methodologies assessed here are ranked according to each criterion on a scale of 1–5 where 1 designates weak support or ability and 5 strong support/ability (a '√' is used to denote that a particular criterion is handled by a methodology.) It is possible that a prospective office automation methodology adopter could attach weights to the various criteria and develop a ranked order of methodologies, choosing the one with the highest ranking. The adopter could also check the robustness of the choice by varying the weights. A methodology which stood up well to weight changes is likely to be desirable. However, the attaching of weights and/or any quantitative analysis on the evaluation data is highly dubious. The numerical data attached to the evaluation are only of an ordinal nature; a rating of '4' does not mean it is twice as good as a rating of '2', only that it is better. The numerical nature of the rating is only to provide a very loose and general quantitative basis by which to evaluate methodologies. Colter (1984), in his evaluation of various systems analysis techniques, used a similar ranking scheme based on a scale of 1–3 where 1 denoted 'no coverage', 2 'weak coverage', and 3 'strong coverage'. The approach used here adds more degrees of variation, although the dangers of carrying the analysis too far are self-evident.

In addition to evaluating the various OA models/methodologies, the methodology appraisal framework attempts to shed additional light on the model/methodology distinction. The framework suggests that upon further analysis, the distinction between model and methodology becomes somewhat less clear. The two, although conceptually separate yet related, are, in practice, like two ends of a continuum. The continuum reflects 'approach' to office system analysis and design. Office models at one end (e.g. OFS, SCOOP, ICN) reflect a more representational and conceptual form of an office and office system. Office methodologies at the other end reflect a more practical, systems analysis-oriented approach to office systems. The framework suggests that while it is important to have elements of both the representational and conceptual types (the office model part) and the practical systems analysis orientation (the office methodology part), what currently exists tends to be either more model oriented or methodology oriented.

It is possible to represent this as a continuum of 'approaches' with models at one end, methodologies at the other. Figure 4.24 depicts the continuum and places the available OA models/methodologies in their respective positions. Table 4.3 adopts the continuum notion as a basis for ordering the various models and methodologies.

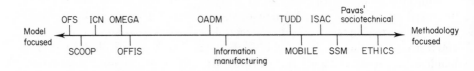

FIGURE 4.24 The OA model/methodology continuum

5. Discussion

On the whole, the approaches which are more 'methodology focused' rate higher using the appraisal framework. This is not surprising since the criteria chosen are biased in favour of more complete approaches to office system analysis and design. Office models (on their own), while perhaps providing a useful basis for representing office activities, are too limited in orientation. They are largely physical design driven. Moreover, their poor showing on the behavioural criteria is a major concern (as will be explained in the next chapter). Office models (or model-focused approaches) cannot, therefore, be recommended as a sound basis for office systems development. Of the office automation methodologies, two score particularly highly: Pava's sociotechnical approach and Mumford's ETHICS. Others such as Checkland's SSM, OADM, MOBILE, and Tapscott's UDD also score well and could be considered. Based on the results of the appraisal, the sociotechnical methodologies are recommended, particularly if an adopter is strongly concerned about the behavioural characteristics of an approach. They score well on most criteria and are clearly superior on the social side. Further, their strong consideration of implementation makes them clear favourites from a social perspective.

There are three caveats about this analysis which need to be borne in mind. One, the evaluation is subjective; it is possible someone else could assign different ratings to the criteria. Further, the quantitative 'feel' of the evaluation

TABLE 4.3

Criteria \ Methodology	OFS	SCOOP	ICN	OMEGA	OFFIS	OADM	Info. Manufact.	TUDD	MOBILE	ISAC	SSM	Pava's socio-technical	ETHICS
(a.1) Function hierarchy	✓	✓	✓	✓	✓	✓	✓	✓	✓	✓	✓	✓	✓
(a.2) Data hierarchcy	✓	✓	✓	✓	✓	✓	✓	✓	✓	✓	✓	✓	✓
(a.3) Interfaces	✓	✓	✓	✓	✓	✓	✓	✓	✓	✓	✓	✓	✓
(a.4) Control flow	✓	✓	✓	✓	✓	✓	✓	✓	✓	✓	✓	✓	✓
(a.5) Data flow	✓	✓	✓	✓	✓	✓	✓	✓	✓	✓	✓	✓	✓
(a.6) Data abstraction	✓	✓	✓	✓	✓	✓	✓	✓	✓	✓	✓	✓	✓
(a.7) Procedural abstraction	✓	✓	✓	✓	✓	✓	✓	✓	✓	✓	✓	✓	✓
(a.8) Parallelism	✓	✓	✓	✓	✓	✓	✓	✓	✓	✓	✓	✓	✓
(a.9) Comprehensiveness	2	2	2	3	1	4	3	4	4	3	4	4	4
(b.1) Understandability	4	3	3	3	4	5	3	5	5	4	4	5	5
(b.2) Comprehendibility	3	2	2	1	2	4	3	4	4	3	4	5	5
(b.3) Transferability	2	1	1	1	1	4	3	4	4	2	4	4	4
(b.4) Reusability	3	3	3	2	3	4	4	5	4	4	4	4	4
(b.5) Computer support	4	3	3	2	4	1	1	1	2	3	1	1	1
(b.6) Life-cycle support	2	1	1	2	2	4	4	4	4	4	4	4	4
(b.7) Project range	1	1	1	2	1	4	4	4	4	3	3	4	4

TABLE 4.3 (continued)

Criteria \ Methodology	OFS	SCOOP	ICN	OMEGA	OFFIS	OADM	Info. Manufact.	TUDD	MOBILE	ISAC	SSM	Pava's sociotechnical	ETHICS
(b.8) Cohesiveness	4	4	4	4	4	5	4	5	4	4	4	4	4
(b.9) Ease of phase transition	4	3	3	3	3	5	4	5	4	3	4	5	5
(b.10) Extent of usage	2	2	2	1	2	3	1	4	3	4	4	3	4
(b.11) Observability	3	3	3	2	2	4	1	4	4	3	3	5	5
(b.12) Controllability	2	2	2	3	3	4	3	4	4	2	3	4	4
(b.13) Relevance	2	2	2	3	2	4	2	3	3	2	4	4	4
(b.14) Consistency	5	5	5	4	5	3	2	3	3	4	2	2	2
(b.15) Complexity	4	5	5	5	4	2	3	2	2	4	3	2	2
(b.16) Modifiability	2	2	2	2	2	4	3	4	4	3	4	4	4
(b.17) Completeness	4	4	4	3	3	3	1	3	3	4	3	3	3
(b.18) Sensitivity	4	4	4	3	4	2	2	2	2	3	2	2	2
(b.19) Formality	4	5	5	4	4	2	1	2	2	4	3	2	2
(b.20) Team work	2	2	2	1	2	4	3	4	4	3	4	5	5
(c.1) Manageability	3	3	3	2	2	3	1	4	3	3	2	2	2

	Form flows	Activities, procedures	Procedures, activities	Procedures, actors	Office objects	Functions, procedures	In-formation products	Tasks	Tasks, procedures	Activities, operations	Problem formulation	Office action	Social interaction
(c.2) Life-cycle benefits	2	2	2	2	1	4	3	4	4	3	4	4	4
(c.3) Cost of use	4	4	4	3	4	2	4	3	3	2	2	2	2
(c.4) cost–benefit analysis	2	1	2	2	2	4	4	4	4	4	4	4	4
(d.1) Structured task capability	4	4	4	4	4	4	3	5	4	4	3	4	4
(d.2) Unstructured task capability	1	1	2	1	1	4	2	2	3	2	4	5	5
(d.3) Social action	1	2	2	1	1	3	1	2	2	2	4	5	5
(d.4) Job design	2	2	2	1	1	3	1	2	2	2	3	5	5
(d.5) Multiple problem perceptions	1	1	2	1	1	2	1	2	3	3	5	4	4
(d.6) Implementation	1	1	2	1	1	3	1	2	3	2	4	5	5
(d.7) User participation	1	2	1	2	2	4	3	3	3	2	4	5	5
(d.8) Primary focus	Form flows	Activities, procedures	Procedures, activities	Procedures, actors	Office objects	Functions, procedures	In-formation products	Tasks	Tasks, procedures	Activities, operations	Problem formulation	Office action	Social interaction
(d.9) Office view	Office activity	Office activity	Office activity	Office semantics	Office activity functions	Office functions	Office functions	Office functions	Office functions	Office activity	Mixed activity	Interpretivist	Interpretivist

might give the wrong impression that additional quantitative analysis is possible. This should be avoided; any such analysis would be highly suspect.

Two, the evaluation criteria have been chosen with care, but they are not exhaustive. For example, one criterion omitted was 'replicability' — that the same result is generated irrespective of the design group or analyst. This was not felt to be meaningful since design is a personal matter; different designers would come up with different designs. Those who advocate replicability imply there is a 'right' design and the methodology should lead to it. Individual differences of analysts should not be permitted to affect the output of the 'right' design. This is not a view shared here. There is no such thing as 'the right' or 'the wrong' design, only interpretations. As people are different so will be their designs. A methodology should allow the design team to be creative and not unduly constrain them. Other evaluation criteria are possible as, for example, used by Colter (1984). In his systems analysis technique assessment, criteria such as structural dimensions, mechanism clarification, functional analysis, procedure detail, input/output detail, level of analysis, communication ability, and analysis perspective were used. Most of these are, however, covered in the appraisal framework used here.

Three, no model/methodology is complete. Each tends to be most appropriate for one part of the systems life-cycle process. Some are best for physical design, others for logical design, some for problem formulation, others for requirements elicitation, and so on. The evaluation carried out here attempted to take into account how well the particular methodology dealt with the complete range of life-cycle needs. However, as Colter (1984) notes:

> ... no single tool, technique, or methodology can support the complete analysis of today's complex systems. Therefore, the analyst must bring a set of tools to a particular analysis task and utilize those approaches which are necessary to produce a complete result. The final product of the analysis is therefore a package of system representations which clarify the multiple dimensions of interest.

Producing good office system designs is not enough; methodologies need to consider how these designs will be implemented, and not just in the technical sense. The social aspects of office system implementation are critical. Methodologies such as Pava's sociotechnical design and Mumford's ETHICS are particularly well suited in this regard, which is a major reason why they have been recommended.

REFERENCES

Aklilu, T. (1981) 'Office automation – office productivity — the missing link', *Office Automation Digest*, AFIPS, Houston, March.
Ballou, D., and Kim, S. (1984) 'A systems life cycle for office automation projects', *Information and Management*, 7.
Barber, G. (1982) 'Embedding knowledge in a workstation', in *Office Information Systems* (Ed. N. Naffah), North-Holland, Amsterdam.

0

Barber, G. (1983) 'Supporting organizational problem solving with a work station', *ACM Transactions on Office Information Systems*, **1**, No. 1, January.

Bracchi, G., and Pernici, B. (1984) 'The design requirements of office systems', *ACM Transactions on Office Information Systems*, **2**, No. 2, April.

Checkland, P. (1972) 'Towards a system-based methodology for real-world problem-solving', *Journal of Systems Engineering*, **3**, No. 2.

Checkland, P. (1981) *Systems Thinking, Systems Practice*, J. Wiley and Sons, Chichester.

Colter, M. (1984) 'A comparative examination of systems analysis techniques', *MIS Quarterly*, March.

Conrath, D., Thachenkary, C., Irving, R., and Zanetti, C. (1982) 'Measuring office activity for Burotique: data collection instruments and procedures, in *Office Information Systems* (Ed. N. Naffah), North-Holland, Amsterdam.

Cook, C. (1980) 'Supporting office procedures — an analysis using the information control net model', *Proceedings AFIPS National Computer Conference*, Anaheim.

Deutsch, K. (1952) 'On communication models and social sciences', *Public Opinion Quarterly*, **16**, No. 3, Fall.

Dumas, P., du Roure, G., and Zanetti, C. (1982) 'MOBILE Burotique: prospects for the future', in *Office Information Systems* (Ed. N. Naffah), North-Holland, Amsterdam.

Ellis, C. (1979) 'Information control nets:: a mathematical model of office automation flow', in *Proceedings of the 1970 Conference on Simulation, Measurement and Modelling of Computer Systems*, Boulder.

Ellis, C., Gibbons, R., and Morris, P. (1980) 'Office streamlining', in *Integrated Office Systems — Burotics* (Ed. N. Naffah), North-Holland, Amsterdam.

Ellis, C., and Limb, J. (1980) 'Office modelling — workshop report, in *Integrated Office Systems — Burotique* (Ed. N. Naffah), North-Holland, Amsterdam.

Ellis, C., and Nutt, G. (1980) 'Office information systems and computer science', *Computing Surveys*, **12**, No. 1, March.

Gehani, N. (1983) 'High level form definition in office information systems', *The Computer Journal*, **26**, No. 1, February.

Gibbs, S. (1982) 'Office information models and the representation of "Office Objects"', *Proceedings SIGOA Conference on Office Systems*, ACM SIGOA Newsletter, **3**, Nos. 1 and 2, Philadelphia, June.

Goldhaber, G. (1976) 'The information communication audit (ICA): rationale and development', *Proceedings of the Academy of Management Conference*, Kansas City, August.

Hammer, M., and Sirbu, M. (1980) 'What is office automation?', *Proceedings First Office Automation Conference*, Atlanta, March.

Hammer, M., and Zisman, M. (1979) 'Design and implementation of office information systems', *Proceedings of the NYU Symposium on Automated Office Systems*, New York, May.

Hirschheim, R. (1984) 'An analysis of participative systems design: user experiences, evaluation and recommendations', LSE Working Paper 84–11–1.0, November.

Keen, P., and Scott Morton, M. (1978) *Decision Support Systems: An Organizational Perspective*, Addison-Wesley, Reading.

Konsynski, B., Bracker, L., and Bracker, W. (1982) 'A model for specification of office communications', *IEEE Transactions on Communications*, **COM–30**, No. 1, January.

Ladd, I., and Tsichritzis, D. (1980) 'An office form flow model', *Proceedings AFIPS National Computer Conference*, Anaheim, May.

Lum, V., Choy, D., and Shu, M. (1982) 'OPAS: an office procedure automation system', *IBM Systems Journal*, **21**, No. 3.

Lundeberg, M., Goldkuhl, G., and Nilsson, A. (1981) *Information Systems Development: A Systematic Approach*, Prentice-Hall, Englewood Cliffs.

Maddison, R., Baker, G., Bhabuta, L., Fitzgerald, G., Hindle, K., Song, J., Stokes, N., and Wood, J. (1983) *Information Systems Methodologies*, Wiley Heyden, Chichester.

Marcus, M., Roubier, J., and Zanetti, C. (1982) 'A trial of office activity methodology application in France', in *Office Information Systems* (Ed. N. Naffah), North-Holland, Amsterdam.

Miller, R. (1973) 'A comparison of some theoretical models of parallel computation', *IEEE Transactions on Computing*.

MOBILE Guide, (1982) 'Equipe Methodologie Kayak', Project Kayak, INRIA, France, January.

Mumford, E. (1981) 'Participative systems design: structure and method', *Systems, Objectives, Solutions*, **1**, No. 1.

Mumford, E., and Weir, M. (1979) *Computer Systems in Work Design — the ETHICS Method*, Associated Business Press, London.

Newman, W. (1980) 'Office models and office systems design', in *Integrated Office Systems — Burotics* (Ed. N. Naffah), North-Holland, Amsterdam.

Olle, T. (1983) 'Information systems design — where do we stand?', *Information Technology Training*, **1**, No. 2, May.

Olle, T., Sol, H., and Verrijn-Stuart, A. (Eds.) (1982) *Information Systems Design Methodologies: A Comparative Review*, North-Holland, Amsterdam.

Pava, C. (1983) *Managing New Office Tchnology: An Organizational Strategy*, Free Press, New York.

Peterson, J. (1977) 'Petri nets', *Computing Surveys*, **9**, No. 3, September.

Richter, G. (1981) 'IML-inscribed nets for modelling text processing and data (base) management systems', *Proceedings Very Large Data Bases Conference*, IEEE, Cannes, September.

Rockart, J. (1979) 'Chief executives define their own data needs', *Harvard Business Review*, March–April.

Rowe, L., and Shoens, K. (1982) 'A form application development system', *Proceedings ACM SIGMOD Conference*, Orlando.

Sirbu, M., Schoichet, S., Kunin, J., and Hammer, M. (1982) 'OAM: an office analysis methodology', MIT, Office Automation Group Memo, OAM–016.

Sutherland, J. (1983) 'An office analysis and diagnosis methodology', Unpublished M.Sc. dissertation, MIT, Mass., February.

Tapscott, D. (1982) *Office Automation: A User-Driven Method*, Plenum Press, New York.

Thachenkary, C., and Conrath, D. (1982) 'The office activities of two organizations', in *Office Information Systems* (Ed. N. Naffah), North-Holland, Amsterdam.

Tsichritzis, D. (1982) 'Form management', *Communications of the ACM*, **25**, No. 7, July.

Wasserman, A., and Freeman, P. (1983) 'Ada methodologies: concepts and requirements', *ACM SIGSOFT Software Engineering Notes*, **8i**, January.

Welke, R. (1981) 'IS/DSS: DBMS support for information systems development', Paper presented at NATO Advance Study Institute on Database Management and Applications, Lisbon, June.

Yao, S., Heuner, A., Shi, Z., and Luo, D. (1984) 'FORMANAGER: an office forms management system', *ACM Transactions on Office Information Systems*, **2**, No. 3, July.

Zisman, M. D. (1977) 'Representation, specification, and automation of office procedures, Ph.D. Thesis, Wharton School, University of Pennsylvania.

Zisman, M. D. (1978) 'Use of production systems to model asynchronous, concurrent processes', in *Pattern Directed Inference Systems* (Eds. D. Water and R. Hayes-Roth), Academic Press, New York.

Zloof, M. (1981) 'QBE/OBE: a language for office and business automation', *IEEE Computer*, **14**, No. 5, May.

Zloof, M. (1985) 'Office-By-Example: a business language that unifies data, word processing, and electronic mail', *IBM Systems Journal*, **21**, No. 3.

Chapter 5
OFFICE AUTOMATION IMPLEMENTATION

INTRODUCTION

The issue of implementation has been a concern of many organizational groups over the years. Whether it is the introduction of a new pay scheme, the building of a new office complex, the operationalizing of a management science model, or the development of a computer-based information system, all are faced with the same task of implementation. As Uhlig, Farber, and Bair (1979) note (in connection with computer systems):

> Implementation is analogous to construction in the building trades where the tools (computer technology and methods) are applied to materials (knowledge/information) to construct a building (application) based upon an architecture (strategy).

This conception of implementation is common in the computing literature. In general, implementation has been thought to simply be the last phase in the systems development process. It has been regarded as little more than the delivery of the developed product to the client. This is however, a view which annoys many people. Eveland (1977), for instance, states:

> Unsophisticated analysts tend to ignore the problem of implementation, and assume that any variance in the innovation after 'adoption' is a form of error to be corrected, rather than the proper subject of study (p. 20).

The concern with such a limited conception of implementation led a number of writers in the 1970s to include the fact that implementation involved change which had to be accepted by those affected. Pressman and Wildavsky (1973), for example, describe implementation in terms of 'getting people to accept innovation and adopt proposed changes' (p. 197). Others, such as Owens (1981), suggest the need to plan for implementation. He writes:

> Successful implementation depends on a match between user needs and systems design. This match is achieved through assessment of organizational and individual variables affecting implementation outcomes. Such an assessment requires extensive planning.

Implementation can thus be defined as the execution and successful effectuation of a planned or designed change.

157

Much of the interest in implementation has stemmed from the large number of less-than-successful computer-based information systems and management science models installed in organizations during the past few decades. Many of these systems that looked good on paper, whose designs were technically elegant, and whose programming faultless, were failing to meet expectations. Many were being used, but ineffectively, while others swiftly fell into disuse (Conrath and du Roure, 1978; Schmitt and Kozar, 1978; and Markus, 1981). Mowshowitz (1976) states that the performance of the data-processing profession has been dismal in terms of the number of 'failed systems'. He notes: '20% are successful, 40% are marginal, and 40% are failures' (p. 70). He attributes these 'appalling statistics' to the naive optimism which was so prevalent among the data-processing professionals in the 1960s. The power of the technology blinded people, causing them to forget about the human dimension in systems. Lucas (1975) possessed a similar belief. He felt many, if not most, systems had been failures in one way or another, due largely to their inappropriate implementation. There were others who felt most failures were of a technical nature, caused by technicians believing the technology had the capability to overcome any human problems (Morgan and Soden, 1973). The area of implementation research developed to study the causes of system failure and ways to overcome them.

IMPLEMENTATION RESEARCH

Out of the need to understand the reasons for information systems failure grew the realization that implementation had not normally been adequately considered. Implementation was not the simple and straightforward process commonly thought. It had a considerable behavioural component and was related to human beliefs, emotions, perceptions, and values. The published product of implementation research has been a proliferation of platitudes based on user involvement, evolutionary change, information analysis, change agents, prototyping, and the like (Bostrom and Heinen, 1977; Feeney and Sladek, 1977; Ginzberg, 1978, 1979; Lucas, 1981). Unfortunately, many of the postulated solutions are superficial, obvious, or both. Alter (1980), for example, proposes an approach for effective systems implementation based on four points: (1) divide the project into manageable pieces; (2) keep the solution simple; (3) develop a satisfactory support base; and (4) meet user needs and institutionalize the system. As noted in Hirschheim, Land and Smithson (1984), approaches such as these are less than complete or coherent implementation strategies; rather they are motley collections of methodological alternatives (e.g. prototyping), obvious essentials for any project (e.g. obtain management support), and dubious advice (e.g. keep it simple).

Recommendations such as these are a direct consequence of a simplistic notion of organizational change. There is an implicit assumption that implementation is a rational, deterministic process, and a belief that the people affected by the change will behave in a manner consistent with the implementer's view of the world. Neither of these assumptions are likely to be true. Gordon, Lewis, and Young (1977), in commenting on implementing policies, write:

> Policy making may be seen as an inescapably political activity into which the perceptions of individual actors enter at all stages. In this case, implementation becomes a problematic activity rather than something that can be taken for granted as in the rational process model; policy is seen as a bargained outcome, the environment as conflictual and the process is characterized by diversity and constraint.

For the implementation of office automation to be successful, it has to be viewed in terms of the more general notion of organizational change. Organizations are social systems, made up of different interest groups each with their own (often conflicting) norms, expectations, objectives, and power. In an environment such as this, it is hardly surprising that the acceptance of change is a non-trivial matter. In fact, it would be surprising if resistance to change was not the norm.

RESISTANCE TO CHANGE

Resistance to change may be defined as an adverse reaction to a proposed change which may manifest itself in a visible, overt fashion (such as through sabotage or direct opposition) or may be less obvious and covert (such as relying on inertia to stall and ultimately kill a project). It could occur fairly quickly, remain latent for a short period of time and then emerge, or lay dormant for a considerable time only to appear later. Resistance should be seen as a normal reaction to change. There is a considerable body of organizational change literature which, either explicitly or implicitly, suggests that the most characteristic individual and group reaction to change is resistance. This is due to the fact that change is normally accompanied by uncertainty or, at least, perceived uncertainty. It is this uncertainty which causes people to resist change.

Fried (1972), for example, contends hostility is the natural consequence of organizational change. Hostility manifests itself in overt, aggressive action which can range from reduced job efficiency to leaving the organization. Fried draws an analogy between people's emotions and reactions to organizational change with the layers of skin on an onion. The outer skin corresponds to a person's overt aggressive actions which he will exhibit due to change. Overt aggressive actions are caused by frustration — the second layer of the onion. He states:

Frustration results when an external barrier stands between a motivated individual and his goal. Frustration is born of the conflicts that arise between the requirement to accept the externally imposed change and the forces driving the individual to reject change. The intensity of the conflict depends on what the individual perceives the impact of change to be on his goals or needs.

Conflict is the third layer of the onion. At the core of the onion is 'the threat to the satisfaction of human needs'. Based on how individuals perceive the change and its effect on their goals, they may adopt a number of dysfunctional behaviours such as regression, aggression, and hostility, or the tendency to blame others.

Sanders (1974) offers a somewhat different argument and sees resistance in a rational light. He claims employees resist change because often they have not been convinced of the merits of the change. Thus resistance is the norm rather than the exception. Sanders feels employees see change as a threat and possess a fear of: losing their jobs, being transferred away from their friends, being unable to acquire the needed new skills, and losing status and prestige. When the organizational change is in the form of a computer-based system, he contends they will react by: withholding data, providing inaccurate data, distrusting computer output, and showing lowered morale. Sanders makes the interesting observation:

> ... changes sought by some may appear to others to be a threat — a threat which prevents them from satisfying certain basic needs or one which decreases the level of their need satisfaction. That a proposed change *does not* actually affect an employee's need satisfaction may be irrelevant from a resistance standpoint. *What is relevant* in this situation is if the employee *believes* that he is threatened.

Ginzberg and Reilley (1957) contend that resistance to change has much to do with an innate conservatism, a reluctance to change the status quo. Inertia, therefore, plays a major role in resistance. They write:

> It must be recognized that many people, though by no means all, do not like to be disturbed. They prefer to stay with the work they know; rather than take on a new assignment (p. 29).

Dickson and Simmons (1970) have attempted to categorize the various dysfunctional behaviours exhibited by people experiencing change. They note three types of behaviour:

1. Aggression — a behaviour which represents an attack (either physically or non-physically) with the intent of injuring or causing harm to the object presenting the problem
2. Projection — a behaviour exhibited when the person blames the systems for causing difficulties

3. Avoidance — occurs when a person defends himself from the system by avoiding or withholding from it

Not everyone believes that resistance to change is a *fait accompli*. Lawrence (1968), for example, feels that resistance is contingent upon how change affects the social aspects of the job, i.e. the established relationships in the organization. Only if there is a change to the social aspects would resistance be likely. Others, such as Markus (1983), contend that resistance is more complex. The basic causes of resistance to change are many and varied, and occur as a tangle of different threads. It is the interaction of the various threads that produce a particular instance of resistance, making it extremely difficult (if not impossible) to see resistance in terms of a simple causal relationship. In contrast to the view held by, for instance, Sanders (1974) and Dickson and Simmons (1970), resistance to change is not a simple acceptance or rejection of a proposed change; there are individual attitudes which colour a person's view of change and degree of acceptance/rejection. Mumford and Banks (1967) noted four sources of these attitudes: (1) variables within the individual, (2) variables in the situation, (3) variables in the change strategy adopted, and (4) the perceived consequences of the change.

Another aspect associated with resistance to change is change by whom? It is likely that depending on who is requesting the change, the range of reactions will be different. This is a point which has not escaped the attention of Eveland (1977) who writes:

> A great deal of what has been characterized as 'resistance to change' is not so much resistance to changing onself as it is resistance to being changed by others (p.4.).

The implementation of office automation represents both a threat and a challenge to individuals and the various interest groups. The threat arises from the disruption of the status quo and a potential attack on the group's interests. The challenge is to improve or defend those interests in the redistribution of resources occasioned by the introduction of the new office system. These resources include departmental budgets, equipment, staff, and territory, and individual authority, status, salary, roles, etc. Moreover, as noted by Pettigrew (1973), Bariff and Galbraith (1978), Bjorn-Andersen and Pedersen (1980), Keen (1981), and Markus (1981), the implementation of a new system may have a direct bearing on the ownership and control of information which has important implications on power.

Resistance to change can be seen as a complex phenomenon whose particular causes and manifestations vary considerably. Machiavelli (1514) may have said it best when he wrote:

... there is nothing more difficult to arrange, more doubtful of success and more dangerous to carry through than initiating change .... The innovator makes enemies of all those who prospered under the old order, and only lukewarm support is forthcoming from those who would prosper under the new. Their support is lukewarm partly from fear of their adversaries, who have existing laws on their side, and partly because men are incredulous, never really trusting new things unless they have tested them by experience. In consequence, whenever those who oppose the changes can do so they attack vigorously, and the defense made by the others is only lukewarm. So both the innovator and his friends are endangered together (p. 51).

PLANNED CHANGE MODELS

In order to overcome resistance to change, a number of commentators have suggested the need for carefully planned implementation approaches. They are based on 'planned change models' and were initially developed by researchers in the organizational development field. Fundamental to these models was the realization of the interaction between organizational elements. Leavitt (1965) postulated that there were four types of interacting elements: tasks, actors, technology, and structure; this gave rise to the well-known Leavitt 'diamond' (see Figure 5.1). *Tasks* were considered the reasons for the existence of the organization; *actors* were people, they undertook tasks; *technology* was the direct, problem-solving mechanisms used by the actors; and *structure* embodied communication, authority, and the system work flow. Leavitt maintained that a change to any one element would cause a change in the other three. He writes:

... the introduction of new technological tools — computers for example — may cause changes in structure (in the communications system or decision map of an organization), changes in actors (their numbers, skills, attitudes and activities) and changes in performance or even definition of task, since some tasks may now become feasible of accomplishment for the first time, and others may become unnecessary.

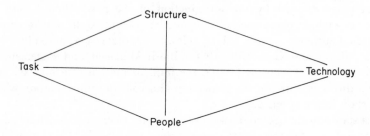

FIGURE 5.1 The Leavitt diamond

Because of the interaction between organizational elements, a number of writers suggested the need to consider the processes involved with change. Implementation, because it involved change, had to be seen as a process requiring successful management. The Lewin/Schein model of change, referred to in Ginzberg (1981), was one of the first to become widely known. It viewed change as occurring in three phases: unfreezing, moving, and refreezing. *Unfreezing* refers to the disconfirmation of existing stable patterns of behaviour. It involves the establishing of a 'felt need' for change and the creating of an environment conducive to individuals feeling they can safely try something different. *Moving* relates to the actual 'action' phase of change. It requires the individual to learn new attitudes and behaviours associated with the change. *Refreezing* refers to the stabilizing of the change and the integration of the new attitudes and behaviours into existing patterns of behaviour.

A more detailed planned change model with seven stages is provided by Kolb and Frohman (1970); it expands and elaborates on the three phases of the Lewin/Schein model (see Figure 5.2). The Kolb/Frohman model is specifically concerned with the intervention process and uses the terms client and consultant rather than user and analyst. In the case of office system development, the client might be the particular stakeholder or initiator and is responsible for the development. The consultant might be an office systems analyst or some form of internal or external facilitator.

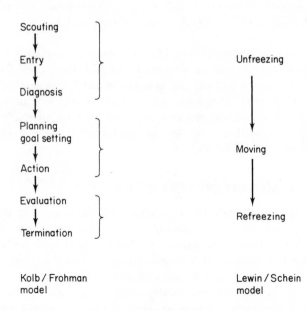

FIGURE 5.2 The Kolb/Frohman and Lewin/Schein models

1. *Scouting* refers to the period where the client and consultant become acquainted. An assessment is made of the fit between the client's needs and the consultant's expertise.

2. *Entry* refers to the stage where a collaborative relationship is formed between the client and consultant. Demb (1979) states: '... it is the collaborative aspect of the change effort which is necessary for organization members to 'own' the change to invest effort in maintaining the result.

3. *Diagnosis* refers to the stage where an assessment of needs is performed. The current situation is described and problems are defined.

4. *Planning and goal setting* refers to the period when a description of the alternative courses of action possible is undertaken. Additionally, evaluation criteria are formulated, applied to the alternatives, and a choice is made.

5. *Action* constitutes the effecting of the chosen 'best' solution from the previous stage. Demb (1979) notes: 'It is important that there is a high level of information exchange, training and communication among all parties' so that the flexibility of the process is ensured.

6. *Evaluation* refers to the stage when an assessment of the implemented system is undertaken to see how well the set objectives have been met. The evaluation uses the criteria developed in stage 4.

7. *Termination* relates to the process of ensuring that the organization is capable of continuing its successful use of the system without the assistance of the consultant. Ginzberg (1978) suggests the primary function of this stage is to make sure the organization is able to maintain the change.

These planned change models provide an interesting approach for dealing with resistance to change and are potentially helpful when considering office automation implementation. They are, however, somewhat general and assume a rationality on the part of organizational members which is unlikely to be valid. Moreover, they miss the plurality of the office. Implementation is more policitcal than these models allow for, as can be noted through the view of counterimplementation strategies.

COUNTERIMPLEMENTATION STRATEGIES

Recent research in the information systems area has suggested that implementation may be thought of in terms of games which people play (Bardach, 1977, Keen, 1981). Often these games are dysfunctional in that they lead to counter games which are applied by those wishing to resist the change. Bardach (1977) refers to the games as 'implementation strategies'.

The notion of implementation strategies grew up out of the desire to overcome people's natural reaction to resist change — particularly change associated with computer introduction. Because of the user reticence to accept computerization, systems analysts and other data processing personnel adopted a number of 'implementation strategies' to mitigate user anxiety. Some of the more common ones are:

1. 'Sell the system'. This is a strategy which asserts that systems designers should strongly sell the system to the user so as to lessen any resistance. Users should be made aware of all the systems' benefits. Schewe, Wieck, and Dann (1977) even went so far as to propose a framework for marketing the system.

2. 'Build a prototype'. This is an approach which attempts to give the users a 'taste' of the system to come through the building of a prototype. The strategy could be said to mirror a philosophy which embraces the phrase 'give them a taste and they will become hooked'.

3. 'I am the expert.' This is a game which some systems designers adopt to overcome resistance. It is based on the fact that most users are unknowledgeable about computers and the systems designer is perceived to be the expert who knows about computers.

4. 'The system is computer based'. This is an approach which promotes the mystique which surrounds computers. It relies on the commonly held belief that computers are efficient, reliable, and error-free; therefore any system which is computer based must be good.

5. 'Appeal to reason'. This is a strategy which contends that since so many organizations and individuals are using computerized systems, they must be valuable and hence readily adopted. Reason dictates it.

6. 'The system will increase prestige and power.' Such a strategy promotes the idea that computer systems are status symbols and can be made a basis for power.

These implementation strategies have been used, to a greater or lesser extent, by many system designers over the years to secure user acceptance. The strategies have, however, met with only limited success. Part of the reason for their lack of success is due to the emergence of counterstrategies adopted by users who oppose the change. Keen (1981) refers to these as counterimplementation strategies.

Counterimplementation strategies are covert and overt attempts by the users to sabotage or make ineffectual the various implementation strategies. Bardach (1977) categorizes three types of counterimplementation strategies: (1) diverting resources; (2) deflecting goals; and (3) dissipating energies. 'Diverting resources' refers to those games played by users which cause resources to be diverted from the system being implemented to some other project. It has the effect of stalling the systems project or forcing the implemented system to be of poor quality because of the lack of resources. 'Deflecting goals' refers to those strategies which attempt to make the systems goals ambiguous. Goal ambiguity leads to less user support as users find it difficult to be enthusiastic about a system whose value to them is questionable. 'Dissipating energies' describes those strategies which attempt to dissipate interest in a system. These games try to draw away support for a system by offering other alternatives or, conversely, by asserting the proposed system is not relevant to particular organizational departments.

These are not the only means by which counterimplementation strategies can be employed. Keen (1981) saw less overt measures which could be used, almost passive resistance in nature. These measures are summarized as follows:

1. 'Lie low'. The less which is done to help or encourage the implementation process along, the greater the chance of failure.
2. 'Rely on inertia.' Given the opportunity to act or not to act, most people prefer not to act. Inertia will often cause most implementation processes to stall or fail.
3. 'Keep the project complex, hard to coordinate, and vaguely defined.' The greater the perceived complexity of the system the more difficult the task of coordination. Similarly, a vaguely defined system makes implementation tenuous.
4. 'Minimize the implementers' legitimacy and influence.' The more the system implementers are seen in an unfavourable light, particularly in terms of a lack of knowledge about the organization's business, etc., the less influence they will be able to command.
5. 'Exploit their lack of inside knowledge.' Systems implementers often have had little prior exposure to organizational politics. Thus, in a political arena, they are at a decided disadvantage.

Because of the well-developed counterimplementation games such as the ones described above, a number of authors have recommended strategies to neutralize these games. Keen calls them counter-counterimplementation approaches. The counter-counterimplementation approach advocated by Keen has five points: (1) make sure that a contract for change has been agreed to by all parties; (2) seek out resistance and treat it as a signal to be responded to; (3) rely on face-to-face contracts; (4) become an insider and work hard to build personal credibility; and (5) co-opt users early.

To these five points, Bardach (1977) would probably add a sixth, i.e. always have a 'fixer' available to smooth out the implementation process. A fixer can be defined as an individual (or group of individuals) who has the prestige, visibility, and legitimacy to facilitate implementation activities effectively.

These counter-counterimplementation strategies, like the planned models, are, however, overly simplistic. While they are more realistic in their assessment of the political nature of change, they fail to provide any meaningful way to deal with it. They offer simplistic platitudes which are unlikely to be very effective, given the complex nature of implementation. Moreover, they perpetuate the notion that implementation is some sort of 'game' people play. The team with the best game strategy will 'win' the implementation battle. A more realistic interpretation is needed.

THE SOCIAL NATURE OF OFFICE SYSTEMS

Office systems, and information systems in general, have been considered as technical systems. Attention has been paid to technological advancement and technical elegance and efficiency. Although lip service has been given to the 'human' aspects of computer-based systems, little real interest has been shown. This is not surprising given the following reasons:

1. Historically, computers had been the expensive resource and people, the inexpensive resource. This has perhaps produced a mentality which focuses on the technology to the exclusion of the individual. Sackman (1971) writes:

   The early computers were virtually one of a kind, very expensive to build and operate, and computer time far more expensive than human time. Under these constraints, it was essential that computer efficiency came first, with people last .... The developing computer ethos assumed an increasing misanthropic visage. Technical matters turned computer professionals on; human matters turned them off. Users were troublesome petitioners somewhere at the end of the line who had to be satisfied with what they got.

2. The self-selection process contributes to the lack of consideration given to human aspects of computerized systems. Bjorn-Andersen and Hedberg (1977) claim systems people lack behavioural skills and concern for human values because of the type of person who is attracted to the systems profession. They write:

   ... people have to be fascinated by technology in order to devote their lives to designing information systems, and if they are fascinated by technology, they are likely to see particularly the technological opportunities and constraints in the design problem which they face. Information systems have benefited from computer developments over the last decades, and it is very likely that people who wanted to work with computers have found it particularly attractive to become systems designers.

3. Systems designers are not rewarded for considering human issues in systems design. Kling (1977) writes:

   Computer staff maintain the most sophisticated technologies available, at the 'frontiers of knowledge' ... computing personnel are usually hired for technological competence and promoted for technological and fiscal success. The latter include meeting deadlines and staying within the budget allocated. The explicit satisfaction of users with particular applications packages, etc., ... is at best, a secondary consideration. Nor is user satisfaction systematically monitored or evaluated like a budget.

A major advancement occurred in the 1970s with the systems profession explicitly recognizing that computer-based systems had social implications. However, this too misses the mark. As Land and Hirschheim (1983) note:

> Information systems are not technical systems which have behavioural and social consequences, rather they are social systems which rely to an increasing extent on information technology for their function (p. 91).

Technology is simply a component of the office system. The emphasis, therefore, must be on the social system. This is a point more and more people are beginning to recognize. Office and factory workers are no longer willing to be treated as technical automata. They want to have a say in any changes which affect them. Kohl, Benedict, and Gerardi (1981) capture the spirit with precision. They write:

> Today's workers, given their experience and education, will not accept a system of distribution of power and status based on traditional definitions. The bottom line is that the manager's right to control the conditions of work and to make decisions without consultation will no longer be accepted, and there are no longer any real differences in his education, life style, or work compared to the worker that can legitimate his right to exclusive control (p. 1472).

Ever since Frederick Taylor (1911) stated 'In the past, the man has been first; in the future, the system must be', organizations have tended to neglect their social systems in favour of their technical systems. Yet with the growth of industrial democracy and the trend for individuals to want more autonomy in respect to both work and leisure, this process will need to be reversed. The need to consider both social and technical systems is preeminent.

SOCIOTECHNICAL SYSTEMS

The concept of jointly considering and 'optimizing' both the technical and social components of implementation is precisely the philosophy of the sociotechnical systems (STS) approach, and is embodied within the implementation approach adopted here.

1. The Approach

The STS approach sees any technological intervention, e.g. office systems/ technology implementation, as having two components: the technical system involving various job tasks and technology, and the social system involving people with their various roles, behaviours, etc. These two systems must be separated from one another, initially, to determine the requirements of each. Once these have been ascertained, the STS process proceeds by recombining the variables in each system in such a way that the two systems are ultimately, jointly optimized. Bostrom (1980) discusses this point succinctly:

> The goal of joint optimization implies the best design alternatives in the technical system and their effects on having the best in the social system are jointly considered. Technical system optimization is usually measured in terms of improvement in task accomplishment (i.e. improvements in productivity) while social system optimization is measured in terms of gains in the quality of working life of the work system's members (i.e. improvements in the ability of employees to satisfy their personal needs, e.g. meaningful and satisfying work, recognition, control and influence, learning opportunities, good wages and working conditions, and the like).

Mumford (1981) defines the sociotechnical approach as a 'design philosophy that produces productivity, quality, coordination, and control; but also provides a work environment and task structure in which people can achieve personal development and satisfaction.

2. Design Principles

It is apparent that the office, which consists of both a technical and social system, could clearly be viewed as a sociotechnical system. People use various bits of technology: typewriters, telephones, photocopiers, etc., in their everyday activities, and the social aspects of work (in general) and office work (in particular) are well known. Therefore, it would appear possible that some form of sociotechnical system approach could be used to achieve an optimal design for both the technical and social parts of an office system. This was precisely Pava's (1983) contention with his STS methodology.

The sociotechnical systems approach has been advocated for quite some time (cf. Trist and Bamforth, 1951; Trist, 1953; and Emery, 1959). Since then, considerable research has been done and the STS approach has evolved accordingly. It has been used in a variety of contexts but has only relatively recently been suggested as an approach to deal with computer-based system introduction (cf. Mumford, 1973, 1974; Bostrom and Heinen, 1977; Mumford, Land, and Hawgood, 1978; Taylor, 1978; and De Maio, Bartezzaghi, and Zanarini, 1979; Kolf and Oppelland, 1979).

One of the developments growing out of the research on sociotechnical systems has been a list of STS design principles (Cherns, 1976). These design principles, it has been claimed, can be used in almost any environment, and therefore could serve as valuable guidelines for the office automation implementation process. The following nine design principles have been adapted from Cherns (1976):

(a) Compatibility. The process of design itself must be compatible with its objectives. For example, if the objective is to develop an adaptable system which embodies individual capabilities and local knowledge, then an opportunity for 'substantive' participation should be given to the users.

(b) Minimal critical specification. The design process should identify what is absolutely essential to be accomplished in a task, but no more. This leaves maximum scope for how the task should be undertaken. Thus, while the design process should be very precise about what needs to be done, it should be very imprecise about the method the employee(s) can use to accomplish the task. A specification which is highly detailed might reduce uncertainty, but is at the expense of flexibility.

(c) Variance. The design process, wherever possible, should allow any variance to be controlled by the employee(s) involved in the process which created the variance. Variance can be defined as the tendency for a task to deviate from the desired standard. If variance cannot be eliminated, then it should be controlled as near to the point of origin as possible. The traditional separated inspection function does less to prevent variance than to correct its consequences. This principle suggests, for example, that word processor operators should be allowed the responsibility to inspect their work rather than having it inspected by others. Therefore, one of the roles of the word processing supervisor would be train the operators on how to inspect their own work accurately.

(d) Multifunctionality. The design process should allow employees to have multifunctional tasks as part of their work. This is based on the realization that for an organization to be sufficiently adaptive to meet a continually changing environment, it is necessary for its members to be ready, willing, and able to perform more than one function, or to perform the same function in a variety of ways. For example, it would be desirable to have administrative secretaries capable of: typing, keyboarding, dictation, organizing meetings, letter writing, and other administrative skills.

(e) System boundaries. The design process must be careful that boundaries drawn from the system do not interfere with the sharing of knowledge or information which are needed for task accomplishment. A word-processing pool, for example, can sometimes erect a boundary between author and typist. The knowledge needed to complete a document successfully has to be conveyed from the author to the typist. The design of a word-processing pool has to insure that such information transfer is not severed.

(f) Information flow. The design process should allow relevant information and feedback to go directly to the person who is responsible for the action or decision. The more information flows through various channels and organizational levels, the greater the chance of distortion and corruption. Direct information feedback contributes to the control of variance and, thus, to superior performance.

(g) Congruence of objectives. The design process should lead to a system which reinforces the behaviours and objectives the organizational structure is designed to produce. For example, if autonomous work groups are introduced then remuneration should be based on group productivity rather than individual performance.

(h) Human needs and values. The design process should produce a system which provides a high quality of working life for its members. This would include: a challenging job content, enhanced job variety and responsibility, enlarged decision-making responsibilities, opportunities for learning and continuous development, social recognition and support from peers, and a satisfying and desirable future. The support of human needs will invariably lead to some disagreement and conflict; thus compromises which maximize the quality of life of the whole would have to be made.

(i) Iteration. Any design is an iterative process. A system is conceived and must continually be reviewed and improved. Thus design is an ongoing process, involving continual assessment. The introduction of personal computing in an organization will necessitate a form of monitoring to see what features are used (and not used), as well as determining what new features (e.g. software) are needed.

These design principles are only guidelines and are far from exhaustive. They do, however, provide a foundation for office automation implementation based on the ideals of sociotechnical systems.

A PARTICIPATIVE APPROACH TO IMPLEMENTATION

One of the more popular ways of implementing the STS philosophy is through participative systems design and implementation involving employees who will eventually have to operate and use the new work system. Lucas (1982) lists six reasons for adopting a participative approach:·

1. Participation is ego enhancing, which builds self-esteem; this results in more favourable attitudes.
2. Participation can be challenging and intrinsically satisfying, leading to positive attitudes.
3. Participation typically results in more commitment to change; commitment in this case should translate into greater system use.
4. Participating users become more knowledgeable about the change. Users are able to control more of the technical qualities of the system and become better trained to use it.

5. Technical quality will be enhanced because participants know more about the old system than any outside analyst.
6. Users retain the control over their activities and should therefore have more favourable attitudes.

To these six reasons, Land and Hirschheim (1983) would likely add two more:

7. Participation allows the interests of the individuals who must use the system to be protected. It is based on the belief that individuals have the right to control (or at least have some say in) their own destinies.
8. Participation provides the mechanism through which individuals can use the system as a basis for a redesign of their jobs and working environment.

The case for participation is intuitively strong and is supported in the wider area of organizational theory (Guest and Knight, 1979; Bate and Mangham, 1981; and Koopmans and Drenth, 1981). Blumberg (1969) writes:

> There is hardly a study in the entire literature (on participation) which fails to demonstrate that satisfaction in work is enhanced or that other generally acknowledged beneficial consequences accrue from a genuine increase in workers' decision making power. Such consistency of findings, I submit, is rare in social research (p. 123).

Yet participation does have its detractors. Child (1977) suggests that participation may not be totally effective when faced with active counterimplementation. He writes:

> One can however expect too much from it. Participation is a way of confronting the political issues involved in change, not a means of avoiding or smoothing over them. If there is a deep seated conflict of interest between parties involved in a proposed change, participation will probably not turn up a mutually acceptable solution. Also, if hidden anxieties and hostilities are present, it may be necessary to introduce a skilled third party, a social consultant, to bring things into the open, where they can be confronted and dissipated. So long as anxieties and conflicts are present, and not totally recognized, participation is likely to prove an unfruitful exercise (p. 198).

Adams (1975) presents a case where users did participate in systems design but had no power to control the direction in which the design progressed. Eason (1977) cites three disadvantages with involving users in the design process: (1) difficulties in developing a system specification understandable to the users, (2) potential delays caused in dealing with multiple groups, and (3) possible suboptimal design because of the involvement of competing user groups. Croisdale (1982) asks how participation is possible when the number of potential participants are measured in the thousands, scattered over a large geographical area. Mumford (1981) doubts whether participation will be effective when the objectives include reducing labour costs by making employees redundant.

Hedberg (1975) asserts that some user participation is dysfunctional. He claims there are two such types: (1) 'hostage', when the participating user groups become shy and introspective because of the technical jargon used by the systems staff; and (2) 'indoctrination', when the user is indoctrinated into the systems group, providing little input. Hedberg suggests that *participation* is not good enough; users must have influence.

Keen and Gerson (1977) present an argument against user participation from the systems analyst's perspective. They believe it leads to political problems — power struggles — which the systems staff are ill-equipped to handle. Kraft (1979) presents a provocative argument against participation. He feels it is a form of manipulation — yet another management tool to usurp further power away from the workers.

Although there has been some dissension regarding the value of participation in systems development, recent studies (Hirschheim, 1983, 1985) have suggested positive results. See also Hedberg (1980) for a compelling treatment on the need for participation in systems implementation.

There are many forms of participation and various ways a participative approach could be implemented. Land (1982) describes three broad categories of participation:

1. Consultative. This is where the participants provide input into the systems design process but where the bulk of the decisions are left to some other group, e.g. systems analysts. The grounds on which the various decisions are reached should be published for the participants to see. In this situation, participation is often confined to particular special interest groups identified as being affected by the proposed system/technology introduction. Normally the kind of input provided by the participants is limited to social system considerations such as job satisfaction needs.
2. Democratic. This is where all the participants have an equal voice in the decisions affecting systems development or at least in the decision-making process. The implementation of decisions, however, is left in the hands of some other group or authority, e.g. senior management. The participants make the decisions, but it is left to another group to approve and make sure they are implemented.
3. Responsible. This is where the participants not only make the decisions but also assume full responsibility and authority for their implementation. In this situation all workers who will use the new system or technology are involved, on a continuous basis, in the development and implementation process. This approach has been described by some as the only true form of participation.

Land contends that the 'responsible' form of participation is the ideal, but that certain situations and environments may militate against this form in favour of some other. Since all organizations are different, no one best form of participation exists. Rather, participation has to be considered in the light of existing organizational realities.

The participative approach to office automation implementation, it is felt, would have much to offer. It could act as a catalyst in getting the various organizational users of the technology thinking about the new social arrangements possible. Remote work, new group and work structures, new activities, and the like, are all facilitated by office technology introduction. Given that organizational members know most about their activities and the tasks they perform, they are in the best position to say what types of arrangements will be best for them. Additionally, any new technology being introduced has a better chance of success (and being used) if its users understand the technology and feel they are in some sense responsible for its introduction. Participation allows for this. Thus, the value of participation in office automation implementation would seem apparent.

1. Components of Participation

Although participation in office automation has been widely accepted as a key aspect of implementation, few authors offer any structural way for participation to take place. Most assume that implementers of the technology should involve the users but fail to specify such issues as: the form of participation, the content of participation, the degree of participation, the groups who should be involved, and the stages where participation should take place. Yet these aspects are important and could very well affect the value of participation. They shall be referred to as the five components of participation.

Forms of participation

There are two forms of participation:

(a) The direct form
(b) The indirect form

The direct form is when each user who has to use the technology or will be affected by it can take part in its discussion. In the indirect form, this is done on behalf of the user by some representative.

Content of participation

There are basically three types of content on which participation can take place:

(a) Long-range issues
(b) Tactical decision making
(c) Operational tasks

Participation associated with the long-term survival of the firm, its ownership, nature of corporate control, etc., is considered to be in category (a). Participation in tactical decisions such as the hiring of managers, setting budgets, or the decision to use some form of office automation would fall into category (b). Participation in operational activities, i.e. those activities which directly affect an employee's task performance and/or working life, is of the category (c) variety.

Degree of participation

This is basically the degree to which participation can influence the actual decision. As was described earlier by Land (1982), it is possible to classify the degree of participation in terms of: (a) consultative, (b) democratic, and (c) responsible.

The groups involved in participation

There have been a number of frameworks by which to categorize the various uses of a specific system of technology, but one useful way is to classify user groups into:

(a) Primary users. These are users who work directly and internally with the system/technology. They have the ability to modify and mould the system/technology while being responsible for its effective and efficient running and operation. They have the job of trying to keep the other users happy. Examples of primary users are computer programmers and analysts.
(b) Secondary users. These are users who work more directly with the system. They provide input to and/or receive output from the system/technology, but have no power (ability) to change it directly. They can, however, influence its operation by indirect means, e.g. asking the programmers and/or analysts to change part of the system/technology. Examples of secondary users are bank clerks and tellers who work with an on-line banking system, and secretaries who use word processors.
(c) Tertiary users. These are users who do not interact with the system/ technology, but are nevertheless affected by it. They may receive some reports from the system, but they neither work directly or indirectly with the system. Tertiary users also have no direct way of influencing the system's/technology's operation. They may write a letter to a manager,

who in turn may request some change, but their ability to change the system is very limited. An example of tertiary users would be a firm's customers. They receive bills, invoices, etc., from the system, but have little ability to make changes.

The stages where participation should take place

Any system or technology must go through a number of stages from the time there is perceived to be a problem, to the time the technology/system is implemented, to the time the system/technology is considered out-of-date and in need of replacement. Often these stages are discussed in terms of the systems life-cycle and involve: (a) project selection, (b) feasibility study, (c) systems analysis, (d) logical systems design, (e) physical systems design, (f) implementation, (g) maintenance, and (h) review and assessment.

2. Contextual Determinants

In addition to the five components of participaton there are three somewhat more macro issues associated with the nature of participation and its potential acceptance. They are referred to as the contextual determinants of participation.

Participation potential of the organization

This is the potential of the organization to allow participation to occur, and is based more on macroorganizational and environmental issues. It assumes that organizations are entities in their own right and possess a number of contextual characteristics, e.g. size, history, structure, age, technical system, and so on.

Additionally, the environment of an organization is also viewed as important. The environment can be thought to consist of the following: (a) physical structure, (b) social structure, (c) ecological structure, (d) legal structure, (e) cultural structure, (f) political structure, (g) economic structure, (h) psychological structure, and (i) international structure (Sethi, 1970). It may be classified as simple or complex, and/or stable or dynamic.

In general, there are four primary organizational factors which contribute to the participation potential of an organization:

(a) *Size.* The propensity to initiate some form of participation process is usually greater in larger organizations than smaller ones. This somewhat surprising point is due to two facts:
   (1) In small organizations there is a tendency towards freedom of action and personal involvement already, so there is less need to embark on a formal participation exercise.

(2) There is a growing trend in the West for workers to demand more autonomy in respect to both work and leisure. This has manifested itself in the emergence of the industrial democracy theme. Larger organizations have been the ones most guilty of providing little worker autonomy in the past and it is in these organizations where the interest in worker participation is most great.

(b) *Nature of technology.* Simpler technologies such as word processing appear to offer a greater opportunity for user involvement than more complex ones. This is because users would be in a better position to understand the technology and, hence, take a greater interest in its design and implementation.

(c) *Nature of the product and labour market.* Organizational control systems are influenced by market forces. The more stable the product market, the more structured and formalized the organizational control system. The more formalized the control system, the less likely the possibility of participation. Guest and Knight (1979), in looking at the labour market, noted that organizations which had relatively low labour costs were usually more willing to agree to direct participation.

(d) *Autonomy.* Highly centralized, bureaucratic organizations usually provide few opportunities for user participation. This is because most jobs in these environments are largely structured and routinized. Edstrom (1977) found that jobs which are more programmed (i.e. structured) provide workers with little scope for participation.

Normally, organizations which have a more decentralized and autonomous structure, have a history of worker participation in decision making, and are more concerned with the growth in industrial democracy will have a high potential for participation in office automation implementation.

User propensity to participation

Not all people want to participate. Participation may be considered to be related to responsibility. The more one participates, the higher the level of responsibility. It has been shown that some people do not necessarily want responsibility or increases in responsibility. Others may want the responsibility but are not capable of participating. Lawrence (1968) asks how do you force or teach people to participate? This is not a skill possessed or even understood by all. Telling a person to participate does not mean 'true' participation will occur. Thus, user propensity to participate will depend on individual factors such as: attitude, perceived power, perceived value, group pressures, knowledge of the subject, interest in the subject, and the like.

In general, there are four particular individual characteristics which play an important role in determining the user propensity to participation:

(a) *Attitudes.* Guest and Knight (1979) report that people who have a flexible personality, a high need for achievement, and a high level of self-esteem would likely have a more favourable attitude towards participation. Participation would be seen as reflecting self-goals.

(b) *Capabilities.* Users who have greater skills and perceived intelligence are more likely to be inclined towards participation. Furthermore, these individuals who have had some experience with participation are likely to desire more.

(c) *Perceived power.* Individuals who perceive they have the power to influence a decision are more likely to participate than those who do not. This is particularly true when they perceive their power to be high relative to others.

(d) *Stakes involved.* Individuals who perceive the stakes involved to be relatively high are more likely to desire participation. This is because they want to protect their own self-interests. Users are often found to be willing and wanting to participate, but needing the proper knowledge of what to do. Pre-training on the various aspects of participation and office automation might, therefore, be advantageous.

Management Acceptance of Participation

Not all managers/superiors are agreeable to sharing their decision-making power. Managerial ideology, values, philosophies, etc., are often at odds with what participation is trying to accomplish. Thus, it is not uncommon to find reticence on the part of management when it comes to participation. Again, the acceptance of participation will depend on their attitudes, capabilities, perceived value, pressures, and the like. (For a further treatment of this subject, see Hoyer, 1980, and Hirschheim, 1983.)

In general, management acceptance of participation is something which can be fostered, but it often needs a catalyst and a sponsor — someone or something to start the process, and someone who is willing to see the participation exercise through to fruition. Management acceptance of participation is the key variable if participation as an organizational approach to office automation implementation is to be successful.

3. Synthesis

Turning now to the five components of participation cited earlier, it can be seen that certain types of participation might be more desirable than others when implementing office systems and technology.

Form of Participation

It is felt that the direct form of participation would be more beneficial in the long run than the indirect form. Office automation can dramatically alter the work and tasks that people perform. Given that most people are somewhat fearful of change — based on not knowing what the future will hold — it is not uncommon to expect and find resistance to change (Lawrence, 1968). A direct form of participation would do much to mitigate the fear as the users would understand much more about office automation and thus be less inclined to resist its introduction. Indirect participation — if the direct form is not acceptable to the organization's management — is better than no participation, but one must be wary of labels such as manipulation and non-representation in indirect participation. (See Hedberg, 1975, for a good treatment of some of the possible dysfunctional consequences of using an indirect form of participation.)

Content of Participation

Participation in office automation implementation, it is felt, should be concerned more with operational tasks and tactical decision making than long-range (or strategic) activities, since most use of office systems would be made by clerical people and managers. Different organizations, however, might have different thoughts on what the content of participation should be. Some might feel participation should be restricted to only operational activities, i.e. those activities which directly affect an employee's task performance. Others might feel participation should be centred around tactical decision making, e.g. whether to implement a local area network or not. Having decided that a particular technology is appropriate, its implementation is left up to the professionals, e.g. the DP department. Yet even though these different approaches to the content of participation exist, it is felt participation in office automation implementation should embrace both tactical actions and operational activities.

Degree of Participation

Ideally, the degree of participation should be 'responsible', i.e. the participants not only make the decisions about office automation implementation but also assume full responsibility and authority over the carrying out of the decisions. It is based on the assumption that only if the participants have responsibility and authority will they feel true participation has taken place. And true participation is the most likely way to ensure that full support of the users is obtained, thus lessening any prospect of sabotage, resistance, avoidance, or other dysfunctional behaviour. Should 'responsible' participation not be possible, then the next best alternative is 'democratic', where all participants have an equal voice in implementaion but exercise no authority or responsibility over its outcome. If this is not possible, then the 'consultative' degree of participation is recommended. This is based on the maxim: 'some participation is better than no participation'.

The Groups Involved in Participation

It could be argued that all three groups of users, i.e. primary, secondary, and tertiary, should be involved in the implementation of office automation. However, the tertiary users — in the main — would be less affected by office automation than the other two groups. Additionally, it would be difficult to have this group participating in the implementation process. Therefore it is felt that the primary and secondary users should be involved in the participation exercise, with perhaps some input by representatives of the tertiary users. It should be noted that identifying all primary and secondary users might not be easy, but their identification is important and is probably worth the time which is needed.

The Stages Where Participation Should Take Place

Research has shown (cf. Hirschheim, 1983) that participation is most valuable at the early stages of the systems life-cycle, i.e. project selection, feasibility, systems analysis, and logical design, although participation would obviously be of value in the review and assessment stage. In the case of office automation implementation, the same would also be true. Most participation would occur in the beginning when deciding whether to implement office automation, what type of office technology and systems to implement, what changes in structural arrangements to make, and so on. Participation would slacken, the further into the systems life-cycle office automation progressed. However, see Lucas (1973) for a treatment on why participation should occur throughout the whole of the systems life-cycle.

4. Participation — How?

One of the great difficulties associated with participation is 'how'. Most recognize its value, but are unsure of how to structure the participation so that it is meaningful. For example, most users — outside the DP department — are not particularly knowledgeable about technical matters, and would find difficulty in determining technical requirements. Similarly, the systems analysts and programmers would have difficulty in determining and analysing social structure requirements for the users of the technology. The solution is to have two groups — as was suggested above: one group for the primary users, a second group for the secondary users. The secondary users would presumably be the non-technical people and would specifically consider the social requirements and alternatives. The primary users, from the data processing department, would consider the technical requirements and alternatives. These two sets of requirements and alternatives would then be matched and evaluated. The result would be an acceptable sociotechnical solution. Figure 5.3, which

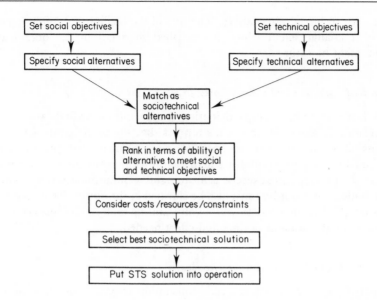

FIGURE 5.3 Participation leading to a sociotechnical solution

has been adapted from Mumford and Weir (1979), depicts the process diagrammatically. It must be noted that the participative implementation process described here is only in skeletal form but see ETHICS in Chapter 4 for more details.

5. Other Aspects of Participation

In addition to the participative issues discussed above, there are a number of important points which have emerged from recent research on participative methodologies (cf. Hoyer, 1980; Mumford, 1982; Hirschheim, 1983; and Land and Hirschheim, 1983). These points are presented as recommendations, which, if followed, should help lead to successful office automation implementation.

Recognize the Need For a Facilitator

A facilitator is someone who can help the participation exercise along. At times the participative approach can get bogged down: people now knowing what to do next, what issues to consider, in what order, and so on. The facilitator should act to keep participation occurring smoothly. Also, the facilitator can act in a liaison capacity between the various groups and can help in the matching of social with technical alternatives. The role of the facilitator is often likened to that of a change agent which is described in detail in the organizational development literature.

Assign Responsibilities and Clarify Commitments

There is a need to have all participating groups and individuals aware of their responsibilities ahead of time. This implies that the participants are assigned responsibilities for the various parts of the implementation process. As was mentioned earlier, responsibilities help guarantee that the individuals' involvement in the participation exercise is meaningful. Commitments in terms of time, effort, budget, and sundry must also be clarified at the outset. Participants must be aware of what the exercise will involve and be under no delusions about its simplicity or the amount of time and effort needed.

A Realistic Plan of Action Must be Developed

The participative approach is a time-consuming activity. Thus it is imperative that realistic timetables, level of work estimates, and budgets for each participative activity are worked out. It must be borne in mind that most of the time-consuming activities will occur at the initial stages. This time will be made up by the shorter lead time to getting the various office technologies and systems totally operative and used by the various organizational members. Participation lessens the amount of formal training needed and there would be less reticence on the part of the others in using the new systems.

Senior Management Support Must be Explicit

Senior management must be seen to be staunchly behind the participative approach and interested in the implementation exercise. Explicit support is a necessary but not sufficient condition for participation to be successful. Senior management's support must be highly visible in more than just a lukewarm or animated fashion. Participation would be most successful when there is perceived to be sincere interest on the part of senior management. Given the importance and potential serious dysfunctional consequences of deficient office automation implementation and use, senior management support should be relatively easy to enlist.

Job and Work Changes Brought about Through Office Automation Must be Seen and Believed to be Positive

As was discussed earlier, people inherently fear the unknown. Beyond the ultimate concern of whether there will still be a job available for an employee after office automation, there is likely to be concern about how the job will be affected. Participation in the implementation process will help reduce the uncertainty of change but institutional measures should be taken so that jobs (and the working environment in general) are not negatively affected. That is, the quality of working life should be positively influenced by office automation.

Such positive influence can take the form of:

(a) *Job enlargement.* This could be brought about by providing increased responsibilities to the tasks performed by the employees. Job enlargement is usually thought to be directly related to job satisfaction, as has been shown in a recent CCTA study (Simons, 1981). In this study — on word processors — a high level of job satisfaction was found to be associated with:

  (1) Development of new skills
  (2) Feeling the job is important
  (3) The job is perceived to be challenging
  (4) Opportunity to use abilities
  (5) Interest in the job
  (6) Interest in the technology associated with the job

(b) *Job rotation.* This is brought about by allowing individuals the mobility to rotate from one job to another. Job rotation can increase job satisfaction as it reduces the monotony of performing just a single or few tasks associated with one job by allowing an individual the flexibility of performing a number of jobs at various times. Additionally, job rotation allows an employee to develop new skills while providing an opportunity to utilize more of his capabilities.

(c) *Job enrichment.* This focuses on the job of the individual employee and attempts to 'enrich' the job by increasing the challenges and responsibilities associated with it. The purpose of job enrichment — particularly in combination with job enlargement and job rotation — is to improve the relationship between the individual and his work.

Office automation, therefore, should lead to a working environment where jobs are enhanced and an increase in job satisfaction is experienced.

Participation is Not Problem-free

According to Hirschheim (1985), individuals who have had experience with participative systems design suggest a number of irritations:

(a) Participation in the systems development process often leads to design delays in the early phases.

(b) The need for a facilitator (preferably someone from outside) who keeps the participative process going is not always easy to find. Moreover when he or she leaves the project, any follow-up seems to vanish.

(c) Resolving disagreements is sometimes problematic as the participative process militates against any 'appeal to authority'. Additionally, it often leads to a great deal of time being spent on resolving relatively minor problems.

(d) Choosing appropriate sized design groups is another difficulty. Too large a group causes difficulty in coordination and endless discussions; too small a group may be felt to be unrepresentative of the user population.

(e) Setting system boundaries is difficult as it is not always clear where a system should begin and end.

To these five, Mumford (1983) would likely add an additional five:

(a) Lack of trust. In certain cases users (e.g. office workers) may be wary of management's reason for involving them in the systems development process, particularly if there is a history of lack of consultation. Participation may be viewed as a manipulative exercise on the part of management.

(b) Selection of the design group. Members of the design group have to be selected somehow and their choice may lead to problems. Management may wish to say how large the group should be and who its members are. Workers may see this as management control and thus be sceptical about the underlying intentions. Democratic elections may be the most desirable as far as the workers are concerned, but management may worry that those elected may be the more militant members of the department.

(c) Conflicting interests. Different people in the participative process have different interests and stand to gain either more or less depending on the outcome. As conflicts are inevitable, they must be quickly and efficiently dealt with. Experience to date suggests this does not always happen. Disagreements quite often drag on, leading to frustration on the part of participants, especially systems personnel. Further, the resolution requires strong communication skills; this is not something which can be easily imparted on the design group members.

(d) Systems analyst role ambiguity. As the role of the systems analyst is changed, there occasionally occurs role ambiguity. Instead of the systems analyst being the key figure in the design process, the users assume this role. This may lead to some systems staff resisting the change.

(e) Role of the departmental manager. It is not clear what role the manager of the participating department should play. If he or she becomes a member of the design group or takes too active a role in the group's operation, it might have an inhibiting effect on discussions. Departmental members may be less willing to express their feelings openly. On the other hand, if the manager is seen to be ambivalent to the participative exercise, the group may feel the process will not lead to any concrete product.

Groups and Individual Needs, Motivations, Pressures, Etc., Will Have a Great Impact on Office Automation and Must be Catered For

The history of computing is rife with examples of computer systems which were built and introduced only to find they were not used because the social elements were not fully considered. Much of this chapter has been devoted to this very point. The use of participation within the context of sociotechnical system development has been proposed as the most appropriate way to deal with these social elements. Yet participation is not enough. There is a need for all to realize that successful office automation implementation and use is contingent upon a myriad of social aspects. For example, individuals may not use an automated office system even though they may have participated in its implementation if their peers perceive its use as socially unacceptable. Group pressures — based on group norms and values — are very powerful forces and must be recognized and somehow dealt with. It is therefore advisable that agreements be made, in advance, so as to lessen pressures arising out of uncertainties. See, for example, Tables 5.1 and 5.2 which describe new technology agreements between unions and employers. Additionally, organizations should set up procedures and mechanisms to resolve conflicts arising out of group and individual pressures associated with new technology implementation and use.

TABLE 5.1 Summary of the New Technology Agreement between APEX and NEI Parsons Ltd. (Sherman, 1980)

* No redundancy
* No subcontracting or agency use without prior discussion
* Constant users of VDUs will have a 20 minutes break for every hour of work
* Training of representatives
* Health and safety technical specifications
* Eye checks every six months
* A joint management/union committee to '... monitor developments, consider and control further introduction of computer aid systems' in addition to changes to office routines

SUMMARY

Implementation has always been — and may always be — a thorny proposition. Implementation research notes that in the past too little attention has been

TABLE 5.2 *Summary of a New Technology Agreement between the Zurich Insurance Company and the Association of Scientific, Technical and Managerial Staff (ASTMS) (Tideswell, 1981)*

KEY POINTS

Work measurement

The management has given a written undertaking that new systems will not be used to measure individuals' work performance.

Access to information

ASTMS will be informed of any research projects or feasibility studies involved in the introduction of new technology. The company will also provide full information on changes in organizational structure, type of new technology proposed, and the introduction date. Union representatives will be offered familiarization training and given adequate time to explain changes to the membership.

Job security

Guarantees are given about security of employment, with no employee being made redundant as a result of the introduction of new technology. Suitable alternative employment, redeployment, or severance terms may be considered.

Job evaluation

A clause covering job evaluation aspects is included in the Agreement. This recognizes that changing skills may require a review of jobs affected, but no loss of salary will be incurred as a result of any downgrading.

Retraining

Both the company and ASTMS agree that retraining is vital and priority will be given to those most directly affected. Salaries will be maintained during training.

Health and safety

Stringent health and safety standards will be maintained and any risks will be minimized prior to introduction.

Peace clause

Finally, a 'peace clause' is also included stating that 'the company undertakes not to introduce the use of new technology and the association agrees not to undertake any form of industrial action until the procedures embodied in this agreement and the procedural agreement have been fully exhausted'.

paid to the issues surrounding implementation. This chapter has attempted to explore these issues, highlighting those issues which are felt to be significant for office automation. The sociotechnical systems approach using participation has been advocated as the most appropriate vehicle for successful office automation implementation. In addition to the STS approach, Appendix B (adapted from the UK Department of Employment's Work Research Unit's (1981) report on new information technology) provides a checklist of key questions to ask when implementing office automation.

REFERENCES

Adams, C. (1975) 'How management users view information systems', *Decision Sciences*, **6**.

Alter, S. (1980) *Decision Support Systems: Current Practice and Continuing Challenges*, Addison-Wesley, Reading.

Bardach, E. (1977) *The Implementation Game*, MIT Press, Cambridge.

Bariff, M., and Galbraith, J. (1978) 'Intra-organizational power considerations for designing information systems', *Accounting, Organizations and Society*, **3**, No. 1.

Bate, P., and Mangham, I. (1981) *Exploring Participation*, J. Wiley and Sons, Chichester.

Bjorn-Andersen, N., and Hedberg, B. (1977) 'Designing information systems in an organizational perspective', in *Prescriptive Models of Organization* (Eds. P. Nystrom and W. Starbuck), TIMS Studies in the Management Sciences, Vol. 5.

Bjorn-Andersen, N., and Pedersen, P. (1980) 'Computer facilitated changes in the management power structure', *Accounting, Organizations and Society*, **4**, No. 2.

Blumberg, P. (1969) *Industrial Democracy*, Schocken Books, New York.

Bostrom, R. (1980) 'A sociotechnical perspective on MIS implementation', Paper presented at ORSA/TIMS National Conference, Colorado Springs, November.

Bostrom, R., and Heinen, S. (1977) 'MIS problems and failures: a sociotechnical perspective — Parts I and II, *MIS Quarterly*, September and December.

Cherns, A. (1976) 'The principles of sociotechnical design', *Human Relations*, **29**, No.8.

Child, J. (1977) *Organization: A Guide to Problems and Practice*, Harper and Row Publishers, London.

Conrath, D., and du Roure, G. (1978) 'Organizational implications of comprehensive communication — information systems: some conjectures', Working paper, Institute d'Administration des Enterprises Centre d'Etude et de Recherche sur les Organizations et la Gestion, Aix-en-Provence.

Croisdale, D. (1982) Contribution to Seminar on Participative Methods, Civil Service College, London.

De Maio, A., Bartezzaghi, E., and Zanarini, G. (1979) 'A new systems analysis method based on the STS approach', in *Formal Models and Technical Tools for Information System Design* (Ed. H. Schneider), North-Holland, Amsterdam.

Demb, A. (1979) *Computer Systems for Human Systems*, Pergamon Press, London.

Dickson, G., and Simmons, J. (1970) 'The behavioural side of MIS: some aspects of the "people problem"', *Business Horizons*, August.

Eason, K. (1977) 'Human relationships and user involvement in systems design', *Computer Management*, May.

Edstrom, A. (1977) 'User influence and the success of MIS projects', *Human Relations*, **30**, No.7.

Emery, F. (1959) 'Characteristics of sociotechnical systems', Tavistock Report No.657.

Eveland, J. (1977) *Implementation of Innovation in Organizations: A Process Approach*, Ph.D. thesis, University of Michigan.

Feeney, W., and Sladek, F. (1977) 'The systems analyst as a change agent', *Datamation*, November.

Fried, L. (1972) 'Hostility in organization change', *Journal of Systems Management*, June.

Ginzberg, E., and Reilley, E. (1957) *Effecting Change in Large Organizations*, Columbia University Press, New York.

Ginzberg, M. (1978) 'Steps toward more effective implementation of MS and MIS', *Interfaces*, **13**.

Ginzberg, M. (1979) 'A study of the implementation process', *TIMS Studies in Management Science*, **13**.

Ginzberg, M. (1981) 'A prescriptive model of system implementation', *Systems, Objectives, Solutions*, **1**, No.1, January.

Gordon, I., Lewis, J., and Young, K. (1977) 'Perspectives on policy analysis', *Public Administration Bulletin*, **25**, December.

Guest, D., and Knight, K. (1979) *Putting Participation into Practice*, Gower Press, Aldershot.

Hedberg, B. (1975) 'Computer systems to support industrial democracy', in *Human Choice and Computers* (Eds. E. Mumford and H. Sackman), North-Holland, Amsterdam.

Hedberg, B. (1980) 'Using computerized information systems to design better organizations and jobs', in *The Human Side of Information Processing* (Ed. N. Bjorn-Andersen), North-Holland, Amsterdam.

Hirschheim, R. (1983) 'Assessing participative systems design: some conclusions from an exploratory study', *Information and Management*, **6**.

Hirschheim, R. (1985) 'An analysis of participative systems design: user experiences, evaluation and recommendations', LSE working paper, January.

Hirschheim, R., Land, F., and Smithson, S. (1984) 'Implementing computer-based information systems in organizations: issues and strategies', *Proceedings of INTERACT '84 Conference*, London, September.

Hoyer, R. (1980) 'User participation — why is development so slow?', in *The Information System* (Eds. H. Lucas, F. Land, T. Lincoln, and K. Supper), North-Holland, Amsterdam.

Keen, P. (1981) 'Information systems and organizational change', *Communications of the ACM*, **24**, No.1, January.

Keen, P., and Gerson, E. (1977) 'The politics of software design', *Datamation*, November.

Kling, R. (1977) 'The organizational context of user-centred software designs', *MIS Quarterly*, December.

Kohl, R., Benedict, G., and Gerardi, R. (1981) 'Can America increase productivity to compete with foreign competition?', *Management Science*, **27**, No. 12, December.

Kolb, D., and Frohman, A. (1970) 'An organizational development approach to consulting', *Sloan Management Review*, **12**, No. 1, Fall.

Kolf, F., and Oppelland, H. (1979) 'A design oriented approach in implementation research: the project PORGI', in *Design and Implementation of Computer-Based Information Systems* (Eds. N. Szyperski and E. Groschla), Sijthoff and Noordhoff, Amsterdam.

Koopmans, P., and Drenth, P. (1981) 'Conditions for successful participation', *LODJ*, **2**, No.4.

Kraft, P., (1979) 'Challenging the Mumford democrats at Derby works', *Computing*, 2 August.

Land, F. (1982) 'Notes on participation', *The Computer Journal*, **25**.

Land, F., and Hirschheim, R. (1983) 'Participative systems design: rationale, tools and techniques', *Journal of Applied Systems Analysis*, **10**.

Land, F., Mumford, E., and Hawgood, J. (1979). 'Training the systems analyst of the 1980s: four new design tools to assist the design process', *Man–Machine Communication*, Infotech State of the Art Report, July.

Lawrence, P. (1968) 'How to deal with resistance to change', *Harvard Business Review*, January–February.

Leavitt, H. (1965) 'Applied organizational change in industry', in *Handbook of Organizations* (Ed. J. March), Rand McNally, Chicago.

Lucas, H. (1973) *Computer-Based Information Systems in Organizations*, Science Research Associates, Chicago.

Lucas, H. (1975) *Why Information Systems Fail*, Columbia University Press, New York.

Lucas, H. (1981) *Implementation: The Key to Successful Information Systems*, Columbia University Press, New York.

Lucas, H. (1982) *Information Systems Concepts for Management*, 2nd ed., McGraw-Hill, New York.

Machiavelli, N. (1514) *The Prince*, Penguin, London, 1961 (originally published in 1514).

Markus, M. L. (1981) 'Implementation politics — top management support and user involvement', *Sytems, Objectives, Solutions*, **1**, No. 4.

Markus, M. L. (1983) 'Power, politics and MIS implementation', *Communications of the ACM*, **26**, No. 6, June.

Morgan, H., and Soden, J. (1973) 'Understanding MIS failures', *Database*, **5**, Nos. 2,3,4, Winter.

Mowshowitz, A. (1976) *The Conquest of Will: Information Processing in Human Affairs*, Addison-Wesley, Reading.

Mumford, E. (1973) 'Job satisfaction: a major objective for the system design process, *Management Informatics*, **2**, No.4.

Mumford, E. (1974) 'Computer systems and work design: problems of philosophy and vision', *Personal Review*, **3**, No.2, Spring.

Mumford, E. (1981) 'Participative systems design: structure and method', *Systems, Objectives, Solutions*, **1**, No.1, January.

Mumford, E. (1982) Paper presented at the working meeting of WG8.2, Copenhagen, April.

Mumford, E. (1983) *Designing Human Systems*, Manchester Business School Publications, Manchester.

Mumford, E., and Banks, O. (1967) *The Computer and the Clerk*, Routledge and Kegan Paul, Henley.

Mumford, E., Land, F., and Hawgood, J. (1978) 'A participative approach to the design of computer systems', *Impact of Science on Society*, **28**, No.3.

Mumford, E., and Weir, M. (1979) *Computer Systems in Work Design — the ETHICS Method*, Associated Business Press, London.

Owens, K. (1981) 'An on-line concept of implementation', *Systems, Objectives, Solutions*, **1**, No.2, April.

Pava, C. (1983) *Managing New Office Technology: An Organizational Strategy*, Free Press, New York.

Pettigrew, A. (1973) *The Politics of Organizational Decision Making*, Tavistock Publications, London.

Pressman, J., and Wildavsky, A. (1973) *Implementation*, University of California Press, Berkeley.

Sackman, H. (1971) *Mass Information Utilities and Social Surveillance*, Auerbach, New York.

Schewe, C., Wieck, J., and Dann, R. (1977) 'Marketing the MIS', *Information and Management*, **1**, No.1, November.

Schmitt, J., and Kozar, K. (1978) 'Management's role in information system development failures: a case study', *MIS Quarterly*, June.

Sethi, N. (1970) 'A research model to study the environmental factors in management', *Management International Journal*, **10**.

Sherman, B. (1980) 'Word processors are human too', *Office Automation*, Infotech State of the Art Report.

Sanders, D. (1974) *Computers and Management: In a Changing Society*, 2nd ed., McGraw-

Hill, New York.

Taylor, F. W. (1947) *Scientific Management*, Harper and Row Publishers, New York, (originally published in 1911).

Taylor, J. (1978) 'Studies in participative sociotechnical work systems analysis and design', Centre for Quality of Working Life, UCLA, CQWL–WP–78–1–A, November.

Tideswell, M. (1981) 'Who's afraid of the microchip?', British Institute of Management, Managers Guide No.3.

Trist, E. (1953) 'Some observations on the machine face as a sociotechnical system', Tavistock Report, London.

Trist, E., and Bamforth, K. (1951) 'Some social and psychological consequences of the Longwall method of goal getting', *Human Relations*, **4**.

Uhlig, R., Farber, D., and Bair, J. (1979) *The Office of the Future*, North-Holland, Amsterdam.

Work Research Unit (1981) 'Introducing new technology into the office', WRU Occasional Paper 20, October.

Chapter 6

IMPLICATIONS OF OFFICE AUTOMATION

INTRODUCTION

Because of the newness of office automation, there is not a great deal of empirical evidence by which to judge what the likely effects will be. That which does exist tends to be contradictory or can be interpreted in many different ways. There are additional problems with attempting to come to grips with the implications of office automation. Firstly, there is the problem of separating office automation from computing; i.e. is there a difference between the effects caused by the introduction of computers and that of office automation? Secondly, how are such effects measured? Anecdotes and case histories are common, but they often lack the rigour and empirical grounding of laboratory and survey studies. Moreover, measuring impact is an extremely tricky business; it can never be proved that a particular cause (e.g. the introduction of a computer) has a particular effect (e.g. an increase in productivity). Was it the introduction of the computer that had that effect or something else (cf. the Hawthorne effect)? Thirdly, much of the literature which does exist on the implications of office automation can be summarized as either one-off case studies which report on the effects in a specific instance or impressionistic reviews which adopt a particular focus. The latter normally promulgate either a favourable or unfavourable view of office automation. There are few reviews which attempt to cover the broad spectrum of office automation impact. Fourth, 'implications' frameworks are rare, nor are they grounded in any epistemological sense. Kling's (1980) 'systems rationalism vs. segmented institutionalism' framework is one laudable exception. Here Kling notes six different perspectives which can be used to analyse the effects of computing: rational, structural, human relations, interactionist, organizational politics, and class politics. But even Kling neglects the epistemological and ontological stances each of these perspectives implicitly adopts.

Although these problems exist, it is felt that some meaningful treatment of office automation impact is still possible. Such a treatment will unfortunately blur the distinction between computing and office automation effects in some cases, but where this occurs, an attempt will be made to alert the reader. Additionally, the studies cited vary in terms of their empirical validity; some are little more than anecdotes, others are based on elaborate laboratory experiments.

The literature on office automation impact can be divided along two dimensions: *methodological base* and *specificity*. *Methodological base* refers to the underlying research method used to elicit impact, and can be partitioned into two categories: empirical (in the sense that it is guided by experience and observation) and non-empirical. The latter tend to be impressionistic reports on how office automation is likely to affect individuals and organizations; the former are more quantitative studies (employing questionnaires, laboratory experiments, and the like) reporting on the implications of one or more applications or technologies. *Specificity* refers to whether a study is specific to one particular application or technology, or covers a broad spectrum. The former are those studies which look at impact in terms of how a specific office automation technology or application has affected a particular environment, e.g. individual, organization, or society; the latter are those reports which are aspecific. They are usually reviews which look at impact across a wide spectrum of office automation applications/technologies.

These dimensions are really complimentary and can be mapped onto one another to produce a framework which permits the office automation impact literature to be classified. Figure 6.1 depicts this diagrammatically.

It can be noted that there are few studies that are of an empirical base and review in nature. This is unfortunate as there is a need to know what the overall implications of office automation are likely to be. It in fact provides the *raison d'être* for this chapter.

	METHODOLOGICAL BASE	
	EMPIRICAL	NON-EMPIRICAL
SPECIFIC		
* Application	Edwards, 1977; Leduc, 1979; Christie, 1981; Hiltz and Turoff, 1981; Zuboff, 1981	Carlisle, 1976; Rule *et al.*, 1980a; Jones, 1982; Brandt, 1983, Rank Xerox, 1983
* Technology	O'Neal, 1976; MSC, 1982	Kelly, 1979; Arnold, 1980; Blackey, 1980; Downing, 1980; Sherman, 1980
SPECIFITY		
ASPECIFIC	Olson and Lucas, 1982	Matteis, 1979; Evans, 1979; Forester, 1980; Toffler, 1980; Abraham, 1981; Martin, 1981; Gregory and Nussbaum, 1982; Poppel, 1982; Burns, 1984

FIGURE 6.1 Office automation implications framework

THE DEVELOPMENTAL VIEW OF OFFICE AUTOMATION

As is the case with many new technological developments: database systems, local area networks, etc., office automation can be conceived as a revolutionary or evolutionary development. The revolutionary/evolutionary argument attempts to portray the development of a technology in an historical context.

Revolutionary technologies are thought to emerge somewhat randomly and are radically different from what existed in the past. They are often thought to provide unique opportunities which were not possible previously. It is not surprising, therefore, that revolutionary technologies are considered to possess the potential for dramatic individual, organizational, and societal consequences.

Evolutionary technologies, on the other hand, are thought to develop in a sequential manner and are direct descendants of some previous technology. They are non-random and are similar to that which previously existed. Evolutionary technologies usually perform similar functions to their predecessors but with greater effectiveness. Their anticipated organizational and societal impact is considered to be far less than their revolutionary counterparts.

Database technology is a good example of a technology which can be thought of as either revolutionary or evolutionary. For writers such as Nolan (1973) and Scott (1976), databases were thought to be the revolutionary development in data management which would free data from application programs, i.e. the provision of data independence. Managers would finally be able to obtain the data they need for *ad hoc* decision making when they needed it. Fry and Sibley (1976) had a different view. They described database technology as an evolutionary development of the data management community which would make data management more efficient and effective. Fry and Sibley would no doubt scoff at the revolutionary view which sees database technology more in terms of a panacea for data management. The point is that technologies which are viewed in a revolutionary light usually cause expectations (and concomitantly fears) to be heightened. It is therefore likely that any technology thought of as revolutionary will have a greater impact than if viewed as evolutionary. It could be expected that the revolutionary view might sensitize the users to the impact or changes brought about (or perceived to be brought about) by the technology and thus lead to a magnified impact. That is, a revolutionary view will cause a negative impact, e.g. deskilled jobs, or a positive impact, e.g. increased job satisfaction, to be more visible and perceived as greater.

It is important to note that the importance of the revolution/evolution argument lies in people's expectations. It is not so much the actual technology which causes a particular impact, rather it is an individual's perception of the impact which is important. Technologies which are promoted as revolutionary will likely give rise to consequences which are perceived to be more extreme than if promoted as evolutionary. Even if a technology, seen as revolutionary, has little organizational impact, its end result might be dramatic. This could come about because of negative feelings towards the technology caused by raised expectations which were unfulfilled.

The revolution/evolution dichotomy is a potentially useful consideration when attempting to assess the organizational and societal consequences of a particular technology. But it is not necessarily complete. There is something of a third alternative which is neither evolutionary nor revolutionary but is more of a combination of the two. It might be termed 'evolutionary-revolution' or 'random-convergence'. This alternative suggests that a particular technology — in this case office automation — is not the homogeneous product implied in the revolution/evolution argument. Rather, office automation is a heterogeneous technology emerging in a random and disparate fashion. Because it is so heterogeneous, its consequences are hard to predict (see the following case study).

'Random-convergence' is not a notion tied strictly to information technology. In an interesting case study Emery and Trist (1965) recounted the history of one organization where seemingly random events occurring over time converged to cause the organization serious problems. Emery and Trist discussed this phenomenon in terms of 'environmental connectedness' but this is very similar to the notion of 'random-convergence'.

The case study centred on a post-war British canned food company whose major product was tinned vegetables. The company planned to expand its operation by building a modern automated factory at the cost of several billion pounds. The company had commanded a lion share of the market (65 per cent) and saw no reason why this would change. Before the factory could even be completed, a series of apparently detached and random events overtook the planned future of the company. When all the factors converged together they made the modern factory totally uneconomic and unnecessary. The order of events was as follows. Due to the ending of wartime controls on steel strip and tin, a number of new small canning firms emerged. Their main product was imported fruit. At first, there appeared to be no conflict with the expanding vegetable canning company. However, in an effort to keep their machinery and labour employed in the off-season, the small fruit canners looked for other alternatives. The United States quick-frozen food industry provided an answer. Much of the US vegetable crop was unsuitable for the frozen food industry but could be used in canning. Since the American farmers had been selling these crops cheaply as animal feed, they were happy and eager to sell them to the new small British canners at a higher price. This mutually advantageous agreement allowed the new canners to undercut the large vegetable canning company. Further, underdeveloped countries exacerbated the vegetable canner's problem by offering to sell their crops to the small canners more cheaply.

Concomitant with the company's problem in the supply market were problems in its product market. Whereas previously a high-quality tinned vegetable product held the top of the market, the quick-frozen products were beginning to supplant this dominance. Because of post-war affluence, frozen vegetables took over the high-quality end of the market leaving the tinned foods with the middle and lower ends. Further, the lower end of the market was quickly absorbed by the smaller canners. The introduction in Britain of the supermarket and chain store posed a new and devastating complication for the vegetable canning company. The supermarket, wanting to enhance their image and increase their share of the tinned vegetable market, sought to establish low-priced house brands. Prior to the war, the house brands accounted for less than 1 per cent of the market; this rose to 50 per cent after the war. Much of the growth was at the expense of the large vegetable canners.

All of the aforementioned events combined to make the consequences of building the new factory deleterious. The company's management had failed to appreciate that a number of seemingly random events were converging to overtake their reasons for planned expansion. The company tried desperately to protect its old market share — and the new factory — without success. 'Random-convergence' had taken its toll.

The point is that technologies which are thought to develop in a 'random-convergence' manner bring with them the realization that predicting consequences, future developments, and the like are extremely tricky — some say impossible — propositions. Further, a more balanced view of the technological innovation is required. The view lies somewhere in between the two extremes 'revolution' and 'evolution' and therefore might lead to a view of impact which is not as extreme as the revolutionary nor as conservative as the evolutionary one.

A conjecture is that technologies such as office automation really *do* develop in a 'random-convergence' fashion, making the prediction of impact problematic. Organizations — particularly the proponents/opponents of the technology (to gather support for their position) — attempt to portray the technology in a revolutionary light. This evokes a counterbalancing response which contends that the technology is evolutionary. Alternatively, the organization adopts a conservative stance, viewing the technology as evolutionary and thereby evoking cries from individuals holding different views asserting the technology is revolutionary. And so the unhappy and unresolvable argument of evolution versus revolution is perpetuated.

In sum, the developmental view of the technology — office automation in this case — has an important bearing on its impact. Revolutionary technologies are thought to produce more dramatic individual, societal, and organizational consequences than evolutionary technologies. Moreover, this section has stressed that it is not whether a given technology *is* revolutionary or evolutionary but how it is *perceived*. Perceptions cause expectations to rise or fall, make the technological change more or less visible, and so on. Thus, whether office automation is perceived to be revolutionary, evolutionary, or a 'random-convergence' development will dictate — to some degree — the nature and extent of its impact.

ALTERNATIVE VIEWS OF OFFICE AUTOMATION IMPACT

Although much has been written about office automation and its likely effects, a considerable portion of it is little more than hype or unfounded speculation. That which is of a more substantial nature, and the subject of this chapter, can be said to reflect one of three alternative positions on impact: optimism, pessimism, and pluralism. These positions represent broad viewpoints about the nature of change and its effects on individuals, organizations, and society. They reflect, to some degree, an underlying value position about technological change — its rightness or wrongness — and how society might or should deal with it. The values are not manifest but intrinsic to the view held. Individuals may not even be aware that the view they hold has a particular value position.

The optimist position asserts that the new information technology will increase the productivity of both managers and staff, create at least as many jobs as it destroys, increase organizational effectiveness, and create exciting new varieties of work. Communication will be enhanced, the quality of working life will improve with fewer menial tasks and more leisure, and medical facilities, television, mail delivery, home life, travel, and education will all be improved through the use of new information technology.

The pessimist position contends that office automation will do little to increase office productivity as most jobs are too unstructured to automate. There is a belief that it will create widespread unemployment, that the remaining work will be deskilled, yielding less job satisfaction, and that the general quality of working life will be deleteriously affected. The technology will also lead to a further centralization of power and a lessening of personal privacy and freedom.

The pluralist or relativist position is neither optimistic nor pessimistic, but a compromise between the two. It proposes that there are possibilities created by office automation which are positive or negative depending on the way the technology is put to use. The pluralist, therefore, is concerned with the development of criteria for social and technological acceptance and the application of 'acceptable' technologies in appropriate circumstances. He does not believe technology is a *fait accompli*.

These three alternative positions on impact are somewhat overstated and oversimplified; they are really generalizations or archetypes. Although they appear distinct from one another, this distinction is sometimes blurred; reality is always more complex. Opinions on impact occasionally cross from one position to another or are not adequately described by any of the three views. Nevertheless, as the following section shows, the views do have a strong theoretical base. Moreover, as a means of summarizing and categorizing fundamental stances on impact, they provide a useful basis by which to explore the organizational and social consequences of office automation.

THEORETICAL PERSPECTIVES OF THE ALTERNATIVE VIEWS

1. Philosophical Roots

Although the three views on office automation impact are fairly apparent, they are rooted in philosophical tradition, which adds substance to the beliefs they hold. For example, each makes certain *epistemological* and *ontological assumptions* within the context of a particular *analytical framework* which leads to the adoption of a specific *scientific paradigm*. No view or position on impact can avoid making philosophical assumptions since, fundamentally, it involves a process of inquiry, which itself is a scientific endeavour. *Ontological assumptions* are concerned with the nature of the world around us — in particular, the 'slice' of reality the researcher chooses to address. There are two basic ontological positions: realism and nominalism. Realism postulates that the universe is comprised of objectively given, immutable objects and structures. These exist as empirical entities, on their own, independent of the observer's appreciation of them. In contrast, nominalism holds that reality is a subjective construction of the mind. Socially transmitted concepts and names direct how reality is perceived and structured; reality therefore varies with different languages and cultures. What is subjectively experienced as an objective reality exists only in the observer's mind.

Epistemological assumptions are concerned with the nature of knowledge and how it is acquired. There are two principal positions: positivism and antipositivism. The former approaches inquiry by concentrating on the explanation and prediction of observable phenomena through the identification of Humean causal relationships. This scientific endeavour searches for causal laws which are presumed to govern the observed sequence of events. It espouses the notion of the unity of science; i.e. the adopted inquiry process is deemed valid for both the natural and social world. A number of variations to and extensions of this view have been proposed, e.g. naive realism, critical rationalism, and logical positivism. Empiricism is often equated with positivism. Antipositivism, on the other hand, denies the appropriateness of the causal model for understanding social or human action except for physiological responses. It holds the belief that when a scientist applies concepts to a particular domain of inquiry, he intrinsically depends on some socially preconditioned understanding of his action. Knowledge about the domain of inquiry can only be improved through the application of the point of view of the individuals who are directly involved in those activities which are to be studied. Knowledge, therefore, is relative to the historical frame of reference of the scientist and the participants. Whatever method of inquiry the scientist tries to use, the results must be understood from the subjective vantage point of the insider rather than from the interpretation of objective measurements taken by some outsider. This leads to an epistemological outlook which questions the existence of objective knowledge.

It is possible to map the epistemological dimensions together to yield four possible scientific paradigms: realist/positivist, realist/antipositivist, nominalist/positivist, and nominalist/antipositivist. These four paradigms have more contemporary names: realist/positivist — functionalism; realist/antipositivist — symbolic interactionalism (or action frame of reference); nominalist/positivist — abstracted empiricism; and nominalist/antipositivist — interpretivism. It should be noted that these four paradigms are not as clear-cut as implied by the above discussion. Rather they are archetypes which exhibit certain characteristics. For example, functionalism and interpretivism are reasonably well-developed schools of thought, although clearly antithetical to one another. The distinction between symbolic interactionalism and abstracted empiricism, however, is a fine one and reflects a much less developed and defined area. Burrell and Morgan (1979) note that the symbolic interactionalist 'views man as living with an essentially "realist" world of symbolic and physical objects' yet 'adopts a more subjectivist position (of inquiry)'. The abstracted empiricist, on the other hand, uses 'a highly nomothetic (empirical) methodology to test a theory which is based upon an ontology ... and a theory of human nature of a more subjectivist kind' (Burrell and Morgan, 1979). Although there can be seen a conceptual difference between the two schools of thought, the practical difference is less clear, as they are both alternatives to — provide something of a middle ground between — the two extreme positions. In fact, the dimensions of epistemology and ontology are really continuums. At one extreme the realist/positivist position, at the other lies the nominalist/antipositivist. Burrell and Morgan (1979) refer to the former as objectivism, the latter as subjectivism. They provide the analytical framework through which knowledge is acquired. Figure 6.2 attempts to depict this diagrammatically.

The scientific paradigms discussed above all hold views about knowledge and its acquisition. For the functionalist, true knowledge is obtained through the application of the scientific method. The functionalist's position is based on four pillars: (a) the belief in the unity of the scientific (hypothetical-deductive) method; (b) the search for causal relationships; (c) the belief in empiricism, i.e. that experience of the senses is the only source of knowledge; and (d) that science (or its process) is value-free. Knowledge, for the functionalist, has an air of certainty about it — only apodictic knowledge is strived for. The interpretivist, on the other hand, rejects all four pillars and searches instead for assertoric knowledge as he does not believe in the notion of infallible knowledge. For the interpretivist, knowledge is conditional: it is a communal achievement and is relative to time and space. Knowledge is thus a matter of community acceptance and agreement. The scientific method used to acquire knowledge is

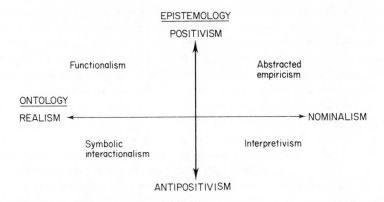

FIGURE 6.2 Scientific paradigms for knowledge acquisition

also a matter of communal agreement and has more to do with a creative search to understand better than the application of some well-used quantitative technique. For the abstracted empiricist and symbolic interactionalist, knowledge and its acquisition is less clear. They tend to see alternatives to the two extreme positions yet realize the merits and shortcomings of both. Their approaches are somewhat of a compromise, providing alternatives which they contend are more appropriate for the acquisition of human knowledge.

The means by which knowledge is acquired is of direct relevance to the view held on office automation impact. That is, beliefs about the likely effects arise from the interpretation of and desire for certain types of information. Those holding an optimistic view of office automation tend to be technologically minded and motivated, and perceive knowledge acquisition within the context of the 'scientific method'. This seems to reflect the technological imperative which the optimist believes in. The optimist, exhibiting a strong predilection towards technology, naturally adopts a functionalist scientific paradigm since this reflects the ethos of the technologist. The history of technological thought drives the optimist's education and enculturation process such that he believes in the notion of a single method of scientific inquiry, i.e. the unity of the scientific method ('scientism' according to Klein and Lyytinen, 1984). For further details see Boguslaw (1965), Mowshowitz (1976), Weizenbaum (1976), Kraft (1977), and Cooley (1980). Moreover, the optimist notes that technology is intrinsically neutral; its analogue in the adopted scientific paradigm is that science is value-free.

Those adopting a pessimistic view of office automation impact not only differ in terms of what they expect the effects to be but also in how such knowledge can be acquired. The pessimist often questions the validity of the 'scientific method', wondering whether this approach can lead to a 'real' understanding of human and mental phenomena. This concern is shared by many contemporary social scientists; see, for example, Berger and Luckmann (1966), Glaser and Strauss (1967), Burrell and Morgan (1979), Van Maanen (1979), Halfpenny (1979), and Clegg and Dunkerley (1980). The pessimist worries that the realist/positivist method of inquiry treats the human as just another research subject, no different from an inanimate object even though human beings possess properties completely different from other objects, e.g. free-will. The writings of the classic antipositivist philosophers support the pessimist's concern as they contend that the acquisition of knowledge about humans requires a different scientific approach. For the pessimist, the use of the 'scientific method' to obtain knowledge on human phenomena would likely lead to the distortion of truth. Yet the pessimist notes that this is precisely what technologically minded researchers do. This gives rise to what Horkheimer (1947) called 'instrumental reason', which is the analytical and logical reasoning process used to acquire knowledge and solve problems. Leavitt (1964) notes that it is built on 'a kind of faith in the ultimate victory of better problem solutions over less good ones ... a pre-Freudian fixation on rationality' (quoted in Bjorn-Andersen and Eason, 1980). Their intentions may be good, but history, the educational system, and the enculturation process all lead to a blinding of the implications of their research and the limitations of their adopted scientific approach. Often they are even unaware that alternative scientific paradigms exist and that their own paradigm has serious philosophical flaws. It is therefore not surprising that the pessimist tends to opt for an alternative scientific paradigm, one which is antithetical to the optimist's. The one most likely to be chosen is that of interpretivism since this puts human understanding at the heart of its scientific inquiry process. Moreover, interpretivism postulates that technology is not neutral. (It should be noted that the pessimist's line of reasoning is also based on historical grounds and may draw heavily on the writings of Marx; cf. Braverman, 1974.)[1]

For the office automation pluralist, the issue of knowledge acquisition and the appropriate scientific paradigm is less clear. The pluralist, in general, recognizes the weaknesses of the hypothetical-deductive method for obtaining knowledge about the human (social) world and therefore leans more towards subjectivist approaches. Often the scientific paradigm adopted is that of

---

1. It must be noted that this conjecture is somewhat at odds with the position adopted in Burrell and Morgan (1979) who posit that radical or dialectic materialism embraces a more objectivist view of knowledge acquisition. The view adopted here is that while Marxists often do use objectivist methods of knowledge acquisition, they need not do. It is not uncommon for them to switch between objectivism and subjectivism depending on the issue at hand. In other words, the choice of the knowledge acquisition approach varies with circumstances (although the dominant form is indeed objectivism). Additionally, it must also be pointed out that pessimists need not be Marxists. In fact, the arguments raised by the pessimists, while consistent with general radical materialist writings, are not driven by them. The arguments quite naturally emerge when a more interpretivist approach to knowledge acquisition is adopted.

symbolic interactionalism, or the action frame of reference. The approach taken normally reflects a desire to use some compromise to the two main alternatives. The pluralist is aware of the historical and cultural reasons behind the optimist's adherence to functionalism and the pessimist's use of interpretivism. The hope of the pluralist is to transcend them and provide a fresh alternative which is based more on the contextual factors of acquiring human knowledge than on historical arguments.

It must be stated that the link between the office automation impact view and scientific paradigm is neither as clear-cut nor as strong as the above discussion might imply. Pessimists do not always embrace interpretivism nor optimists functionalism. Pluralists usually favour more subjectivist paradigms but this is not always the case. The link is a conceptual one, based partly on historical grounds and partly on practical implementation. Certain scientific paradigms lend themselves to certain arguments and points of view. The point to the argument is simply that the views on impact have a philosophical base.

2. Pragmatic Roots

In addition to the philosophical underpinnings of the three alternative views, there is a pragmatic aspect which is useful to consider. That is, an essential criterion for determining the value of the views lies in the practical consequences they bring about. To better understand what these consequences might be, it is important to look at how the views perceive, interpret, and treat the two underlying components of impact: technology and man. It is possible to describe their approach to impact in terms of *root metaphors* — one for technology, one for man. (The concept of root metaphor is taken from Pepper, 1942; however, its use here is somewhat more limited.) For the optimist, the root metaphors are: technology as a tool, man as craftsman. Technology is thought to be a tool in the hands of the workers. It is used when and where appropriate, to make their work more efficient, and to raise the quality of life in general. The tool is of itself neutral and can be used in many ways. Man is looked upon as a craftsman who scans the surroundings, choosing the most appropriate tools for the task at hand. The craftsman is skilled and can therefore apply the tools to advantage. Should the tools be unsatisfactory, the craftsman can modify them or choose not to use them. Through time, the tasks that the craftsman performs are likely to become more sophisticated; he then comes to rely on new and better tools for help. The development of new tools often drives the development of new skills and crafts. The relationship between craftsman and tool is that of master–slave.

For the pessimist, the root metaphors are: technology as governor or controlling device, man as machine. Technology is the controlling device used to govern the operation of some task(s). It is used to regulate the flow of work regardless of changes in power, fuel, etc. For the governor to work properly, the tasks have to be highly structured so that all possible variances can be responded to. The governor is applied to a machine which performs activities in a structured and routinized way. Machines are built (trained) to engage in certain tasks and are provided with the appropriate fuels and materials. When machines wear out, they are discarded and usually replaced by more modern and better ones. Machines are incapable of thought, only action. They cannot suggest improvements in the types of activities to be performed nor how they are carried out. They are under the control of the governor which regulates what they can and cannot do. The governor is not neutral in that it is set by those who are ultimately in control. The relationship between machine and governor is also master–slave, except that in this case it is technology which is the master while man is relegated to the role of slave.

The pluralist adopts the root metaphors: technology as malleable agent, man as gatekeeper or controlling agent. Technology is the malleable agent or raw material which is chosen and then moulded into a usable resource. It has little value on its own but takes on significance once it is applied to the appropriate task. The controlling agent or gatekeeper decides what types, how much, and when to use the malleable agent. The gatekeeper uses his experience, based on the collective knowledge of the community, to make these decisions and sometimes has to make hard choices and thus seeks the advice of the community, which often sets the criteria for judging the malleable agent which is to be applied. The malleable agent may or may not be neutral. Since the gatekeeper can decide which materials to let through, those which are non-neutral can be kept out. Unlike the other two sets of metaphors, the relationship between gatekeeper and malleable agent is more symbiotic. They coexist and can be said to be mutually beneficial to one another.

Table 6.1 summarizes how the three alternative views relate to one another along the philosophical and pragmatic dimensions discussed above. Included in

TABLE 6.1 *Comparison of the optimist, pessimist, and pluralist views*

	OPTIMIST	PLURALIST	PESSIMIST
ONTOLOGY	Realism ◄──────────────► Nominalism		
EPISTEMOLOGY	Positivism ◄──────────────► Antipositivism		
SCIENTIFIC PARADIGM	Functionalism ◄──────────────► Interpretivism		
ANALYTICAL FRAMEWORK	Objectivism ◄──────────────► Subjectivism		
ROOT METAPHOR			
*Technology as:	Tool	Malleable agent	Controller
*Man as:	Craftsman	Gatekeeper	Machine
Kling equivalent	Rationalist	Human relations/ interactionist	Class politics

the table is an attempt at relating Kling's (1980) 'theoretical perspectives' with the views proposed here.

3. Additional Underlying Differences

As can be seen from above, the optimist, pessimist, and pluralist all hold irreconcilably different beliefs not only about the consequence of office automation but also such fundamental notions as man, technology, knowledge, and its acquisition. There are, however, a number of other underlying differences which are worth noting.

Politics

To the optimist, office automation (and new technology in general) is essentially apolitical. There are no intrinsic properties which make it political or ideological by nature. It could be used for political advantage but that is not the technology's fault; it is fundamentally neutral. To the pessimist, nothing could be further from the truth. Technology in and of itself is political, since it is simply another instrument by which those in charge maintain or increase their control over the workers. It is designed, developed, and paid for with that specific intention in mind. The pluralist does not necessarily agree that the technology is intrinsically non-neutral yet worries about its political use. Technology does have to be treated in a political way and therefore only those technologies which are widely accepted as 'appropriate' or applied in 'appropriate circumstances' should be adopted.

There is an important relationship between politics, societal values, and the acquisition of knowledge which has been recognized by a number of social scientists. That is, how and what knowledge is acquired has a direct bearing on political practice. Fay (1975), for example, notes that scientific inquiry and political practice are inextricably linked. He contends that it is naive to think knowledge can be separated from what it is used for. Since the relationship between knowledge and the scientific inquiry process by which it is discovered is a strong and important one, it is imperative that societal values be in-built and explicit within the adopted paradigm. This argument is well developed in the literature on critical social theory: Habermas (1973, 1974), McCarthy (1982), and Lyytinen and Klein (1984). For further details see Feyerabend (1978) and Apel (1980). The fundamental point of the argument is that so-called 'value-free' scientific paradigms are not really value-free and therefore it is critical to provide an opportunity for deciding what the values should be. Habermas calls for the discussion of the values to occur in a 'rational discourse' where all affected parties participate equally, without external domination. By assuming that technology and science are essentially apolitical and value-free, the optimist presents a dangerously naive view according to the pessimist and pluralist.

Volition

The role of volition is another interesting difference between the office automation impact views. The optimist holds the view that new technologies like office automation offer unique opportunities which should be exploited. They are, more often than not, chance developments which somehow surface, are spotted by key organizational actors, and then applied to perceived organizational problems. Volition has apparently little to do with this view as technology is either noted or not. Once spotted, the choice is usually not whether to adopt a given technology, but how it can be most effectively applied. Similarly, the pessimist's position also has little volition. As the technology is developed, it is immediately adopted since it facilitates the furthering of rationality and control. There is little discussion about which technologies to embrace as those in charge (the elite) see them as desirable vehicles for pushing their own agendas, which either deliberately or coincidentally work against the interests of the workers. The pluralist's view, however, is strongly volitional. Since technology is seen as raw material which has to be moulded into shape to be used, individuals can choose: (a) if they wish to use the material and (b), if so, how they wish to mould it. In this case it is the community which chooses. Provided a list of acceptable or appropriate criteria is established by which to judge the technologies, then only those which are deemed 'appropriate' would be adopted.

Technology Development

Technologies such as office automation develop in some particular fashion and are applied to organizational problems. Where such developments come from is not generally questioned. For the optimist, technological growth is a mixed bag of evolutionary and revolutionary developments. They are often seen as 'lucky breaks' which should be used to the best of the organizations' abilities since the competitors will invariably adopt the new technology and potentially gain advantage. The pessimist, on the other hand, does not see the technological developments as random events. Instead, they are planned, well thought out occurrences. There is no mystery in where the technology comes from nor how it will be put to use. Should a random technological development occur which could be beneficial to the workers, the elite will find some way to modify it to suit their ends. For the pluralist, technological developments arise in an *ad hoc* way and are therefore hard to predict or know how to use to the best advantage. Moreover, technologies such as office automation are not the homogeneous product or concept which most think; rather they are much more heterogeneous and have emerged in a largely random, disparate fashion. This is the notion of 'random convergence' as discussed earlier.

A somewhat related concept to that of 'random convergence' was proposed by Simon (1977) who noted that instead of new technologies arising in response to particular organizational needs or problems, they can be viewed as potential problem solutions waiting for some adherent to find the relevant problem to apply them to. Simon refers to this as 'problemistic search'. The usual result is the application of some technology to an unclearly specified set of problems. The consequences are also unclear although it is not unusual to find the technology being little used, particularly in those environments where the end user has a choice of whether or not to use the technology.

SURVEY OF THE IMPLICATIONS

1. The Optimist Position

> The fact is that the industrialized world has already reached the point where it can no longer survive without using computers .... (They) have not arrived on the scene for aesthetic reasons, but because they are essential to the survival of a computer society ... (just as) food, clothing, housing, education and health services (Evans, 1979).

> Faced with the dilemmas of our age, it is imperative that we employ benevolent technologies to tackle our problems and build a better world .... It is technology that has created these dilemmas, and yet the only way out of the dilemmas is more technology (Martin, 1981).

Quotes such as the two above epitomize the optimist position. Technology is believed to be the only way forward in an increasingly dynamic and unstable environment. The argument is simple. The more dynamic, uncertain the environment, the more information an organization needs (Galbraith, 1973). The more information it needs, the more processing it has to do, and the more processing an organization has to do, the more it needs some form of assistance. This assistance, the optimist asserts, must be technology.

This line of reasoning is sometimes referred to as 'the technological imperative' and has many followers. The argument has a certain elegance in its simplicity and there is considerable evidence to support it. The following areas are where the optimist sees office automation as having beneficial and important effects.

Productivity

Office productivity is one of the key areas of organizational concern. As was discussed in Chapter 2, this is perhaps the primary impetus behind office automation and arises from the perception that office workers' productivity is low relative to their factory counterparts.

In general, office productivity is discussed in terms of two broad categories of office workers: principals and non-principals. Principals refer to those occupations which are managerial or professional (e.g. doctors and lawyers) in nature. Non-principals are those jobs which are secretarial or clerical in nature:

(a) Non-principal office workers
Office automation is thought to have a dramatic impact on the productivity of the non-principal office worker, primarily because the nature of this work is relatively structured. Since a considerable portion of the non-principal's activities involve typing, technologies such as word processing should prove valuable. This argument is fairly strongly supported by the available experience. For example, the British Insurance Company Willis, Faber and Dumas, have reported productivity increases in terms of 'key rates' in the order of 50 per cent in the early stages of word processing introduction rising to 90 per cent within two and a half years (Kelly, 1979). The Illinois' National Bank of Springfield, Illinois, announced typing productivity had increased by 340 per cent while turnaround time decreased by 75 per cent due to word processing (O'Neal, 1976). Other reports on word processing suggest a similar trend on improvements in productivity, but many do not attempt to quantify these improvements. This is succinctly expressed in a recent UK Manpower Services Commission Report on 'Organizations and their staff':

> Whilst, overall, it was recognized that productivity had increased as a result of the introduction of WP, hard measurements were difficult to obtain .... The majority ... had experienced some improvement in productivity but few could quantify the increase they had achieved (MSC, 1982).

(b) Principal office workers
The optimist position contends the major advantage of office automation will likely be the major improvements in the principals' productivity. Given that the principals' share of office costs is roughly 73 per cent (according to Booz, Allen and Hamilton), productivity gains here could make a substantial difference to the organization.

Unfortunately, there has not been a great deal of empirical research done on this area, partly because of the newness of the technology and partly because measuring productivity improvements is extremely difficult. In fact, even putting into operation the notion of principal productivity is problematic (cf. Sutton and Kaye, 1983). There do, however, exist a few studies which report increases in productivity. Curley (1984) summarizes seven case examples where office principal's productivity increased. A well-known Booz, Allen and Hamilton study (reported in US Comptroller General, 1984) notes that productivity improvements in the order of 15 per cent could be obtained, based on their study of fifteen organizations. Edwards (1978), analysing data collected on the use of a computer-based messaging system (NLS), reports a significant increase in productivity. Wainright and Francis (1984) purport similar findings based on their study of four organizations.

Moreover, numerous conceptual arguments exist which support the contention that office automation will lead to an increase in the principal office workers' productivity.

Abraham (1981), as noted in Chapter 2, sees productivity improving because office automation leads to:

(1) Fewer transfers of control over work
(2) Fewer media transformations
(3) Decreased travel
(4) Decreased formal meetings
(5) Decreased interruptions and better control over events
(6) Decreased number of telephone calls
(7) Elimination of many unproductive functions, e.g. searching for incorrectly filed documents
(8) More effective and timely communication

Uhlig, Farber, and Bair (1979) suggest that because office automation can replace or augment present tasks, a savings of 2 hours 45 minutes per working day can be obtained. This could lead to a 35 per cent increase in the principal's productivity. Similar points of view have been expressed by Carlisle (1976), Burns (1977), Bair (1978), Haider (1979), Price (1979), Poppel (1982), and Strassman (1982).

Employment

The issue of employment — particularly how it is affected by new technology — is a topical and controversial one given the current world-wide problem of rising unemployment. The optimist position contends that the application of technology has never reduced overall employment in the long run so the same should be expected with the new technology. The supportive arguments for this contention are varied. Four of the more popular ones are summarized below:

(a) For those who believe history is the best indicator of what will happen in the future, the past has shown that technological introduction has not led to a lessening of overall employment. The types of jobs have changed, however, with a substantial shift to service sector employment.
(b) Technology creates improved productivity which leads to an eventual increase in demand for labour (cf. Simon, 1980).
(c) In a turbulent environment — such as the one we now live in — organizations need to process much more information than before. Technology will facilitate the processing of this information but there will be an increasing need for more and better skilled people to help process and make use of the information for the organizations.

(d) Although technology will displace people from certain jobs, it will give rise to a myriad of new occupations which are directly related to the new technology. (See, for example, Vyssotsky, 1980, who expects two new organizational careers arising from office automation: 'methods and procedures' and 'data administration'.)

The view that office automation (and new information technology in general) will not lead to a reduction of employment is held by numerous individuals, cf. Sleigh *et al* (1979), and there is some supportive evidence as well. In an early OECD report on 'Manpower aspects of automation and technical change' (OECD, 1966) it was stated that there was an average 8 per cent increase in the total number of office employees following the introduction of new office technology and systems in the United Kingdom. Similarly, Pearl Assurance Company (*Computertalk*, 1978) reported that they employ more staff with a word processing centre than they did in the past with the conventional typing pool. Further, in a number of instances the introduction of new office technology had no effect on overall office employment (cf. Kelly, 1979; and MSC, 1982).

The optimist position on the effect of office automation on employment is summarized by John Kendrick, Chief Economist of the US Department of Commerce, in his statement:

> There is a significant positive correlation between industry rates of change in productivity and in output. ... Thus, despite temporary problems of labour displacement, it would appear that technologically progressive industries create more jobs on net balance than the backward industries which are more vulnerable to dynamic change (Robinson, 1980).

Work

The possibilities of new working arrangements, new varieties of work, and the like, brought about by office automation are very great indeed. To the optimist, these possibilities look attractive. For one, office automation can relieve the drudgery of performing many menial and repetitive tasks. For another, it provides the ability for remote office work. Further, office automation should provide the office worker with better control over what he does and when he does it. Each of these is explored in more detail.

(a) Relief from drudgery
Many of the tasks performed by office workers — particularly the non-principals — are routine, repetitive, and menial, i.e. boring. Dialling telephone numbers, writing standard letters, correcting typing errors, trying to reach someone by telephone, and filing are all examples of such tasks. New office technology, according to the optimist, would do away with these menial operations in that they would be performed (or at least facilitated) by the

technology. This would then free up the time of the office worker to engage in more intellectually stimulating activities.

(b) Remote office work
One of the more unhappy consequences of our society is commuting. People travel great distances every day to get to work as most offices are located in the inner core of our cities while most employees live in the suburban areas. Thus a tremendous amount of time, effort, and money (not to mention stress) is associated with getting people from home to the geographic place where they work (the office). Remote office work possibilities provided by office automation, therefore, would seem to possess considerable appeal.

Olson (1981) lists four types of remote work options:

(1) *Satellite work centres.* This is where relatively self-contained organizational divisions are physically relocated away from the inner core of the city to a more remote site. Employees of these divisions would also be relocated so that they would live within a convenient commuting distance to their work. The satellite work centre would be large enough to provide the necessary social interaction required by workers while maintaining some form of hierarchical structure to support adequate management.

(2) *Neighbourhood work centres.* This is structurally similar to the satellite work centre in that employees go to their local centres to work. The difference, however, is that the neighbourhood work centre is not structured along divisional or organizational boundaries; in fact, there is (relatively speaking) no specific structure. Neighbourhood centres are set up in populated areas and employees from one or more different organizations travel to their nearest centre to work. In addition to the savings associated with freedom from commuting, the neighbourhood centre also provides economies associated with the shared use of office equipment and services, e.g., facsimile, LANs, printers, and teleconferencing. Because of its structure, employee supervision is more difficult than in satellite work centres. Moreover, it is more complex to set up because of the cooperation needed among a number of organizations.

(3) *Flexible work arrangements.* These are arrangements which provide employees with flexibility in the scheduling and location of their work. It is more based perhaps on the realization that an individual's personal and family needs require accommodation in a work arrangement rather than on any new technology. Flexi-time and job sharing are two types of flexible work arrangements. Additionally, there is a growing trend towards occasional alternative work arrangements, particularly for principal office workers. These are arrangements whereby people stay at home to perform important activities, such as the writing of reports, to get away from the normal office distractions. It is likely that with office automation these kinds of arrange-

ments will surge as employees will be encouraged to take computer terminals and microcomputers home with them at nights or over weekends.

(4) *Work at home.* This is the most extreme case of the remote office work options, where employees work at home on a regular basis. It could range from one day a week to virtually full-time. Work at home provides maximum flexibility but offers little in the way of social interaction.

(c) Better control over work

One of the great problems associated with office work is the general lack of control the worker has over outside interruptions — telephone calls, unscheduled meetings, and the like. These distractions make work more dynamic than many would like. With office automation many of the random events can be controlled, thereby leading to a more stable environment. For example, with electronic mail, messages can be held until an appropriate time when they can then be read and responded to. Travel, with all inherent uncertainties, can be minimized through the use of teleconferencing. Additionally, as the number of media transformations associated with production of a document decreases so, too, the chance of delay.

Many of the means by which an office worker can gain better control of his work probably existed before office automation. For example, one way to stop telephone interruptions is not to answer the phone! Nevertheless, the advent of office automation has largely been responsible for people paying more attention to the need for better control over office work.

Support for the optimist position on work is considerable. Reports on new types of work arrangements brought about — or facilitated — by office automation abound (cf. Matteis, 1979; Olson, 1981; Rank Xerox, 1983). Yet much of it is anecdotal in nature. Little empirical evidence exists upon which to corroborate the notion that work will improve. Nevertheless, as the arguments suggest the potential for improved work and work arrangements is apparent, then office automation should be embraced on the basis that work will improve as long as it is carefully considered in any office automation strategy.

Communication

One of the primary functions of the office is that of communication. People working in offices spend a considerable portion of their time exchanging information with one another. (Datapro, 1981, reports that managers spend over 75 per cent of their time in oral communication.) Therefore, any means by which communication can be improved is desirable. To the optimist, office automation provides such a means for enhanced communication. In particular, new office systems and technology provide a number of opportunities which appear quite attractive.

(a) More communication

Technologies such as teleconferencing, audioconferencing, electronic message systems, and the like, offer the opportunity of greater intra- and interorganizational information exchange. Tele- and audioconferencing allow communication between individuals who are geographically dispersed. Instead of one group having to travel to the site of another, they can all remain in their respective locations and communicate with one another via the conferencing facility. This not only saves time and money but offers the opportunity of greater frequency of meetings and the concomitant increase in information exchange. Electronic message systems and electronic mail provide for a similar increase in communication in that they permit non-simultaneous communication to take place. Studies have shown that over 50 per cent of business telephone calls involve one-way communication such as calls to distribute or request information. This kind of communication does not require simultaneous contact and would seem to be precisely where electronic message systems are of value. Moreover, much of the simultaneous communication people engage in is of the 'social etiquette' variety which is ostensibly non-productive. Electronic message system proponents also argue that a much greater proportion of office communication could be done just as effectively in a non-simultaneous mode, meaning a higher proportion of time could be spent communicating with more people. These systems also provide the capability of sending a particular message to a variety of sources; so instead of the telephone where a message is delivered to one person, an electronic message can be sent to many people inside and outside the organization.

(b) More thoughtful communication

One of the potential drawbacks of telephone conversation is the lack of time a person has to respond to queries. A question is asked and the responder must say something within a few seconds. Quite often individuals are compelled to respond at that moment with some statement even though they are not sure they are saying the 'right' thing; in retrospect, they may have regretted what they said. This is the nature of simultaneous communication and many people find it difficult, particularly in an argumentative situation. Take, for example, a public relations clerk who has to deal with complaints. The clerk is under constant pressure in a face-to-face or telephone complaint because he has to respond in real-time — there is little time to think and he runs the risk of saying something at the spur of the moment which he may regret later. Politicians being interviewed face the same pressure. In simultaneous communication stress and strain can be heightened and researchers have noted that this form of communication favours the individual who is articulate, quick thinking, and better educated (generally speaking).

Non-simultaneous communication provides a more open environment for all in that people are not required to respond immediately to a query. They can take their time and think about what it is they want to say. This could very well lead to communication which is more accurate. Moreover, they can choose when they want to respond. This could facilitate more thoughtful communication and lessen the inherent advantages of people who are quick thinkers, articulate, etc.

(c) Greater community feeling

Leading on from the advantages of non-simultaneous communication discussed above, people given the opportunity to think before they respond may very well be willing to enter into more organizational discussions. This may be particularly true in those cases where individuals wanted to participate more actively in organizational decisions but were too timid because they felt they were not articulate enough. Electronic message systems might be considered a technology which promotes better organizational dialogue and thus leads to a greater sense of organizational unity.

Conferencing systems could also lead to a greater community feeling in that more organizational members could be involved in a meeting through the use of this technology. Instead of having to travel to some distant site, the individuals could take part in a meeting through the conferencing system. It has the effect of drawing geographically dispersed sites closer together, resulting in a greater awareness of the rest of the organization and more community spirit.

(d) Written record of all communication

One of the often-mentioned drawbacks of voice communication (unless it is recorded) is the lack of any record of what was actually said. Telephone conversations can be particularly irksome. One person remembers one aspect of the conversation but not another while someone else is just the reverse. Considerable misunderstanding often occurs in simultaneous communication and there is no record of what was said. Further, people forget. What might have been perfectly clear when a conversation takes place becomes vague or forgotten a short time later. Because of these concerns, individuals sometimes write letters or memos to keep a written record of what is to be communicated. But these take time to be received by the recipient and usually there is no record that the message was received. Electronic message systems offer the capability of storing copies of all messages sent and received. Thus, fewer misunderstandings are likely to occur, leading to an overall improvement in organizational communication. Further, the potential of a stored record of all messages could lead to: (1) more thought being given before any communication is initiated and (2) the exclusion of meaningless or redundant information being sent.

(e) Reduction of paper

The use of conferencing and electronic message systems provides the potential for reduced paper flow both in and out of the organization. Instead of individuals writing letters, memos, and reports which need to be typed, proofread, photocopied, and then distributed, office technology allows the information to be stored and transmitted electronically without the need for paper. Given the astronomical amounts of paper produced every working day in offices (10 million miles of paper according to *Computing*, 1980), any reduction would be welcomed.

(f) Greater people accessibility
Electronic communication has the potential of providing greater access to people. With conferencing systems it is possible to communicate with individuals who might normally be too difficult to communicate with because of distance. Electronic message systems allow a subordinate who might be too timid to contact a superior using a simultaneous communications means to communicate with the superior through electronic means. Electronic message systems also provide access to a greater number of people than through other means. *EDP Analyzer* (1978) reports an interesting case where they were able to communicate with an individual even though he was out of town when they rang his office. Instead of the usual next-day response, they were able to communicate with him in two hours. His secretary had entered a message into his file stating *EDP Analyzer* had rung. Although he was a number of time zones away, he apparently checked his file with a portable terminal, noted the message, and rang back *EDP Analyzer*. The benefits are particularly clear when the desired communication is to take place over a number of time zones, e.g. between London and San Francisco.

The optimist has considerable support for his view that communication will be enhanced through office automation. A number of studies have reported improved information exchange through the use of electronic message and mail systems. See, for example, Edwards (1977, 1978), Bair (1978), *EDP Analyzer* (1978), Leduc (1979), Hiltz and Turoff (1978, 1981), Conrath *et al.*, (1981), and Trauth, Kwan, and Barber (1984).

Quality of Working Life

Somewhat related to all of the above areas is the notion of quality of working life (QWL). This is a broad concept which most people speak rather loosely about. It is loosely spoken about because QWL is difficult to define. Although related to job satisfaction it is not synonymous with it. Dyer and Hoffenberg (1975) state:

> The phrase 'quality of working life' invokes a sympathetic response among many, but consensus has not yet developed on a definition of the problem that is implied. Thus those who attempt to improve the quality of working life are grappling with

an ill-defined problem that occurs in the context of complex systems, and no generally accepted basis exists for the evaluation of their efforts.

Nevertheless, this has not stopped people from discussing QWL issues and, particularly, how QWL is affected by new technology. In general, the quality of working life can be thought to include a number of criteria. Walton (1975) lists eight such criteria.

(a) Adequate and fair compensation. As a major impetus to work is to earn a living, compensation in the form of salary must be felt to be 'adequate' as determined by societal standards and 'fair' in relation to pay received for other work.
(b) Safe and healthy working conditions. Workers should not be exposed to physical working conditions and/or working times that are unduly hazardous or detrimental to their health.
(c) Immediate opportunity to use and develop human capacities. Workers should have jobs which enable them to use and develop their skills and knowledge, have some degree of autonomy and control over their work, and are challenging.
(d) Opportunity for continued growth and security. Workers should have jobs which can lead to career advancements. This would involve jobs which allow workers to expand their capabilities, have the potential to apply new skills and knowledge in future work assignments, provide for advancement opportunities, and offer employment security.
(e) Social integration in the work organization. Workers need to have a positive self-image in their workplace. This would include freedom from prejudice, upward mobility possibilities, supportive work groups, interpersonal openness, and a sense of community with others in the organization.
(f) Constitutionalism in the work organization. Workers should have the right to privacy, free speech, equitable treatment in all matters, and due process.
(g) Work and the total life space. Workers should not have jobs which cause serious negative consequences on other spheres of their lives. There must be a balance between work schedules, career demands and travel requirements, and the workers' total life space.
(h) Social relevance of work life. Workers should feel that their work is socially relevant and acceptable — that it fills some social need. Moreover, workers should be able to believe their organizations are socially responsible in terms of, for example, waste disposal, marketing techniques, employment practices, and so on.

As can be seen from above, the quality of working life concept is a rather grand one, capable of being discussed at a broad level but problematic on a more detailed level. It is perhaps, therefore, not surprising that most tend to operationalize the QWL concept in terms of job satisfaction. The rationale is straightforward: the better the QWL climate the greater the employees' job satisfaction. Thus, although job satisfaction is not equal to quality of working life it is, nevertheless, a reasonable surrogate. The optimist sees office automation as providing the opportunity for a better quality of working life and a commensurate increase in job satisfaction. Office automation can increase task variety and skill requirements as well as improve job feedback, which may lead to higher perceived status and greater job satisfaction (Olson and Lucas, 1982). Moreover, the optimist would argue that office automation leads to improvements in most, if not all, of the eight criteria described above. For example:

(a) Improved compensation in terms of higher salaries
(b) Better working conditions in that work can be undertaken in a variety of places, e.g. at home, during travel
(c) Better control over their work and greater autonomy
(d) Improved prospects for career advancements and the opportunity to learn many new desirable skills
(e) Greater community spirit (discussed above) through the use of electronic message systems and conferencing sytems
(f) Greater chance for constitutionalism in the work organization through a better sharing of information
(g) Improved total life space through better control
(h) No negative effect on the social relevance of work life

Although the optimist's position with respect to quality of working life is logically consistent, the supportive empirical evidence is not very great. The UK Manpower Services Commission study on text processing (MSC, 1982) is one of the few studies reporting improved job satisfaction and interest due to office automation. However, see Edwards (1978), Attewell and Rule (1984), and Wainright and Francis (1984) for additional empirical support. Other supportive evidence tends to manifest itself in terms of anecdotes and inference or implication, cf. White (1977), Matteis (1979), and Simons (1981). The optimist might no doubt point to the fact that there have been few studies which have addressed the issue of quality of working life on job satisfaction and thus it should not be surprising there is little supportive empirical evidence.

Society

Society, in this context, is meant to connote the broad spectrum of additional areas (outside the organization) where office automation — or more generally new technology — is likely to have a positive impact. The optimist sees the new technology as providing a far better quality of life for virtually everyone in society. Technology, the optimist contends, can enhance the operation of most, if not all, societal operations. And there are good reasons for the optimists' beliefs, as will be summarized below. It is therefore not surprising that there is a rich and abundant literature base for the optimist. See, for example, the writings of Evans (1979), Dertouzos and Moses (1980), Forester (1980), Toffler (1980), Burns (1981), and Martin (1981).

The optimist notes that office automation, and new technology in general, will have the following societal effects.

(a) Education

Education will play a more influential role in society than ever before. This is because as the environment changes at an increasing rate, traditional skills and knowledge will become dated and irrelevant very quickly. Individuals will need to update their knowledge and learn new skills rapidly. Education, therefore, will have to be continuous and perpetual; it will be a life-long activity. The strain this will place on our present educational system will be considerable and there will be a need to improve our education abilities — particularly in the areas of retraining and refresher courses. Technology is seen as the answer.

Television is conceived of as part of the solution in that educational material can be broadcast over the existing television network. This is precisely what is done in Britain via the Open University, which provides the means for millions of people to get an education while sitting at home. Television is also used in industry and at home for the playing of training material pre-recorded on videotape or videodisk.

This is sometimes referred to as 'distance learning' and provides individuals with the ability to learn while being geographically distant from the instructor.

Computer-assisted instruction (CAI) is another development which could help mitigate society's educational problem. It uses a computer to support instruction. The computer assumes the role of the instructor, presenting material, answering queries, and testing the person's knowledge of the material covered. CAI is interactive providing the student with an environment which is conducive to learning. CAI software is becoming relatively inexpensive and its availability on popular microcomputers means that it is within the reach of many families.

Other educational developments based on new technology such as interactive television, interactive videodisks, home terminals with access to view data systems, and the like, will allow the education industry to flourish and thus meet the needs of today's and tomorrow's society.

(b) Health and medical care

Medical care could change dramatically due to new technological developments: in particular, telecommunications links between doctors and patients who are geographically apart, computer diagnosis, and access to medical records and specialized medical databases.

Martin (1981) presents an interesting example of health care provided to patients who are geographically separate from the doctors. It was based on an experiment conducted between Boston's Logan Airport and the Massachusetts General Hospital. Doctors at the hospital were provided with a telecommunications link to Logan Airport. Persons taken ill at the airport went to the airport's medical station where they were tended to by the resident nurse in combination (when necessary) with doctors at the Massachusetts General Hospital. The doctors were in contact with the airport via a telecommunications link which provided visual and audio communications. The experiment proved the viability of this kind of arrangement where a doctor need not always be present for health care. For remote communities and small towns away from medical facilities, remote health care such as that provided at Logan Airport would appear to offer a better standard of medical care for the entire population.

Computer diagnosis also promises to provide improved medical care in that computers could have access to a far greater variety of information than possessed by a physician. Medical expert systems have already proven themselves as capable diagnosticians because they possess the 'knowledge' of experts who acquired their knowledge over many years of practising medicine. Although the computer diagnosis system may never replace the physician, its value as an aid in medical diagnosis is unquestionable. It is likely that these kinds of systems will lead to improved medical diagnosis and thus raise the overall quality of health care.

Computer-based medical systems can improve medical care through their ability to immediately access a patient's complete medical history. At present, patients may have multiple sets of medical records, due to moving from one city to another, none of which is complete, making diagnosis more difficult. With a computer-based system access to complete patient records (either from a centralized store or through some form of distributed patient records) becomes more likely. Additionally, these kinds of systems may permit access to specialized databases on drugs, illnesses, other patient records, etc., which may also enhance health care.

New technology is already being heavily used to aid the handicapped and new uses are being developed daily. There are, for example, devices for the blind which read text and produce audio output, 'intelligent' wheelchairs with robotic capabilities, and various appliances which are voice activated.

(c) Home

The home is likely to be the place where the greatest changes will occur. Much of this is due to the fact that the home market is an enormous one with hundreds of millions of homes in the industrialized world. Thus, considerable effort is being (and will continue to be) exerted in developing new and existing products for the home. It has been suggested by numerous authors that virtually no aspect of traditional home life will escape the effect of new technology. This would include: home banking and shopping, computer games, security, world-wide news access, environmental control, 'intelligent' washers, refrigerators, and the like. (See Martin, 1981, pp. 124–127, for an impressive list of likely services in the home provided by technological developments.)

Davis and McCormack (1979), quoted in Burns (1981), offer the following optimistic scenario of the futuristic home:

> Houses will contain sensors built into walls, roofs, furnaces and pipes. These sensors will, in turn, be hooked in to the home's computers. Any leak, any potential problem in wiring or heating will be instantly relayed to the home's computer that will, in turn, notify you of the need for repairs or maintenance. The automatic fire alarm will sound at almost the instant smoke is detected, and the automatic phone hook-up will simultaneously notify police and fire departments.
>
> The home computer system will probably be used to turn lights, appliances and entertainment equipment on and off at set times. Your computer, for example, can control your tv cassette recorder, allowing you to watch 'The Tonight Show' at eight in the morning. Do you like coffee when you first get up? The computer will turn on the coffee pot, wake you up, and run your bathwater. If you enjoy games, your home computer will provide a partner for chess, a dealer for blackjack, or a wheel for roulette.
>
> Burglaries probably will plague society in the future, as they do now, but your home computer system will be connected to sensors placed in windowsills, doors and other likely points where an intruder could enter your home. Even if the burglar alarm system were disarmed, it is possible to set up a fail-safe second line of defense. Equipment exists to create an electronic field and to sense any disturbance of that field. By simply moving in the house, the burglar would trigger the alarm. Your system will sound a signal, dial the police, turn on the lights, and play a recorded tape of vicious-sounding Doberman Pinscher barks and growls.
>
> This same system might be set to turn on your oven, defrost your refrigerator, and water your plants. It might remind you, too, of maintenance tasks only you can perform, such as changing your storm windows or raking leaves.

It should be noted that the optimist sees the development of these new home products which provide comfort, excitement, safety, efficiency, etc., as extremely beneficial as a considerable proportion of a person's time is spent at home and indications are that this proportion is rising. This is particularly important given that office automation permits the worker to spend more time at home.

(d) The media

Both television and newspapers are experiencing considerable upheaval due to the new technology, and the implications for society are likely to be profound. The development of cable television, viewdata, pay television, interactive television, and special applications like video dating present interesting possibilities for the future. Cable television provides the cable subscriber with interference-free reception leading to sharp, clear television pictures and more pleasurable viewing. Viewdata merges telephone technology with televisions, providing subscribers with access to extensive databanks containing a variety of information, e.g. news, weather, stock market data, etc. Pay television provides subscribers with special programs which are not normally available on the standard networks, e.g. first-run full-length feature movies, reporting events, and the like. Pay television subscribers normally pay a monthly fee for the privilege of receiving these special programs. Interactive television possesses the capability of two-way communication between the viewer and the sender. Both viewers and sender are usually hooked together on a closed-circuit network which allows simultaneous two-way speech and video communication. Interactive television is particularly valuable for educational uses.

Special applications such as video dating offer intriguing opportunities. Here, prospective clients are videotaped. Information about themselves and their preferences are fed into a computer and once a 'match' is found, the 'matched couple' is instructed to watch a video transmission. Applications such as these are usually run on a cable television network.

Newspapers are also experiencing changes. It is now technically possible to produce a particular newspaper, e.g. the *New York Times*, at any place in the world. So instead of a one- or two-day delay in reading the *New York Times* in, say, Singapore, it could be available (theoretically) in Singapore before the newsagents in New York received their copies. Another change surrounds the availability of information retrieval systems. A number of newspapers have their own information retrieval systems which allow information searches on any topic. Abstracts of all news stories are stored on the computer. When a search is desired, keywords are entered and the abstracts searched for a match. Many of these information retrieval systems are not tied strictly to just one newspaper, rather they contain abstracts and reports from a number of important newspapers and magazines. A third possible change is the prospect of sending the news electronically to a person's home and having it printed out on a home printer. This could save the newspaper companies large sums of money as two-thirds of their expenses are attributable to newsprint, production, and distribution.

To the optimist, the technology promises to improve the quality and effectiveness of the media. Both television and the newspaper industry should find the prospects exciting and the results satisfying.

There are a number of other areas where the optimist sees office automation and new technology making a large, beneficial impact. Electronic funds transfer systems will gradually relieve society of the need to have and carry cash around to buy goods. Electronic mail is a fast and efficient means of communicating with someone and its cost will be less than the cost of first class post. Travel will be reduced as more work can be done outside the formal office, and, as was discussed above, conferencing systems can also lessen the amount of travel. As Martin (1981) contends, 'the wired society' will have at its disposal world television, world news, multiple cultures, global corporations, and world-wide communication. The new technology will provide a vast array of exciting options for society which can only barely be contemplated at present.

Summing up, the optimist sees office automation, and new technology in general, as providing a better world. Productivity will increase, employment will rise (or at least not fall), new and interesting varieties of work will emerge, comunication will improve, the overall quality of working life will be enhanced, and society at large will experience a better quality of life. Burns (1981) captures the optimist's position cogently:

> The basis of this optimistic view is that if change is inevitable, as appears to be the case, then there is no reason why it should not be for the better.
> As people in an information society gain more knowledge they will have greater control over their own lives and more freedom from the state. But to get the most from this technical revolution, attitudes must change and quickly; society must be sufficiently adaptable so that this image of a golden future will be realized. In particular, the wealth created through widespread use of efficient microelectronic based machinery and services must pass to the population at large, who will then buy the goods and use the services necessary to sustain the economy. A truly brave new world is ahead.

2. The Pessimist Position

> Computerization has to be considered as a process intimately linked to the conditions of economic stagnation and crisis. It is a strategy management uses to react to unfavourable conditions in the environment of business organizations. In a social system which is based on the exploitation of living human labour this strategy produces over-whelming negative consequences for the working class. (Briefs, 1980).

> The remarkable development of machinery becomes, for most of the working population, the source not of freedom but enslavement, and not of broadening the horizons of labour but the confinements of the worker within a blind round of servile duties (Braverman, 1974).

Quotations such as these epitomize the pessimist position. Information technology is seen as the latest in an unending stream of tools and techniques which are used to maintain — indeed improve — control over the working class. The pessimist worries about the inevitability of the technology — that it is a *fait accompli*, that technology only benefits the privileged sector of society. Because few people really know anything about the technology, there can be little influence exerted by the population at large about its use. Further, the pessimist anguishes over how society will be able to cope with the inherent cultural upheaval associated with rapid technological development and use. As can be expected, the pessimist has antithetical views from the optimist on how office automation will affect individuals, organizations, and society.

Productivity

Although the pessimist would agree with the optimist that productivity is an important organizational concern, he or she would tend to disagree with how it is likely to be affected by office automation. Whereas the optimist feels fairly confident that productivity would increase, the pessimist thinks otherwise. (This is true for both principal and non-principal office workers.) The arguments for the pessimist's position are many and varied. A particularly important one is the underlying assumption about office workers. The optimist points to the low level of productivity growth experienced by the office worker over the past decade and cites this as a primary reason for office automation. The pessimist, on the other hand, would be more cautious. He or she might contend that if office workers were fairly productive ten years ago, then it would be incorrect to expect any great rise in productivity from them. So although there is agreement about the importance of productivity, there may be disagreement about whether office workers are a relatively productive or unproductive lot. The pessimist also holds different views on the impact of office automation on non-principal and principal office workers.

(a) Non-principal office workers

Because the tasks performed by the non-principal worker are thought to be more or less structured in nature, it has been widely thought that office automation would lead to increased productivity. The pessimist argues this notion is too simplistic. For one, it is highly likely that the presumed structured tasks are much less deterministic than most assume. Research by Mintzberg (1973), Stewart (1971a), and others points to the fact that managers' jobs are inordinately unstructured (see the next section on principal office workers). As they are unstructured they are not deterministic, and thus incapable of being automated. Moreover, according to Hammer and Sirbu (1980) the research on managerial work is germane to non-principal office workers as well. Their research shows office activities are distributed both in terms of space and time, are constantly changing, and are highly interactive. That is, they are hard to predict. Therefore, the job of the non-principal is more unstructured than the optimist contends and thus less amenable to automation. Additionally, there are studies which report decreases in non-principals' productivity due to office technology; e.g. Goldfield (1978) who noted a drop in productivity due to word processing (see also Walton and Vittori, 1983).

For another, the pessimist would contend that even if certain parts of the non-principal's job are structured and could be supported by technology, the resultant consequences are dysfunctional, in terms of job deskilling, unemployment, etc. (more on these later). These dysfunctional consequences would not only more than offset any productivity gains accrued, but could likely rebound on productivity such that in the long term productivity would actually decline (through high absenteeism, poor quality of work, etc.).

Additionally, there is a concern about the deleterious consequences which could arise out of trying to structure activities and jobs which are in fact unstructured. See, for example, Burke and George (1979) and Land and Kennedy-McGregor (1981) who describe the dysfunctional consequences which can occur when there is an attempt to formalize informal procedures through computerization. (See, also, the discussion on bureaucratic rationalism which follows later in the chapter.)

(b) Principal office workers

It is widely recognized that the activities performed by principal office workers are not particularly structured. However, beyond this recognition, the optimist and pessimist differ markedly. The optimist sees office automation as supporting or augmenting the tasks of the principal. Those tasks, or portions of tasks, which are deterministic could be automated, with the resultant increase in productivity. The pessimist sees this view as at best a waste of time and at worst, dangerous. The pessimist contends the nature of the principal's work is inherently unstructured. So much so that attempts to automate particular aspects of work would meet with failure. There are two reasons for this contention: (1) the work is so unstructured that it is not amenable to automation — not even in parts — and (2) any attempt at formalizing (attempting to put structure on) informal activities would be met with either passive or active resistance. (This latter point was briefly discussed above.)

Mintzberg (1973) provides convincing evidence to support the first point. In a comprehensive study on the nature of managerial work, he found six primary characteristics of the manager's job:

(1) Much work is done at an unrelenting pace. The manager is constantly active with little time for pause and reflection.

(2) Work is characterized by brevity, variety, and fragmentation. The manager does not normally follow a task from start to finish; rather he performs a number of activities in parallel and there is considerable variety in what he does.

(3) Preference for live action. Given the choice, managers will opt for face-to-face or verbal communication rather than written communication.

(4) A communication node. Managers are the nerve centre of the organization; information passes to them and they direct and redirect it as they see fit.

(5) Preference for verbal communication. Managers virtually always prefer communication to be verbal rather than written. This allows communication to be in real-time and more powerful with less effort.

(6) Blend of rites and duties. Much of the manager's job involves ceremonial activities which are intrinsically unstructured in nature.

Similar results are reported by Stewart (1971a), regarding management in general, and Hammer and Sirbu (1980), in relation to office activities. Thus, the pessimist wonders whether office automation can really have much of an impact given the highly unstructured nature of the principal's work. Moreover, the pessimist worries about attempts to take the unstructured tasks and turn them into more structured ones. This has a tendency to cause goal displacement, blinkered problem definitions, difficulty in adapting to a changing environment, and so on. (These will be discussed in more detail in the section on bureaucratic rationalism.)

In sum, the pessimist feels office automation will likely have, at best, no effect on the principal's job, but at worst, serious dysfunctional consequences brought about by individuals resisting any attempt at formalizing processes and procedures which are informally handled. Similar concerns are voiced about the impact on the non-principal's job.

Employment

> If religion was the opium of the masses then work is the castor-oil of the population (Jenkins and Sherman, 1979).

This topical and polemical issue causes the pessimist great concern, for he sees unemployment providing potentially cataclysmic consequences. For the pessimist, work — particularly in the form of a formal job — is an endemic part of our culture. When people are asked what they are, they typically respond in terms of their occupation — a student, a dentist, a housewife, etc. Take away work and the individual loses part of his identity. Unemployment is a traumatic experience, one which perhaps only those who have been unemployed can fully comprehend. The stigma, sense of failure, loss of identity associated with being unemployed all contribute to the great concern the pessimist attaches to new technology. For the pessimist, office automation (and new technology in general) will categorically lead to greater unemployment. It is this loss of employment which frightens the pessimist. Large-scale unemployment, which many feel will occur due to new technology, would have a destabilizing effect on society and could lead to massive social unrest. Mike Cooley (1979), past president of the white collar trade union TASS, said:

> We expect that many of the big electrical companies will reduce their total employment by up to thirty per cent in the early 1980s, even though their total production may be double what it is now. It may improve the profit for the corporations but it's going to cause massive problems in this country.

Similar concerns have been expressed by numerous individuals. Stonier (1980) has suggested that by early next century, only 10 per cent of today's labour force will be required to provide for all of society's material needs. Professor Crossman of Oxford University was reported to have stated:

> There seems little doubt that unemployment due to automation will grow steadily over the next few decades, perhaps centuries, and in the end it is likely to reach a very high figure, say ninety per cent of the labour force, unless radical changes are made in the present pattern of work (Sadler, 1980).

Numerous studies from all over the world performed over the past few years offer similarly gloomy employment forecasts. Siemens (1978) suggests that 40 per cent of office jobs in Germany could be lost by 1990 due to new technology. Nora and Minc (1980) report that there is likely to be a 30 per cent reduction in banking and insurance jobs in France in the next ten years. Barron and Curnow (1979) state unemployment in the United Kingdom will rise to 10 to 20 per cent over the next fifteen years, mainly through the loss of secretarial, typing, clerical, and managerial jobs. Jenkins and Sherman (1979) predict a 30 per cent displacement of information processing jobs by 1990. Virgo (1979) asserts that 40 per cent of clerical and administrative jobs could be lost in the 1980s. Similar predictions exist for most of the countries of the industrialized world.

Empirical support for the position that office automation leads to a reduction in employment is considerable; see, for example, APEX (1979), Markoff and Stewart (1979), Downing (1980), McMahon (1980), Craig (1981), and PSI (1983). In fact, there is considerably more evidence to suggest that the new technology displaces more jobs than it creates — at least in the short term.

Work

Whereas the optimist sees the work opportunities brought about by office automation as positive, the pessimist sees things differently. Instead of providing relief from boring tasks the pessimist worries that the new technology will in fact create *more* boring and routine tasks. Office automation, and its inherent embracing of the ideals of 'scientific management' (the rationalization of work), would lead to jobs which are more structured, routinized and less creative, i.e. boring, and this is particularly the case in the principal's work. Cooley (1980) sums this up succinctly:

> The computer is the Trojan Horse with which Taylorism is going to be introduced into intellectual work.

The fear is that with the myriad of new opportunities created by office automation, the temptation to take a relatively unstructured job, reduce it to a number of tasks, and then rationalize these tasks so they become appropriate for automation will be irresistible. Thus office automation will lead to more drudgery for the manager not less. The same is true for the non-principal office worker. Arnold (1980) states:

Typists tend to have their work deskilled by the introduction of word processors. Word processors relieve the operator of many aspects of typing which create some variety (and introduce some 'space') in the work, such as layout and presentation skills. The technology is designed to maximize the amount of time which the operator spends performing the part of the typing task which the machine cannot do, namely, operating the keyboard.

The pessimist also wonders whether the new work possibilities, e.g. remote work, will be beneficial to the worker. Arrangements such as 'work at home' may save on commuting costs and offer great flexibility, but at what cost? The social isolation and role ambiguity can cause enormous emotional stress and strain. For example, a man with a family who works at home suffers from the ambiguity of being a company employee and a father at the same time. He faces role pressures while working at home which he would not experience at the office. Moreover, with technologies such as portable computers, the pressures on an employee to do extra work at home in the evenings and on weekends could be great — particularly for a job which is behind schedule, or happens to be a pet project of the boss, etc. Whereas this possibility of extra work at home has existed before the new technology, the ease of working at home may now be a temptation which is too difficult for an employee to refuse — particularly if he is an aspiring young executive. The potentially damaging effect this has on family life is cause for concern, and worries the pessimist.

Support for the pessimist's concern about the deleterious consequences of office automation on work comes from a number of sources: cf. Mumford (1970), Weizenbaum (1976), Briefs (1980), Cooley (1980), Mowshowitz (1980), Craig (1981), Zuboff (1981), and Gregory and Nussbaum (1982). However, as was the case for the optimist, there is not a great deal of empirical evidence to support the pessimist's contention. This is probably due to the newness of office automation. Nevertheless, studies performed by Glenn and Feldberg (1977) (reported in Gregory and Nussbaum, 1982), Bjorn-Andersen and Eason (1980), and Cooley (1980) do support the contention that office automation leads to work which is more mechanical and rationalized.

Communication

Communication is unquestionably a primary function of the office. Both the pessimist and optimist agree on this point. They differ, however, on the way it is likely to be affected by office automation.

(a) More communication
The pessimist concedes that office automation will increase office communication but does not feel that this is necessarily desirable. Numerous researchers, see particularly Ackoff (1967), have asserted that the problem for management is not that they lack information (for decision making, etc.); quite the reverse, they suffer from information overload. If this is true, and there is considerable

support for this contention, then an increase in communication will only exacerbate management's problem. Therefore, the pessimist does not see an increase in communication as inherently beneficial.

(b) More thoughtful communication
Although non-simultaneous communication, in the form of an electronic message system, does permit individuals to consider carefully what they want to say and how they will word their statements, it also provides the means for information exchange to be slowed down. Instead of a real-time response to a query, such as occurs in face-to-face or telephone communication, a responder is at liberty to take whatever time is needed to respond — which could be problematic if a response is wanted quickly. Additionally, non-simultaneous communication provides a vehicle for stalling or deliberately making a response vague if a responder so wishes. Although it is possible to stall for time with simultaneous communication, it is more difficult.

(c) Greater community feeling
The pessimist might contend that the use of electronic message systems might have just the opposite effect from what the optimist expects. Instead of creating greater community feeling, the new technology could lead to less community spirit. This might come about because electronic message systems could supplant face-to-face and voice communication, thereby leading to a greater sense of remoteness. Visual and audio communication are far more socially cohesive modes of communication.

(d) Written record of communication
Although electronic message systems provide a means for keeping a record of communication, this may not be desirable in all circumstances. Individuals are likely to be much more reserved about what they say if there is a written record. It is unlikely that communication will be as free or as open in this kind of environment. Moreover, the communication itself will suffer because the communication means, i.e. written text, is not as powerful as either voice or visual contact.

(e) Reduction in paper
The pessimist is more apt to see increased communication leading to more paper not less. In fact, indications are that offices rarely experience a reduction in the use of paper (except, perhaps, when the company goes bankrupt). The trend appears irreversible. The pessimist, therefore, would find it hard to believe that office automation would lead to a reduction in paper.

Finally, the pessimist would contend that the anticipated use of office automation for office communication is grossly overestimated by the optimist, for a number of reasons. Firstly, as Mintzberg (1973) points out, managers prefer verbal and face-to-face communication whenever possible. These modes of communication are powerful and efficient in that far more information can be conveyed in a much shorter period of time. This is precisely what the manager needs as his work is characterized by fragmentation and constant activity. Secondly, as numerous authors have pointed out, most managers have a strong dislike of keyboards. Typing is associated with secretarial work and is therefore looked down upon. Moreover, as few managers possess typing skills, keyboarding is considered a waste of time, as it is something they cannot perform efficiently. Thirdly, as a manager's job is highly unstructured, much of the information exchange entered into is of an informal nature. Office automation, on the other hand, is most appropriate for formal activities. Given the apparent mismatch, there should be little expectation that office automation will be of much use to the manager. The pessimist, therefore, sees office automation use for office communication to be substantially less than the optimist. Studies done by Edwards (1978) and Trauth, Kwan, and Barber (1984) suggest that communication does not always improve with the use of computer-based messaging systems.

Power

Power — both organizational and individual — has been the subject of considerable research and speculation. How individuals acquire power and how they hold on to it has fascinated many researchers.

French and Raven (1959), for example, in their study of power conclude that there are many types of power. They suggest five categories: reward, coercive, referent, legitimate, and expert. Reward power refers to the belief held by an individual that someone has the ability to give rewards for a particular behaviour. Coercive power refers to the recipient's belief that someone has the ability to hand out punishment for undesired actions. Referent power is based on the desire of the recipient to be associated or identified with the source of the power. See, for example, sports fans who want to be identified with a particular team. Legitimate power stems from the belief of the recipient that the source has a legitimate right to exert influence; e.g. a parent's influence over his/her child. Expert power is derived from a recipient's perception that the sources possess special knowledge or expertise. More recently, the notion of power has been extended from one of 'power over someone', i.e. command (cf. Dahl, 1957; French and Raven, 1959), to one which includes 'power to do something', i.e. leadership (cf. Ackoff, 1983).

Whatever the view on power, one point is absolutely clear: information (and its possession) is an important source of power (cf. Pettigrew, 1973; Bariff and Galbraith, 1978, Conrath and du Roure, 1978, Markus, 1983, and Mintzberg, 1983.). Because information is closely linked to both knowledge and power, its possession can dramatically alter the interaction between individuals. Those in possession of information look for ways to safeguard its acquisition and retention; those not in possession look for ways to obtain it. Stewart (1971b) argues that people look for ways to access new information in an attempt to abolish the mystique and associated power connected with possession of information of another. Sircar (1978) notes new information acquisition can lead to the uncovering of mistakes of others; and so on. It is therefore apparent that anything which has the ability to change information access and possession is itself a power resource. It is this very point which worries the pessimist.

For the pessimist, office automation is yet another tool through which greater and greater quantities of information are made available to senior management in organizations. Information is made to flow up the organization in an increasing measure, with the result being less discretion available to the lower organizational levels. Office automation is seen as providing yet another means of controlling (or improving the control over) the workforce leading to a further centralization of power. Support for this contention abounds as most studies which have looked at computers and power suggest a positive correlation, i.e. computer systems seem to increase the power of those already in power (cf. Bariff and Galbraith, 1978; Bjorn-Andersen and Pedersen, 1980, and Markus, 1981, 1983).

The optimist might contend that office automation would have just the opposite effect in that information could be more readily available to lower organizational levels. That is, information sharing would be enhanced as access would be facilitated. Thus, instead of centralizing power, office automation would lead to a better distribution of power. The pessimist would strongly disagree with this contention as he feels it to be naive. Office automation would only be used if it indeed did lead to a further centralization of power. If it did not, it would be abandoned. Conrath and du Roure (1978) provide graphic support for the pessimist's position. In their study on the implementation of a logistics system in the US military, the authors report on how the new system had a deleterious effect on the power base of the senior officers. The new system provided junior officers with access to information which was previously unavailable to them. Gradually, as the senior officers perceived the system as eroding their power, they became alarmed until eventually they found a way to neutralize the system.

Office automation is seen by the pessimist as inevitably leading to power struggles. Although they are part-and-parcel of organizational and social life the new office technology and systems provide the opportunity for far greater (and more damaging) power struggles than ever before.

Personal Privacy

For many decades, individuals have worried about personal freedom and privacy. Large bureaucratic systems seem to possess an insatiable desire for more information about their subjects. This desire, in combination with the developments of telecommunications technology, has given rise to a fear of an Orwellian 1984. As technology advances and the potential for ever greater and more sophisticated databanks arise, so the fear of a 'Big Brother is watching' syndrome becomes more acute (cf. Warner and Stone, 1970, and Rule *et al.*, 1980a).

Personal privacy is the social expectation of an individual (and, by extension, a group of individuals, an institution, or, taken collectively, all of society) to be able to have some influence in determining how information about the individual is used or communicated to others; be assured of openness and fairness in relations with any record-keeping organization that holds data about the individual; and be protected against unwelcome, unfair, improper, or excessive collection or dissemination of information about the individual.

Personal privacy, although an emotive subject where there is apparent unanimous agreement about its importance, nevertheless tends to attract little attention in comparison to other socially important issues. Ware (1980) writes:

> Privacy is not a flashy and visible social issue like energy and pollution. It is not as noticeable and its effects are subtle and everywhere. The sense of this comment — namely pervasiveness and subtlety — tends to characterize most situations that involve information, its flow, use, control, or management.

For the pessimist, this lack of attention is worrying, for office automation is seen as contributing to the reduction of personal privacy. Further, the pessimist's argument is based on some well-known fundamental notions. It is as follows. Modern society is composed of formal organizations who strive to keep track of the more or less unpredictable aspects of their environments by obtaining as much information as possible — information about competitors, the government, individuals, etc. This organizational drive for more information leads, the pessimist contends, to the growth of large databanks and is worrisome because of the implications on social control. Rule and his colleagues (1980b) state:

> Thus, the growth of vast, bureaucratic personal data systems, both computerized and conventional, often marks the development of characteristically modern forms of *social control*. By this we mean direct patterns of influence by organizations over the behaviours of individuals. Such influence may be benign ... or coercive .... The systematic collection and monitoring of personal information for purposes of social control we term *surveillance* .... The development of efficient systems of mass surveillance and control is one of the distinctive sociological features of advanced societies.

Moreover, the pessimist worries that organizations will demand and develop new forms of surveillance systems to provide more information. This surveillance must lead to an inevitable long-term decline in personal privacy and autonomy, centralization of social control, and a concomitant weakening of other forms of social control such as families and communities. Rule *et al.* (1980b) write:

> Thus, a fundamental trend in modern, highly developed societies is the progressive centralization of social control in large bureaucracies, and the incorporation of more and more personal information in these bureaucratic systems to guide the workings of control.

The optimist might contend that people would never allow surveillance to grow to such an extreme state that it could be used for social control. The pessimist, however, would dismiss this argument as pure naivete. Rule *et al.* (1980b) state:

> People do indeed protect what they consider 'unfair surveillance', often in the same breath in which they demand more vigorous surveillance for purposes which they support.

As for safeguards — legislated or otherwise — history has shown their ineffectiveness, e.g. Nixon in the White House and J. Edgar Hoover in the FBI. Rule *et al.* (1980b) note:

> ... creating pluralistic rules of the game by which individuals are accorded some influence over treatment of their data is desirable in itself, but it has no effect beyond the point where participants stop playing by the rules.

Office automation, acccording to the pessimist, poses a new threat to personal privacy — a threat which has been enlarging rapidly since the advent of the computer.

Bureaucratic Rationalism

A notion related to the two previous points is that of bureaucratic rationalism. Bureaucratic rationalism refers to the movement of organizations towards more bureaucratic structures in their drive for higher degrees of rationalism. The concept is related to what Weizenbaum (1976) calls 'instrumental reason', which is defined as the analytical and logical reasoning process used by scientists and technologists in addressing their problems. Technologists, when viewing organizational problems or opportunities for improvement, tend to use this analytical and logical reasoning process to develop solutions. What this leads to is more 'rational' decision-making processes within more 'rational' organizational structures. A 'rational' decision-making process is where less reliance is placed on human intuition, judgement, and politics, and rather more emphasis is placed on the analysis of empirical data and the calculation of a 'best' solution. A 'rational' organization structure is defined by Bjorn-Andersen and Eason (1980) as:

... one which aims at overriding the confusing, overlapping and often implicit networks of relationships that usually exist in an organization and replacing this with an unambiguous and explicit structure systematically related to specific organizational goals.

Mowshowitz (1977) offers three reasons why this movement towards bureaucratic rationalism is dysfunctional:

(a) The difficulty in adapting to change. Bureaucratic rationalism inherently leads to organizational structures and routines which are more bureaucratic and rational. While this may facilitate the processing and handling of routine, structured events, it can seriously obstruct adaptation to non-routine, unstructured events. For those organizations existing in very stable environments this may prove satisfactory, but, for the rest, this must be highly unsatisfactory.

(b) The problem of goal displacement. Bureaucratic rationalism leads to the development of organizational goals which are more easily operationalized, quantified, and analysed, e.g. goals related to resource optimization. However, what about those goals which are not readily operationalized? It is likely that the pursuit of the more readily operationalized goals may have a deleterious effect on the pursuit of other goals.

(c) The process of problem definition. The existence of new technology may lead individuals to view problems in a blinkered fashion, i.e. viewing a problem only in terms which are compatible with the existing technology. Bjorn-Andersen and Eason (1980) state:

> There is a risk that, having a marvellous tool available which facilitates a particular definition of the problem, people will tend always to define problems in ways which are compatible with the computer. This may lead to only those aspects of the problem being considered which lend themselves to logical analysis, whereas, when all aspects are considered we need to use judgement, intuition and creativity.

For the pessimist, any tool or technique which leads to a furthering of bureaucratic rationalism should be avoided. As office automation is perceived by the pessimist to be such a tool, its adoption would have dysfunctional consequences.

Support for the pessimist's contention can be found in Bjorn-Andersen and Eason (1980) who report that computerization had led to greater bureaucratic structures and more rational decision-making processes in the organizations who participated in their study. The authors therefore conclude:

> ... computerization is a driving force behind the growth of bureaucratic rationalism.

Further corroboration comes from Mowshowitz (1977) (quoted in Bjorn-Andersen and Eason, 1980) who states:

> Information technology is an extension of the tools of bureaucratic rationalism ...
> computers are instruments, but they are not neutral; their instrumentality is
> contingent on social and historical possibility.

Quality of Working Life

It is easy to surmise, based on the previous points, that the pessimist sees the
overall quality of working life deteriorating through the introduction of office
automation in organizations. With jobs becoming fewer in number, more
routinized and structured with less autonomy and control, the pessimist sees
only a bleak future. Of particular concern is the prospect of job deskilling with
its concomitant lessening of job satisfaction. Blackey (1980), for example,
discussing word processing notes:

> There is a change in the role for the present generation of typists, some of whom
> have claimed that the change has meant a reduction in job satisfaction, a loss of
> personal skill and therefore a loss of status .... Unfortunately, the very nature of
> the word processing equipment design is such that the typists' job is partly
> deskilled. The decision making process is removed in a lot of cases and taken over
> by the machine.

A similar point is made by Price (1979) who writes;

> Traditional typist training has had the objective of teaching the production of
> good copy at the first go (along with), teaching good letter and report layout.
> Word processors are tending to devalue these skills. Corrections can be made
> using minimum effort before the work is committed to paper. House styles for
> letters can be defined as a standard format within which word processor operators
> work.

It is not, however, just the jobs of non-principals that the pessimist feels will
be deskilled by office automation, but the principals' as well. This is a point
written extensively on by Cooley (1980) who describes vividly how skilled
draughtsmen were deskilled by computer-aided design equipment. Similar
concerns have been expressed by others — Rosenbrock (1977), Briefs (1980),
and Craig (1981).

Additionally, the pessimist sees office automation increasing alienation and
causing the self-image of the worker to be lessened. This would lead to higher
job absenteeism, more errors, apathy, and a general lack of community spirit
between employees and the organization.

Empirical support for the pessimist's contention that office automation will
lead to less job satisfaction and therefore a lower quality of working life is
considerable. See, for example, *Computing* (1981), Craig (1981), Zuboff (1981)

and Gregory and Nussbaum (1982). See also Maldes' (1980) study where office automation was seen to have a negative impact on five of the seven variables associated with job satisfaction.

Summing up, the pessimist sees office automation, and new technology in general, as worsening the lot of the vast majority of people. It is only the privileged few who would benefit. The pessimist asserts productivity will at best remain the same (when taken in total), employment will fall dramatically, work will become more tedious and boring, communication may increase but this would not be to the advantage of most, power will become more centralized, personal privacy will be reduced, bureaucratic rationalism will continue at an accelerated pace, and the overall quality of working life will be adversely affected. Dodswell (1983) presents the pessimists' concern cogently:

> The danger of the (optimists') arguments ... is that of self-deception. First, because technology must always amplify man's efforts and this must mean that current foul-ups of life that exist can only be increased (because when things go wrong the technology will multiply the effects of that wrongness) not reduced, by technological developments. Second, we already know the kinds of society we live within, so we know how technology will be put to work. It is disingenuous to argue that the abhorrent aspects of any technology ... may not be applied. We know they will: by someone, somewhere, sometime.

Table 6.2 summarizes how the pessimist and optimist differ on the major areas of office automation impact.

TABLE 6.2 Comparison of the optimist and pessimist positions

Area of concern	Optimist	Pessimist
Productivity	Marked improvement	Little increase
— principals	— increase	— no change
— non-principals	— large increase	— some increase
Employment	Increase or no change	Steady decline
Work	Better	Worse
Communication	Better	Mixed
Quality of working life	Improved	Deteriorated
Power	Implied better power sharing	Further centralized
Personal privacy	No change	Decreased
Neutrality of technology	Neutral	Not neutral

3. The Pluralist Position

> Technology is not apolitical; the micro may be compared to the building block, which is itself neutral but when part of a working structure, it reflects the desire and wishes of whoever designs or controls the system (Burns, 1981).

> Man cannot live without science and technology .... What needs the most careful consideration, however, is the *direction* of scientific research ... the direction should be towards non-violence rather than violence (and) towards a harmonious cooperation with nature rather than a warfare against nature (Schumaker, 1974).

Quotes such as the ones above epitomize the pluralist's concern. It is in some ways a compromise between the optimist's and pessimist's position in that the pluralist believes office automation creates possibilities which are positive or negative depending on the way it is put to use. That is, it is *how* office automation is used that determines whether it is beneficial or not. Thus, the pluralist is less concerned about the technology *per se* and more concerned about the appropriate criteria by which to judge the technology. This is a subtle but extremely important point and underscores the difference in orientation between the pluralist and the others. Whereas the optimist and pessimist seek to define a technology as good or bad somewhat independently of a specific application, the pluralist attempts to define what criteria would need to be satisfied in a given application for that technology to be considered positive. The pluralist, therefore, devotes attention to the development of criteria for social and technological acceptance and then the application of 'acceptable' technologies in appropriate circumstances. It follows that the pluralist does not believe that office automation, or new technology in general, is a *fait accompli*. Since the pluralist does not believe technology (or office automation) in itself will lead to either more or less productivity, job satisfaction, etc., he tends to concentrate on a different set of issues. These are discussed below.

Black Economy

The pluralist sees new technology facilitating, and indeed a driving force behind, the growth of the so-called 'black economy' (or sometimes referred to as the 'underground or hidden economy'). This is the portion of economic activity which is unreported and undeclared, i.e. hidden from official/government sources (Dahrendorf, 1982). Most sources report a dramatic increase in black economy activity with figures varying considerably about the actual level of activity. Some have gone so far as to suggest that the black economy is as large as the formal economy. Whatever the real level, most sources acknowledge that it is considerable. For the pluralist, the black economy is inevitable. It is a natural reaction against a society which becomes more formal and bureaucratic aided by the new technology.

The black economy, moreover, tends to bring with it a change in orientation about the notion of work. Instead of work being associated with just some formal activity or set of activities, e.g. going to work in an office, it takes on a broader meaning, one which encompasses any activity which leads to economic gain. Temporal and spatial aspects of work become less structured and less of a concern as black activities are generally informal.

Overall, the black economy (the alternative of the official economy) promises to grow rapidly through the use of office automation and other forms of technology for two reasons:

(a) The new technology creates many new work prospects which were not possible before.
(b) Alternative (unofficial) work is seen as man's natural right as a counterbalance to the increasing degree of social bureaucratization which new technology has helped bring about.

It should be noted that the pluralist does not necessarily see the growth of the black economy as undesirable as it helps relieve the pressures of the formal economy. For example, as unemployment rises (particularly in times of world recession) the black economy provides an outlet for individuals to do something with their time. It can be thought of as a pressure valve which opens when the pressure of the system is too great. Individuals who are unemployed or underemployed use the opportunities afforded by the black economy to engage in some form of remunerative work. As was mentioned previously, people seem to have an inherent need to engage in some type of work; sever the opportunity for work and pressure will be inevitable. The black economy provides a vehicle for the relieving of the pressure.

Participation

The pluralist believes that the only way to successfully deal with new technology is through the participation of all affected parties. The arguments for participation are fairly well known (see the last chapter) and so will only be summarized here.

(a) Participation allows the interests of the individuals who must use the new technology to be protected. It is based on the belief that individuals have the right to control (or at least have say in) their own destinies.
(b) Participation provides the means through which individuals can use the technology as a basis for a redesign of their jobs and working environments.
(c) As activities are ultimately controlled by those who perform them, people who do not have a say in the decisions about activities may choose not to abide by them. Participation, therefore, facilitates compliance with the results of decision making.
(d) Participation leads to positive perceptions as individuals participating in new technology decisions are likely to identify with the technology.
(e) Participation permits the various skills and knowledge of the individuals who will use the technology to be incorporated in it.
(f) Participation facilitates individual learning. Individuals participating in

new technology decisions will learn much about the technology as well as acquiring new skills (interpersonal relations) and knowledge.

One of the leading advocates of participation is Russell Ackoff (see Ackoff, 1970, 1974, 1979). Ackoff argues that participation is absolutely essential, particularly in planning for the future. His plea of 'plan, or be planned for' was the theme adopted by the blacks in Philadelphia during the city's redevelopment in the early 1970s. His support for the participation process is based on the belief that the major benefit of planning comes from engaging in it. 'In planning, process is the most important product' (Ackoff, 1979). He suggests two important implications based on this belief:

> It implies that no one can plan effectively for someone else: that it is better to plan for yourself, no matter how badly, than to be planned for by others, no matter how well.

And secondly:

> The participation principle also implies that planners should not emulate medical doctors by diagnosing the ailments of others and prescribing for them. Rather they should be like teachers who, although they cannot learn for their students, can facilitate their students' learning for themselves.

For the pluralist, participation is a necessary (although not sufficient) condition for office automation to be considered acceptable. This is a theme which has been adopted by many. A number of countries have even gone so far as to guarantee the right of participation of trade unions and employees through legislation; see, for example, the Norwegian 'Data Agreements' Bill of 1975, Sweden's Co-determination Law of 1976 and West Germany's 'Works Council' Bill (for more information see Jonasson, 1980). Other countries have adopted a more reserved stance, but even in these participation is strongly encouraged. In Britain, for example, a number of trade unions have signed what are called 'new technology agreements' (NTA) with various companies (see the last chapter for two such examples). Trade unions in other countries are following a similar path. Generally speaking, the view held by most unions regarding new technology agreements is the same as the British trade union ASTMS who state:

> Technology conferences between management and unions will be held at regular intervals. They will be formal meetings with agreed minutes. The subjects under discussion will be the introduction of defined new technological systems, even where this relates to finished products or components. Work arrangements, the type and method of purchase and the siting of new equipment will be discussed, as well as any possible health and safety aspects. Training and retraining, recruitment policies, and manpower forecasts, will all be on the agenda, as will training and time off for union representatives (Sherman, 1980).

Participation in office automation introduction, however, may not be enough. Participation cannot guarantee a consensus will be reached, even though that is a primary objective. And even if a consensus is reached, there is no guarantee that it is an authentic one, i.e. reached in good faith with each side possessing equal knowledge of the situation. In fact, this is one of the major problems with participation — it may lead to an agreement but it may not be 'fair'. One side often possesses more knowledge about, say, technology than the others and thus the participation process does not necessarily lead to an equitable arrangement. The discussion must be free of human domination, mental distortions, and injurious psychological compulsions and must approximate (as much as humanly possible) the conditions of ideal speech. These conditions include: free access to the debate for all, equally informed and equally powerful participants, with no taboos limiting the range of the agenda under discussion. For an elaboration of these conditions see Habermas (1973), Apel (1980), and Klein (1981). See Land and Hirschheim (1983) for a more detailed treatment of some of the potential problems associated with obtaining meaningful participation.

The pluralist realizes the difficulties inherent in participation yet feels it is the only way to effectively deal with new technology. He advocates the conditions of ideal speech, in particular, that knowledge of the new technology and the organizational situation be known in advance by all participating groups.

Ethical and Social Acceptability

Following on from the ideals of participation, the pluralist believes in the need to define some criteria by which to judge the social and ethical acceptability of office automation or new technology in general. As was stated previously, technology, in and of itself, is neither accepted nor rejected automatically. Rather it has to be judged in the context of its setting and use. Therefore, the pluralist spends considerable time developing such criteria and then testing the technology against it. Only if a particular technology satisfies the various conditions (criteria) is it deemed appropriate or acceptable.

For office automation to be considered acceptable, it must meet specific social and ethical conditions. One such set of criteria for social acceptability is presented below. It is based on the list of human needs set out in Etzioni (1967).

PRIMARY NEEDS

FREEDOM (autonomy, independence, self-determination, liberty)
AFFECTION (solidarity, cohesion, love, warmth)
RECOGNITION (success, achievement, respect, etc.)
MEANING (orientation, identity, consistency, etc.)
CONTINUITY (repeated gratification to avoid frustration)

SECONDARY NEEDS (derived from primary needs and can be used to set requirements for the structuring of social conditions)

STABILITY (expectation of a consistent environment)
VARIANCE (opportunity for differentiation to meet individual differences)

It should be noted that this list does not include man's physiological needs but rather those needs which tend to differentiate man from other animals. Thus, for a technology to be considered socially acceptable, it must provide the opportunity for man's social needs to be fulfilled.

Developing criteria for ethical acceptability is more problematic in that there is no universally agreed upon code of ethics. What is considered ethical by one is unethical to another. Nevertheless, this has not stopped people from discussing and writing about ethics. Rawls' (1973) *A Theory of Justice*, for example, is one of the most oft-quoted and best sources of such discussion. The criteria on ethical acceptability presented below have been adopted from Burns (1981) and are generally consistent with the principles offered by Rawls. That is, for any technology to be considered ethically acceptable by the pluralist, the following conditions would need to be met:

(a) The technology and/or its function should be intelligible to the community as a whole.
(b) The technology itself or the use of the technology should be available and at a price affordable by most individuals.
(c) It must fulfil a socially useful purpose.
(d) It should be under the operational control of the local workforce.
(e) It should, wherever possible, use indigenous resources and skills.
(f) It should not create unemployment.
(g) Its production and use should present no undue health hazards or risk.
(h) Wherever possible, it should be non-polluting, ecologically and aesthetically sound, and use recycled materials.
(i) It must not lead to external cultural domination.
(j) Wherever possible, it should permit fulfilling, flexible, and innovative use.
(k) Its cost should not overburden the community as a whole.
(l) It should contribute to social conditions which can be defended by principles of justice (cf. Rawls, 1973) or at least it should not contribute to the perpetuation of social structures which are widely recognized as unjust.
(m) It should not disturb the existing social order or conditions if these are preferred by many, and widely accepted as just and fair (as circumstances permit).

For the pluralist, only technologies which satisfy the conditions outlined for social and ethical acceptability would be considered 'appropriate'. And it is only 'appropriate' technologies which should be adopted.

Education

The pluralist, like the optimist and pessimist, sees education playing a much more important role than ever before. But there is a difference. Whereas the optimist tends to concentrate on how the technology will improve our educational abilities, the pluralist concerns himself with the role education will play in our lives. The most fundamental change, as noted by Burns (1981), is that 'knowledge is no longer the sole province of "the elders"'.

In the past, knowledge was acquired through experience and during the course of life. The older the individual, the more knowledge (at least theoretically) was acquired. (This accumulation of knowledge is at the very heart of why traditionally many cultures respect their elders). The development of new technology and the concomitant growing dynamicism of our society has meant that much — if not most — acquired knowledge becomes dated rapidly. This means that the role that age plays in knowledge acquisition is dramatically altered. Individuals find the need to do more reading, attend seminars and refresher courses, and the like in an attempt to keep their knowledge up-to-date. Moreover, this exercise is an ongoing and life-long one. The importance of education in this process is therefore clear to the pluralist. Society will need to place a greater emphasis on education and this will mean many more people will be employed in the educational services sector of the economy (cf. Stonier, 1980).

A larger educational system is seen by many as a boon for society in that it:

(a) Creates employment by providing new jobs for people.
(b) Provides the opportunity for people to keep their knowledge up-to-date.
(c) Provides a vehicle through which the working class can advance into the middle class.
(d) Offers more people the possibility of becoming literate with a capacity for independent thought.

As Thomas Jefferson was reported to have said:

> To expect a nation to be ignorant and free is to expect something which never has been and never can be.

To the pluralist, education — perhaps above all — is the key to whether technology and office automation will work to our advantage. Individuals need to possess knowledge on a variety of subjects in order for them to engage in meaningful participation; to determine whether a particular technology is 'appropriate' and whether it should be implemented; to decide how best to redesign and restructure jobs; to decide who should use the technology; and so on. Take away education and the pessimist's concerns become reality. Provide expanded educational services to the masses, and the dreams of the optimist move one step closer to reality. As Jones (1982) writes:

> Every technological change has an equal capacity for the enhancement and degradation of life, depending on how it is used.

The plea of the pluralist is 'make sure that any technological use is appropriate'. To achieve this aim, the pluralist advocates participation, expanded and extensive educational services, and the acceptance of only those technologies which satisfy the conditions of social and ethical appropriateness.

ANALYSIS

In analysing the alternative views for consistency and veracity, it becomes apparent that they are more ideological positions than actual empirical reality. Because of this, their internal consistency is high but their veracity is questionable. Ideologically based arguments and positions do not easily lend themselves to empirical testing. What appears to be the case is that researchers have an *a priori* view about impact, adopt a scientific paradigm apapropriate to their view, and then interpret research results in terms of their *a priori* beliefs. Positions, because of their ideological bias, can never be refuted as any disconfirming evidence is rejected, modified, or ignored. Self-deception becomes something of an intrinsic property. Since the optimist and pessimist views are the more strongly ideological, they are subject to the most distortion. Their beliefs about office automation impact become self-fulfilling promises. It is for this reason that research reports which suggest strongly optimistic or pessimistic results need to be carefully scrutinized.

If the literature on impact is closely analysed, it becomes apparent that most studies take a highly simplified view of technology and impact. This is a point which has not escaped the attention of Kling and Scacchi (1982) who write:

> ... most scholarly and professional examinations of the social and economic repercussions of new computing developments are based on a highly simplified concept of computing and social life. This conception focuses on certain explicit economic, physical, or information processing features of a technology ... (but ignores) the social context in which the technology is developed and used, and the history of participating organizations.

These studies assume what Kling and Scacchi call 'discrete-entity' models which assume rationality on the part of all organizational actors, a direct translation of technical attributes into social consequences, and a general neglect of the social and cultural context which fostered the technological development. They call for the application of 'web' models which attempt to take account of these issues through the use of four conceptual elements: 'lines of work and going concerns' — what people actually do in organizations; 'infrastructure' — the support of basic services; 'production lattices' — the chains of social, organizational and work dependencies; and 'macrostructures' — important constraints imposed by outside forces. Unfortunately, research involving web models is time-consuming, complex, foreign to most researchers, and requires something of a paradigmatic shift away from objectivism towards subjectivism.

Another major problem with the research on office automation impact is differentiating office automation from computing; the two are obviously inextricably linked. The question is basic: are the social implications of computing the same for office automation? One possible answer suggests this is the wrong question. Since there is no generally agreed upon list of social implications of computing, it is not possible to make any comparison even if such a list existed for office automation. This interpretation assumes there exists a difference between the two. What might be argued from a conceptual level, however, is that office automation is really a special case of the general area of computing (provided the term 'computing' is used in its widest sense). Office automation, therefore, includes only a fraction of the technologies embraced by computing. From this viewpoint, there is no difference in implications; the social implications of computing are the same for office automation and vice versa. It would appear that the interpretation is dependent on the view of impact held. For example, the optimist might likely contend that the two are different; office automation is a new technology which opens up many new avenues and produces numerous opportunities which were not previously available. The pessimist would see little difference in that both come out of the same mould and are used for the same purpose. The pluralist would likely conceive of office automation as an extension of computing.

Based on the literature surveyed in this chapter, it might be reasonable to conclude that the latter interpretation, i.e. there is no difference in the implications of computing and office automation, is the most likely. Although office automation may provide new opportunities, they are really simply extensions of what currently exists. There is little 'real' evidence to support any dramatic difference.

Whatever the results of any discussion on the difference between computing and office automation, one point seems painfully clear: our collective understanding of the social impact of technology — whether office automation or other — is highly deficient. The implications written about are largely guesses or hunches. There is a pressing need for further research. Kling and Scacchi's (1982) proposal for studies based on 'web' models appears to be one fruitful way forward. Others are Walton and Vittori's (1984) 'organizational impact statement' approach and Kling's (1984) 'social impact analysis'. Another is the 'consequentialist perspective' (based on hermeneutics) discussed in the next chapter. It presents one way forward in the serious attempt to produce a better understanding of the implications of office automation.

CONCLUSION

The arguments put forward by the three protagonists are fairly forceful, yet need to be considered in the light of a few facts. One, predicting the consequences of any new technology is an extremely tricky proposition. History is full of embarrassing examples of this fact. Winston Churchill, upon hearing about the discovery of X-rays while in India, is reported to have said 'The X-ray will lead to the end of privacy'. Professor Aiken, who is often credited with the development of the first computer in the United States, predicted that 'the world demand for computers will be approximately six'. All this lends support to the famous Chinese proverb: 'Prediction is a difficult art ... particularly when the future is concerned. Further evidence on the difficulty of predicting how new technology would affect jobs comes from the numerous reports in the late 1950s and early 1960s about the demise of middle management due to computers. Many felt that the middle manager would largely be replaced by the computer. This, of course, never happened. Two, people are remarkably robust. They have a capacity for absorbing change which many fail to appreciate. Individuals, organizations, and society itself have usually managed to adapt to change in the past, using ingenious ideas which could not necessarily have been predicted. This adaptability appears to be an innate ability of man. Therefore, many feel man will survive the latest round of change, e.g. office automation, satisfactorily using these ingenious ideas which we cannot even begin to predict.

REFERENCES

Abraham, S. (1981) 'The impact of automated office systems on the productivity of managers and professionals', *Proceedings of the Office Automation Conference*, Houston, March.

Ackoff, R. (1967) 'Management misinformation systems', *Management Science*, **14**, No.4, December.

Ackoff, R. (1970) *A Concept of Corporate Planning*, Wiley-Interscience, New York.

Ackoff, R. (1974) *Re-Designing the Future*, Wiley-Interscience, New York.

Ackoff, R. (1979) 'Resurrecting the future of operational research', *Journal of the Operational Research Society*, **30**, No.3, March.

Ackoff, R. (1983) Paper presented at the Systems in OR Conference, Henley — The Management College, May.

Apel, K. (1980) *The Explanation: Understanding Controversy in Transcendental-Pragmatic Perspective* (in German), Theorie-Diskussion, Suhrkamp, Frankfurt.

APEX (1979) *Office Technology: A Trade Union Response*, Association of Professional, Executive, Clerical and Computer Staff Report, March.

Arnold, E. (1980) 'Word processing, the job', in *Office Automation-Analysis*, Infotech State of the Art Report.

Attewell, P., and Rule, J. (1984) 'Computing and organizations: what we know and what we don't know', *Communications of the ACM*, **27**, No. 12, December.

Bair, J. (1978) 'Productivity assessment of office information systems technology', *Proceedings of the IEEE Symposium on Trends and Applications in Distributed Processing*.

Bariff, M., and Galbraith, J. (1978) 'Intraorganizational power considerations for designing information systems', *Accounting, Organizations and Society*, **3**, No.1.

Barron, I., and Curnow, R. (1979) *The Future with Microelectronics*, Francis Printer, London.

Berger, P., and Luckmann, T. (1966) *The Social Construction of Reality: A Treatise in the Sociology of Knowledge*, Doubleday, New York.

Bjorn-Andersen, N., and Eason, K., (1980) 'Myths and realities of information systems contributing to organizational rationality', in *Human Choice and Computers* (Ed. A. Mowshowitz), Vol.2, North-Holland, Amsterdam.

Bjorn-Andersen, N., and Pedersen, P. (1980) 'Computer facilitated changes in the management power structure', *Accounting, Organizations and Society*, **4**, No.2.

Blackey, B. (1982) 'Word processing, the job', *Office Automation-Analysis*, Infotech State of the Art Report.

Boguslaw, R. (1965) *The New Utopians*, Prentice-Hall, Englewood Cliffs.

Brandt, S. (1983) 'Working-at-home: how to cope with spatial design possibilities caused by the new communication media', *Office: Technology and People*, **2**.

Braverman, H. (1974) *Labour and Monopoly Capital — The Degradation of Work in the Twentieth Century*, Monthly Review Press, New York.

Briefs, V. (1980) 'The effects of computerization on human work — new directions for computer use in the work-place', in *Human Choice and Computers* (Ed. A. Mowshowitz), Vol. 2, North-Holland, Amsterdam.

Burke, F., and George, R. (1979) 'How top executives perceive their choices among information sources for decision', Paper presented at IFIP TC8.2 Conference, Bonn, June.

Burns, A. (1981) *The Microchip: Appropriate or Inappropriate Technology?*, Ellis Horwood, Chichester.

Burns, A. (ed.) (1984) *New Information Technology*, Ellis Horwood, Chichester.

Burns, J. (1977) 'The evolution of office information systems', *Datamation*, April.

Burrell, G., and Morgan, G. (1979) *Sociological Paradigms and Organizational Analysis*, Heinemann, London.

Carlisle, J. (1976) 'Evaluating the impact of office automation and top management communications', *National Computer Conference Proceedings*.

Christie, B. (1981) *Face to File Communication*, John Wiley, Chichester.

Clegg, S., and Dunkerley, D. (1980) *Organization, Class and Control*, Routledge and Kegan Paul, Henley.

Computertalk (1978) 'Certainly not at Pearl', 27 August.

Computing (1980) 'Soul searching task of office automation', 14 February.

Computing (1981) 'Automation: office work has unpromising future', 21 May.

Conrath, D., and du Roure, G. (1978) 'Organizational implications of comprehensive communication — information systems: some conjectures', Working paper, Institute d'Administration des Enterprises Centre d'Etude et de Recherche sur les Organizations et la Gastion, Aix-en-Provence.

Conrath, D., Higgins, C., Irving, R., and Thackenkary, C. (1981) 'Determining the need for office automation: methods and results', CECIT working paper, University of Waterloo.

Cooley, M. (1979) 'Computers, politics, unemployment', *Politics and Computing*, Infotech Conference.

Cooley, M. (1980) *Architect or Bee? The Human/Technology Relationship*, Hand and Brain Publications, Slough.

Craig, M. (1981) *Office Worker's Survival Handbook*, British Society for Social Responsibility in Science, London.

Curley, K. (1984) 'Are there any real benefits from office automation? *Business Horizons*, July/August.
Dahl, R. (1957) 'The concept of power', *Behaviour Science*, July.
Dahrendorf, R. (1982) *On Britain*, University of Chicago Press, Chicago.
Datapro (1981) 'Evolving office of the future', Datapro Reports, June.
Davis, W., and McCormack, A. (1979) *The Information Age*, Addison-Wesley, Reading.
Dertouzos, M., and Moses, J. (Eds.)(1980) *The Computer Age: A Twenty-Year View*, MIT Press, Cambridge.
Dodswell, A. (1983) *Office Automation*, J. Wiley and Sons, Chichester.
Downing, H. (1980) 'Word processors and the oppression of women', in *The Microelectronics Revolution* (Ed. T. Forester), Basil Blackwell, Oxford.
Dyer, J., and Hoffenberg, M. (1975) 'Evaluating the quality of working life — some reflections on production and cost and a method for problem definition', in *The Quality of Working Life* (Eds. L. Davis and A. Cherns), Vol.1, Free Press, New York.
EDP Analyzer (1978) 'The automated office: Part 1', **16**, No.9, September.
Edwards, G. (1977) 'An analysis of usage and related perceptions of NLS — a computer based text processing and communications systems', Bell Canada Report, October.
Edwards, G. (1978) 'Organizational impacts of office automation', *Telecommunications Policy*, June.
Emery, F., and Trist, E. (1965) 'The causal texture of organizational environments', *Human Relations*, Free Press, New York.
EOC (1980) 'Information technology in the office: the impact on women's jobs', Equal Opportunities Commission Report, September.
Etzioni, A. (1967) *The Active Society*, The Free Press, New York.
Evans, C. (1979) *The Mighty Micro*, Victor Gollancz Publishers, London.
Fay, B. (1975) *Social Theory and Political Practice*, George Allen and Unwin, London.
Feyerabend, P. (1978) *Science in a Free Society*, Doubleday, New York.
Forester, T. (Ed.) (1980) *The Microelectronics Revolution*, Basil Blackwell Publishers, Oxford.
French, J., and Raven, B. (1959) 'The bases of social power', in *Studies in Social Power* (Ed. D. Cartwright), Institute for Social Research.
Fry, J., and Sibley, E. (1976) 'Evolution of data base management systems', *ACM Computing Surveys*, **8**, No.1, March.
Galbraith, J. (1973) *Designing Complex Organizations*, Addison-Wesley, Reading.
Glaser, B., and Strauss, A. (1967) *The Discovery of Grounded Theory*, Aldine Press, Chicago.
Glenn, E., and Feldberg, R. (1979) 'Technology and the transformation of clerical work', Working paper quoted in Gregory and Nussbaum (1982), November.
Goldfield, R. (1978) 'The new word processing manager', *Datamation*, September.
Gregory, J., and Nussbaum, K. (1982) 'Race against time: automation and the office', *Office: Technology and People*, **1**.
Habermas, J. (1973) *Legitimation Crisis*, Suhrkamp Verlag, Frankfurt.
Habermas, J. (1974) *Theory and Practice*, Heinemann, London.
Habermas, J. (1979) *Communication and the Evolution of Society*, Heinemann, London.
Haider, P. (1979) 'Planning for office automation', *Proceedings of the Infotech State of the Art Conference on Convergence*, Vienna, April.
Halfpenny, P. (1979) 'The analysis of qualitative data', *Sociological Review*, **27**, No.4.
Hammer, M., and Sirbu, M. (1980) 'What is office automation?', *Proceedings of the 1980 Office Automation Conference*, Atlanta, March.
Hiltz, S., and Turoff, M. (1979) *The Network Nation*, Addison-Wesley, Reading.
Hiltz, S., and Turoff, M. (1981) 'The evolution of user behaviour in a computerized conferencing system', *Communications of the ACM*, **24**, No.11, November.

Horkeimer, M. (1947) *The Eclipse of Reason*, Seabury Press, New York.

Jenkins, C., and Sherman, B. (1979) *The Collapse of Work*, Eyre Methuen Publishers, London.

Jonasson, S. (1980) 'Computerization and human and social requirements' in *Human Choice and Computers* (Ed. A. Mowshowitz), Vol.2, North-Holland, Amsterdam.

Jones, B. (1982) *Sleepers, Wake! Technology and the Future of Work*, Wheatsheaf Books, Brighton.

Kelly, J. (1979) 'The use and usefulness of word processing', *Proceedings of the Infotech State of the Art Conference*.

Klein, H. (1981) 'Design ideals and their critical reconstruction', Paper presented at the TIMS/ORSA meeting, Toronto, May.

Klein, H., and Lyytinen, K. (1984) 'The poverty of scientism in information systems', *Proceedings of IFIP WG 8.2 Conference, Information Systems Research Methodologies — A Doubtful Science*, Manchester, September.

Kling, R. (1980) 'Social analyses of computing: theoretical perspectives in recent empirical research', *Computing Surveys*, **12**.

Kling, R. (1984) 'Assimilating social values in computer-based technologies', *Telecommunications Policy*, June.

Kling, R., and Scacchi, W. (1982) 'The web of computing: computer technology as social organization', in *Advances in Computers*, Vol.21, Academic Press, New York.

Kraft, P. (1977) *Programmers and Managers: The Routinization of Computer Programming in the United States*, Springer-Verlag, New York.

Land, F., and Hirschheim, R. (1983) 'Participative systems design: rationale, tools and techniques', *Journal of Applied Systems Analysis*, **10**.

Land, F., and Kennedy-McGregor, M. (1981) 'Effective use of internal information', *Proceedings of FEWIST — First European Workshop on Information Systems Teaching*, Aix-en-Provence, April.

Leavitt, H. (1964) 'Applied organization change in industry: structural, technical and human approaches', in *Management and Motivation* (Eds. V. Vroom and E. Deci), Penguin Books, Harmondsworth.

Leduc, N. (1979) 'Communicating through computers: impact on a small business group', *Telecommunications Policy*, September.

Lyytinen, K., and Klein, H. (1984) 'Critical social theory as a basis for the theory of information systems', *Proceedings of the IFIP WG 8.2 Conference, Information Systems Research Methodologies — A Doubtful Science*, Manchester, September.

McCarthy T. (1982) *The Critical Theory of Jurgen Habermas*, MIT Press, Cambridge.

McMahon, F. (1980) 'Office drudges and the bosses who can't spell', *Computing (Europe)*, 8 March.

Maldes, J. (1980) 'Human aspects of office automation', *Office Automation*, Infotech State of the Art Report.

Markoff, J., and Stewart, J. (1979) 'The microprocessor revolution: an office on the head of a pin', *In These Times*, 3–17 March.

Markus, M. L. (1981) 'Implementation politics — top management support and user involvement', *Systems, Objectives, Solutions*, **1**, No.4.

Markus, M. (1983) 'Power, politics and MIS implementation', *Communications of the ACM*, **26**, No.6, June.

Martin, J. (1981) *The Telematic Society*, Prentice-Hall, Englewood Cliffs.

Matteis, R. (1979) 'The new back office focuses on customer service', *Harvard Business Review*, March–April.

Mintzberg, H. (1973) *The Nature of Managerial Work*, Harper and Row, New York.

Mintzberg, H. (1983) *Power in and around Organizations*, Prentice-Hall, Englewood Cliffs.

Mowshowitz, A. (1977) 'Computers and the mechanization of judgement', Technical Report, Department of Computer Science, University of British Columbia.

Mowshowitz, A. (1979) *The Conquest of Will: Information Processing in Human Affairs*, Addison-Wesley, Reading.

Mowshowitz, A. (1980) 'Ethics and cultural integration in a computerized world', in *Human Choice and Computers* (Ed. A. Mowshowitz), Vol. 2, North-Holland, Amsterdam.

MSC (1982) 'Text processing — the implications of the new technology', Manpower Services Commission Report, March.

Mumford, L. (1970) *The Myth of the Machine: The Pentagon of Power*, Harcourt, Brace and Jovanovich, New York.

Nolan, R. (1973) 'Computer data bases: the future is now', *Harvard Business Review*, September–October.

Nora, S., and Minc, A. (1980) *The Computerization of Society*, MIT Press, Cambridge.

OECD (1966) 'Manpower aspects of automation and technical change', OECD Final Report.

Olson, M. (1981) 'Remote office work: implications for individuals and organization', Working Paper CRIS 25, GBA 81–56 (CR), Graduate School of Business, New York University.

Olson, M., and Lucas, H. (1982) 'The impact of office automation on the organization: some implications for research and practice', *Communications of the ACM*, **25**, No.11, November.

O'Neal, J. (1976) 'We increased typing productivity by 340%', *The Office*, February.

Pepper, S. (1942) *World Hypotheses*, University of California Press, Berkeley.

Pettigrew, A. (1973) *The Politics of Organizational Decision Making*, Tavistock Publication, London.

Poppel, H. (1982) 'Who needs the office of the future?', *Harvard Business Review*, November–December.

Price, S. (1979) *Introducing the Electronic Office*, NCC Publications, Manchester.

PSI (1983) 'The electronic office: progress and problems, Policy Studies Institute Research Paper 83–1, April.

Rank Xerox (1983) 'Networking — the distributed office: a new venture in modes of employment', Rank Xerox Document.

Rawls, J. (1973) *A Theory of Justice*, Oxford University Press, Oxford.

Robinson, A. (1980) 'Electronics and employment: displacement effects', in *The Microelectronics Revolution* (Ed. T. Forester), Basil Blackwell, Oxford.

Rosenbrock, H. (1977) 'The future of control', *Automatica*, **13**.

Rule, J., McAdam, D., Stearns, L., and Uglow, D. (1980a) *The Politics of Privacy*, New Maerica Library, New York.

Rule, J., McAdam, D., Stearns, L., and Uglow, D. (1980b) 'Preserving individual autonomy in an information-oriented society', in *Computers and Privacy in the Next Decade* (Ed. L. Hoffman), Academic Press, New York.

Sadler, P. (1980) 'Welcome back to the "automation" debate', in *The Microelectronics Revolution* (Ed. T. Forester), Basil Blackwell, Oxford.

Schumacher, E. (1974) *Small is Beautiful*, Abacus Press, Tunbridge Wells.

Scott, G. (1976) 'A data base for your company', *California Management Review*, **19**, No.1, Fall.

Sherman, B. (1980) 'Word processors are human too', *Office Automation*, Infotech State of the Art Report.

Siemens (1978) *Report on Employment*, reported in *Computing (Europe)*, 6 March 1980.

Simon, H. (1977) *The New Science of Management Decision*, Revised Edition, Prentice-Hall, Englewood Cliffs.

Simon, H. (1980) 'What computers mean for man and society', in *The Microelectronics Revolution* (Ed. T. Forester), Basil Blackwell, Oxford.

Simons, G. (1981) *Introducing Word Processing*, NCC Publication, Manchester.

Sircar, S. (1978) 'The importance of data base management systems', *The Business Quarterly*, Summer.

Sleigh, J., Boatwright, B., Irwin, P., and Stanyon, R. (1979) 'The manpower implications of microelectronic technology', Report for HMSO.

Stewart, R. (1971a) *How Computers Affect Management*, Macmillan, London.

Stewart, R. (1971b) 'Do you know what you want?', *Data Processing*, May–June.

Stonier, T. (1980) 'The impact of microprocessors on employment', in *The Microelectronics Revolution* (Ed. T. Forester), Basil Blackwell, Oxford.

Strassman, P. (1982) 'Information technology and organizations', Paper presented at the IT'82 Conference, London, December.

Sutton, M., and Kaye, A. (1983) 'Factors related to productivity for professionals and managers', *Working Paper SCE–83–13*, Carleton University, Ottawa, November.

Toffler, A. (1980) *The Third Wave*, William Collins Sons and Company, London.

Trauth, E., Kwan, S., and Barber, S. (1984) 'Channel selection and effective communication for managerial decision making', *ACM Transactions on Office Information Systems*, **2**, No. 2, April.

Uhlig, R., Farber, D., and Bair, J. (1979) *The Office of the Future*, North-Holland, Amsterdam.

US Comptroller General (1984) 'Strong central management of office automation will boost productivity', *Systems, Objectives, Solutions*, **4**.

Van Maanen, J. (Ed.) (1979) Special edition on Qualitative Methodology, *Administrative Science Quarterly*, **24**, December.

Virgo, P. (1980) Report on Employment, 1979; reported in *Computing (Europe)*, 6 March.

Vyssotsky, V. (1980) 'The use of computers for business functions', in *The Computer Age: A Twenty-Year View* (Eds. M. Dertouzos and J. Moses), MIT Press, Cambridge.

Wainright, J., and Francis, A. (1984) *Office Automation, Organization and the Nature of Work*, Gower, Aldershot.

Walton, R. (1975) 'Criteria for quality of working life', in *The Quality of Working Life* (Eds. L. Davis and A. Cherns), Vol.1, Free Press, New York.

Walton, R., and Vittori, W. (1983) 'New information technology: organizational problem or opportunity?', *Office: Technology and People*, **1**.

Ware, W. (1980) 'Privacy and information technology — the years ahead', in *Computers and Privacy in the Next Decade* (Ed. L. Hoffman), Academic Press, New York.

Warner, M., and Stone, M. (1970) *The Data Bank Society: Organizations, Computers and Social Freedom*, George Allen and Unwin, London.

Weizenbaum, J. (1976) *Computer Power and Human Reason: From Judgement to Calculation*, Freeman and Company, San Francisco.

White, R. (1977) 'A prototype for the automated office', *Datamation*, April.

Wynne, B., and Otway, H. (1984) 'Information technology, power and managers', *Office: Technology and People*, **2**.

Zuboff, S. (1981) 'Psychological and organizational implications of computer-mediated work', CISR Report 71, Centre for Information Systems Research, Sloan School of Management, MIT, June.

Chapter 7

APPRAISING TECHNOLOGICAL CHANGE IN THE OFFICE

INTRODUCTION

The successful application of new technologies in the office holds the promise of great advances, not only in boosting productivity but also in improving the quality of working life in its widest sense. The reasons supporting these beliefs are straightforward: technology appears capable of automating away what is boring and making work more rewarding. Most people wish to lead productive lives and contribute to the welfare of coworkers and society by remunerative work, and if technology can help to get more work done with less tedium in the same time then it should be seriously considered. There are, however, some nagging doubts about these promises, as raised in the previous chapter.

The concern is a simple one yet of paramount importance. Given the great amount of theoretical research and experience testifying to the inherent difficulty of developing computer-based information systems which truly satisfy users and other system stakeholders (such as management, clients, and creditors), there is little reason to believe that developing successful office systems will be any less difficult. In fact, it is likely to be harder. Thus, it is necessary to have a better understanding of the potential impact of new office technologies on the various organizational stakeholders before there is any attempt to implement office automation.

The last chapter sought to outline the possible organizational implications of office automation which have been reported in the literature. As can be noted, however, there is considerable disagreement about what those impacts are between the three alternative positions of optimism, pessimism, and pluralism. Moreover, the reported impacts are *ex post facto* and descriptive — interesting, perhaps, from an academic standpoint but of little value unless they can be used in a predictive sense. Organizations need to be able to predict in advance what the consequences of a given intervention will be. This chapter explores the issue of the consequences of prediction.

THE NEED FOR A CONSEQUENTIALIST PERSPECTIVE

The information systems literature is replete with examples of failed computer-based systems (Morgan and Soden, 1973; Lucas, 1975; Conrath and du Roure,

248

1978; Schmitt and Kozar, 1978; Markus, 1981; and Walton and Vittori, 1983). The postulated reasons for the failures are many and varied. For example: (1) failure to take into account organizational issues (Argyris, 1970, 1971; Pettigrew, 1973; Mowshowitz, 1980; Argyris and Schon, 1978; and Bjorn-Andersen and Eason, 1980); (2) failure to consider individual differences (Mason and Mitroff, 1973; Mintzberg, 1976; Dickson, Senn, and Chervany, 1977; and Podger, 1976); (3) failure due to inadequate technology (Deen, 1977; Davenport, 1978; and Lieberman *et al.*, 1982); (4) failure due to inadequacies in the systems profession (Mumford, 1970; Sackman, 1971; Hedberg and Mumford, 1975; Mumford and Pettigrew, 1975; Pettigrew, 1975; Bjorn-Andersen and Hedberg, 1977; and Kling, 1977; (5) failure to realize the process nature of implementation (Zmud and Cox, 1979; Ginzberg, 1978a,b, 1979, 1981; and Lucas, 1981); (6) failure to appreciate the true nature of managerial work (Stewart, 1971; and Mintzberg, 1973, 1975); and (7) failure due to 'myths' held by the systems professional, e.g. that systems have measurable objectives (Huysmans, 1970), managers will use terminals (Keen, 1976), managers suffer from a lack of information (Ackoff, 1967), and problems are known and can be articulated (Kilmann and Mitroff, 1979). (These are, of course, only a limited set of reasons, offered in the literature, on why information systems have failed. For a more detailed treatment, see Lucas, 1981, and Hirschheim, 1982.)

Although these reasons provide a variety of perspectives on information systems failure, they all boil down to one fundamental reason for failure: the inability of the systems developers to adequately predict, in advance, the consequences of the implemented system. Either there was no consideration given to the organizational consequences or there was a mismatch between what was predicted and what actually occurred. In this field, intended effects have a habit of giving way to unintended ones. Hoyer (1979) notes the challenge is in bringing about desired instead of *ad hoc* effects. He writes:

> Technological change as represented by systems development has a structural impact upon the work organization, and generally alters significant properties of the jobs of employees affected by the change. An important challenge is obtaining better control of these change processes, so that desirable rather than random consequences are the result (p. 235).

Hoyer contends that many systems developers produce systems such that the negative effects are presumed to be offset by the positive ones, a process akin to Lindblom's (1959) 'muddling through'. But why should the process be random? Many people clearly believe it is possible to predict and control the impacts of computerized systems. Walton and Vittori (1983) state:

> While many of the human consequences of this technology are complex and subtle, they are largely predictable, given an appropriate analytical effort (p. 252).

On the other hand, if prediction was straightforward, it is unlikely that the number of failed systems would be as high as the 40 per cent suggested by Mowshowitz (1976).

Prediction involves the analysis of what would be likely to happen if a particular change is made. The change could literally be anything: the building of a new highway, the implementation of a computer system, the institution of a new policy, and such like. However, the process of prediction is likely to be different depending on the nature of the change. For example, predicting the optimal mixture of sand, water, stone, etc., to make concrete for building a highway is different from predicting how people would react to the highway. The former is certainly more deterministic than the latter. The cause–effect relationships are known in the first case but probably not in the second. More fundamentally, the whole notion of cause and effect becomes problematic when the subject of study is human beings. The method of knowledge acquisition and hence the approach to predicting consequences becomes a decided philosophical issue — and the subject of considerable debate (Mumford *et al.*, 1985). The stand taken here is that there are two basic types of prediction mechanisms: mechanistic–causal, and humanistic–interpretive (or simply 'hermeneutic'). The former is appropriate for those types of situations which are mostly, if not entirely, deterministic in nature. Prediction involves known, or knowable, cause–effect relationships. The latter is appropriate for those situations which are unstructured and non-deterministic. Cause–effect relationships are unknown — indeed, many do not even exist. Predicting the consequences of office automation introduction, it is argued, is of this latter variety. As such, human–interpretive prediction is necessary.

The fundamental issue raised in this chapter is the need to consider the human and social consequences of technology introduction before any office system implementation is attempted. This is an amazingly simple plea but one which has apparently not been heeded, or at least not successfully heeded, by the information systems community. It is likely that if there were attempts to predict the impacts of computer-based information systems, they used an inappropriate method of consequence determination (i.e. a mechanistic–causal approach) to consequence prediction.

THE BIAS TOWARDS A MECHANISTIC–CAUSAL APPROACH TO CONSEQUENCE PREDICTION

The difference between the mechanistic–causal and humanistic–interpretive approaches to prediction are pronounced, particularly in their underlying philosophical beliefs. The Burrell and Morgan (1979) framework, described in Chapter 6 and Appendix A, provides a useful vehicle for discussing the differences and for structuring the tacit presuppositions used by the information systems researchers in attempting to measure impact. The framework has two dimensions: a subjectivist–objectivist one and a cooperative–conflict one. The former is concerned primarily with epistemological issues and ontological assumptions (see Figure 6.2 of the previous chapter). The latter reflects whether organizational and human behaviour can be categorized as generally stable or in a state of conflict (see Table 7.1). Mechanistic–causal analysis reflects an objectivist-cooperative interpretation of consequence prediction. By focusing specifically on issues such as efficiency, productivity, and the like, information systems researchers have exhibited a clear disposition towards an integrationist (cooperative) model of organizations. The attention paid to the phenomena to which the right half of Table 7.1 refers has been minimal. Almost no work draws on, for example, critical social theory (Marcuse, 1964; and Habermas, 1981) or the psychoanalysis school (Fromm, 1955; Klein, 1959; and Bion, 1968). Consequence prediction has been based almost totally on an integrationist perspective. Secondly, there has been a clear predilection towards what Goldkuhl and Lyytinen (1982) refer to as 'reality modelling' — an unreflected commitment towards an objectivist ontology and epistemology. This latter bias prevents the individual attempting to predict consequences from absorbing the lessons of, for example, hermeneutics and phenomenology in understanding human behaviour. The problems associated with consciousness and free-will are simply ignored in an objectivist perspective.

In principle, the consequentialist perspective adopted here attempts to strike an eclectic balance between the various philosophical positions. The bias, however, is more on the subjectivist–integrationist paradigm which is felt to be more appropriate when the subject of consequence determination is human beings rather than machines.

TABLE 7.1 *The integrationist versus conflict models of organizations (adapted from Burrell and Morgan, 1979, and Dahrendorf, 1959)*

Core concept of: integrationist or regulation model of organization behaviour	Core concept of: conflict or power-coercion model of organization behaviour
Stability and equilibrium	Change and unpredictability
Integration	Conflict and disintegration
Consent	Dissent
Order	Anarchy (pluralism)
Compliance	Freedom and independence
Functional coordination	Laissez-faire
Consensus and support	Power and coercion
Cooperation	Resistance

EXPLICATION OF THE CONSEQUENTIALIST PERSPECTIVE

The label 'consequentialist' connotes that the desirability of an act — its merit — is to be determined by weighing its consequences. The consideration of intent associated with the act is secondary. A simple example may show the difficult issues involved here: if a young child accidentally poisons his brother or sister while intending to feed him or her, then the consequence is the same as that of intentional murder. While no one would wish to argue that therefore the child is guilty of murder, one can nevertheless agree that the act as such is still objectionable, because its consequences are undesirable. Reasoning along similar lines, taking a consequentialist perspective in systems development means, essentially, that the desirability of a proposed change is to be judged by the consequences it brings about regardless of whether these were intended or unintended.

Taking a consequentialist perspective requires at least four conceptually separate steps:

1. Establishing that, in principle at least, it is possible to identify the *actual* consequences. (That this is in principle possible will be doubted by someone believing in a probabilistic universe or the possibility of human freedom. Causal determinism involves the denial of human freedom; this is one of Kant's (1964) famous antinomies. But if users are granted the possibility of free choice then it must be recognized that they can react in a basically *unpredictable* fashion to the developer's action.)

2. *Perceiving* a subset of the actual consequences, given that they are predictable in principle.

3. *Evaluating* the predicted and perceived consequences.

4. Developing a *method of inquiry* which permits the identification of consequences.

1. Identifying Actual Consequences

The identification of actual consequences is difficult at best and impossible at worst for two basic reasons: the issue of causation and the difficulties with measuring important aspects of human behaviour. Both of these issues arise in predicting the impact of a technological intervention in the office because offices are of sufficient complexity to exhibit many of the dynamics of sociotechnical systems. The purpose of raising the issue of freedom versus determinism is not to provide the arguments for a total rejection of the causal approach to predicting social impacts, but rather to shed light on its difficulties, and thereby to provide the grounds for a possible alternative to causal modes of thought: hermeneutic analysis.

There are two problems which must be faced by anyone attempting to predict human behaviour. One is the question of whether the cause–effect mode of analysis is as applicable (in principle) to the 'understanding' of human behaviour as it is to animal behaviour. The fundamental issue is to what extent, if at all, human behaviour is 'determined' by causal laws — and hence predictable by positivist inquiry — and to what extent it is the result of an 'indeterminate' human will, i.e. the result of conscious and free choices for which the agent (and not some law of nature) is responsible. Even if one believes that the former is true, then there is a second difficulty which needs to be resolved, i.e. measuring the cause–effect relationships. As Hume (1740, 1748) pointed out, we cannot observe cause–effect relationships, only the succession of certain events in time. Hence the causal mode of thinking is only a heuristic device by which one hopes to find regularities among the disjointed sense impressions which are partly concurrent with one another and partly following one another. In defining cause, Hume essentially says that causation means that two events tend to follow each other, or that 'upon the appearance of one, the mind anticipates the senses and forms immediately an idea of the other. We may consider the relation of cause and effect in either of these lights; but beyond these we have no idea of it (Hume, 1748, p. 90).

The fundamental question of this 'measurement problem' is how to select those events which are causally related and not merely sequentially correlated.

Causality versus Free Choice

There exist a number of very convincing epistemological arguments to suggest that the causal mode of thinking is misleading, or at least insufficient for the analysis of human behaviour. For instance, it is a common observation that there appears to be a fundamental difference between 'explaining' why a stone would drop from the edge of a cliff and 'understanding' why a person would jump from that same cliff. When it comes to 'predicting' whether a stone will drop or a person will jump (commit suicide), the meaning of prediction in the first case has very little to do with the kind of analysis that is needed in predicting the second event. When using the first approach to prediction, such terms as 'causal mode of analysis' or 'causal explanation' will be employed. In the case where the focus of analysis is on conscious human choice or 'free' choice, such phrases as 'hermeneutic mode of analysis', 'hermeneutic understanding', or simply 'human understanding' will be used. To be consistent with this terminology, in the example above it could be said that physics can 'explain' why a stone falls off a cliff, but someone might (or might not) 'understand' why someone jumped off the cliff.

The consequentialist position notes that it is unnecessary to take a stand on this rather controversial issue of whether there is a difference between 'explanation' and 'understanding' (for pertinent summaries of this debate see Manninen and Tuomela, 1975, and, more recently, Apel, 1979). It is sufficient to note that there is a 'causal' and a 'hermeneutic' mode of analysis. The contention here is that both can be used to predict the consequences of technological interventions in the following ways: (a) there may be situations where one is appropriate but not the other; (b) there may also be cases where both can be used and the results compared for cross-validation. If they match it would increase our confidence in their validity. However, as will be discussed in the next section, there is reason to believe that causal analysis may be appropriate in only very limited circumstances. Hermeneutic analysis, on the other hand, appears more generally suited to prediction when the subject of study is the human being.

The Measurability of Actual Consequences

Given that the mode of causal analysis in principle is said to apply, then the second fundamental issue is that of measurement, or more precisely: how and what should be measured when the desire is to attribute cause with effect in the social sciences? The fundamental problem is to devise analytical methods which can separate the effects of multicausation or 'coproduction': how can it be assured that the consequence assumed to be caused by, for example, the introduction of word processing are in fact caused by it and not something else? Is it possible to positively attribute consequences to a particular cause? In an epistemological sense, the answer is no. In the natural sciences, however, the adopted scientific paradigm has allowed such issues to be dealt with effectively (cf. Popper, 1965). Unfortunately this is not necessarily true in the social sciences. Lessnoff (1974) suggests the reason why; he states that the major difference between the physical and social sciences is that the latter deals with people — particularly people's behaviour. It is behaviour which is at the centre of the problem. People, Lessnoff states, have conscious minds, which means they act differently from the rest of nature. Therefore, the adoption of the physical science paradigm is inappropriate.

In the physical sciences, measurement is less of a problem in that various observable features of objects are studied: shapes, sizes, colours, etc. With the notable exception of particle physics, it may not be very problematic in the natural sciences to assume that the properties to be measured do exist independently of the observer and that the measurement process does not create or change them. This is quite different in the social sciences, which are after all concerned with consciously reacting people — those observed are in turn observers. As the reactions of the observed are dependent on the state of mind, the social sciences must somehow deal with the phenomena of the human mind, e.g. intuition, beliefs, desires, purposes, and values. Yet how does one measure the 'phenomena of the human mind'. For example, whether a proposed office system change is a change for the better is to a large extent in the eye of the beholder. How can one predict the favourable or unfavourable reaction which an intervention will 'cause' in the minds of all possible affected subjects. Even if one assumes that the subjects' memory contents are known to some extent, there is still one further difficulty: measurement controls are needed to prevent the very act of measuring from influencing the subjects' attitudes towards the proposed change, as was witnessed in the Hawthorne experiments. Hence the same system change could produce positive or negative human reactions, depending on whether attitude measurements are taken or not.

When transplanting the causal mode of analysis from the physical to the social sciences the usual approach is to assume that mental phenomenon can be measured and studied through the observation of overt phenomena, i.e. behaviour. In other words, behaviour is used as a surrogate for mental phenomena. In general, social scientists appear to believe in this surrogate, and have therefore developed a strong predilection towards empiricism. Various social scientists have elaborated on the notion of empiricism as is evidenced by the writings of Emile Durkheim. Durkheim (1938), for example, noted a distinction between 'ways of thinking' and 'ideas' in human minds. He claimed the former are data for the social scientist, while the latter are not. This is so because the former manifest themselves through written creeds, written laws, and other forms of observable behaviour, such as speech. In modern language one would refer to 'ways of thinking' as the patterns or logic of human thought as it is discernable in documented output. In other words, people's 'ways of thinking' are expressed in language (i.e. symbols) which can be studied by the methods of empirical science. In addition, Durkheim made the assumption that symbolic behaviour (e.g. speech and writing) can be substituted for observable behaviour.

Unfortunately, this view that *observable* human behaviour can be used as a sufficient basis for the explanation of human behaviour, and therefore the understanding of the mental phenomena of the mind, is fallacious. The description of the physical aspects of behaviour does *not* describe human action, only people performing activities. Mere causal analysis fails to analyse what lies behind 'man as an appearance' (Kant, 1964). In order to see an event as a human action, it is necessary to interpret its empirically observable features in terms of mental categories. It is the purposive (i.e. goal-seeking) aspect of behaviour, not its physical aspects, that constitute the unity of action. It is this purposive aspect of behaviour that needs to be understood and measured if mental phenomena of the mind are to be understood. No matter how well the patterns of observable behaviours have been identified, they will fall short of the 'real' understanding of human actions. Description, explanation, and under-standing are categorically different. A similar point is also made in speech act theory. Searle (1979) argues, for instance, that understanding natural language relies on a sufficient appreciation of the speaker's intent or purpose. Meaning within language cannot be fully derived from the symbolic context of the text to be interpreted, but must depend on a pre-understanding of the speaker's purpose — no matter how tentative or incomplete. The realization of this provides the basis for the advocation of hermeneutic analysis.

The issue of purposive behaviour is also problematic. Some have argued that the goal directedness of an individual can be determined by the results which his or her actions bring about (see, for example, the office semantics view in Chapter 3). This argument, however, is also fallacious. The purpose of an action is indeed the goal to which it is directed, but this cannot be identified with the results it brings about because this would involve two assumptions which are not necessarily true: (a) the individual believed — correctly— that his or her movements would have that result and (b) the individual consciously desired that the result should come about. (Note that the issue of understanding an individual's action is much more complicated than this brief treatment has suggested. Goal-seeking behaviour, for example, must be considered in a social context. That is, an individual is a member of a community — hence an understanding of the community's culture, e.g. its language, customs, institutions, and the like would be necessary.) The difficulties involved here are self-evident.

It is thus clear that the issue of attaching consequences — particularly human consequences — to a proposed technological intervention, such as the introduction of office automation, is equivocal. Consequences embody, in some way or another, the changing of human minds; as has been described above, its measurement is fraught with problems.

2. The Issue of Perceiving Actual Consequences

Another problem noted by the consequentialist perspective is that of perceiving actual consequences. Consequences have to be perceived by someone, and there is no certainty that one person will perceive the same consequences as someone else. The particular consequences perceived depends on an individual's experiences, environment, learned beliefs, desires, frame of reference, political ideology, and the like; i.e. a person's 'world view' (Weltanschauung). From this it is obvious that the perception of actual consequences is not independent of the interests, goals, and values which guide human behaviour. March and Simon (1958) state: 'What a person wants and likes influences what he sees; what he sees influences what he wants and likes' (p. 151).

In practice, the perception issue is 'resolved' by the choice of a measurement method, but the question of just what criteria should guide the choice of a method which is 'appropriate' for information or office systems development is rarely asked. Whatever tools and techniques are applied will condition the perception of the subset of consequences that actually enter the analyst's focus of awareness.

3. Evaluating Consequences

How to determine which values are to be attached to the consequences is not one which lends itself to straightforward analysis. It leads to such questions as: what is desirable, for whom, in whose eyes, for what purposes, and so on? This raises the question of how to deal with value judgements. The consequentialist position advocates that a methodology for system development should give explicit consideration to addressing the value question. The concern in developing an appropriate evaluation approach must be with 'emancipating' the interests of the system stakeholders, such that the resulting system design is sensitive to both the human needs of the stakeholders and to the 'ethics of the system as a whole', as this latter concept has been defined by Churchman (1968). Further details are discussed in Klein (1981).

In Chapter 6, two sets of criteria were proposed as a basis for judging the ethical acceptability of a technical intervention. These criteria are also appropriate for evaluating consequences. Desirable consequences are those which are judged 'ethically and socially acceptable' in terms of the specified criteria. Office automation should only be introduced if such 'acceptable' consequences result. To these, two additional types of objectives should be met: (a) epistemological neutrality and (b) political neutrality. The former refers to the desire for the intervention *not* to cause a fundamental change in the way people perceive the world. How an individual interprets sense impressions should not be altered in such a way that they can only be interpreted in the way the intervention's owner dictates. A person's epistemological perspective should not be forced to reflect someone else's unless the change comes about through social agreement. Political neutrality refers to the belief that a person's value system should not be altered because of a technical intervention, unless that is his wish. The change should not alter the behavioural equilibrium and power balance of the interest groups except through mutual agreement.

For such types of neutrality to be maintained, the 'rationality' (Habermas, 1981) of the intervention must not be undermined. It must be free of: (a) *subjective bias* which includes lack of understanding; (b) *information suppression* due to physical constraints; and (c) *information distortion* due to social conditions, in particular through the effects of hierarchy and power on the human willingness to communicate accurately. The consequentialist perspective advocates a value position consistent with the desire for such rationality.

4. A Pluralist Conception of Inquiry

The method of inquiry relates to how consequences are to be identified. Hermeneutic analysis has been proposed as the most appropriate approach, given the social and behavioural nature of the subject of study. From an epistemological and ontological perspective, what is advocated is largely a subjectivist/interpretivist method of inquiry. However, according to Burrell and Morgan (1979), there is also a need to consider a second dimension: viz. the nature of behaviour. The basic choice available in Table 7.1 is between the 'integrationist' and 'conflict' paradigms. Whatever paradigm is chosen as a conceptual basis for reasoning about social consequences should be flexible enough to absorb valid insights from the other. This is referred to as a *pluralist conception of inquiry*. The critical 'integrationist' approach welcomes both the need for regulative order and the need for change. It also recognizes that changes implies conflict and resistance.

> Allowing for various but limited degrees of order and disorder, consensus and dissensus, social integration and disintegration, solidarity and conflict, need satisfaction and frustration, the overall endeavour is to provide an explanation of why the social fabric of society tends to hold together (Burrell and Morgan, 1979), p. 107).

The social phenomena to which this quote relates must, in one form or another, be part of the agenda of office automation consequence determination.

The danger with the integrationist emphasis on understanding 'the regulated nature of human affairs' is, of course, that it could degenerate into an ideology. It could be misused for merely rationalizing the status quo as the only one permitted by 'an order and coherence similar to that found in the natural world' (Burrell and Morgan, 1979, p. 107). However, by choosing a conceptional base which can be given dialectically opposed interpretations, it is possible to escape this danger. The consequentialist perspective's preference for the integrationist frame of reference is more of a contingent judgement regarding its usefulness as a heuristic and promising approach to consequence determination. Moreover, as is clear from a perusal of the literature, the integrationist paradigm is the most developed in the study of organizations. It is therefore felt that an approach based on integrationism provides the best chance to deal with the issue of selective perception and measurement of consequences in an organizational setting.

5. Conclusion

The consequentialist perspective appreciates the difficulties and limitations of addressing the human and social consequences of implementing office automation. It does, however, take the position that some treatment — no matter how difficult — is better than no treatment at all.

The consequentialist perspective also notes the need for an alternative approach to predicting consequences when humans are an essential part of the system under study. The recommended alternative to causal prediction is hermeneutic analysis. Such an analysis pays a price, in that some of the advantages of causal analysis (such as reproducibility, experimental controls, etc.) are given up. Yet this price may not be very high. Causal analysis has not shown itself to be a particularly effective means of understanding human behaviour. The advocation here is to approach the task of human consequence determination through the use of hermeneutic analysis while embracing a pluralist conception of inquiry.

HERMENEUTIC ANALYSIS OF HUMAN BEHAVIOUR

The difficulties of predicting human behaviour cited above contrast sharply with the relative ease by which people successfully anticipate the likely reactions of others in everyday life. Techers are often able to predict how students will react to course changes, politicians to how their constituency will respond to policy changes, and so on. On the personal side, a good friend might fear (with good reasons) that a colleague was likely to commit a crime, spouses usually know how each other will react to a multitude of circumstances, and so forth. It appears that this kind of human predictive capacity is based on a different type of reasoning than causal analysis — something more innate.

Support for a terminological distinction between prediction based on a causal explanation and hermeneutic understanding of human behaviour can easily be found in recent philosophical writings (e.g. Wright, 1971; Manninen and Tuomela, 1975; Gadamer, 1977; Habermas, 1981). The most basic characteristics of hermeneutics is its reliance on human 'pre-understanding' of a situation or text to bootstrap the mind into an improved understanding. The techniques used in hermeneutics were first discussed under the heading of 'rhetoric' by the Greek sophists, and later amended to cope with the interpretation of difficult texts such as holy scriptures or codes of law. One example of a hermeneutic tool is a concordance or cross-listing of terms (cf. Gadamer and Boehm, 1979) — the precursor of the modern data dictionary. Here, the interest is in the practical application of hermeneutics, and therefore no further consideration of its philosophical roots or recent methodological justification is provided.

To explore its possible practical use in predicting behavioural consequences, several types of predictive scenarios are introduced whose common feature is that they all rely on the hermeneutic understanding capabilities of the human mind. After reviewing these examples, an attempt is made to extract the operational characteristics of hermeneutic prediction which are necessary for its application to office automation consequence determination.

The hermeneutic exercise described here does not make use of any sophisticated philosophical 'methodology of hermeneutics', but relies instead on the hermeneutic skills which are part of the native intelligence of all people. It suggests a way to improve upon a totally unaided application of this skill, as in everyday life, by the use of a role-playing exercise. Note that the hermeneutic mode of prediction as proposed in the following is compatible with Mason and

Mitroff's (1981) concept of stakeholder analysis. Hermeneutic procedures can supplement stakeholder analysis by strengthening its predictive components. In order to explain how scenarios, role playing, and similar devices may improve the native capacity of people to predict the behaviour of their fellow human beings, it is useful to look at some well-known applications of this very general human skill.

1. Typical Applications of Hermeneutics for Prediction of Human Behaviour

The need to predict the effectiveness of a specific change has, through the ages, been an important concern of the military. The time-honoured procedure for testing the likely reactions of friend and foe to new combat weaponry and tactics is, of course, the manoeuvre. In the area of information systems development, manoeuvres are rarely possible. It is, however, worth while to consider how manoeuvres make use of the hermeneutic skills of their participants and to ask how these skills could be activated for predicting the likely reactions to new office technology.

In principle, game theory provides a frame of reference for predicting enemy behaviour. Game theory, however, presupposes a completely rational opponent. This raises the question of whether one's own strategy is to be designed assuming the most likely enemy response (using intelligence about his intentions) or the most damaging response that the enemy is capable of (using intelligence about his resources). In a manoeuvre, likely enemy reactions are tested by putting some of one's own troops into the enemy's situation. The general feature here is that one set of people is used to predict the behaviour of another simply by letting them assume a different role, with its associated human interests, rules of inference, and other constraining considerations. For the sake of brevity, a group assuming a certain role or set of roles will be referred to as the 'predictor' group. The 'target' group is the set of people whose behaviour is to be ascertained by the predictor group.

In an office environment, it might be possible to use either internal or external predictor groups to assess the potential reactions of systems stakeholders to technological change. Both have advantages and disadvantages. External predictor groups are likely to be most appropriate if the primary concern is to test the possible impact of a system change without disturbing the current operation of the organization. This might be the wish if, as the result of the consequence prediction exercise, it could be decided to remain with the status quo. No internal expectations would have been raised and little disruption would have occurred. The disadvantage is that the external predictor groups are likely to know less about the actual system stakeholders, the organization's and office's culture, and the like. Using internal predictor groups would improve the group's understanding of the office and organization environment but at the cost of potentially reinforcing both the status quo and various organizational myths. Greater organization disturbance is also likely.

There is no *prima facie* evidence to prove, however, that internal predictor groups will lead to more accurate consequence predictions even though this is apparently a belief widely held. See, for example, the use of prototypes as a means to assess user reactions to change. The prototype is a classic instance of the use of internal predictor groups. Experiments are conducted with a mock-up of the operational system in order to obtain user reactions. However, this approach is more mechanical; consequences are generalized on the basis of a few persons' reactions to the prototype. Prediction is based more on a simplistic cause–effect model of human behaviour and does not use the innate hermeneutic skills of people. Organization development role-playing exercises using internal predictor groups have been shown to be effective (cf. Hall *et al.*, 1975) but this does not prove they would be more effective in the attempt to determine the impact of technological change in the office.

External predictor groups, as will be shown later, do possess the ability to yield useful results, but this does not mean that any group of people can serve as a predictor group for any set of stakeholders. Two necessary requirements for a good predictor group are: (a) a sufficient level of understanding of the state of mind of the target group, e.g. their interests and beliefs which make up their particular world view, and (b) proper identification with the target group. These conditions make it likely that the predictor group is willing and able to see the implications of the proposed change from the perspective of the target group. Essentially, the predictor group members must feel motivated to become actors who will 'take on' the interests of the characters which they play. If done properly the members of the predictor group will begin to feel and think like that target group. Apart from the identification with the interests and values of the target group they must be in a position to understand the context and presuppositions on the basis of which the members of the target groups will act. Otherwise the hermeneutic skills of the predictor group cannot operate effectively.

A characteristic of the manoeuvre is that real systems are used by the predictor groups. This is not always possible in an office environment given the great expense of office technology and other types of IS development projects. Hence another application of hermeneutic analysis is needed to get around this difficulty: scenario playing. This is very much like a manoeuvre, except that it relies much more on the imagination of the participants. Actions are taken 'on paper' as opposed to real terrain using real combat weaponry. This potentially introduces an additional error margin, but may nevertheless be the only alternative to letting a small group of people (e.g. analysts or management) decide how future users will react given a set of totally implicit assumptions (which often turn out to be rather unrealistic, as is pointedly noted by Bostrom and Heinen's, 1977, 'seven deadly sins'). Some improvements in this very basis approach are possible through the use of prototyping and system simulators which can be introduced when the exercise is set up.

2. Comparison of Hermeneutic Prediction Methods with the Status Quo

The current practice of predicting human consequences appears to be based on an intuitive and unchecked interpretation of human behaviour which is used for 'analysing' the consequences of technological interventions. It is hypothesized here that a properly chosen group, whose attention has been focused on the role of one stakeholder group and whose imagination has been prepared to have an adequate appreciation of the potential of information technology, will be a good predictor of the likely behaviour of stakeholders in a system change. Having several such groups interacting in a manoeuvre-like fashion should prove a useful basis for assessing the likely impact on all stakeholders. This is the notion of hermeneutic role playing.

A HERMENEUTIC ROLE-PLAYING EXERCISE: THE PREDICTION OF CONFLICTS ABOUT OFFICE TECHNOLOGY

A hermeneutic role-playing exercise should proceed in four phases:

1. Identification of the predictor group and assessment of its hermeneutic pre-understanding relevant to the phenomena to be predicted.
2. The improvement of the pre-understanding and the identification of tools to support the imagination of the predictor group(s). If there is a lack of understanding or motivation to play, a hermeneutic role-playing exercise will fail. In phase two these conditions need to be carefully assessed.
3. The prediction exercise is undertaken resulting in various documented outputs — opinions, observed behaviours, and the like.
4. The critical evaluation and discussion of these results.

Each of these four steps completes a major hermeneutic cycle by which the understanding accomplished in the previous cycle is used as a basis for improving one's knowledge of the situation as a whole. In each major cycle, various minor cycles may exist, as will become evident in the example to be reported.

1. The First Hermeneutic Cycle: Identification of Qualified Predictor Groups

The experiment described below was part of a workshop looking at the implications of technological change in the office, and was not pre-planned. In fact, the theoretical basis suggested here for explaining the effectiveness of the exercise was not fully understood by the participants at the time when the exercise was performed. This should not be viewed as a disadvantage, because it safeguards against an unwanted 'researcher bias'. However, as a result of this, the first phase of hermeneutic role playing was replaced by a general discussion of how to proceed in the workshop.

The exercise began with a discussion whose goal was the identification of the various office stakeholders and their interests. In practice this part can be improved by applying a proper stakeholder analysis. Under the given circumstances it was decided, after some discussion, that the following stakeholder groups needed consideration: *top management, middle management, clerks and their union,* and *technologists.* The outcome of a hermeneutic experiment is very sensitive to the correct identification of stakeholders — witness the split of management into two distinct groups. This phase, like some parts of the next, benefited by the workshop members' familiarity with the general issues and technology of office automation. In another case, the preconditioning of the participants could be achieved in a variety of ways (such as extensive briefings or a preceding instructional workshop), and might need more attention than in this pilot study.

Next, the workshop members were split into four sections, each serving as a predictor group for one of the identified stakeholders. Top and middle management were each represented by two participants, and the clerks and technologists each by five. The choice as to which participants were to play which roles was arbitrarily determined.

2. Improving the Hermeneutic Pre-understanding of the Predictor Groups

In order to prepare each predictor group for the role-playing exercise, it was agreed that each group identify and list the possible technological tools of the future, their functions in the office, and their possible consequences. Some groups chose to represent this information in the form of a matrix, the essential purpose of which was to support the imagination of the role players in the absence of any real system to experiment with. It is possible to think of various means to improve this part, such as using a simulation laboratory, but the easy availability and cost-effectiveness of the approach chosen is difficult to surpass. It is important to note that each group originally constructed its own matrix, focusing on a description of technological components (the matrix rows) in a language which was most relevant to its professional view, but filling in the consequences (in the columns) as seen from the viewpoint of the stakeholder target group.

In order to facilitate discussion, each group used flipcharts, which were posted next to each other on a wall during the role-playing session.

3. Description of the Role-Playing Exercise and Hermeneutic Results

The purpose of the previous phase was to create a mental set which focused attention on the following three topics:

(a) Identify and list the office technologies of the future.
(b) Identify their functions or applications.
(c) Identify the possible consequences of applying these technologies.

This prepared the way for engaging in the principal stage of the predictive exercise. This is best described by explaining how the four predictor groups interpreted their role.

Top Management

This group interpreted the exercise in terms of how new office technologies could enhance the profitability of the company. The individuals playing the roles of top management were concerned with corporate growth and stability. They made assumptions regarding what would be a reasonable rate of return on investment, and how this rate could (or would) be enhanced by any new office technology. Consideration was given to how a new technology might affect the amount of work obtainable from the clerks. Increased throughput was envisaged, as efficient, predictable automation could replace, or at least enhance, inefficient and unpredictable humans. Additionally, top management gave thought to the benefits of technology to areas of the organization other than the office. Considerable attention was given to a variety of technologies, such as viewdata (Prestel) and teleconferencing, and how these technologies could be useful to the organization. In summary, top management's primary concern was with increasing profits; whether this would be done at the expense of the firm's clerks was not an issue. It must be added, however, that top management did not consciously avoid the worker issue or see it as not important; rather it was not perceived by top management as an issue. In fact, no 'real' mention was ever made as to how the clerks might react to a change in their jobs brought about by any new office technology.

Middle Management

In contrast to top management's lack of consideration of worker reactions to office technology, middle management was concerned with how implementing new technology might cause reactions from the clerks, and also the clerks' union. On the one hand, middle management had to be concerned with the firm's profitability, as this would be the primary yardstick of their worth to the firm in the eyes of top management. On the other, they had to be concerned with the people who they managed. They perceived themselves as a buffer between top management and the clerks; as such their role was one of conflict resolution. Middle management, in their attempt to address the possible new office technologies and their impact on the firm, had difficulty in articulating what should be done. They appeared to be keenly aware of the impending worker problems inherent in any large-scale office automation implementation and hence were a bit reticent in recommending anything major. However, they also recognized the value of some of the new technology. They therefore took a somewhat 'middle-of-the-road' approach in their attempt to keep both top management and the clerks and their union satisfied.

Clerks and Their Union

The clerks and their union took a totally different view of office technology from top management. They recognized that new technology might be valuable to the firm, but this would not be a primary consideration for them. The clerks' major interest was that of job satisfaction, and how their job satisfaction needs could be met. It followed that they were concerned with how the technology might affect their jobs, and thus them. For this reason the clerks wanted some say in how the technology would be used. They desired to be part of any design team which would consider the implementation of any new office technology. The clerks did not address the various types of new office technologies available. In essence, they did not care; their concern was not with any specific technology, only with how the technology might affect them. The overall design of how the technology would be used was their major concern.

Technologists

Unlike their counterparts, who were concerned primarily with company profitability or dehumanized jobs, the technologists addressed the issue of new technologies and their possible applications in the office. The technologists viewed themselves as externals, i.e. salesmen, whose task was to produce a suitable marketing plan to sell management on the virtues of new technology. They developed a listing of various new technologies, where they could be used in the office, and why they should be obtained. The strategy was geared for management as issues such as possible effects on workers' jobs were not raised. Instead, the technologists produced a selling plan which reflected management's concern with profitability and stability.

4. The Squeezing of Middle Management and Other Conflicts

The role-playing session followed. Each group got up in front of the others to act out what had been discussed and agreed to in each group's private sessions. The order of presentation turned out to be important although this was not envisaged at the outset. The session began with top management describing their views. Their presentation centred on how the firm's first and foremost consideration must be with profitability. If new office technology would enhance the firm's financial position it should be considered seriously. Top management pleaded ignorance when it came to concrete new technology recommendations; it was up to middle management to 'know about these things'. Top management concluded by stating new office technology could be beneficial to the firm, and that middle management should begin a program to see in what areas the new technology would be useful.

The technologists followed. Having listened to top management's willingness to consider and desire for new technology, the technologists seized this opportunity and oriented their presentation around the issues raised by top management. They went step by step through the various technologies available, where and how they could be used in the firm, and how they would save the firm money in the long run. This was exactly what top management wanted to hear, and a rather pronounced dialogue developed between these two groups. Middle management would occasionally add a word of caution to top management's optimism, but the impact appeared negligible.

Middle management next presented their discussions. Right from the very beginning a sense of pressure could be felt. It appeared as though what had been discussed in private sessions had to be modified somewhat. Middle management had sensed top management's enthusiasm for the new office technology, and thus had to temper their remarks to keep their enthusiasm fueled. On the other hand, middle management knew the clerks had to be considered in any new technology decision but were unclear on how to bring this point to the attention of top management without drawing their wrath. This had a definite 'squeezing effect' on middle management. They wanted to show the clerks that they had been considered by middle management but they did not want top management to think they were not concerned with the firm's profitability. The resulting presentation was one of ambiguity, tension, and conflict. Clearly middle management was thrust into a no-win situation. Pro-top management support would be viewed with anger by the clerks, pro-clerk support would be viewed with contempt by top management, and a noncommittal approach would risk the distrust of both top management and the clerks. Middle management unquestionably had a dilemma which they could neither solve nor ignore.

The clerks then followed. Sensing the uneasy environment, they attempted to make known their concern over any new office technology implementation, but they attempted to present their case in what they thought would be the least offensive manner. They brought up concerns about what constituted reasonable working conditions, and what kinds of opportunities they desired. It was clear they were concerned with the human aspects of work, and not about any particular kinds of technology. All they really wanted was to be considered and involved in any technological innovation which would affect their working environment or, more specifically, their jobs. To this end the clerks drew up a design principle (see Table 7.2) which addressed this need. Unfortunately, the clerks' presentation fell on deaf ears. Middle management was busy planning how they could convince top management that they were concerned about the firm's profitability and not allied with the clerks and their union. Top management did not understand what the clerks were worried about since they felt they had always had concern for their employees even though it had not always been explicitly stated. Top management felt the clerks' presentation was inaccurate and thus inappropriate. The technologists were interested in selling their technology and since it was not the clerks who were buying the technology they had little reason to listen to them. The clerks presentation was thus irrelevant as far as they were concerned.

5. Synthesis

The results presented above represent one level of hermeneutic understanding. It provides the basis for an additional iteration when the information which each group produces is fed back to the other groups and a conscious attempt is made to evaluate it in the context of its wider implications. In the described role-playing exercise, this led to three major insights:

(a) Major technology changes in the office will inevitably cause conflict due to the different goals and needs of the stakeholders.
(b) The question of why conflict is inevitable led to the identification of three antagonistic views of the nature of technological change in modern society.
(c) These general insights led to a commonly recognized need for the development of conflict-handling methods and managerial strategies which would minimize destructive side-effects of conflicts about technological change.

(a) The Inevitability of Conflict

The message which arose as a result of the role-playing exercise is that conflict inevitably arises due to the various goals and needs of the different interest groups. Each group had determined what was important for it and what would be strived for. Unfortunately, these needs and goals which are deemed important by the group's members do not always match those of other groups; in fact, they rarely do. Therefore conflict is inevitable. How a firm deals with this conflict is likely to affect how successfully the firm operates. The choice of looking at office technology is only one example of an almost infinite number of possible conflict-producing situations.

The realization that a great deal of the role-playing exercise involved the raising of conflicts led to the discussion and subsequent need to include conflict-saving methods in the office system design process. It was suggested, as a preliminary conclusion, that technology will only be effectively used if it is adaptive enough to meet the needs and interests of all the different interest groups in the situation. Given that power is somewhat distributed, then strategies to influence the acceptance of new technology will essentially be negotiating and conflict resolving rather than the traditional planning approach, which assumes that a specific rationality serves all parties best.

An assumption embedded in the preliminary conclusion was that power is 'somehow' distributed in offices (or companies in general). Nothing was said of the evenness or fairness of distribution, however. This led one of the participants to state that '... there is an overshadowing power relationship between workers and entrepreneurs that also covers the dialectics of introducing new technology'. From this evolved the citing of three views about the consequences of applying new technologies in the office. They were described as the 'utopian', 'pluralistic', and 'repressive' views. (Note the similarity with the three views discussed in the last chapter.)

(b) Technological Consequences: Three Views

The utopian view stated that with growing technological advancement (as in the present time of tremendous computer-based development), technology is flexible enough to be used to the advantage of the entire society, including all groups affected. Moreover, the intrinsic flexibility in it will ensure that the flexibility is actually used.

With a pluralistic view a critique was launched against the optimistic view as to its lack of taking into account the existence of conflicting interests and of a non-uniform power distribution. Although technologists themselves may want to promote 'positive' ways of using technology, other groups usually decide what specific technologies to develop and to apply, as well as how to implement and use them. In other words, specific characteristics of a society, such as its level of technology and its distribution of power, will greatly influence the manner in which technology is used.

Participants claiming a repressive view pointed to what they perceived as the actual power distribution between workers and owners of the means of production in the capitalist societies and the great danger of new technologies being used as a repressive tool against workers, not for the sake of repression itself, but as a means of increasing control over the working process. Flexibility is two-sided, and it is a power question if such technological flexibility will be used for improving working conditions whenever this does not at the same time reduce costs.

(c) Strategies to Promote the Utopian View

Neither of the three proposed views could be unanimously adhered to by all participants. There was no doubt, however, as to what direction the group wanted the actual use of technology to be changed. Actions to promote the design and use of technology as suggested by the utopian view were considered. The four major strategies that were assumed to give positive contributions in this direction are listed below.

(1) Participation in technological choice and design.
(2) Experimentation, in particular with new forms of work organization.
(3) Increasing workers' consciousness about technological change. (This is also a prerequisite for successful participation. Research conducted or controlled by workers and their unions is also part of this strategy.)
(4) Increasing systems analysts' consciousness about human and social consequences.

It was underlined that what could be obtained through these strategies would be to use certain unused degrees of freedom which are already embedded in the existing societal structures. Humanization and democratization strategies (such as outlined above) can only operate within certain limits given the existing power distribution. None of these strategies is sufficient to move these limits. Thus, although there exist technologies and technological applications which might serve workers and society better, they will not be developed under the present conditions.

It was also recognized that problem-solving methods need to be consistent with the kind of problem to be solved: traditional planning and causal models for dealing with purely technical problems; dialectical inquiry, participative group techniques and conflict-handling procedures for dealing with complex issues involving multiple human interests. These latter methods were considered most appropriate for promoting the utopian view.

DISCUSSION

The squeezing of middle management in this exercise has a wider and symbolic significance. It not only suggests the inevitability of conflict because of the different and antagonistic interests, but also the negotiation and process of conflict resolution which must take part for the organization to survive. Middle management were thrust into this role and had to provide something of a compromise to the competing views. Their role was interpretive by definition in that they needed to understand and interpret the actions and interests of the various social actors. This underlies a major theme advocated in this work, viz. the need to adopt an interpretivist office perspective. Office work is full of conflicts due to competing interests; the squeezing felt by middle management is endemic to organizational life. It is only through the adoption of a more social or interpretive orientation that this reality can be adequately dealt with.

CRITICAL EVALUATION OF HERMENEUTIC ROLE-PLAYING

How much confidence can one have that the results produced in this pilot study are 'reasonable' and therefore worth considering? The same question must be asked about any model-based prediction. Even if the model is accurate, in the sense that the relationships which were used in its construction are 'empirically true', the predictions still need not be true because of the issue of self-falsifying predictions: if one predicts that his car is on a crash course then he will take purposeful corrective action and the prediction will hopefully turn out to be false.

As was described earlier, it was agreed as a starting point that each group should address three topics: appropriate technologies, their functions, and the consequences of their application. It turned out that the technologists adhered very closely to this original plan, while other groups deviated considerably. Tables 7.2 and 7.3 contain some of the workshop notes of the clerks/union and top management predictor groups. From these notes it is evident that as far as these two groups are concerned they 'emancipated' themselves from the original instructions in such a way that one might be inclined to say they redefined their mandate. If this can happen, what can be said about the trustworthiness or validity of the results?

An answer to the question of trustworthiness seems to depend on one's assumptions of the reasons why some groups deviated while others stuck with the original plan. Two interpretations seem possible:

1. The original plan was inappropriate and the groups modified it to reflect a new understanding of the problems which arose during the course of the hermeneutic procedure. If this was the case, it is valuable that the groups emancipated themselves from misleading instructions and made the best of them as they saw fit. But why then did the technologists group stay with the original plan? One possible answer is that the technologists were more loyal to the original plan and made it more of an unquestionable assumption than the other groups. This would be in line with the observation that the training of technologists is generally thought to be more conformist. It would mean that the information generated by the technologists is less trustworthy because it rests on assumptions that were not critically evaluated. There is, however, a second interpretation which is more likely to be the correct one.

2. The original plan was dominated by the way technologists tend to think. To express it differently: the technologists' world view was the one on which

TABLE 7.2 Transcript of notes from the clerks and union predictor group

General design principle

Organizations need to think out their values and their goals and ensure that the design of technology fits these values and goals.

We as clerks expect that our organizations will have humanistic values and make our job satisfaction one of their important goals.

Clerks job satisfaction needs

Knowledge needs	Use skills
	Learn new skills
Psychological needs	Job security
	Adequate pay
	Status
	Social contact/relationships
	Shorter work hours/year—overtime restrictions
	Clerks control machines
	No machine recording of human performance
Task needs	To take decisions (creative)
	Judgement
	Discretion
	Routine work: reduce, distribute optimally
Organizational needs	Flexi-structure
Personnel policies	Equity
	Influence on what personal data to be recorded
Legislation	
TU/employment agreements	To protect our interests

the first pre-understanding of the problem rested. It provided the anchoring point. If this is the case one would hope that the results could be independent of the anchoring point. That is, no matter what the first pre-understanding is, over the course of the several hermeneutic circles an iterative convergence towards an appropriate interpretation occurs. Under this view it seems natural that the technologists were unable to transcend the original plan. The onus of the convergence rests primarily on the other groups.

Under this interpretation, it is confidence inspiring that the other groups managed to emancipate themselves from the original instructions, as it shows these groups managed to switch their thinking towards the beliefs and interests

TABLE 7.3 Transcript of notes from the top management predictor group

Assumptions

— we, as the senior management for this organization, have assumed the following objectives:
  - 5–8% growth in profit yearly
  - increase market share to 12% by 1985
  - minimize risk whenever possible; this leads us to be interested in increasing efficiency (technology might be appropriate in this case)
— more competition
— uncertainty caused by resource scarcity, e.g. energy, raw materials, etc.
— high labour turnover
— increased awareness of unionization
— difficulty in recruiting good quality staff
— already had computerized many DP functions, but still had many to go
— DP budget is 3.4% of turnover
— stagnant customer growth
— overheads rising as a proportion of costs

Technical opportunities

EFTS
— direct debit looks promising in the short run
— improvements in cash flow can reduce our indebtedness to approximately 3 or 4 days from the present 10
— there may be a risk however in the loss of goodwill

Marketing through PRESTEL
— we perceive our catalogue to be on Prestel which could then expand the number of customers available
— we would like a preliminary study done, however, and possibly some experiment
— the general feeling is we would like access to a larger market; Prestel may offer us this

Word processing
— may provide us the opportunity to produce multiple catalogues for special markets
— connection with databases could allow us to reorganize the way we handle customers. This could lead to a more personalized service

Computerized warehouse
— Seems like a good idea. Previously this was looked at and was deemed not economical; now, however, we should look again in light of the recent microtechnology

In general:

— we, as senior management, are happy with our computing services. We view them in a 'line' capacity rather than 'service' and are more than happy to let them deal with technical innovations. They have the authority to call in consultants if they feel this is necessary of those whom they attempted to represent. If this is accepted then any advice to tighten the hermeneutic procedure by imposing controls on the flexibility of the predictor groups, e.g. to prevent them from redefining their mandate as they see fit, would seem inappropriate.

There is some external evidence that this latter interpretation is a valid one. The literature on management tends to show that an open-ended and 'organic' style of leadership is preferable for the management of innovation (cf. Burns and Stalker, 1961). This style of leadership encourages the growth and development of human creativity, e.g. independent thought, sharing of ideas, initiative, and responsibility taking. A 'mechanistic' style of management, on the other hand, encourages defensive behaviour. Given the ill-defined nature of behavioural consequence prediction, it seems appropriate to advocate a more 'organic' form of approach, i.e. hermeneutic role-playing. Instead of ending up with a list of technological applications and their possible consequences spelled out in detail, the hermeneutic procedure came up with a better understanding of the conflict-laden nature of changing office technology — a qualitatively different kind of knowledge, but one which is highly pertinent to the issue at hand. This shift in perspective is a credit to the procedure which was able to bring it about. Hermeneutic role-playing can thus be considered a valuable approach to assessing the consequences of technological introduction in the office.

CONCLUSIONS

The application of new information technology in the office provides the potential for numerous benefits — both for the employees and the organization as a whole. The realization of these benefits through the appropriate application of new technology, however, will not be easy. The consequences of introducing office automation could be very great. It has become apparent that there is a need for a better understanding of what these consequences might be. Unfortunately, predicting behavioural consequences is not straightforward. The orthodox method of prediction — mechanistic–causal analysis — has been shown to be deficient in the social sciences, and thus an alternative approach — hermeneutic analysis — has been proposed. The application of hermeneutic analysis has been documented in the form of a role-playing exercise with promising results. A much better understanding of the potential consequences of office automation, and how to deal with them, was gained.

It should be noted, however, that the hermeneutic experiment reported here has the character of a pilot study. No substantive claims can be made regarding the reliability of this method. Rather, it should be looked upon as a heuristic device, one which is capable of generating a better understanding of possible technological effects. Further research could address the reliability issue by various means, such as testing with an actual project (using action research) and the use of control groups.

REFERENCES

Ackoff, R. (1967) 'Management misinformation systems', *Management Science*, **14**, No.4, December.
Apel, K. (1979) *The Explanation: Understanding Controversy in Transcendental-Pragmatic Perspective*, Suhrkamp, Frankfurt.
Argyris, C. (1970) 'Resistance to rational management', *Innovation*, **10**.
Argyris, C. (1971) 'Management information systems: the challenge to rationality and emotionally', *Management Science*, **17**, No.6, February.
Argyris, C., and Schon, D. (1978) *Organizational Learning: A Theory of Action Perspective*, Addison-Wesley, Reading.
Bion, W. (1968) *Experience in Groups*, Tavistock Publications, London.
Bjorn-Andersen, N., and Eason, K. (1980) 'Myths and realities of information systems contributing to organizational rationality', in *Human Choice and Computers* (Ed. A. Mowshowitz), Vol.2, North-Holland, Amsterdam.
Bjorn-Andersen, N., and Hedberg, B. (1977) 'Designing information systems in an organizational perspective', in *Prescriptive Models of Organizations* (Eds. P. Nystrom and W. Starbuck), Vol.5, TIMS Studies in the Management Sciences.
Bostrom, R., and Heinen, S. (1977) 'MIS problems and failures: a socio-technical perspective', *MIS Quarterly*, September and December.
Burns, T., and Stalker, W. (1961) *The Management of Innovation*, Tavistock Publications, London.
Burrell, G., and Morgan, G. (1979) *Sociological Paradigms and Organizational Analysis*, Heinemann, London.
Churchman, C. (1968) *Challenge to Reason*, McGraw-Hill, New York.
Conrath, D., and du Roure, G. (1978) 'Organizational implications of comprehensive communication — information systems: some conjectures', Working paper, Institute d'Administration des Entreprises Centre d'Etude et de Recherche sur les Organizations et la Gestion, Aix-en-Provence.
Dahrendorf, R. (1959) *Class and Class Conflict in Industrial Society*, Routledge and Kegan Paul, London.
Davenport, R. (1978) 'Data analysis for database design', *Australian Computer Journal*, **10**, No.4.
Deen, S. (1977) *An Introduction to Database Management Systems*, Macmillan, London.
Dickson, G., Senn, J., and Chervany, N. (1977) 'Research in management information systems: the Minnesota experiments', *Management Science*, **23**, No. 9, May.
Durkheim, E. (1938) *The Rules of Sociological Method*, The Free Press, New York.
Fromm, E. (1955) *The Sane Society*, Fawcett Publications, Greenwich.
Gadamer, H. (1977) *Philosophical Hermeneutics* (edited and translated by D. E. Linge), University of California Press, Berkeley.
Gadamer, H., and Boehm, G. (Eds.) (1979) *Seminar on Philosophical Hermeneutics*, 2nd ed., Suhrkamp, Frankfurt.
Ginzberg, M. (1978a) 'Steps towards more effective implementation of MS and MIS', *Interfaces*, **8**, No. 3, May.
Ginsberg, M. (1978b) 'Redesign of managerial tasks: a requisite for successful decision support systems', *MIS Quarterly*, March.

Ginzberg, M. (1979) *A Study of the Implementation Process*, Vol.13, TIMS Studies in Management Sciences.
Ginzberg, M. (1981) 'A prescriptive model of system implementation,' *Systems, Objectives, Solutions*, 1, No.1, January.
Goldkuhl, G., and Lyytinen, K. (1982) 'A language action view on information systems', *Proceedings of the Third International Conference on Information Systems.* Ann Arbor, Michigan, December.
Habermas, J. (1981) *Theory of Communicative Action*, Suhrkamp, Frankfurt.
Hall, D., Bowen, D., Lewicki, R., and Hall, F. (1975) *Experiences in Management and Organizational Behaviour*, St. Clair Press, Chicago.
Hedberg, B., and Mumford, E. (1975) 'The design of computer systems: man's vision of man as an integral part of the system design process, in *Human Choice and Computers* (Eds. E. Mumford and H. Sackman), North-Holland, Amsterdam.
Hirschheim, R. (1982) 'Information systems failures revisited', LSE working paper WP 82–07–1.1.
Hoyer, R. (1979) 'Information systems supporting organization development', in *EURO-IFIP 79* (Ed. P. Samet), North-Holland, Amsterdam.
Hume, D. (1740) 'A treatise of human nature' in *David Hume on Human Nature and the Understanding* (Ed. Anthony Flew), Macmillan, London.
Hume, D. (1748) 'An inquiry concerning human nature', in *David Hume on Human Nature and the Understanding* (Ed. Anthony Flew), Macmillan, London, 1962.
Huysmans, J. (1970) 'The effectiveness of the cognitive style constraint in implementing operations research proposals', *Management Science*, 17.
Kant, I. (1964) *Groundwork of the Metaphysic of Morals*, Harper Torchbooks, New York.
Keen, P. (1976) 'Interactive computer systems for managers: a modest proposal', *Sloan Management Review*, Fall.
Kilmann, R., and Mitroff, I. (1979) 'Problem defining and the consulting intervention process', *California Management Review*, Spring.
Klein, H. (1981) 'Design ideals and their critical reconstruction', Paper presented at the TIMS College on Management Philosophy, Toronto, May.
Klein, M. (1959) 'Our adult world and its roots in infancy', *Human Relations*, 12.
Kling, R. (1977) 'The organizational context of user-centered software design', *MIS Quarterly*, December.
Lessnoff, M. (1974) *The Structure of Social Science: A Philosophical Introduction*, George Allen and Unwin, London.
Lieberman, M., Selig, G., and Walsh, J. (1982) *Office Automation: A Manager's Guide for Improved Productivity*, Wiley–Interscience, New York.
Lindblom, C. (1959) 'The science of muddling through', *Public Administration Review*, 19.
Lucas, H. (1975) *Why Information Systems Fail*, Columbia University Press, New York.
Lucas, H. (1981) *Implementation: The Key to Successful Information Systems*, Columbia University Press, New York.
Manninen, J., and Tuomela, R. (Eds.) (1975) *Essays on Explanation and Understanding*, Dordrecht-Holland, Amsterdam.
March, J., and Simon, H. (1958) *Organizations*, J. Wiley and Sons, New York.
Marcuse, H. (1964) *One-Dimensional Man: Studies in the Ideology of Advanced Industrial Society*, Beacon Press, Boston.
Markus, M. L. (1981) 'Implementation politics — top management support and user involvement', *Systems, Objectives, Solutions*, 1, No.4.
Mason, R., and Mitroff, I. (1973) 'A program for research on management information systems', *Management Science*, 19, No.5, January.

Mason, R., and Mitroff, I. (1981) *Challenging Strategic Planning Assumptions*, J. Wiley and Sons, New York.

Mintzberg, H. (1973) *The Nature of Managerial Work*, Harper and Row, New York.

Mintzberg, H. (1975) 'The manager's job: folklore and fact', *Harvard Business Review*, July–August.

Mintzberg, H. (1976) 'Planning on the left side and managing on the right', *Harvard Business Review*, July–August.

Morgan, H., and Soden, J. (1973) 'Understanding MIS failures', *Data Base*, **5**, Winter.

Mowshowitz, A. (1976) *The Conquest of Will: Information Processing in Human Affairs*, Addison-Wesley, Reading.

Mowshowitz, A. (1980) 'Ethics and cultural integration in a computerized world', in *Human Choice and Computers* (Ed. A. Mowshowitz), Vol.2, North-Holland, Amsterdam.

Mumford, E., Fitzgerald, G., Hirschheim, R., and Wood-Harper, T. (Eds.) (1985) *Research Methods in Information Systems*, North-Holland, Amsterdam.

Mumford, E., and Pettigrew, A. (1975) *Implementing Strategic Decisions*, Longmans, London.

Mumford, L. (1970) *The Myth of the Machine: The Pentagon of Power*, Harcourt, Brace and Jovanovich, New York.

Pettigrew, A. (1973) *The Politics of Organizational Decision Making*, Tavistock, London.

Pettigrew, A. (1975) 'Strategic aspects of the management of specialist activity', *Personnel Review*, **4**, No. 1.

Podger, D. (1976) 'The human factor in small business computer systems: a design method', *Personnel Review*, **5**, No. 4.

Popper, K. (1965) *The Logic of Scientific Discovery*, Revised Edition, Hutchinson, London.

Sackman, H. (1971) *Mass Information Utilities and Social Excellence*, Auerbach, New York.

Schmitt, J., and Kozar, K. (1978) 'Management's role in information system development failures: a case study', *MIS Quarterly*, June.

Searle, J. (1979) *Expression and Meaning: Studies in the Theory of Speech Acts*, Cambridge University Press, Cambridge.

Stewart, R. (1971) *How Computers Affect Management*, Macmillan, London.

Walton, R., and Vittori, W. (1983) 'New information technology: organizational problem or opportunity?', *Office: Technology and People*, **1**.

Wright, G. von (1971) *Explanation and Understanding*, Konigstein, London.

Zmud, R., and Cox, J. (1979) 'The implementations process: a change approach', *MIS Quarterly*, June.

Chapter 8
CONCLUSIONS

INTRODUCTION

The primary motivation of this work has come from the desire to have a more balanced treatment of office automation. The field abounds with technical treatments of the subject, but relatively little has been written about the social side of OA. And most of what has, is either extremely superficial and naive or more psychological rather than sociological in orientation. Serious social treatments are virtually non-existent. Rhee's (1968) classic treatment is one exception but it is now almost twenty years old; the technology has moved on considerably since then. Kling's (1980, 1984) cogent analyses are another exception but even here there are weaknesses. For example, Kling makes no reference to the philosophical underpinnings of his work. They are either taken for granted, or not felt to be of sufficient importance to warrant attention. In either case, this is thought to be a mistake. It is not possible to` disregard epistemological and ontological assumptions from any serious attempt at a social analysis of office automation (or any technology for that matter). Philosophical considerations provide the foundation for all inquiry. As Fay (1975) notes, there is a clear linkage between the philosophical roots of inquiry and its product or output.

This point is extremely important and a good part of this work has been devoted to defining the philosophical notions underlying the various social aspects of office automation. The social theoretic approach adopted here has a firm foundation in the more 'interpretivist' philosophical camp. This is based on the belief that as the unit of analysis is the human being, positivistic conceptions of inquiry are inappropriate. Human beings: have free will; possess an intersubjective conception of reality; perform social action which is mediated through language; possess ideals, values, beliefs, etc., which can only be understood from the perspective of that individual; and attach great significance to myths and rituals which are likely to appear irrational to outside observers — all of which make 'normal science' dubious. The motivation for adopting an interpretivist philosophy in such circumstances is straightforward and has been written up in an extensive fashion in Hirschheim (1985a).

Why should office systems be studied using the tools and techniques of social science inquiry? Because office systems are fundamentally social systems. An office system has been defined not as a technical system which had social implications, but as a social system which increasingly relies on new information technology for its effective operation. It is this social system orientation which is lacking in most treatments on office automation.

It is not surprising that the technical side of OA has received considerable attention. The technology of office automation is exciting and company managers see the potential for improved productivity through its use. Vendors and consultants see a huge market and are quick to point out the economic advantage of embracing the new technology. Academics, by and large, have also stressed the technical aspects of OA, although there has been a rising number of more social or behavioural-oriented writings. However, even these provide only a limited — and often simplistic — alternative to the technically based material. Although their numbers may be on the increase, due no doubt to the growing recognition of the importance of the human and social dimension of technological introduction, their substance has, by and large, been weak. To provide an alternative, this work has concentrated exclusively on the social side of office automation. The primary areas of concern have been: (1) the office, (2) the models and methodologies available for office systems development, (3) the issue of implementation, (4) the potential individual, organizational, and societal implications of office automation, and (5) the issue of consequence prediction. These were felt to be the key areas where a social analysis was necessary and would help in providing a richer understanding of office automation.

SYNTHESIS

The social analysis undertaken in the preceding chapters leads to a number of conclusions about the fundamental issues of OA.

1. Office System

An office system, like its more general counterpart — the computer-based information system — is best conceived in terms of a social system. The technological tools it embraces are little more than instruments in the hands of skilled craftsmen, i.e. the office workers. As a social system, people engage in social action which helps them to construct a largely shared sense of reality. Leavitt's (1965) 'diamond' provides one interpretation of a social system where complex relationships are thought to exist between its four components: people, tasks, structure, and technology. A change to one component causes the others to change as well. A somewhat similar notion is presented in Klein and Hirschheim's (1985) 'pentagon' where a social system is viewed in terms of five core concepts: power, knowledge, consensus, individual interests, and collective interests. These five concepts exist in a precarious equilibrium in any social system; the slightest change to one will force the others to readjust. The delicate balance which exists is altered by, for example, the introduction of new office technology. It takes some time for a new equilibrium to be achieved. This is similar to a mobile, where the suspended items eventually return to a steady state despite disruptions. Whichever social system interpretation one holds, it is clear that a social system is a complex entity, involving many relationships with many disparate and conflicting elements.

The social system view of an office system appears a more promising way for understanding office automation. The technology of OA in itself is of little consequence; it is the social setting into which it is placed that is of significance.

2. Office Conception

Viewing office systems as social systems leads directly to the exclusion of certain interpretations of the 'office'. Conceptions such as offices as 'information handlers and processors' or 'activity centres' are felt to be too simplistic and, thus, inappropriate. They treat offices as rational, organizational goal-seeking bodies which follow a mostly deterministic set of rules. There is some difference in interpretation regarding whether the rules are manifest or needing to be drawn out from the office workers. In the former case, the rules are articulated and set out in organizational documents. In the latter, they have to be elicited. This can be done by interviewing the appropriate organizational personnel, tracing organizational responsibilities and accountabilities (such as might be suggested in the 'office functions' view), or backtracing from office work behaviours to implicit rules (such as advocated in OMEGA).

A number of researchers have noted the difficulties inherent in discovering office rules. They are not simply discovered by asking people or looking at organizational charts. Panko (1984), for example, suggest the only way to understand the operation of the office is to look at it in terms of the wider organizational setting. He writes:

> But office tasks and roles can be understood only if they were viewed as parts of larger organizational processes (p. 228).

This, however, just perpetuates the simplistic and rational notion of the office. Instead of realizing the social nature of the office, it attempts to explain behaviour by appealing to the more global nature of the office — it is part of a larger process (the organization) and it needs to be viewed as such. By analysing the operation of the organization, an understanding of the behaviours of the office can be understood. From a social theoretic perspective, such a conception is pure naivete. Offices are not 'rational' and manifestly rule following, they are social arenas where power, ritual, and myth predominate. The set of rules or procedures followed in an office are not a simple empirical reality existing 'out there' to be discovered by classic empiricist means; rather it exists in the minds of the social actors and is intersubjectively determined. Sheil (1983) brings out this point cogently. He writes:

> I had approached those offices convinced ... that office procedures were, at least in principle, clearly defined methods of processing information. I assumed that they *existed*, independently of my enquiries. And that is fantasy. The office worker is under no such delusion (p. 300).

Moreover, if one attempts to draw out the procedures followed by an office worker through normal means, e.g. interviews, questionnaires, and the like, the result will be little more than a distorted picture of the office. Sheil states:

> ... office workers construct different descriptions of what they do around a common core of fact, for consumption by different groups of outsiders. By controlling those groups' beliefs about his work, the office worker can cause them to interact with him in a way that he finds advantageous (p. 300).

Based on this analysis, it is apparent that only an interpretive perspective offers any hope at capturing the richness of the office. Conceptions such as the transactional or language action view hold the most promise for understanding the office, but it is likely that neither of them provides a complete picture. Further research must be done to elaborate the views and make them more specific for the office domain.

3. Office Models and Methodologies

Because office systems and the office itself are best conceived in terms of social entities, formal and deterministic models and methodologies appear inappropriate. While models such as SCOOP, ICN, OFS, and OMEGA, and methodologies such as OADM and ISAC have merit in structured and deterministic environments, they are not considered very appropriate for office system development. Based on the evaluation performed in Chapter 4, methodologies and models which are less formal and more participative in nature are likely to be most appropriate for office automation. Three particular approaches score well and could form the basis of office systems development: Checkland's (1981) soft systems methodology, Pava's (1983) sociotechnical design, and Mumford and Weir's (1979) STS-based ETHICS. Each has its own strengths and weaknesses but all are felt to be appropriate for office automation. It is likely that some combination of the approaches may even be better than a single one on its own. For example, Checkland's methodology is particularly strong in problem formulation and reaching a consensus on what might be done (e.g. introducing word processing or the like). It is less strong on the design and development phases. Pava's and Mumford and Weir's approaches, on the other hand, are strong on these phases, but perhaps weaker on the initial phases.

Thus, the use of soft systems methodology at the outset to clarify problems and opportunities followed by ETHICS or Pava's sociotechnical methodology during office system design and development may provide an optimal approach. There is some support for this contention. Wood-Harper, Episkopou, and Flynn (1985) report on the successful use of an amalgamated approach, called the multiview methodology, for computer-based information systems development. It combines components of Checkland's soft systems methodology, Rock-Evans' data analysis, and Mumford's sociotechnical approach, along with appropriate 'man/machine interface' notions.

4. Implementation

The social analysis of office automation leads to the inescapable conclusion that implementation is not simply the last phase in systems development, but a process which continues throughout the whole of office systems development. Implementation strategies, such as those discussed in Bardach (1977) and Keen (1981), provide a simplistic view of the process and perpetuate the myth that implementation can be viewed as a game. Planned change models capture the spirit of change but not its intensely political and 'irrational' nature (Robey and Markus, 1984). The most appropriate basis for office automation implementation is on worker participation. Not only has it been shown to be effective for computer-based information systems (Hirschheim, 1983, 1985b) but for other forms of organizational intervention as well (Blumberg, 1969; Guest and Knight, 1979; and Koopmans and Drenth, 1981). Since the office 'reality' can only be understood by its actors, it is incongruous to think outside analysts can effectively develop systems for an environment they know little about. Participation provides the vehicle for incorporating the views, needs, belief, values, etc., of the office workers into system design, and, thus, is the most appropriate means by which to develop and implement office automation. Participation is also consistent with the ideals of sociotechnical design; it proves to be one of the most effective ways of making operational the STS concept. Moreover, given that the most highly rated OA methodologies were STS-based and have been shown to be successful in the literature (Ranney and Carder, 1984; and Sydow, 1984), participation is an obvious choice for implementation.

5. Implications

Office automation has been shown to have a variety of impacts. Claims that OA will increase productivity, improve the quality of work life, and the like have been offset by counterclaims that just the reverse would happen. As there is empirical data to support both positions, it can be concluded that the relationship between office automation and its implications is a more complex one than is currently thought. The apparent widespread belief that office automation has certain effects, leads to increases in job satisfaction, promotes better decision making, etc., appears too simplistic. The basic cause–effect model may be totally inappropriate. This would certainly be supported by· Attewell and Rule (1984) who question the belief that a certain technological intervention *will* cause certain consequences. They write:

> There is no reason why (office automation) should not result in deskilling in some settings and the enhancement of job content elsewhere ... we see no reason to believe that any simple set of theoretical relationships can account for all the data that one might expect empirical inquiry to bring to life on these subjects (p.1190).

However, it would also be wrong to suggest that office automation had no effect. Chapter 6 clearly shows that changes *did* occur when OA was introduced. If it was not the technology that caused the effects, then it must have been something else; it is unlikely that changes were entirely random. Boddy and Buchanan (1984) purport to have the answer. They contend that the impacts of new technology are directly related to 'managerial decisions about why and how it is used' (p.233).

Technology is merely a tool in the hands of management. It is their choices regarding how the technology is used, how it is to be implemented, how individual workers are to be evaluated, and so on, which ultimately determines what the effects of office automation will be. The pessimist is likely to share this conception. As management's primary motivation is profitability, they will use office automation to further control the workforce.

The best way to ensure that office automation will have positive effects is to have an agreed set of objectives: not just economic criteria such as reduced costs, but social considerations such as quality of work life as well. The best way for this to occur is through adopting a pluralist conception of OA implications. For the pluralist, the key concerns are social and ethical acceptability, and participation. Office automation *may* lead to positive and desirable changes on its own (although this view would not be shared by the pessimist), but a better way to ensure they come about is to embrace the ideals of the pluralist. Adopt OA only if: (a) it achieves a high degree of social and ethical acceptability (using the criteria from Chapter 6); (b) an authentic consensus can be reached about its use and objectives; and (c) a participative approach is used throughout.

6. Consequence Prediction

As noted above, office automation will have consequences which are not random. The goal is to maximize the intended consequences while minimizing the unintended. Although adopting the ideals of the pluralist is felt to be the most appropriate way of ensuring positive OA impacts, the ability of being able to predict the likely consequences of any change is highly desirable. Even with the best intentions, an agreed set of objectives, and the use of a participative approach, it is never certain that positive effects will come about. Because of the need for consequence prediction, Chapter 7 explored how this might be effectively done. Causal analysis, which relies on the orthodox cause–effect model, is thought to be inappropriate in this circumstance for two reasons. One, as noted above, it is not the technology which causes the particular manifest effects, but the rationale behind its implementation and use. Thus, it would not be possible to predict the consequences of OA unless this rationale was known. Two, the impacts are social and behavioural in substance and thus the prediction approach must be able to deal with the qualitative nature of the substance. Hermeneutic analysis, which is based on an interpretive epistemology and ontology, has been advocated as an appropriate approach. The interpretive nature of hermeneutic analysis fits in well with the general interpretive perspective used in this social theoretic treatment of office automation. The approach discussed here was a hermeneutic role-playing exercise which was shown to be effective as a vehicle for consequence prediction. Moreover, valuable insight was gained by the iterative nature of the hermeneutic analysis when the various groups came together after the role-playing to discuss the exercise. It proves to be an exceptional knowledge acquisition technique when the subject of inquiry is the human being.

AVENUES FOR FURTHER RESEARCH

The social theoretic perspective adopted here has been used to provide an alternative conception and treatment of office automation. The importance of the social nature of OA has been highlighted with the view that additional research will be undertaken to continue this stream of thought. There are a number of areas where further research is needed.

1. Office Conception

Present conceptions of the office, as discussed above, are totally incapable of providing sensible interpretations. Their rational account of office operation leads to an unacceptably simplistic view of office work; yet they are widely used. Kling (1977) writes:

> ... although sociologists no longer believe that the classical theory provides a credible account of the ways that large organizations are or can be managed, it is commonly adopted as an analytical posture in the computing literature.

Alternative conceptions such as the work role, transactional, and language action views possess the potential for providing a much richer social account of the office and office work. These views, however, are still in the formative stages. Considerable effort is still needed to refine them and then test their veracity in the office domain.

More emphasis should be placed on anthropological and sociological studies. These fields have a long tradition in human study yet, with little exception (Suchman, 1983; and Suchman and Wynn, 1984), have been largely ignored by the OA community. Additionally, the methods of inquiry (e.g. ethnomethodology and phenomenology) used by these fields should be considered in understanding the office. At present, only orthodox methods based on a positivist conception of knowledge acquisition have been used.

2. Office Automation Methodologies

Current methodologies need further work. Even those which were deemed appropriate by the appraisal in Chapter 4, need refinement and extension. Most were developed with the specific intention of analysing and designing information rather than office systems. STS-based approaches seem to have most to offer and additional work could help them reach their potential. Combined approaches also have much promise. As was mentioned above, approaches such as the multiview methodology which embrace features of a number of methodologies could be developed specifically for office automation. Considerably more work is needed in providing a relatively comprehensive approach which would allow the designers the ability to choose the particular tools necessary in any given circumstance. That is, a structure would be provided but a large number of OA development tools would be available to be used as, if, and when needed.

3. Implementation

Although there has been considerable effort on the part of implementation researchers to develop approaches for successful organizational intervention, there is still much to learn. As was mentioned in Chapter 5, much of what passes as valuable insight for implementation, e.g. planned change models and counterimplementation strategies, is little more than simplistic conceptions or common sense. Implementation based on sociotechnical systems ideals and participation appears the most promising avenue, but much more research is needed. STS ideas still need to be successfully translated into the office environment. Although Pava (1983) and Ranney and Carder (1984) suggest how this can be done, examples of its application are still somewhat rare. Similarly, more research is needed to determine which type of participation is the most appropriate in a given circumstance.

4. Implications

This work has proposed a conceptual foundation by which to better understand the nature of OA implications. Simple cause–effect relationships are considered an inappropriate way of conceiving impact. Philosophical, political, pragmatic, and ideological assumptions are a more appropriate base by which to understand reported OA impact. Research is now required to either corroborate or refute these claims. Further refinement is also thought possible on the framework itself.

The pluralist position is offered as the most desirable of the three alternatives, but this position needs more work. The criteria for ethical and social acceptability could be refined to include the insight of others with similar conceptions (e.g. Kling, 1984; and Burns, 1984). Ideas from, for example, critical social theory, could also be included.

5. Consequence Prediction

The hermeneutic role-playing exercise described here as the basis for office automation consequence prediction has been presented as an alternative to classic causal analysis. The movement away from more positivist modes of inquiry was felt appropriate given the subject of inquiry — the human being. Causal analysis, while powerful for predicting physical science phenomena, has not been shown to be overly effective in the social sciences. The exercise described in Chapter 7 using hermeneutic analysis provided insight which could not have been obtained with cause–effect methods. However, one case example is not sufficient to prove the contention. Additional hermeneutic role-playing exercises are required to test the value of such an approach. Experimentation with internal and external predictor groups should be undertaken as well.

CONCLUDING REMARKS

In Chapter 1, the *raison d'être* for this work was discussed in terms of the need for a dialectical treatment of office automation, to give primacy to the social and organizational rather than the technical aspects of the subject. This has been undertaken through the adoption and application of the social theoretic perspective. The perspective has proved valuable in its ability to generate insight into the social nature of office systems. It is likely, however, that the conclusions reached by this study might to some seem either obvious or irrelevant — obvious because everyone already 'knows' that the behavioural side of office automation is important or irrelevant because the philosophical and conceptual arguments raised have no place in the business world; they are just more 'ivory tower' thinking. Both criticisms have been levelled against research works of similar kind, and thus there is a need to anticipate and respond to these points at the conclusions of this work.

The first criticism is one raised with some regularity in response to most, if not all, work done on the social aspects of information technology. It is raised by 'enlightened' individuals who note that the behavioural dimension of new technology needs to be addressed and it *is* through the research on man/ machine interaction and the like. Many individuals contend that the systems developed today do take into account the social dimension of information systems: users are involved through techniques like the structured walk-through; the systems developed now have user-friendly interfaces; the products out on the market have been carefully designed so they are ergonomically sound, and so forth. The social side has been recognized as being important and it has been catered for. This criticism, however, is fairly easy to refute. While it is clear that some progress has been made on the social aspects of office and information systems development and implementation, it is minimal and probably misguided. Firstly, the social dimension involves social interaction — people engaging in joint action, sense making, and the like. The meanings associated with social action are intersubjectively shared. This has little to do with user-friendly interfaces and ergonomic sophistication. These palliatives are psychologically driven and, while not wanting to deny their beneficial effect, they do little to address the social environment of office work. Secondly, the view that users are involved in systems development because they take part in structured walk-throughs or similar 'involvement' exercises is misguided. They are to some extent involved but only to a very limited degree. Moreover, the type of involvement is often little more than token. The contention that the social environment of office work is satisfactorily dealt with through these forms of user involvement cannot be supported. Meaningful user participation can only be obtained through the adoption of approaches such as Pava's sociotech-nical method or Mumford's ETHICS. Only then could the richness of social interaction begin to be addressed.

The second criticism — the lack of practical relevancy — is perhaps more difficult to refute. Critics may claim that computer-based systems have had considerable success over the past thirty years without undue concern for the social domain. Systems analysts obtain an understanding of the manual system and then produce a design of a new computer-based information system which replaces or augments the current operation. The design takes into account the existing 'social' needs. Epistemological and ontological assumptions are considered irrelevant. Individuals holding this belief find it hard to see the relevancy of the arguments raised by the social theoretic perspective. There are, however, two primary fallacies associated with this criticism which need discussion.

1. Information Systems Have Been Successful

The first fallacy has to do with the belief that past information systems have been widely effective and successful. As noted earlier, particularly in Chapter 5, there is considerable reason to treat this belief with scepticism. The information systems literature abounds with examples of failed systems. (Until recently, there was even a specific journal — *Systems, Objectives, Solutions* — whose primary purpose was the reporting of systems failures.) The simple truth is that if information systems have not been particularly successful in the past, there is no reason to assume office systems will be any different. Historical reason leads to the inescapable conclusion that unless there is some change in the development process, office systems will meet with the same fate as their information systems predecessors.

2. The Office Environment is Largely Structured

The second fallacy involves a more subtle and fundamental issue, viz. the degree of determinism or structure intrinsic to the office domain. This is perhaps the most basic issue of all and the root cause of the different views of office automation. Individuals holding the belief that a social perspective is irrelevant for successful OA tend to adopt a conception of the office domain which is largely deterministic. People perform certain tasks in specified ways because that is how they accomplish the jobs they are employed to do. They are accountable and responsible for specifiable and rational functions; analyse these functions to discover the tasks and activities which the workers need to undertake. The function of the analyst is to discover the underlying structure of the office. This view simply believes that there is a largely structured and deterministic foundation to the office. Although there exists much in the way of unstructured activities, the predominant share of office work is in fact determinant — both for the principal and non-principal office worker. Moreover, there is a fundamental belief that that which is unstructured is probably inefficient. Formalizing the unstructured activity would likely lead to improved productivity by removing wasteful and unnecessary actions. The ultimate goal may indeed be the complete restructuring and formalizing of office work. Once done, automation could likely take over to gain maximum productivity. In sum, this belief holds that there is an underlying and enduring structure to the office; once discovered, new technology can be applied to great advantage.

This view is believed to be fallacious because there is considerable evidence to suggest that the office domain is anything but structured. Sheil (1983), Suchman (1983), and Suchman and Wynn (1984), as noted earlier in the chapter, discovered just how unstructured it is. True, there are many office tasks which are somewhat deterministic, but this is the exception to the rule. From a social theoretic perspective, office work is conceived of in terms of social interaction. The only so-called 'enduring' structure is the one which guides social action (e.g. social norms, rules, and conventions), but even this is continuously changing and often only known to those who take part in the interaction. Moreover, the desire to impose structure on such a domain can only be counterproductive; see, for example, the arguments on bureaucratic rationalism in Chapter 6.

It is possible to conceive of this 'office structure' argument in terms of a continuum. Those believing the office is largely structured contend that a very high proportion of office work (perhaps 60–80 per cent) is structured. Those adopting a social theoretic perspective suggest the figure is probably closer to 10–30 per cent. A fundamental conclusion which emerges from this work is that dysfunctional effects are likely if the former view is adopted. Developing office or information systems under the mistaken belief that a very high proportion of work is deterministic leads to systems which: (a) have to deal with great quantities of 'exceptions'; (b) force people to perform tasks or operations which are unnatural to them; and (c) cause a blinkering effect where all data are viewed in only prespecified ways. This leads to considerable anxiety on the part of the users, and inevitably to system failure. This work has hopefully allowed the reader to obtain a richer understanding of the office domain and, hopefully, the ability to avoid office system failure.

REFERENCES

Attewell, P., and Rule, J. (1984) 'Computing and organizations: what we know and what we don't know', *Communications of the ACM*, **27**, No.12, December.

Bardach, E. (1977) *The Implementation Game*, MIT Press, Cambridge.

Blumberg, P. (1969) *Industrial Democracy*, Schocken Books, New York.

Boddy, D., and Buchanan, D. (1984) 'Information technology and productivity: myths and realities', *Omega*, **12**, No.3.

Burns, A. (Ed.) (1984) *New Information Technology*, Ellis Horwood, Chichester.

Checkland, P. (1981) *Systems Thinking, Systems Practice*, J. Wiley and Sons, Chichester.

Fay, B. (1975) *Social Theory and Political Practice*, George Allen and Unwin, London.

Guest, D., and Knight, K. (1979) *Putting Participation into Practice*, Gower, Aldershot.

Hirschheim, R. (1983) 'Assessing participative design: some conclusions from an exploratory study', *Information and Management*, **6**, No.6, December.

Hirschheim, R. (1985a) 'Information systems epistemology: an historical perspective', in *Research Methods in Information Systems* (Eds. E. Mumford, G. Fitzgerald, R. Hirschheim, and T. Wood-Harper), North-Holland Amsterdam.

Hirschheim, R. (1985b) 'An analysis of participative systems design: user experiences, evaluation and recommendations', LSE Working Paper, January.

Keen, P. (1981) 'Information systems and organizational change', *Communications of the ACM*, **24**, No.1, January.

Klein, H., and Hirschheim, R. (1985) 'Fundamental issues of decision support systems: a consequentialist perspective', *Decision Support Systems*, **1**, No.1, January.

Kling, R. (1977) 'The organizational context of user-centred software designs', *MIS Quarterly*, December.

Kling, R. (1980) 'Social analyses of computing: theoretical perspectives in recent empirical research', *Computing Surveys*, **12**, No. 1, March.

Kling, R. (1984) 'Assimilating social values in computer-based technologies', *Telecommunications Policy*, June.

Koopmans, P., and Drenth, P. (1981) 'Conditions for successful participation', *LODJ*, **2**, No.4.

Leavitt, H. (1965) 'Applied organizational change in industry', in *Handbook of Organizations* (Ed. J. March), Rand McNally, Chicago.

Mumford, E., and Weir, M. (1979) *Computer Systems in Work Design — the ETHICS Method*, Associated Business Press, London.

Panko, R. (1984) 'Office work', *Office: Technology and People*, **2**.

Pava, C. (1983) *Managing New Office Technology: An Organizational Strategy*, Free Press, New York.

Ranney, J., and Carder, C. (1984) 'Sociotechnical design methods in office settings: two cases', *Office: Technology and People*, **2**.

Rhee, H. (1968) *Office Automation in Social Perspective: The Progress and Social Implications of Electronic Data Processing*, Basil Blackwell, Oxford.

Robey, D., and Markus, M. L. (1984) 'Rituals in information system design', *MIS Quarterly*, March.

Sheil, B. (1983) 'Coping with complexity', *Office: Technology and People*, **1**.

Suchman, L. (1983) 'Office procedure as practical action: models of work and system design', *ACM Transactions on Office Information Systems*, **1**, No.4, October.

Suchman, L., and Wynn, E. (1984) 'Procedures and problems in the office', *Office: Technology and People*, **2**.

Sydow, J. (1984) 'Sociotechnical change and perceived work situations: some conceptual propositions and an empirical investigation in different office settings', *Office: Technology and People*, **2**.

Wood-Harper, T., Episkopou, D., and Flynn, D. (1985) 'Research methods in information systems using action research', in *Research Methods in Information Systems* (Eds. E. Mumford, G. Fitzgerald, R. Hirschheim, and T. Wood-Harper), North-Holland, Amsterdam.

Appendix A

SELECTED ORGANIZATIONAL THEORY FRAMEWORKS AND THEIR RELATIONSHIP TO OFFICE VIEWS

INTRODUCTION

The notion of 'office perspectives' in the framework outlined in Chapter 3 has a direct equivalent in organization theory where, over the past decade, considerable effort has been expended to formulate frameworks by which to understand 'the organization'. Given that offices can be considered as parts of organizations, these frameworks might provide additional clues or guidance on how best to conceive of the office. It should be noted that frameworks are really conceptual mechanisms by which to classify the available literature of a field. They attempt to pinpoint the underlying similarities and differences existing in the literature. In so doing, they often artificially simplify: drawing boundaries where there are none and portraying a field in a somewhat disjointed and discontinuous fashion. Nevertheless, their value is unmistakable. Frameworks provide a simplified way of grasping the diversity and similarity of the field. The importance of such an apparatus for understanding the office is apparent.

PFEFFER'S FRAMEWORK

Pfeffer (1982) suggests there are a number of major theoretical perspectives that populate the field of organization theory. He classifies them along two dimensions: (1) perspective on action taken and (2) level of analysis. The first dimension refers to how organizational action is either implicitly or explicitly conceived. Pfeffer notes three alternatives. (a) Action seen as purposive, boundedly or intendedly rational, and prospective. Human behaviour is construed to be chosen, based on a set of consistent preferences, which is presumed to have occurred prior to the action itself. The actions are consciously chosen based on some anticipated consequence, i.e. they are goal directed. (b) Action seen as externally constrained or situationally determined. Here, human action is seen as the result of externally induced constraints, demands, or forces which the social actor is likely to have little control over or even awareness of. This is in contrast to the previous view where action is conceived of as the end product of conscious and purposive choice. Behaviour, in this context, is 'retrospectively rational' — explained (after the fact) to be rational. (c) Action seen as a somewhat random, emergent process. Here, human action is seen as emerging from the synthesis of people, problems, and solutions which come together to give meaning to a situation. This view denies either an internally directed or externally determined rationality of behaviour. Goals and preferences are thought to emerge from action rather than guide action. Organizational reality is a socially constructed system of shared meanings which produce an understanding of the social world.

The second dimension in Pfeffer's framework refers to the level of analysis by which organizational activity is studied. There are two categories: (a) where the organization is treated as a unit, as an undifferentiated collectivity (macrolevel), and (b) where it is dealt with in terms of smaller social units such as the individual (microlevel). This is the so-called individualist–structuralist controversy. Individualists such as Weick (1969) contend that 'organizations do not behave, people do'. By focusing on larger collectivities researchers neglect the individual processes that occur which produce the observed results. Collins (1981) argues that the activities of the larger collectivity are simply aggregates and are insufficient as empirical explanations of social processes. Structuralists, on the other hand, contend just the opposite. Collectivities are more than simply the aggregation of the individuals or activities which constitute them. They possess emergent properties which cannot be explained through an individualist interpretation (Mayhew, 1980).

Table A.1 summarizes Pfeffer's framework, placing the various organizational schools of thought in their respective positions.

VAN DE VEN AND JOYCE'S FRAMEWORK

In a somewhat less sophisticated vein, Van de Ven and Joyce (1981) categorize the major organizational theory perspectives into seven distinct areas. These seven perspectives may alternatively be seen as research programs, which suggests a somewhat less theoretical more pragmatic way of classifying various streams of organization theory research. They are:

(1. The *sociotechnical systems perspective* which is based on two fundamental premises. Firstly, that organizations can be seen as purposive systems where people perform both social and technical functions. The organization is made up of two coexisting systems: a social and a technical system; their successful joint operation is what makes the organization function. Secondly, sociotechnical systems operate in both hospitable and inhospitable environments which are influenced by culture, values, history, and accepted practices. In order to understand the sociotechnical system (particularly the social system) it is important to have an appreciation of the environmental forces which operate on it.

2. The *quality of work life perspective* which attempts to understand the nature of work life. In particular, it has been concerned with the development of

TABLE A.1 Pfeffer's categorization of theoretical perspectives in organization theory. Reprinted with permission from Jeffrey Pfeffer, Organizations and Organization Theory (Marshfield, Ma: Pitman Publishing Inc., 1982), p. 13

		PERSPECTIVES ON ACTION		
		Purposive, intentional, goal directed, rational	Externally constrained and controlled	Emergent, almost-random, dependent on process and social construction
LEVEL OF ANALYSIS	Individuals, coalitions, or sub-units	Expectancy theory Goal setting Needs theories and job design Political theories	Operant conditioning Social learning theory Socialization Role theories Social context effects and groups Retrospective rationality Social information processing	Ethnomethodology Cognitive theories of organizations Language in organizations Affect-based processes
	Total Organization	Structural contingency theory Market failures/ transaction costs Marxist or class perspectives	Population ecology Resource dependence	Organizations as paradigms Decisions process and administrative theories Institutionalization theory

mechanisms through which management and unions may learn about and apply social science knowledge to accomplish a significant improvement in the conditions of work within an organization (Seashore, 1981). The notion of planned organizational change is essential. Areas for study include: job and task characterization, individual work attitudes and perceptions, work group processes, pay and performance evaluation, intergroup relations, and individual differences.

3. The *Aston studies perspective* concerns itself with the context and bureaucratic dimensions of organizational structure. It is an example of what Pfeffer referred to as a 'structuralist' approach. It studies the activities and structural properties of organizations in relation to various contextual variables — in particular, the social and economic context in which the organization is found.

4. The *decision-making perspective* which grew out of the pioneering work of Herb
    Simon where the behaviour of an individual is viewed as intendedly and
    adaptively rational. However, due to cognitive limits the individual exhibits
    'bounded rationality' and 'satisfies' rather than 'maximizes' his choice in
    decision making. Moreover, the decision-making process can be made
    routinized by programming the premises of decision making. This perspec-
    tive is also concerned with providing alternatives to what March (1981)
    refers to as the three assumptions of classical organizational choice theories:
    the irrelevance of the way decisions are actually made, the wilfulness of the
    purposive nature of decision makers, and the primacy placed on the results
    of decisions.
5. The *organization assessment perspective* which is concerned with explaining the
    performance of complex organizations through the way they are organized
    and the environments in which they operate. In making sense of the
    complexity of organizational life, Van de Ven (1981) identifies a number of
    qualitatively different kinds of subsystems which exist in complex organiza-
    tions. These subsystems are based on 'performance programs' (systema-
    tized, discretionary, and developmental) and the different functions which
    different levels of organizations perform (technical, managerial, and institu-
    tional).
6. The *organization environment perspective* which posits that the only way an
    organization can be successful is if its design is consonant with the
    characteristics of the environment in which it operates. Lawrence and
    Lorsch (1967) introduced the notion of 'contingency theory' which showed
    that organizational performance was related to how well the organization
    coped with the level of uncertainty encountered in its environment.
    Moreover, they suggested that the psychological correlates of structural
    differentiation and their attendant problems were important for achieving
    the integration of organizational activities.
7. The *markets and hierarchies perspective* which sees the organization (i.e.
    hierarchy) as just one of several forms for carrying out transactions. The
    transaction is the basic unit of analysis and follows on from classical
    'institutional economics'. This perspective is based on Williamson's (1975)
    'new institutional economics' and has been extended by Ouchi (1979) (see
    the transaction view discussed in Chapter 3). Fundamentally, this
    approach suggests that the basic way to deal with organizational design is
    through organizing transactions so as to economize on bounded rationality
    while minimizing the impact of individual 'opportunism'.

ASTLEY AND VAN DE VEN'S FRAMEWORK

Astley and Van de Ven (1981) present a framework for classifying approaches
to organizational theory which has some similarity to Pfeffer's. They note two

underlying factors or dimensions which are the basis of their framework: the level of organizational analysis and the relative emphasis placed on deterministic versus voluntaristic assumptions about human nature. The first dimension — the level of analysis — is the same one noted by Pfeffer. It refers to the focusing on either micro- or macro-organizational characteristics — the 'individualist versus structuralist' perspective. The second dimension — deterministic versus voluntaristic orientation — relates the classic duality of social determinism versus free-will — the notion that the action of human beings and their collectivities are either determined by exogenous forces or are freely chosen and created. Astley and Van de Ven map these two dimensions onto one another and come up with four possible schools of thought: macro-level analysis/determinism — the 'natural selection view'; macro-level analysis/voluntarism — the 'system-action' view; micro-level analysis/determinism — the 'system-structural' view; and micro-level analysis/voluntarism — the 'strategic choice' view.

The *system-structural* view has its basis in the conception that individual freedom needs to be controlled through rational procedures for the good of the organization. It has been the dominant mode of study and had its foundations laid in the work of Frederick Taylor and his principles of scientific management. Although there is considerable diversity in the various organization theory approaches which make up this view, there are many similar underlying premises. In particular, they share a deterministic orientation towards social structure and behaviour which is consistent with both the 'structural-functionalism' and 'systems' schools of thought (Burrell and Morgan, 1979). The fundamental unit of analysis is the organizational position, which is structured in such a way as to constrain human behaviour so that organizational goals can be realized. Decision making is seen more as a technology (Lindblom, 1981), and the focus is on gathering information to make rational choices.

The *strategic choice* view is largely founded in the work of Child (1972) who criticized the determinism inherent in the systems-structural view. He suggested that organizational design was not simply a reflection of operational contingency but rather a strategic event which embodies the value positions of the involved actors and the political process through which they engage. Organization structure is largely designed to suit the preferences of those in power. The organization is best seen in terms of coalitions with vested interests who manipulate the environment to their own advantage. The strategic choice view, according to Van de Ven and Astley (1981):

> ... draws attention to individuals, their interactions, and their perceptions, as opposed to positions and their interrelations and functions. ... Both environment and structure are enacted and embody the meaning of action of people, particularly those in power (p.437).

The *natural selection* view relies on the biological evolution analogy of Darwin to explain social organization. The organization is perceived as deterministically given — an evolutionary development governed by natural 'ecological' laws. Environmental (economic) competition and resource scarcity are the primary external forces which cause the selection of a particular form of organization. This environmental determinism is similar to one embraced by the systems-structural view, except that it sees organizational change as a product of internal adaptation whereas the natural selection view sees it as the product of external selection. Organizations, according to this view, have little ability to act independently; the environmental forces totally overwhelm any possible action, channelling and determining their overall fate.

The *collective system* view focuses on the network of semi-autonomous organizations and stakeholders who join together (as a social system) to construct their collective domain. The actions of the organizational parties are symbiotically related, creating roles and expectations of each other. The structure of the parties is such that it acts as a unit, making decisions to attain collective goals. Perrow (1981) notes that such symbiotic action is the result of political agreement and social definition rather than economic fiat. The norms implicitly agreed to are symbolic outgrowths reflecting common experiences encountered in the collective action for existence. It is a pluralistic conception of social and organizational action.

Figures A.1 and A.2 provide summaries of the Astley and Van de Ven framework.

VAN DE VEN AND ASTLEY'S FRAMEWORK

In an updated version of the Astley and Van de Ven framework, Van de Ven and Astley (1981) try to explore in more detail the reasons why various perspectives exist. This analysis led them to conclude that a refined framework would better explain the existence of the many organizational theory perspectives. Their updated framework attempts to take into account the change in organization structure and behaviour over time. It makes four substantive changes from their earlier classification scheme: (1) the deterministic–voluntaristic orientation is reconstituted to focus more on the 'object of study' — in particular, on the structured forms and personnel actions within organizations; (2) the level of analysis dimension is also reconstituted to focus on 'part or whole' (the 'me–we' frame of reference); (3) the addition of fundamental concepts central to each perspective for understanding 'structure, behaviour, and performance'; and (4) the inclusion of 'time' to reflect the dynamic quality of organizations. Figure A.3 represents the Van de Ven and Astley framework diagrammatically.

	Focus on structural configurations	Focus on personnel actions, processes
Macro level (populations or networks of organizations, industries communities)	Natural selection view 1 Societal evolution 2 Scientific Marxism 3 Population ecology 4 Institutional economics (current views)	Collective action view 1 Societal guidance 2 Critical Marxism 3 Social ecology 4 Pluralism collective bargaining
Micro level (individual organizations, groups and persons)	System-structural view 1 Structural-functionalism 2 Human engineering 3 Social systems theory 4 Structural contingency theory	Strategic choice view 1 Quality of working life 2 Strategic policy formation 3 Decision theory 4 Interaction theory

Deterministic ·Voluntaristic

FIGURE A.1 Classification of major schools of organization design and behaviour (Van de Ven and Astley, 1981)

BURRELL AND MORGAN'S FRAMEWORK

In a more sociological and philosophical approach, Burrell and Morgan (1979) offer an interesting framework by which to classify the various schools of thought. Their framework is based on two dimensions: assumptions about the nature of social science and assumptions about the nature of society. The former relates to the various assumptions which underlie the different approaches to social science. Burrell and Morgan list four primary sets of assumptions: ontological, which relate to the nature of the phenomena under investigation; epistemological, which relate to the theory of knowledge, i.e. how knowledge is acquired; human nature, which concerns itself with whether humans respond in a deterministic or non-deterministic (voluntaristic) fashion; and methodological, which describes the mechanisms used to acquire knowledge about the social world. These assumptions are reformulated to yield a 'subjectivist–objectivist' dimension, the two extremes of philosophical inquiry. (For further details on

Macro level	Natural Selection View	Collective Action View:
	Structure: Like all natural things, social organization is given by nature. Environmental competition and carrying capacity select and deselect organizational forms	Structure: Networks of semi-autonomous partisan groups that interact to modify or construct their collective environment, rules and options. Organization is collective action controlling, liberating, and expanding individual action.
	Change: A natural evolution of environmental variation, selection, and retention of organizational forms, which must either fit their environmental niches or they fail	Change: Collective bargaining, conflict negotiation and compromise through partisan mutual adjustment.
	Behaviour: Random, natural environmental selection	Behaviour: Reasonable, collective moral selection and construction
	Manager role: Inactive or alienated.	Manager role: Interactive.

Micro level	System-Structural View:	Strategic Choice View:
	Structure: Roles and positions hierarchically arranged to efficiently achieve the function of the system.	Structure: People and their relationships organized and socialized to serve the choices and purposes of people in power.
	Changes: Divide and integrate roles to adapt subsystems to changes in environment, technology, size, and resource needs.	Change: Environment and structure are enacted and embody the meanings of action of people in power.
	Behaviour: Determined, constrained, and adaptive.	Behaviour: Constructed, autonomous, and enacted.
	Manager role: Reative.	Manage role: Proactive

Deterministic orientation . . . . Voluntaristic orientation

FIGURE A.2 Summary of four views of organization and behaviour (Van de Ven and Astley, 1981)

the various ontological and epistemological positions, see Chapter 6.) Burrell and Morgan's second dimension relates to the dichotomous view about society, viz. order or conflict. The 'order' or 'integrationist' view of society emphasizes stability, integration, functional coordination, and consensus. The 'conflict' or 'coercion' view stresses change, conflict, disintegration, and coercion. Burrell and Morgan note that the order/conflict dimension is more of a continuum, as is the subjectivist/objectivist dimension. When the two dimensions are mapped onto one another four paradigms emerge: 'functionalist' (objective/order);

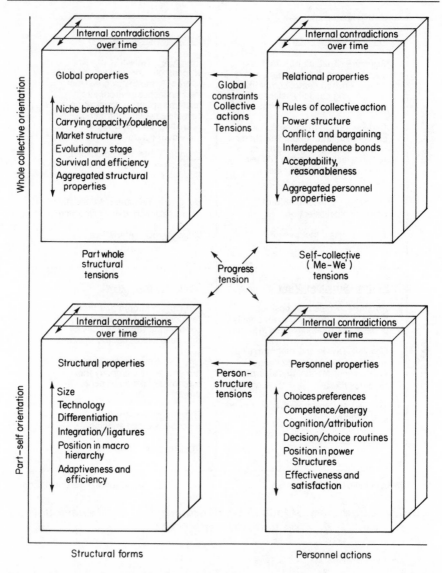

FIGURE A.3 Van de Ven and Astley's framework (Van de Ven and Astley, 1981)

'interpretivist' (subjective/order); 'radical humanist' (subjective conflict); and 'radical structuralist' (objective/conflict) (see Figure A.4).

The functionalist paradigm (the dominant framework of organization theory) is concerned with providing explanations of the status quo, and social order,

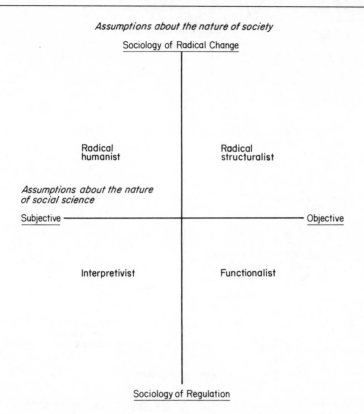

Assumptions about the nature of society

Sociology of Radical Change

Radical
humanist

Radical
structuralist

*Assumptions about the nature
of social science*

Subjective ———————————————————————— Objective

Interpretivist

Functionalist

Sociology of Regulation

FIGURE A.4 Burrell and Morgan's paradigms (Reproduced by permission of Gower Publishing Company Ltd from Burrell and Morgan, 1979)

social integration, consensus, need satisfaction, and rational choice. The interpretivist paradigm seeks explanation within the realm of individual consciousness and subjectivity, and within the frame of reference of the social actor as opposed to the observer of the action. From the perspective of this paradigm: 'social roles and institutions exist as an expresion of the meanings which men attach to their world' (Silverman, 1970, p. 134). The radical humanist paradigm has a view of society (and organizations) which emphasizes the need to overthrow or transcend the limitations placed on existing social and organizational arrangements. The radical structuralist paradigm seeks radical change, emancipation, and potentiality, and stresses the role that different social and organizational forces play in understanding change. The paradigm focuses primarily on the structure and analysis of power relationships. Figure A.5 suggests how the various schools of organizational thought fit into the Burrell and Morgan framework.

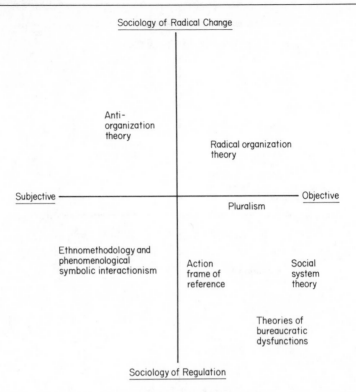

FIGURE A.5 The relationship between schools of organizational thought and Burrell and Morgan's framework (Reproduced by permission of Gower Publishing Company Ltd from Burrell and Morgan, 1979)

DISCUSSION

Although these frameworks differ from one another, there is some similarity between them. The first four (to a greater or lesser extent) concern themselves with the level of analysis in terms of the structuralist–individualist dichotomy. The determinism–voluntarism concept underlies all the frameworks. Methodological issues are implied by all. The more interesting aspect, however, is the relationship between the organizational theory frameworks and the office perspectives/views of Chapter 3. Although their focus is different — the former concentrates on organizations while the latter is concerned with offices — there are some similarities. For example, the analytical office perspective is closely allied to Burrell and Morgan's objectivist position, while the interpretivist perspective is similar to their subjectivist position. Their 'order–conflict' dimension, however, has little significance in the office arena. More specifically,

TABLE A.2 Comparison of organizational frameworks with office views

Office view / Framework	Pfeffer	Van de Ven and Joyce	Astley and Van de Ven	Van de Ven and Astley	Burrell and Morgan
Office activities	Purposive, rational/individualist	—	System-structural	Structural – part	Functionalist
Office semantics	Purposive, rational/individualist	—	System-structural	—	Functionalist
Office functions	Purposive, rational/structuralist	Organizational assessment and Aston studies	System-structural	—	Functionalist
Work roles	Externally constrained/individualist	Sociotechnical and quality of working life	Strategic choice	Personnel–part	Functionalist/interpretivist
Decision making	Externally constrained/individualist	Decision making	Strategic choice	Personnel–part	Functionalist
Transactional	Purposive, rational and emergent, social construction/structuralist	Markets and hierarchies	Natural selection and collective action	Structural and personnel–whole	Functionalist/interpretivist
Language action	Emergent, social construction/individualist	—	Strategic choice	Personnel – whole and part	Interpretivist

the office activity view has much in common with Pfeffer's purposive, rational/individualist perspective, Astley and Van de Ven's system-structured view, and a mixture of Van de Ven and Joyce's organizational assessment and Aston study perspectives. The office semantics view shares properties of Pfeffer's purposive, rational/individualist perspective, and Astley and Van de Ven's system-structural view.

Interpretivists' views reflect a different orientation. For example, the work roles view reflects Pfeffer's externally constrained/individualist perspective, Van de Ven and Joyce's sociotechnical systems and quality of working life perspectives, Astley and Van de Ven's strategic choice view, and Van de Ven and Astley's personnel/part perspective. The decision-making view has similarities with Pfeffer's internally contained/individualist perspective, Van de Ven and Joyce's decision-making perspective, Astley and Van de Ven's strategic choice view, and Van de Ven and Astley's personnel/part perspective. The transactional view reflects a combination of Pfeffer's purposive-rational and emergent, social construction/structuralist perspectives, Van de Ven and Joyce's markets and hierarchies perspective, a mix of Astley and Van de Ven's natural selection and collective action views, and similarly a mix of Van de Ven and Astley's structural and personnel/whole perspectives. Lastly, the language action view relates to Pfeffer's emergent, social construction/individualist perspective, Astley and Van de Ven's strategic choice view, and a mix of Van de Ven and Astley's personnel/whole and personnel/part perspectives. Table A.2 summarizes and compares the organizational theory frameworks with the various office views.

It is interesting to note that just as Pfeffer's purposive, rational/individualist, and Astley and Van de Ven's system-structural view are the most popular perspectives in the organizational theory literature, so too is their analogue in office automation — the office activities view. By comparing the organizational theory frameworks with the available office views it is hoped that the range of office conception possibilities has been made richer.

REFERENCES

Astley, W., and Van de Ven, A. (1981) 'Central perspectives and debates in organization theory', Wharton School Discussion Paper 101, University of Pennsylvania, Philadelphia.

Burrell, G., and Morgan, G. (1979) *Sociological Paradigms and Organizational Analysis*, Heinemann, London.

Child, J. (1972) 'Organizational structure, environment and performance: the role of strategic choice', *Sociology*, **6**.

Collins, R. (1981) 'On the microfoundations of macrosociology', *American Journal of Sociology*, **86**.

Lawrence, P., and Lorsch, J. (1967) *Organization and Environment*, Harvard University Press, Cambridge.

Lindblom, C. (1981) 'Comments on decisions in organizations', in *Perspectives on Organizational Design and Behaviour* (Eds. A. Van de Ven and W. Joyce), J. Wiley and Sons, New York.

March, J. (1981) 'Decisions in organizations and theories of choice', in *Perspectives on Organizational Design and Behaviour* (Eds. A. Van de Ven and W. Joyce), John Wiley and Sons, New York.

Mayhew, B. (1980) 'Structuralism versus individualism: Part I, Shadowboxing in the dark', *Social Forces*, **59**.

Perrow, C. (1981) 'Markets, hierarchies and hegemony', in *Perspectives on Organizational Design and Behaviour* (Eds. A. Van de Ven and W. Joyce), John Wiley and Sons, New York.

Pfeffer, J. (1982) *Organizations and Organization Theory*, Pitman, Boston.

Ouchi, W. (1979) 'A conceptual framework for the design of organizational control mechanism', *Management Science*, **25**, No.9, September.

Seashore, S. (1981) 'The Michigan quality of work program: issues in measurement, assessment, and outcome evaluation', in *Perspectives on Organizational Design and Behaviour* (Eds. A. Van de Ven and W. Joyce), J. Wiley and Sons, New York.

Silverman, D. (1970) *The Theory of Organizations*, Heinemann Educational Books, London.

Van de Ven, A. (1981) 'The organization assessment research program', in *Perspectives on Organizational Design and Behaviour* (Eds. A. Van de Ven and W. Joyce), J. Wiley and Sons, New York.

Van de Ven, A., and Astley, A. (1981) 'Mapping the field to create a dynamic perspective on organization design and behaviour', in *Perspectives on Organizational Design and Behaviour* (Eds. A. Van de Ven and W. Joyce), J. Wiley and Sons, New York.

Weick, K. (1969) *The Social Psychology of Organizations*, Addison-Wesley, Reading.

Williamson, O. (1975) *Markets and Hierarchies: Analysis and Antitrust Implications*, Free Press, New York.

Appendix B

CHECKLIST OF KEY QUESTIONS FOR OFFICE AUTOMATION IMPLEMENTATION

The Work Research Unit of the UK Department of Employment has developed a comprehensive set of questions on office automation implementation which it feels can be used equally well in any environment. The list below, which is adapted from the Work Research Unit's report on information technology (Work Research Unit, 1981), provides a summary of the myriad aspects of office automation implementation.

Technical considerations

What objectives does the equipment need to meet?
What are the most important priorities, in terms of technical, social, human requirements?
What are the volumes of work?
What are the time-critical pressures?
What equipment is available to meet the defined operational needs?
What equipment should be considered?
How reliable is the equipment?
Are servicing arrangements satisfactory?
Is internal maintenance required?
Is the technical infrastructure sufficient to support the new system?
Can it be upgraded to meet the future needs of the business?
How does it fit in with other systems within the organization?
What are the cost implications?
Can we afford it?
What will we save?
Are the costs worth the gain?
Should we wait until mass production and competition forces prices down further?
Should we buy, rent, or lease?
How flexible is the system to future changes in need?
What is the life-span of the equipment?

Organizational considerations

How will the new technology actually change the nature of the organization's business?

What use will be made of the information available?
How will it affect the flow of information?
What will be the impact on the number of jobs?
How will hierarchical or organizational structures be affected?
How will the overall physical arrangement of the office need changing?
Will authority levels need changing?
Will basic departmental structures need altering?
Is there full senior management commitment?
Is there full employee and trade union commitment?
Is the organization ready for change?
Will the organizational climate accept change?
Who will take the initiative for piloting the change through?
Can the organization cope with anticipated conditions and results?

Communication considerations

What are the existing means of communication and consultation?
How effective are these channels?
Can problems be identified early enough?
Do people have a chance to express their views?
Are they told what is expected of them?
Are they told how well they are doing?
Do they have a chance to talk to colleagues?
And to their bosses? And do their bosses listen?
Are there regular communications meetings?
Do people know what is going on?

Job design considerations

Can new jobs be designed such that the tasks combine together to make up
   satisfying total jobs?
Is each job such that tasks are not too tiring or repetitive?
Is feedback provided on performance levels?
Do jobs contain sufficient variety?
Do jobs contain an element of challenge?
Does the job-holder have responsibility for his own work?
Does the job ensure that the skills of the job-holder are well used?
Does the job provide the job-holder with reasonable discretion in decision
   making?
Is there suitable discretion over when the job-holder can take breaks from
   work?
Does the job have well-defined objectives?
Does the job provide the job-holder with the visible results of labour?

Are there clear relationships between the tasks which make up the job and can they be seen by the job-holder?

Does the job provide the opportunity of social interaction with workmates?

Work group considerations

Is there a clearly defined work activity for the work group?

Will the work group have the ability to help set work targets?

Will the work group be involved in evaluating performance?

How reliant will the work group be for task achievement on others?

What degree of influence will the work group have on routine and non-routine decision making?

Job considerations

What jobs will be affected?

Are jobs likely to disappear?

What jobs will disappear?

What new jobs will be created?

What functions will be merged?

How many, and which, jobs will be changed?

Do we want to avoid de-skilling?

How can we avoid de-skilling?

Can new or remaining jobs be enriched or enlarged?

Are there problems of boredom?

Do the jobs create any kind of stress?

What are the frustrations?

How can the adverse factors be eliminated?

Recruitment and training considerations

How will the changes affect recruitment, selection, and retirement patterns?

What kind of people will be needed for the future?

What people will need to be redeployed or relocated?

What extra skills will be required?

What training will be needed to meet these skill requirements?

How can we best use our existing people, by retraining or redeployment?

Who will need training?

What type of training is available, and from whom?

How can increased responsibility be given to people?

Are they equipped for it?

Will new supervisory patterns create training requirements?

Are age patterns important?

Are there likely to be any changes to the male/female mix?

Does this present any particular training problem?

Are there some people not suited to the new system, either physically or temperamentally, in spite of all efforts to retrain or redeploy them?

What should be done about them?

Are there clear career structure and progression paths?

Have we identified which factors influence career progress or promotion?

Participation considerations

What are the systems of participation at present?

Do these need to be improved?

Are people involved in issues that affect them?

Are they being consulted specifically about the introduction of new technology?

Are their views properly represented?

Is involvement early enough?

Regular enough?

What account is taken of what people say?

Can the system be altered to accommodate suggestions for improvement?

Ergonomic and safety considerations

Is the new equipment safe?

Does it provide proper levels of comfort?

Is it tiring to use?

Is lighting adequate?

What method of lighting is needed?

Are there problems of screen reflections or glare?

Is there sufficient room for all operations and maintenance to be carried out safely and comfortably?

Are seating arrangements satisfactory?

Is ventilation and heating good enough?

Are noise levels acceptable?

Is there any fire risk?

Are any electric safeguards such as isolation switches required?

Are there problems with static electricity and how can they be overcome?

Are VDU screens readable, flicker free, and properly illuminated?

Are the keyboards detachable and ergonomically sound?

Is the response time of the system within an acceptable limit?

Is the equipment capable of adjustment?

Is there any opportunity for privacy?

Are general work conditions satisfactory?

Can they be improved?

Employment and remuneration considerations

Are pay systems perceived by all employees as being fair?
Are general conditions of employment satisfactory?
Is the time right for change?
What will be the effects on payment, grading, promotion of the proposed changes?

Evaluation considerations

Does the system meet the objectives set for it?
Is it efficient?
Is it cost-effective?
Will it meet the organization's future needs?
What modifications/upgrading are necessary?
Has it improved people's jobs?
Has the quality of working life been improved?
What further 'people' changes are called for?
What lessons can we learn from the changes?
How can we be more effective in future?

Future considerations

Where do we go from here?
What additional changes are required?
How can we improve our new way of operating further?
How can we involve people in future decision-making procedures?

REFERENCES

Work Research Unit, 'Introducing new technology into the office', WRU Occasional Paper 20, London, October 1981.

Author Index

Abraham, S.   32, 207
Ackoff, R.   225, 227, 236, 249
Adams, C.   172
Aklilu, T.   59, 140
Aldrich, H.   41, 49
Allison, G.   68
Alter, S.   158
Apel, K.   203, 237, 254
APEX   224
Argyris, C.   44, 61, 249
Arnold, E.   224
Astley, W.   293, 294, 295, 302
Attardi, G.   54, 57, 58
Attewell, P.   215, 282

Bair, J.   12, 14, 33, 157, 207, 213
Ballou, D.   87
Bamforth, K.   169
Banbury, J.   61, 63
Banks, O.   161
Barber, G.   46, 56, 57, 58, 101, 102
Bardach, E.   164, 165, 166, 281
Bariff, M.   161, 227, 228
Barron, I.   224
Bate, P.   172
Bell, D.   20, 21, 37
Benedict, G.   168
Berger, P.   200
Bion, W.   251
Bjorn-Andersen, N.   4, 161, 167, 200, 225,
   228, 230, 231, 232, 249
Blackey, B.   232
Blumberg, P.   172, 281
Boddy, D.   282
Boehm, G.   259
Boguslaw, R.   199
Bostrom, R.   158, 169, 261
Boulding, K.   60
Bracchi, G.   81, 86, 87, 88, 91, 139
Branscomb, L.   21, 22, 31
Braverman, H.   200, 220

Briefs, V.   220, 225, 232
British Insurance Company   206
Bronsema, G.   66
Buchanan, D.   282
Burke, F.   222
Burns, A.   216, 220, 233, 238, 239, 285
Burns, J.   22, 207
Burns, T.   273
Burrell, G.   44, 73, 198, 200, 250, 258, 294,
   296
Business Week   26

Carder, C.   281, 284
Carlisle, J.   207
Carter, L.   39
Checkland, P.   45, 47, 67, 84, 86, 105, 127,
   145, 150, 280
Cherns, A.   169
Cheung, C.   46, 54
Child, J.   172, 294
Christie, B.   41, 51
Churchill, Winston   242
Churchman, C.   65, 257
Ciborra, C.   69, 70
Clegg, S.   57, 60, 70, 200
Coates, S.   31
Colley, M.   224
Collins, R.   6, 291
Colter, M.   149, 154
Commons, J.   68, 69
Computertalk   208
Computing   213, 232
Conrath, D.   41, 53, 139, 158, 213, 227,
   228, 248
Cook, C.   41, 94
Cooley, M.   199, 223, 225, 232
Cox, J.   249
Craig, M.   224, 225, 232
Croisdale, D.   172
Curley, K.   206
Curnow, R.   224
Cyert, R.   68

309

Subject Index